Philip Watson is Editor-at-Large [illegible] the Condé Nast international publishing empire. *GQ* was established nine years ago and has been widely acclaimed for the quality of its reportage and feature writing. *More Than a Game* includes writings from some of the best sports journalists of the last decade, such as Simon Barnes, Richard Williams, Pete Davies, Jim White and Julie Welch, among many others.

MORE THAN A GAME

GQ on Sport

PHŒNIX

A Phoenix Paperback
First published in Great Britain by Orion in 1997
This paperback edition published in 1997 by Phoenix,
a division of Orion Books Ltd,
Orion House, 5 Upper St Martin's Lane,
London WC2H 9EA

A CIP catalogue record for this book
is available from the British Library

ISBN: 1 85799 938 X

Printed and bound in Great Britain by
Guernsey Press Ltd, Guernsey C.I.

CONTENTS

PREFACE

Ian Botham

Sport has been my life since I was a kid. From a very young age I wanted and intended to play sport for a living, and when I got thrown out of school at the age of fifteen I turned professional straight away. For many years there was little else I thought about; I used to eat, drink, sleep, walk, smell and breathe cricket. Sport for me has always been much, much more than just a game.

Luckily, I had a gift – you have to have some kind of ability to play a hard leather ball travelling at 100 mph. And I've always thought that it's a great privilege and honour to have that gift. Many people would give up a great deal for it. How many schoolboys dream of playing football for Manchester United or cricket for England? Well, only eleven can, so you have to make the most of that ability.

The sportsmen and women in this collection have two things in common: a very solid backbone and total self-belief. You need tunnel vision if you want to succeed in sport. There's only one route to being the best and you have to ruthlessly put everything else out of the way. Sport is cut-throat and no one else is going to do it for you. It's sink or swim.

Negative thoughts are something I've tried to avoid throughout my career, and my life, but without sport I'd probably be doing 25 years on the Isle of Wight as a guest of Her Majesty's Government (well, at least that's what some people tell me). Sport has taught me personal discipline and determination, but it can also teach you the value of working as one of a team. Cricket allows and encourages you to excel individually, yet it will always be a team game and you have to learn to balance the two. It's very much like life – you can succeed as an individual, but you must never forget there are others around you.

Sport has given me a great deal – and not just financially. It's opened doors and opened my eyes, and I've seen things around the world that others will never see. But you also give up a lot for those perks. You have to have total commitment. You have no family life; you are on the road for eleven months of the year. I was in Australia when my wife Kathy discovered she was pregnant with Liam. I missed my daughter Sarah's birth because I was on tour. For many years, Viv Richards and I joked that we knew each other better than we did our wives.

Sport can hurt physically, too, and I have had my fair share of injuries. In fact, as some of these articles powerfully show, sport can kill – it comes with the territory. But if you're facing a very quick bowler you cannot let yourself stop to think for one moment that you might get killed; if you have doubts or fears you shouldn't be out there. My one great advantage as a batsman was that I could also dish it out as a bowler. In my prime I was certainly fast enough to worry most lower order batsmen. And they knew I'd do it – and I did do it. If a guy's hanging around, stick it on his nose. I had no remorse; it's part of the game. Make him think that if you can't bowl him out, you're going to knock him out. These are the facts of sport; cricket is a tough game.

As much as sport is a business, a global entertainment industry, it can also be a matter of personal principle and honesty. It's hard to keep politics out of sport, as it is with most things, and cricket has had its share of controversies. Many cricketers were attacked for playing in South Africa during the eighties, but I'll tell you one thing: sportsmen break down more barriers than politicians ever will because the public knows that sportsmen are basically honest people.

Still, for all the bad press I've got over the years I've received much more favourable attention, and I think the quality of the sportswriting in Britain is second to none. At its best, sports journalism conveys all the passion and depth of emotion of sport. It communicates the sheer enjoyment of playing and watching it. I've always thought that sport should be played as competitively as hell – you don't give an inch, and you don't expect an inch – but when you come off the pitch you've got to be able to slap each other on the back and have a laugh.

That's why of all the pieces in this collection, perhaps the one that illustrates the point best is *Village People*, the article on the local cricket team in Leicestershire. This, to me, is what cricket is all about. It's about guys who've worked hard all week relishing their Saturday or Sunday game. It's about guys who want to have a bit of rivalry, a bit of fun and who dream of pumping a six out of the ground or of taking a vital wicket with a late inswinger. Oh, and just as importantly, it's also about having a few beers afterwards.

INTRODUCTION

Simon Barnes

'Fuck you. You are a great champion.'

This was the seven-word tribute of Larry Holmes to Mike Tyson, when at last Holmes rose from the canvas following their World Heavyweight Championship fight in Atlantic City in 1988.

It is a line that sums up all of boxing – rivalry, sordidness, brutality, grudging respect – and with it, perhaps, all of sport. And every one of us newspapermen there on that unpleasant night knew it. We discussed it afterwards, and agreed: yes, it was probably the great boxing quote of all time. But none of us was able to use it.

F*** you? —— you? It's not the same, is it? It doesn't work if it isn't 'Fuck'. Without the word spelt out in full, it means fuck all.

That is newspapers for you: offices and pubs are full of casual obscenity, but most newspapers are . . . well, not necessarily careful about language, but careful about bad words, anyway. The phrase 'family newspaper' is an ineluctable part of our lives. Newspapers are not in the business of giving gratuitous offence. It is a limitation of newspaper writing, and one everybody in the business, whether writing or reading, understands, and accepts. There are may other necessary limitations, and most of these concern time and space.

Newspapers have dominated sportswriting for years, and have produced their own totem figures and doyens. Panting distantly in their wake have been the writers for specialist sports magazines: those who tend to cater for the Anorak Tendency. Sportswriting has, in short, been set about with restrictions. A 'long' piece in newspaper terms is a thousand words; a long deadline is the Sunday man's week-to-week routine.

But ten years ago, a new player entered the game. This was the phenomenon of men's magazines. A monthly magazine for men that had actual words in it – words for actually reading. *GQ* was the pioneer and, in my totally unbiased opinion as the long-term author of the magazine's sports column, it leads the way still, leaving the rest panting distantly in its wake.

Sport is, of course, a blindingly obvious subject for a men's magazine – but it could not be tackled in a blindingly obvious way. Certainly, one of the first things *GQ* was able to offer was a new way of writing about sport; but this was not so much a cunning plan as a necessity. The magazine was doomed, as it were, to offer a whole suit of new freedoms to its sportswriters. Heady and rather alarming freedoms.

Freedom of vocabulary was simply the most obvious one and, inevitably, it appealed to the schoolboy within us. But space and time were the others, and these possibilities meant that the craft of sportswriting had to be reinvented.

Unlike newspapers, a magazine can offer an author a decent length of time to research and to write. These are, you would think, luxuries – especially to those of us who are often required to read an 800-word match report over the telephone to a deaf-mute copy-taker the instant the final whistle has gone. Such a discipline is nerve-wracking, but as long as you can get it done *at all*, you have done a good job. No one expects a masterpiece under such circumstances. In some ways, the ferocious restrictions make the job easier.

But a long magazine deadline gives you the disconcerting and agoraphobic freedom to research, to write, to *think*. And time, for a magazine, involves a further restriction: that of, to use a spot of jargon, lead-time. The logistics of producing a colour magazine insist that copy is filed, not on the final whistle, but about three months before the whistle is blown for the kick-off.

You can make of this what you choose. But the best way to react to such a restriction is to use it as a freedom. You are not responding to the news, a salivating Pavlov's dog leaping up at every clang of the bell, every blast of the whistle. No, you must anticipate, still better, *create* the story before it happens.

Thus, we have Ayrton Senna, musing upon life and death as he prepared for a new season with a new team. An extraodinary man, Senna, and it produced remarkable copy. His death, an event I still find utterly shocking, more or less coincided with the appearance of the piece in *GQ*. But far from making a fool of the magazine and the author of the piece, it added a deep and fascinating insight into the life and death of the most extraordinary sportsman I have ever met.

A magazine like *GQ* has plenty of pages to fill and, as I say, fill them for people who are actually going to read them. I remember Ben Elton talking about the old-style men's magazines like *Playboy*. 'Nobody reads the articles in 'em about biplanes do they? Why not? Because these magazines are for masturbation.'

Thus we who write for *GQ* live in the ever-present danger of being read, and not necessarily by wankers, either. And to fill those pages with all those words – 'oh, the usual 3,000 or so' – takes a bit of thought.

Well, thoughts – plural – really. To write a piece for newspaper, or a magazine, at about a quarter of this massive *GQ*-length, you require a single thought. The best method is to find a really good idea, and then to pursue it remorselessly to the end, where ideally you make a nice joke and bale out stylishly. If this is an interview piece you look for a few good quotes, and if you get them, that's your piece written for you.

For a long, feature piece, you have to stretch your mind a little bit more: look a little further. You must seek the non-obvious. This is a good quality in the best of newspaper writing, but an absolute essential for any writer who hopes to complete the terrifying amount of words that *GQ* demands. If you write for *GQ* you are condemned to try and join the best. There is no other way.

In other words, a writer, and for that matter a reader, has the freedom to use his mind. And there is a further freedom, too: freedom of subject matter. Most traditional forms of sportswriting involve the star performers of mainstream sports. Indeed, there are plenty of them in these pages, though handled with a leisurely, discursive freedom you cannot find in the traditional places.

A magazine reader does not have the same expectations. If Alan Shearer scores a hat-trick, a newspaper reader will expect to read about him the next day. But a magazine reader, and more especially a *GQ* reader, is hoping for a series of stimulating surprises. He *might* find an incisive and thoughtful piece about Shearer's inner demons, but he's more likely to discover a much better and more revealing piece about the demons of, say, Kevin Keegan. Or, indeed, he might find a feature on bare-knuckle boxing or surfing or village cricket.

A magazine is not restricted by the same conventions of reader expectation. You can supply something not found elsewhere. You need not worry about offending people or alienating them; the whole ethos of the magazine, is that readers are there to be challenged. This is the tradition of the magazine, largely established by my late friend Michael VerMeulen, and carried on zestfully by his successor as editor, Angus MacKinnon.

Thus for example, the cosy clubbability of rugby union is challenged by an acerbic piece on violence in which the game's code of *omerta* is set aside. There will be readers who would find such a piece offensive or even impossible in a newspaper, or even in a different magazine. But the same reader will read the piece in *GQ* and find it enthralling. That is because the magazine is always slightly uncomfortable to be with. It is not like a cosy member of the family, nor even like a friend. It is the strong, self-opinionated person that you can never quite make up your mind whether you like or not. You admire him, but you are slightly uneasy with him. The people around him might not altogether approve of everything he says; some might not care for him at all. But they feel compelled to listen. The self-confidence is too compelling. And just when you think he is beginning to become rather a bore, he surprises you with his genuine intelligence. He makes a broad joke, and then suddenly he is demanding you follow him in the turning of an intellectual somersault.

All of this does not constitute a revolution in writing. But it has been a vast change for sportswriting. Sport is a big subject these days, and one used by politicians and media moguls as the fast track to power. Sport has long been a central aspect of cultural history, and it becomes more so with every passing week. In *GQ* magazine, it is possible to come to terms both with sport's essential triviality, and with its extraordinary and increasingly powerful place in the world. The pieces gathered here reflect that – as will the stories in the current issue of the magazine. Writing on sport for *GQ* is always a stimulating and challenging business. And I will tell you something else: it is bloody good fun, too.

Sporting Life

BLOOD SPORT

Robert Ashton

July, 1995

In the theatre of violence the script is predictable but compelling. *Crack*. A head butt, delivered with a sickening crunch, bloodies a nose. *Thwack*. A carefully aimed elbow is swung with bone-crushing intensity. *Smack*. A knee connects with a groin. And the mob howls in appreciation, springing to its feet, eyes popping, veins pumped.

This no-holds-barred human cockfight in a modern amphitheatre in Charlotte, North Carolina, is legal. Winner pockets a $52,000 purse; loser faces intensive care. Six thousand enthusiasts have come to see blood spilt, hear bones snap, and maybe pick up a couple of busted teeth for souvenirs. 'Rip his head off,' brays a rabid meathead. 'Kill the muthafucker!' Two fighters trapped inside an eight-sided chain-link fence – The Octagon – seem prepared to oblige. With a sickening, repetitive thud, bare knuckles beat a steady rhythm against bleeding skull.

Bludgeoned to a pulp, the fallen contender is carried from the caged pit under the harsh lights of cameras beaming to 220,000 TV viewers. A couple of blonde girls in ass-skimming shorts hop up and down between bouts, drawing enthusiastic whoops from the audience. The hollering swells when some stodgy guitar work, accompanied by a rock 'n' roll light show, kicks in and another pair of brawlers take the stage.

This is not just wrestling or boxing. Neither contender is wearing gloves, there hasn't been a weigh-in and there are no judges or scoring system. A sign on the wall boasts: THERE ARE NO RULES.

That's not strictly true – there's a stiff penalty for eye-gouging and biting is frowned upon, but merciless kicks, elbow and knee shots and joint-popping locks and choke holds are *de rigueur*. It's a knockout contest: there are eight carefully selected contestants, and whoever is left standing advances to the next round, which means the winner will fight up to three times in one night.

This is the Ultimate Fighting Championship V. Not since the legendary John L Sullivan pickled his fists in turpentine and fought bare-knuckle bouts at the beginning of the last century has the world seen anything like it. While boxing in Britain undergoes another of its periodic exercises in self-examination following Gerald McClellan's possible brain damage at the hands of Nigel Benn, America is upping the ante. 'In Western culture we look for the *It* girl, whether she's Marilyn Monroe or Madonna,' foams Art Devie, the Brooklyn-born motormouth promoter of the UFC. 'And we also look for Superman. We want to know who *the toughest guy in the world is*.'

Charlotte is a dreary little town. Bang in the middle of the Carolinas, flanked by Tennessee to the west and the Atlantic to the east, this Old South stronghold's place in the Bible Belt is unrivalled. Only a few miles down the road, disgraced TV evangelist Jim Bakker built a resort for his followers, a sort of Godneyland theme park, next door to Billy Graham's childhood home.

Bible punchers and beefy sluggers make strange bedfellows. Public outcry against these ungloved dust-ups is curiously muted, but the political lobby isn't convinced the quest for Superman should take place within the city limits. John McCain, the Republican Senator for Arizona, has made several overtures to North Carolina Governor Jim Hunt to have the UFC outlawed. And, fearing the folksy backwater will be tarnished by what he calls a 'barbaric blood sport', the state's attorney general, Mike Easley, searched the statute books to find a way to ban it. Unfortunately for him, North Carolina is one of only a handful of US states which doesn't have a boxing commission with the powers to regulate anything-goes bare-knuckle fighting.

When Easley's efforts failed, he pleaded with the town's mayor, Richard Vinroot, to beef up its local laws to see off the invasion of hulking ruffians with a hungry media circus in tow. 'It's something we don't really want to have in our city, but we don't have an ordinance that can stop it,' grumbles Vinroot. 'I'm sure the promoters are absolutely delighted.'

Art Davie revels in stirring up some pretty powerful nests. The 48-year-old Vietnam vet and former adman is part of a steely triumvirate (which includes Hollywood bigshot John Milius and Brazilian law graduate Rorion Gracie) who are responsible for breathing life back into the sort of savage prize mills which largely died out with the introduction of the Queensberry Rules in 1867.

But the trinity claim a nobler tradition than the manly pugilism practised by granite-fisted bulls in Regency London. Their inspiration is the Greek *pankration,* a vicious free-for-all blend of boxing and wrestling, where combatants stopped opponents by breaking limbs or killing them outright. 'We live in times where we are meant to be politically correct,' asserts Davie. 'There doesn't seem to be a place for the warrior spirit, it is an anachronism. But I don't think this should be engineered out of human experience.'

Far from regarding such organised brutality as a breakdown in civilisation, Davie justifies the UFC with the conviction of an evangelist. 'Cultures go through a maturation process and wind up repeating at their later stages some earlier forms,' he blithely insists. 'That's why we're bringing back the kind of fighting they had in Ancient Greece. It's not the end of the West, it is the renaissance of the West.'

Spreading the word, the pay-for-view production company Semaphore Entertainment Group came on board in 1993 to broadcast the fighting live to the nation. The team is already looking at staging similar events in Europe, South America and Japan.

Davie's partner Rorion Gracie brought something else to the party: his lean, mean, fighting-machine younger brother, Royce, defending UFC champion. The Gracies are part of a Brazilian warring dynasty, headed by the 82-year-old patriarch Helio. This white-haired grandfather has been a fighter all his life, learning his craft in the back streets of Rio. Although only five-foot-eight in his socks and 140 pounds wet, Helio developed his own unique fighting style, Gracie Jiu-jitsu, and became revered as a national hero.

Considering his father's pedigree, Royce's career options were cast. 'When my father was younger he had to prove himself and would take on *anyone* – we grew up watching that,' explains the brooding 28-year-old, before trotting out the Gracie claim that no member of the family has lost a fight in 65 years.

Royce is one reason the fighters have converged on Charlotte. They want to take him out. However, this time that privilege falls solely to a tough bird called Ken Shamrock, whose dynamite blow earned him the nickname One-Punch Shamrock. Because Shamrock has not had the opportunity to avenge his defeat to Royce in the very first UFC, tonight they are fighting a one-off grudge match separate from the three-round eliminator.

The softly spoken, meditative Shamrock, one broken neck and a multi-break nose to his credit, can't wait. 'I finally get to meet Royce Gracie,' he says, flexing 205 pounds of battle-scarred hardware. But more powerful forces than Shamrock would need to be summoned to make Gracie sweat. 'I'll just pull enough stuff and see what juice comes out,' he growls, sharpening his gameplan on a punch bag at a local hardcore gym. 'Put the devil in the other side of the ring and I will walk in to meet him.'

The eight contenders (and four stand-ins, in case of injuries) on the bill have all had full-contact experience, cracking bones in prizefights in Mexico or bouncing troublemakers at clubs. Invariably they've been plucked from the 400 hopefuls who sent Davie their CVs and videos because of their prowess in the martial arts. 'I've had applications from people who claim their art is so deadly they can't reveal it,' he cackles. 'Every month, I get to hear from someone who has defeated a wild bull.'

With furrowed brows and bull necks, their intimidating biceps folded, the gladiators stare stoically ahead at the pre-fight meeting. Gracie, Canadian Dave Beneteau and Russian Oleg Taktarov provide the international flavour. The other muscle has been marshalled from everywhere between New Jersey and California. Many are married with kids and mortgages and – apart from a few youthful digressions – have led pretty blameless lives. At least three fighters profess to be God-fearing souls.

Why do it? Pride. And the money. It costs about $750,000 to stage a UFC, but with pay-for-view TV at $19.95 a pop, ticket sales, merchandising and licensing agreements, Davie estimates it generates 'mid-seven figures' revenue. Considering he has wisely taken the precaution of arranging insurance to cover death during combat, the total pot of $100,000 begins to look paltry.

But that's big bucks for those who juggle jobs like firefighting and paramedic work with martial arts instruction. 'I do this stuff so my kid can have a better life,' says Joe Charles, aka The Ghetto Man. When he's not knocking out people, Joe's knocking on school doors selling educational software. 'My mom wanted me to stop all this fighting, but now that I'm getting paid she's standing behind me.'

They also consider themselves to be natural-born fighters. 'I love competition. I like to fight,' proclaims Shamrock, a father of three, whose chosen method of shootfighting has made him a *manga* cartoon hero in Japan. 'To be a good fighter you've got to be born with it in your system, the ability to overcome fear.'

None of the fighters appears to be troubled by fear. Waiting for his tilt at Royce, Shamrock hops around, chirpy as you like. He looks more in tune for a dinner date with his wife Tina than preparing to go the distance with one of the most dangerous men on earth. 'If a guy stares you down in a bar, adrenalin will start going through your body,' he says, a one-time troublemaker who spent his teenage years in and out of juvenile homes. 'Some people interpret that as fear, but I use it to get psyched up. When I'm fighting everything becomes numb to me and I don't feel any pain.'

Showtime. Time to step up and dance. The arena is about two-thirds full, but the UFC has got stiff competition. The Eagles are playing across town. Some of the crowd look like they've done a fair bit of sparring themselves, but there's also the beer-bellied backwoods boys wrapped in baseball caps, plaid and tattoos, and a smattering of women. 'All those close clinches, the muscles ... it's a goddamn, freakin' turn on,' giggles 23-year-old Casey.

The evening's entertainment opens at a savage pace when Dave Beneteau pins down Cancio, a Miami-based Kung Fu practitioner, and rains at least two dozen blows on his face, which quickly turns to mush. It's all over before the redneck in the 'I'd just kick your butt' T-shirt has time to eat his pizza.

'How ya'll doin'?' Tracy sidles up to get a better view. 'I wanna see heads busted up,' she confides. It looks a distinct possibility as a giant called Jon Hess proceeds to batter Andy 'The Hammer' Anderson. This rumble stays on its feet despite the monster's bowling ball-sized fists quickly bloodying the smaller man's ear. But with no protective gloves there's a limit to how many times a man can drive knuckles into solid cranium without them breaking. Hess finds out the hard way. He wins the bout, but a fractured hand puts him out of business.

And so it goes on. But when a lake of blood fails to materialise on the canvas during the grudge match between Gracie and Shamrock, Tracy and the rest of the audience lose patience. The bout turns into a 33-minute war of attrition, and its relatively mild brutality is not nearly enough to quell the mantra-like chant 'bullshit, bullshit, bullshit'. Sensing the pay-for-view audience might be reaching for the remote control, the fight is declared a draw.

The Michigan-based Greco-Roman wrestler Dan Severn peps things up in his semi-final clash with Oleg Taktarov. Severn turns his rival into a floor mop before cudgelling him with a combination of pistol-cracking piledrivers and knee blows. The Elvis-loving Russian is renowned for being able to take a shot, but this is extreme punishment and his head begins to turn into something resembling chopped liver. The fight is stopped and a lackey wipes up the blood.

On a roll, Severn dispatches the other finalist, Beneteau, in double-quick time to become king of The Octagon. As the herd teems into the carpark, they reflect on the evening's blood-letting and $15 well spent. At about a penny a punch, the lust for witnessing real violence from the safety of a plastic seat has been satisfied – for now. But there's precious little debate about the morality of the spectacle. 'Who cares, man?' asks a gangly youth.

Davie hurries past, mentally pencilling in his next batch of willing fodder. He can't have missed a banner proposing the definitive challenge: TYSON VERSUS ROYCE GRACIE. Iron Mike against Superman. Unmissable.

HARD RUCK

Frank Keating

February, 1989

The other Saturday I was ordering a tea-time round of drinks in a Welsh rugby clubhouse after a bloodthirsty local 'derby' between neighbouring village teams when I broke off to join in the applause for an ugly brute with cauliflower ears who had just returned from a token visit to the hospital. The opponent he had deliberately 'done over' on the pitch a couple of hours before was being prepared for an emergency operation to reassemble his broken jaw and slashed cheekbone.

The cheers were not for this visit of sorrow or contrition – but for the *macho* skulduggery itself. I was later horrified to realise that I too had joined in the guffawing backslaps for the hard-man hero as he recounted with an almost satisfied grin how many stitches his opponent had needed. 'Nobody messes around with our Ivor and gets away with it', was the general smug and triumphant consensus. And these were compatriots and neighbours: there wasn't even the excuse of hyped up nationalism. To adapt Dr Johnson – 'The Welsh are a fair people; they *never* act kindly towards one another.'

You notice I don't name names. It is inadvisable these days. Rugby players have become writ happy. Already this season, to my knowledge, there have been three High Court actions over injuries sustained on the rugby field. In France, a player was killed in a pitch brawl, and the opposing club had to defend *en masse* charges of manslaughter. One of Britain's leading experts on sport and the law, Edward Grayson QC, says that not only the culprit thugs could be liable to legal action 'but also referees who allow a game to degenerate into violence through lax control, or coaches who over-motivate players to such an extent that serious injury might be caused as a result'.

This spring, on March 18, a vengeful match takes place at Cardiff. The last time Wales (in the sporting jargon) 'entertained' England at the National Stadium was on March 7, 1987. Inside five minutes, the English lock and Lancashire police constable (no less), Wade Dooley, broke the cheek-bone of the Welsh forward, Phil Davies, with a purler of a right hander.

Afterwards, Dooley and three other England players, including the captain, Richard Hill, were dropped from the team for the next match. The irony of Dooley's chosen profession seemed totally to have escaped his masters. Indeed, that same month in Wales, a Cardiff police constable, Richard Johnson, was dismissed from the Force and jailed for six months for *biting off the ear of a fellow cop* in the match between Cardiff and Newport Police. Not many weeks before, the Pontypool and Wales scrum-half, David Bishop, was jailed for a month, later suspended on appeal, after pleading guilty of assault by taking a running kick at a floored Newbridge player, Chris Jarman.

Off the field, Bishop has twice been charged with assault. He phrases exactly the double standards his games have so long fostered and hidden behind: 'I'm no bad boy at all. Nor do I pretend I'm an angel. It's a hard game and you've got to play it hard; it's a physical game and you've got to play it physical. Tempers boil over sometimes – so what, you can only regret it when they do. But basically, as well as a test of skill and speed, rugby is also a test of manhood. What's wrong with that? It's just the shit press that blows it up out of all proportion.'

Aye, there's the rub – that thin line between heroic *manhood* and mean-spirited *machismo*. It has always been the dilemma for rugby. It could have been any Saturday afternoon of the century, couldn't it, that the muscle-preening prop stood naked in the showers admiring his rippling physique? 'Look at Adonis,' chaffs a caustic team mate. 'What do you mean,

"Adonis"?' answers the self-admiring thicko – '*the* Donis!'

Ever since the 14-year-old committee of the Rugby Union demanded in their Rules of 1885 that the referee be sole arbiter of fair and unfair play, the macho men have, by definition, had licence to examine the limits they could get away with – though those earliest Rules contained such parentheses as, 'though it is lawful to hold an opposing player in the scrimmage, it is not legal to attempt to *throttle* or *strangle* an opponent' ... or to 'hold a player and *hack* him at the same time'.

In the bar afterwards, rugby has never entertained squealers. Wimps in the clubhouse get as short shrift as randy nymphs outside it. One of rugger's first lily-livered wets to dare go public was the poet Rupert Brooke, who submitted these lines to, of all magazines, the *Rugby School Annual*, when he was 17 in 1904:

> 'When first I played I nearly died,
> The bitter memory still rankles –
> They formed a scrum with *me* inside!
> Some kicked the ball and some my ankles,
> I did not like the game at all,
> Yet, after all the harm they'd done me,
> Whenever I came near the ball,
> They knocked me down and stood upon me.'

There, you see, you've got to laugh, haven't you, at the utter, pansified drippiness of yon simpering Wupert Bwooke? The complexity of this hooligan game is such, too, that even those whose spirits are embedded close and warmly to the heart of the freemasonry itself find enormous satisfaction in letting you count their own stitches and bruises acquired in ancient battles – like the actor Richard Burton's classic, tongue-rolling, lip-smacking litany of verbs that describe his treatment during the last club rugby match he ever played, when he was 28, against a neighbouring village team of Welsh colliers – '... troglodytes burned to the bone by the fury of their work, bow-legged and embittered because they weren't playing for or hadn't played for and would never play for Cardiff or Swansea or Neath or Aberavon, men who smiled seldom and when they did it was like a scalpel . . . and I was elbowed, gouged, dug, planted, raked, hoed, kicked a great deal, sandwiched, and once humiliatingly taken from behind with nobody in front of me when I had nothing to do but run 15 yards to score.'

Burton had to play *Hamlet* at the Old Vic the following Monday – but such, he recalled, were his muscle cramps after the experience, 'I was compelled to play the Prince of Denmark as if he were the hunchbacked Richard III.'

All good stuff for the clubhouse yarns – but it leaves you none the wiser as you attempt to pin rugby's two-faced philosophies to the noticeboard. I've been a hanger-on through the last three tours by the British Lions and loitered on the fringes of club rugby for some three decades now. But I'm still none the wiser about the acceptable levels of violence.

I played the game for a few years as a kid. I left school as a fancypants scrum-half and had a trial for Gloucester, then as now a rampaging collection of toughs. The old myths and mystiques, I notice, still abound. Beat out that old gospel! The old jokes are always the best. Halfway through that first trial match almost 30 autumns ago I was shovelled up from the touchline and carted off to Gloucester Infirmary. Thus ended my first-class rugby career. But my concussion was mild enough to allow me to remember the pre-match exhortation by Gloucester's England forward, a bald, demonic, agate-eyed warrior called Peter Ford.

'If it's dark and moves, kick it; it might be the ball. If it's dark and still, either rake it back with your studs or just stand on it. If it squeals, say a loud "Sorry" in earshot of the ref.'

The doughty Peter, still a legend all over Gloucester, became an England selector when he retired from playing. One of his front-row stokers in that fearsome old Gloucester pack was Roy Fowker, a bargee on the nearby Sharpness Canal. The whole county knew him just as 'Our Fowker'. He imparted his wisdom to me with relish; it had stood the test of time. 'If one of them other buggers in the backs drops the thing and you find yourself first to get there, just pick it up, and charge like a battering ram at the nearest bloke who gets in the way; but if someone of their side goes to pick it up first, then just drive your bloody boot in at his fingers; that'll learn him.'

The philosophy, I fancy, has not changed one jot, however much the coaches who've been to study PE at Loughborough College might nowadays wrap it up in academic semantics. It's called 'taking out your man'.

Our Fowker also showed me how the cultural divide can increase violence on the field. Not only north-south, but east-west, too. Like Gloucester would – and still – always play their hardest (*i.e.* dirtiest) against the presumed hooray-Herberts from, say, Harlequins, the snooty London club based at the middle-class shrine of Twickenham itself. One time (by then I was safely behind the touchline myself, as a paid observer on the Gloucester *Citizen*), Roy had so thunderously duffed up a Harlequin winger with pretensions to play for England that I suggested he made amends in the clubhouse afterwards.

Pint nursed by his giant's mitt, Fowker approached his poor, prancing adversary of the afternoon. The still quivering Quin had won his Blue at Oxford and was now one of the country's most promising barristers. The conversation went like this:

Fowker: 'What be y'doin' furra livin' then?'

QC Quin: 'Actually, I work at the Bar.'

Fowker: 'Which one?'

QC Quin: 'Lincoln's Inn, actually.'

Fowker: 'What be 'ee there then? Potman, is it?'

So, any suggestion of a cultural gap can inspire violence in rugby. There is also the generation gap – that is, the old buffer in the clubhouse forever tut-tutting about the meekness of today's youth and the comparative namby-pambiness of strict refereeing. A few years ago at Cardiff there was an almighty punch-up between the two macho forwards Geoff Wheel of Wales and Willie Duggan of Ireland. Wheel had, by all accounts, thrown the first left-hook after Willie had fraternally warned him with mischievous Kilkenny cunning that if he tried any strong-arm stunts he'd be carted from the field of play, not as Geoffrey Wheel, but as Meals on Wheels.

Bomph! Crack! The two of them went at it hell for whatever –

till the ref sent them packing. At which point, as half of us in the pressbox licked our pencils and became all po-faced about the game being besmirched and all that, the other half – mostly former players – started attacking us for being so pathetically prim about a man's game, a physical contact sport. I remember Wilf Wooller, rampaging old Welsh centre of 50 years before, was next to me. I feared for my own chin as Wilf thundered:

'By God! If they'd sent players off for punching so punily in my day, there wouldn't have been one player left by the half-time whistle. Punches are part and parcel of the game. When we played Ireland we'd spend the next eight hours licking each other's wounds over pints of Guinness in the bar. Wheel v Duggan could have been staged at a vicarage tea party!'

So is a major determining force the need for new generations to prove their manhood to the bellicose ancients who went before them, gruff old warriors like Wooller who wear their rugger scars like campaign medals?

I asked the best prop forward in Britain, David Sole, who used to play for the crack English side, Bath, before returning to his native heath in Edinburgh to be nearer his international colleagues. 'Oh, sure,' says David, 'there are a few front-row psychopaths around, especially in Wales.' There are ways, he says, of calming them:

'Go in *really* hard in that first scrum. Stags charging to show who's boss. If someone really whacks you in the first set-to, you can't let them get away with it, you must whack them back.'

Had he ever maliciously felled an opponent on purpose? A long pause, then the eyes twinkle. 'Probably ... but never to do as much damage as the fellow concerned might have done in the first place. And to actually run straight up to an opponent, pre-meditated, and whack him or boot him in the head, no, never.'

For Bath, Sole packed down alongside the England prop, Gareth Chilcott, a four-square personification of the brick outhouse, 17 stones and standing just five feet and a fagpaper, with a Wormwood Scrubs 'haircut' framed by two voluptuous cauliflower ears – but as gentle and good-natured a soul as you could wish to meet off the field. Gareth has been sent off for a string of misdeeds: butting, punching, kicking, and stamping – ('What do you mean,' asked a girlfriend of mine, 'stamping on people's *toes*?' 'No,' admitted the man they call Coochie, 'stamping on much more sensitive parts, I'm afraid!'). But since the second of his England caps Chilcott has been a reformed character – 'though you've still got to play it physical, especially in those first two or three close-quarter exchanges. You've just got to prove you ain't no babby-ass boy.' And he says no more, though leaving a lot, still, to the imagination. Babby-ass, indeed.

Chilcott was one of the England players temporarily dropped after the Dooley duff-up in Cardiff – unfairly, many said, for he was convicted on his reputation rather than being the sinner who repenteth. Most blame was fixed on the England captain that day, Richard Hill. He has never played for England since. He agrees there might have been too much adrenalin flowing.

'But that's me, I'm a combative little fellow. There's nothing worse than a dull, lifeless dressing-room. I tend to strut about firing everyone up, shouting at blokes, geeing them up, whacking their backsides to get the blood flowing. Especially the forwards. It's good when you see the glint come in their eyes, it means they're ready to go – though I agree there's a fine line about it, and the danger can be that they get so worked up they go out there and charge about like headless chickens, whacking everything that moves. As for me actually whopping someone, well, I'm only a little bloke aren't I, I'm not going to hurt anyone seriously, am I?'

His replacement, Richard Harding, far from gloating at the crack-down on dirty play that led to him being given the job, closed ranks within the freemasonry like the best of them:

'I feel extremely sorry for anyone who takes the rap, who are made scapegoats for something that goes on every day of the week in rugby – so does every player in England. Far worse than a few punches has been going on for years. And as for the piety and pomposity emanating from Wales after one of their chaps got hit, well, they've had a heck of a lot of psychopaths strutting about their rugby fields for years, haven't they?'

Harding's Bristol club was involved – against Newport – on the only occasion in first-class rugby when a referee, George Crawford, sent *himself* off for dirty play. Two years ago, after 20 minutes of scrapping, gouging and punching between the two sides, Crawford got fed up with issuing final warnings, turned tail and awarded himself an early bath, cancelling the match.

'It was sheer lunacy,' recalls Crawford, who also happens to be a Metropolitan Police Superintendent, 'a running fist-fight. Can you imagine the sheer horror of watching players who had been friends half an hour beforehand, tearing into each other with their faces contorted in hate? To hear the blows was sickening. Given a single death from violent action and this once marvellous game could be placed alongside the victim in the same grave. Any parent should be concerned about their child playing.'

And what happened to the peaceable Superintendent? He was given a severe reprimand by the game's governing body, the RFU at Twickenham, for abdicating his responsibilities. Other referees would sympathise. England's finest Union official, Colin High, had eight seasons as a senior ref before he sent his first two blackguards off three years ago. 'One was for putting the boot in with malice; the other simply measured the opposite guy, and though the punch only travelled that far' – and he holds out his hand like a fisherman boasting about a medium-sized trout – 'it was viciously intended to inflict maximum damage, which it did. Mind you, it's really all a matter of degree; if you sent everyone off just for throwing a measly punch, then I don't think we'd have anyone left on the field of play.'

Where does that leave us? The rise in sendings-off through the decade – in Wales (207 clubs) 137 in 1980–81, 211 last year; in England (1,903 clubs) 1,184 in 1980–81, 1,378 last year – does not mean much except, most players will tell you, that a few more refs got out of bed on the wrong side that morning.

Or is it a necessity for them to live up to all the old clubhouse myths of derring-do and the heroic dirty deeds of legend? Is violence whipped up by the captains, with their Henry V exhortations in the dressing-room; or the touchline coaches whose bellowing *'Take him out!'* can mean only one thing – render an opponent physically ineffective for the rest of the game?

Or might it be that rugby players – for the sake of not being wet and unmanly – never *ever* apologise to an opponent for losing their rag; unless getting blind drunk with each other serves always as a tacit apology?

Not quite true. The only man I've ever known apologise for dirty play on the rugby field was Andy Ripley, of Rosslyn Park and England. Last season, when I did a farewell interview with Andy after he had retired from 20 years as a credit to the game, he asked if he could add one line of his own. Sure, I said. 'Could you publicly apologise for me to Bob Anderson, of Gosforth, the only man I knowingly fouled in my career.' Ah, sweet, eh?

So is rugby an enduring, honest game full of Andy Ripleys, fun and good fellowship, comradely challenge and chivalry, ruined only rarely by the odd playground bully?

'Most certainly not,' says John Davidson, the Moseley prop who was forced to retire from the game after his jaw and cheekbone were smashed by a Swansea opponent's punch – 'the club circuit in England and Wales includes about a dozen players who are, quite simply, psychopathic thugs: it's the only way to describe them; they are bonkers and they are very dangerous.'

Thus, on the whole, I think the Psychopathic Thugs have it.

PATRIOT GAMES

Andrew Walpole

October, 1995

'Hrvatska! Hrvatska! Let's go Croatia! Let's go!' crackles a guttural-sounding voice over the in-flight intercom as the Croatian football team's plane begins its slow descent into the sun-drenched Ukrainian capital of Kiev.

'Blazevic . . . Prosinecki . . . Beli . . . Suker . . . Ivic . . .' intones the voice, proceeding to reel off a long list of unfamiliar sounding names amid a chorus of cheers – and the odd catcall – from the passengers on board flight 490 from Zagreb. The master of ceremonies behind the microphone is Zorislav Srebric, the Croatian Football Federation's Mr Fixit. Finally, after paying tribute to all manner of players, officials, fans and hangers-on, he reaches a surname which is vaguely familiar to British ears. 'Boban!' cries Srebric loudly. 'Zvonimir Boban!'

This name belongs to the man lazily sprawled out in his seat at the rear of the plane. He acknowledges the applause with a wry smile before joining the rest of the team in idly leafing through various Croatian newspapers.

His name is all over the back pages. Not just in Croatia either. At 27, Zvonimir Boban is a sure-fire candidate for inclusion in anyone's World Football XI. Not only is he an integral part of the all-conquering Italian side AC Milan, he's also captain of a Croatian national team which many rate the best in Europe on current form.

A mark of Croatia's rising status was to have been this month's game against England at Wembley, a fixture now cancelled. However, on October 8, they will secure a place in next year's

European Championships when they take on Italy – a team they have already beaten once and left trailing behind them in their qualifying group. But for now, we are in the Ukraine, where Croatia are playing a crucial qualifying game against their hosts.

Despite their status, the blank-faced youth in uniform keeps the team waiting for an age in Ukrainian customs before they are finally given a cursory wave through. Even the mighty Boban barely merits a second look as he hands over his passport. In Croatia, Boban gets the red-carpet treatment wherever he goes: fans call him 'The Duke'; the press revere him as a kind of sporting renaissance man; and his picture – even in this predominantly Catholic country – probably hangs on more bedroom walls than the Pope's.

Closer inspection of Boban's appearance reveals a small clue about the reason for his god-like status back home. Alone among the tracksuited throng, he is the one wearing his baseball cap turned round the wrong way with its peak nearly touching his shoulders. This is reminiscent of another complex individual, Eric Cantona, a man who betrays his fierce streak of independence by always wearing his shirt with the collar turned up – while his Manchester United team-mates, to a man, turn theirs down.

The comparison with Cantona is apt. Just as the Frenchman's kung-fu kick at a Crystal Palace fan at Selhurst Park is indelibly etched into the memory of every Briton, no Croat will ever forget the moment when Boban kicked a Serbian policeman who attacked him during a full-scale riot between rival Dinamo Zagreb and Red Star Belgrade fans in Zagreb in May 1990. The ethnic violence which ended that match was a harbinger of one of the twentieth century's bloodiest and most bitter civil wars; a conflict which has so far claimed the lives of around 10,000 people, made thousands more homeless and resulted in Serbs controlling nearly a third of Croatian territory.

During a bumpy ride from the airport in a rickety bus which probably first saw service when Stalin still ruled, the full significance of Boban's retaliatory lunge begins to sink in. When we finally arrive at the towering concrete monument to bad design which will serve as the team's hotel for the next three days, he is asked if he ever regrets lashing out in the way that he did in front of a TV audience of millions.

'No, I would do exactly the same thing again if I had to,' he explains quietly in passable, if halting, English. 'The Serbian police were attacking our fans in the most incredible way. When I asked them to stop, one of them called me "a son of a bitch". He was just a boy, so I did nothing, but then another policeman tried to hit me in the stomach and I just reacted in the same way as anyone would. I defended myself.'

Boban peers thoughtfully into the gloomy hotel lobby and admits that this kick was possibly a turning-point in his life. 'It was like an explosion,' he says. 'I felt all my nationalistic feelings coming to the surface and in that moment, I knew that I had balls.'

Afterwards, he spent three weeks in hiding because striking a policeman carried a sentence of hard labour. 'I really thought that I might have to go to prison,' he says. 'But in the end the policeman was punished because he had attacked me in my place of work.'

The main reason Boban has no regrets about this incident is because such a powerful Croatian side has emerged from the wreckage of the former Yugoslavia; a phoenix-from-the-ashes team built around the crop of exciting young Croatian players who played with him in Yugoslavia's World Youth Championship winning side of 1987: the full-back Robert Jarni; the striker Davor Suker; the midfielder Robert Prosinecki.

Four years ago, the presence of this promising Croatian quartet (coupled with the talented Montenegrin Savicevic) made Yugoslavia strong favourites for the 1992 European Football Championships, until the outbreak of war forced their withdrawal. Now the same foursome are holding the reins of a good dark-horse bet for Euro '96. Only this time they are a team of exiles. It's not just Boban who flies in from abroad for their games: Jarni comes from Juventus, Suker and Prosinecki from their respective Spanish clubs, Seville and Oviedo. So do others – like Gazza's former Lazio team-mate Alen Boksic and the German-based pair, Slaven Bilic and Elvis Brajkovic.

What draws this raggle-taggle band of footballing gypsies home is a burning desire to pull on the distinctive red-and-white-checked shirts of Hrvatska-Croatia. 'It just does not compare with playing for Yugoslavia,' says Boban. 'The Croatian team is where my heart is now.'

Passion and pride are often hollow words in football circles. But in this case, Croatia's results bear them out: since they first stepped onto the international football stage in 1990, Croatia have played twenty, won twelve, drawn four, and lost four. Which is a remarkable record for a country that wasn't even on the world map five years ago. Especially when you consider that initially the team had to pay their own air fares and hotel bills in order to balance the Croatian Football Federation's shoestring budget. Even now, the players only get expenses and will have to wait for their appearance money until qualification for Euro '96 is guaranteed.

'I don't think any team has ever been admitted to FIFA under such difficult circumstances,' says the Croatian Football Federation's General Secretary Ante Pavlovic. Just persuading world football's governing body to let them play home games in the capital Zagreb – which has been largely untouched by the war – took an age. They still can't play in Split – home of the country's most successful club, Hadjuk – because it's deemed to be unsafe.

Then there was the sheer mental strain that an unceasing toll of death and destruction placed on the team. 'Every player was afraid that one day they would get a call saying that his friend or a member of his family had been killed,' says Pavlovic, casting his mind back to the bleak winter of 1991–2 when the fighting was at its peak.

One squad member, Nenad Pralija, lost a brother. So did the team's number-one fan, 39-year-old Zelgko Katavic – a long-haired, gap-toothed, fifteen-stone truck driver from Osijek whose sizeable beer gut has earned him the nickname 'Beli'.

But shouldering the burden of grief together has forged a close bond between players, coaches, fans and administrators; one which is extremely rare in the money-driven world of professional football. Boban has paid for operations on Croatian civilians injured in the war and donated money to a bomb-ravaged church. Boksic organised collections for humanitarian relief at his Lazio club. And when, earlier this year, the legendary Beli made a marathon 72-hour trek overland through five countries to watch the team's game in Estonia, all the players had a whip-round to pay for his flight home.

Over drinks at a reception at the Croatian Embassy in Kiev, the team's 62-year-old technical director Tomislav Ivic lauds his players' newfound sense of patriotism and social responsibility. 'All the players want to contribute something to the building of a new country. They see it as their duty,' says the former Ajax and Paris St Germain coach. 'They know that there isn't one ambassador in the world who can do what they can to promote a new Croatia.'

But the man the Croatians call 'Little Napoleon' only really wants to talk about football, or to be more precise, formations. Putting his arm around me, he demands a full breakdown on England's likely starting line-up and tactics for this September's friendly. Then, grabbing my notebook and pen, he draws page after page of diagrams illustrating how Boban played a crucial role in countering the threat of Roberto Baggio during Croatia's tumultuous win over Italy in Palermo last year. 'Boban is so important to this team,' he says. 'He is a natural leader not just on the pitch, but in the dressing room, in the training ground, even in the hotel.'

The owlish Zdravko Reic, a close confidant of Boban's and a veteran Croatian football correspondent who has covered four World Cups and seven European Championships, paints an even grander portrait. 'Boban is a man of great culture and humanity. He doesn't just read sports papers, he reads novels and philosophy,' he says. 'If he wasn't a footballer, he could have been a government minister or a professor.'

Or maybe even a priest. 'I do read a lot of books, but I always come back to the Bible – especially the New Testament,' says Boban quietly. 'It's my guiding principle in life. I have had a great religious feeling inside me since I was about fifteen.' Which is why, presumably, he pays for churches to be repaired and shattered limbs mended. 'It gives me a good feeling inside – yes. I want to set a good example, of course. But I don't like to talk about things like that too much. Somehow they become plastic – not real – when journalists write about them.'

But five years on from that infamous kick, can he find forgiveness in his Christian heart and cultured head for the Serbs? Boban cites his friendship with his AC Milan colleague Savicevic who hails from Montenegro, Serbia's ally. 'You can't generalise and say all Serbs are bad and all Croatians good,' he says. They often discuss the war: 'We are a long way apart – but he does not agree with attacks on civilians. He is not an "ultra".'

As a cluster of painfully thin Ukrainian boys crowd round our table begging for an autograph, Boban turns his mind to the following day's game. The omens are not good. He clutches his groin which has been troubling him for weeks. Worse still, he has also lost a precious necklace which was a wedding present and is engraved with an image of his favourite bird – the seagull.

His gloomy prognosis is based on reason as well as superstition. It's the end of a long, hard season and the team are not in the best of spirits: Prosinecki is suspended, Jarni is also carrying a niggling injury and there is universal annoyance that the Federation hasn't brought its own supplies of food to a city which is close to the site of the Chernobyl nuclear disaster.

Twenty-four hours later, the lack of atmosphere in the Ukraine's national stadium appears to deaden the team's spirit further. Twenty years ago, when Dinamo Kiev were among the most feared sides in Europe, this ground was frequently a seething cauldron filled to the brim with 100,000 spectators. But today's game clashes with a religious festival in Kiev, resulting in a crowd of barely 5,000 – and a large proportion of them are in uniform too. 'It's like a cemetery,' says the Ukrainian press attaché wearily.

Led by the imposing figure of Beli, the small band of Croatian fans try hard to add colour to the drab spectacle by draping a series of huge red and white banners over the rows of empty seats. In the press box, the mood is equally patriotic; the Croatian journalists all stand when their own national anthem is played. Their Ukrainian counterparts stay seated – to the fury of the press attaché. 'Stand up, you fucking bastards, stand up,' he shouts. 'Show some respect.'

Croatia opt for a defensive 5–3–2 system, they concede an early goal and then have their goalkeeper sent off for the second game in a row. Boban, playing in a deeper position than usual, shows only flashes of brilliance. He nearly scores with a curling 25-yard drive before his groin gives way and he is substituted just before half-time. Without him, his team-mates fail to reduce the deficit and at the end of 90 minutes, the bottle of champagne the Croatian pressmen had brought is quietly packed away.

On the plane back to Zagreb, the talk is not of Euro '96, but the minutiae of Croatian football politics. Will 'Attila' (the team's manager Miroslav Blazevic) and 'Little Napoleon' still be at the managerial helm this time next year? Or will the Federation's new vice-president Vlatko Markovic, who is not only the team's ex-manager, but also a good friend of the country's football-mad President Franjo Tudjman, get his old job back?

But the whispering stops as £10-million worth of talent comes loping down the aisle in the shape of Gazza's former Lazio team-mate Alen Boksic. He stops in front of the beer-guzzling Beli, punches him playfully on the chest and ruffles his hair like a lion playing with an oversized cub. Their banter is temporarily drowned out by the sound of the in-flight intercom. It's the Federation's Srebric rallying his weary troops again with the now all too familiar war cry of 'Let's go Croatia! Let's go!'

Like Srebric, Boban's confidence in the team remains undented by the temporary setback in the Ukraine. 'We will learn from this defeat,' he says. 'Perhaps it will teach us that we need to be better prepared before we go into a big tournament where you play maybe three games in seven days. But if we can get our preparation right then we will have a very good chance. We already believe that we can beat anyone in the world in a one-off.'

This is not mere sabre-rattling; some of the wisest football sages in the world agree with Boban. England's Terry Venables has gone on record saying that Croatia are the continent's best team on current form; Arrigo Sacchi, national coach of Italy, has made no secret of his admiration either. 'Croatia are the European team who have made the biggest leap in the FIFA rankings,' he said recently. 'They have a lot of very good players.'

The former England international Steve Coppell takes an even more bullish view of Croatia's chances next year: 'Given the nationalistic fervour that they take into every game with them now, I am sure they will be a real force to be reckoned with. Boksic is a terrific player and in Boban they have a very talented individual who can win a game by himself. I think they are well capable of doing what Romania and Bulgaria did in the World Cup last year – and surprising a few of the big names.'

KURDS UNITED

Gareth Smyth

November, 1993

It is a pleasant spring afternoon in Arbil in north-eastern Iraq. Mohammed Khalil leans forward on the bench at the town's football ground as he watches two local sides and scouts for promising young players. Mr Mohammed is a calm, broad man of 53. His hair is carefully parted, his moustache neatly brushed and he wears an immaculate cream tank top. But his brow is furrowed and he fiddles nervously with his prayer beads. In short, he seems preoccupied. As well he might. Mr Mohammed has much on his mind. It is not easy being manager of Arbil, the leading football team in Iraqi Kurdistan.

'We are suffering financially, physically, morally,' he says. 'Our players must learn new ways. Some special circumstances make it difficult for them to play their best.' This is something of an understatement. Five years ago Mr Mohammed led Arbil to promotion into the top division of the Iraqi league. Since then, Iraqi Kurdistan has been devastated, and is today under economic siege from all its neighbours. Football is played in the shadow of Saddam Hussein, amid an uneasy armed truce between Kurdish guerrillas and the Iraqi army. And since Iraqi teams from outside Kurdistan are not allowed to come to an area which Saddam says is run by 'bandits, Zionists and US imperialists,' Arbil must play all their games away from home in territory controlled by the Iraqi government.

Arbil is the Kurdish equivalent of Milan or Liverpool. Football here is fever. As mothers hang out washing and grandfathers smoke pipes, small boys chase balls or stones along hot, dusty streets until their fathers call them in at dusk. Arbil's fans understand Mr Mohammed's difficulties and are pleased simply that his team still plays competitive football. But most were disappointed when Arbil finished last season seventeenth in Iraq's premier league of 24 clubs. Arbil's fans expect success.

At the entrance to Arbil's ground, and supported by two outsize concrete footballs, stands a painting depicting the Football Martyr. The glazed, timeless face of eternal youth belongs to former player and Kurdish guerrilla Mursil Hussain Mursil, who was killed by an Iraqi helicopter gunship in 1978 while fighting in the mountains. The Kurds call their fighters *peshmerga*, which means 'those who face death'. The hero is remembered respectfully as fans file past.

Inside the dusty ground, only the heavy concrete plinth and surround remain of the larger-than-life portrait of Saddam Hussein, which once dominated the field. The image of Iraq's president has been obliterated by the defiantly generous spray of Kalashnikov fire. Expunging the thousand faces of Saddam was a priority when, as the allies created a so-called safe haven in the wake of the Gulf war, Iraqi troops fell back behind a 320-mile 'green line' and Kurdish guerrillas took over a swathe of 50,000 square kilometres in the north-east of Iraq.

Kurds make few forward plans. Too many fathers, sons and brothers died at the hands of the Iraqi regime or in the long war against Iran. Too many children were buried when more than a million Kurds fled across mountain passes to Turkey and Iran as Saddam crushed the uprising of 1991. Landmines still regularly blow off victims' legs, and some 4,000 villages remain in ruins. More sheep grazed the hillsides this year than last and more land was cultivated, but food shortages are endemic. Cross-border smuggling is a lifeline to this once prosperous land which remains under a strict trade embargo from both the United Nations and Saddam.

Rumours travel fast and feed uncertainty. Faith in the Western allies is weakening, while the fear grows that Saddam's troops and security police, or *mukharabat*, will return. As it is, the *mukharabat* or its recruits are blamed for a spate of bombs in the cafés and streets of Arbil, and the murder of several foreign aid workers. The two-year equilibrium of 'free Kurdistan' on Iraqi soil is ultimately unstable. This is a surreal 'normality'. Saddam still pays the workers at the massive Dokan dam, south-east of Arbil, since they transfer hydro-electric power to the Iraqi regime, which, in return, supplies intermittent electricity to the Kurds. Similarly, the pro-government newspapers *al-Iraq* and *al-Thaura* – with Saddam's face beaming out from their front pages – are freely available in Arbil's bazaar.

Frequently, mass graves of bound skeletons are unearthed and remind the Kurds of the horrors of Saddam's 'Anfal' campaign of 1987–8, in which perhaps 180,000 men, women and children were eliminated. Yet flickery Rambo films are all the rage in Kurdish cinemas, and refugees sleep, eat and wash up in the torture chambers of former prisons. Life goes on. The Kurds settle back into their traditional pursuits of farming, raising children, and wiling away the day in tea shops. The passion for football stirs.

The mountains of northern Iraq, bordering Turkey and Iran, rise to nearly 12,000 feet. This rocky, inhospitable terrain has provided refuge for the Kurds through centuries of conflict with hostile neighbours. South of the former mountain resort of Salahuddin, the road wends steeply downwards. Arbil is the first city south of the mountains, nestling between the Greater and Lesser Zabs, two main tributaries of the mighty Tigris river, in one of the most fertile tracts of agricultural land in the world. The rolling plain which leads to Baghdad and beyond is suitably flat for playing the world's most popular game.

A sign in English, put up by the Iraqi Ministry of Tourism, proclaims Arbil the longest continuously inhabited city in the world. Archaeological research dates Arba Elo ('city of the four gods') to at least 5,000 BC, making it contemporary with, or even preceding, Ur, Babylon and Nineveh, the great cities of ancient Mesopotamia, one of the world's first civilisations. As the gateway to the mountains and routes east, Arbil was a natural trading centre and stopping-off post: in 401 BC the 'ten thousand' of the

Athenian Xenophon dropped in on their march back to Greece following an away defeat in Persia.

In today's geopolitics, Arbil is the capital of the statelet and fledgling democracy of 'free Kurdistan'. The reassuring buzz of allied jets is heard almost daily – evidence that the football ground is just north of the 36th Parallel and so within the 'no-fly zone' created to stop Saddam bombing the Kurds. But the positions of the Republican Guards, the crack troops left mostly unscathed by the Gulf war, are fewer than twenty miles away across the plain, and Saddam's embargo is slowly strangling everyday life.

When Mohammed Khalil uses the standard manager's excuse for the team's poor form – circumstances beyond his control – he has a better case than most. It is not, for example, difficult to believe his players' claims that Baghdad referees will not award penalties or offsides to Arbil. At the same time, the blockade rules out the high-protein, high-carbohydrate diet beloved by footballers the world over: while the team eat better than many Kurds, their staple fare is still bread, rice and tea. And they cannot recuperate adequately because they are constantly travelling to and from fixtures.

Arbil used to perform before home gates of 20,000 noisy fans. No longer. Since no other team in the Iraqi premier division can come to the Kurdish zone, Arbil play all their 'home' games at Mosul, the Iraqi government-controlled city 70 miles away. For every game – whether 'at home' in Mosul or away in Baghdad, Basra or Najaf – the players' ancient Nissan bus must pass the checkpoints of the 'green line'. It is a very stressful journey. On one side of the line are lightly armed, nervous Kurdish *peshmerga* in loose-fitting brown garb and Korean-made trainers; on the other side, more than 100,000 combat-ready Iraqi troops backed up by tanks and heavy artillery.

Kurds pass across the line in both directions, mainly visiting relatives, but getting through has become more difficult as Saddam has tightened the embargo. Few concessions are made to Arbil's team bus and its occupants. If the Iraqi soldiers on duty are sympathetic, the players may be waved through quickly, but if not they may have to wait in line for hours before being frisked and having their kit bags turned out.

For supporters, the crossing is even more fraught. Fewer and fewer brave a trip which can involve many hours' delay, if not detention, questioning and beatings. Most of the handful who continue to make the journey are boys too young for the military call-up: Saddam's troops guarding the checkpoints sometimes amuse themselves by conscripting older fans for the Iraqi army.

At several points on the line, the *peshmerga* and Iraqi soldiers glower at one another from barely 100 yards apart. North-west of Arbil, Iraqi troops have taken to burning petrol confiscated from returning Kurds: the billowing, sinister smoke visible for miles serves both to demonstrate the plentiful supply of petrol south of the line and to intimidate. If that weren't enough, the occasional shell flies over. The 'green line' is no place for the faint-hearted.

Kamiran Mohammed, Arbil's 26-year-old midfield playmaker, scored eleven goals last season in 44 games. Handsome and clean-cut, he is married with two small sons. He sports designer stubble, wears fashionable clothes with turn-ups on his trousers and accepts the adoration of young boys with an embarrassed smile. No doubt he would be a heart-throb, too, if women in this Muslim land watched football.

Open-mouthed fans gather behind the grille surrounding the pitch as we talk. Their fascination is as much with the pale-skinned Western reporter as with their footballing hero, and they strain to catch every word of the translated exchange. Kamiran is softly spoken, polite, and happy to answer questions. His ambitions, he says, with a gentle shrug of the shoulders, are 'to remain a good player, to train and practise, and to serve my country and people'. His ideal player, he says, is the German midfielder Lothar Matthaus, but off the field he comes across more as a Kurdish Gary Lineker.

Kamiran recounts what might have turned into the standard rags-to-riches story. He began with a small rubber ball in the street, his potential was recognised at school and by the age of fourteen he was playing for Arbil's youth team. As he moved rapidly into the first eleven, it was clear that Kamiran's talent could make him a star of Iraqi football.

The Brazilian Romereo, imported to manage the Iraqi national side, took an early interest in the 'number ten from Arbil'. Kamiran flourished. He became the linchpin of the Iraqi youth team and was top scorer when they won the 1985 Jordan Independence championship. He played for the full national side in March 1986 in two friendlies against Ipswich Town. Racking his brain, he can remember one name from Bobby Ferguson's outfit, that of defender Terry Butcher. 'He was a good player, their captain, the number five. When I dribbled past him, he kicked me!' (Ipswich won the first game one-nil, and the second was a nil-all draw.)

Kamiran was included in the Iraqi squad for the 1986 Gulf Championship in Bahrain, but Romereo left shortly afterwards, reportedly disillusioned by the way Iraqi football was run. Kamiran was never picked again. Arbil supporters believe fervently that Kamiran's international career was cut short because he is a Kurd, and not an Arab. Behind Kamiran's smile and charm lies a deep disappointment. 'I hoped I would be the best player in Iraq,' he says, 'but those in Baghdad have not given me the chance'.

'Those in Baghdad', Saddam and his circle, dominate football as they dominate everything else in Iraq. Despite an official policy of respect for Kurdish rights, the reality is discrimination and favouritism – generally in favour of Sunni Arabs over Shia Arabs or Kurds, and specifically in favour of Sunni Arabs from Tikrit, Saddam's birthplace. The head of both the Iraqi football association and the country's Olympic committee is Udai Hussein, the president's eldest son and former deputy head of Iraq's intelligence service. Udai was appointed to these posts straight after graduating from engineering college with a 99.5 per cent grade. His career was briefly thwarted when, in 1988, he bludgeoned to death a presidential food-taster who had acted as go-between for Saddam and a lover (the ex-wife of the chairman of Iraqi Airways). Udai's action, apparently in respect for his mother's honour, threatened to make the dalliance public and so dent Saddam's image as a devoted husband and family man. An angry Saddam threw his son into jail. But Udai's mother intervened. 'Why arrest him?' she reportedly asked her husband. 'After all, it is not the first time he has killed. Nor is he the only one in his family who has killed.' She had a point. Before slaughtering the food-taster, Udai had killed two army officers, one who had resisted his attempts to seduce his daughter and one who had resisted his attempts to seduce his wife.

Saddam relented. After a spell of luxurious exile in Switzerland, Udai resumed his position in charge of Iraqi sport. During the Gulf war he flew Kuwaiti footballers to Baghdad in an unsuccessful attempt to persuade them to play for Iraq – Kuwait was, after all, Iraq's 'nineteenth province'. Following the war, Udai announced that Iraq's 'victory' would be honoured annually by a 'Mother of all Battles' football championship.

In the anti-Saddam uprisings which followed the Gulf war, according to Shia sources, in the southern city of Basra, Udai personally selected and then executed dissidents in front of large numbers of detainees. In May 1992, three spectators were killed when Udai ordered his bodyguards to open fire on a football crowd chanting anti-Saddam slogans at a match in Baghdad. Udai now heads Iraq's bid to qualify for next summer's World Cup finals in the United States.

Sniffing around Arbil's ground, decked out in the traditional baggy trousers, is the diminutive Sadiq 'Gichka' ('The Small') Sa'aid, aka 'the sports encyclopaedia'. Gichka is in his late forties, but has a boyish enthusiasm which rarely leaves him silent. The gusto in his defence of the law forbidding back-passes to the goalkeeper makes the curled ends of his moustache vibrate. He salivates and sighs while reeling off the names of the 1970 Brazilian World Cup team – Pele, Tostão, Jairzinho, Rivelino ... he knows them all. His eyes radiate as he recalls the contrasting styles of the Charlton brothers. His face drops as he mourns Bobby Moore. He sees the funny side of Paul Gascoigne, collapsing in near hysterics over a long tale whose punchline is an Italian referee giving Gazza some gum: 'He found a new way to keep him quiet!'

Gichka has been a sports reporter since 1976, working 'underground' in the days when the punishment for working on an illegal newspaper was an unpleasant death. These days he works for *Briety*, one of the two new Kurdish daily newspapers, and also broadcasts a sports spot on local radio. Although Gichka is now too afraid to attend Arbil's games, manager Mohammed Khalil can't relax, because the newspaperman's absence doesn't prevent him writing columns offering comment and advice on tactics.

But Gichka's hyperactivity is, in part, a withdrawal symptom from not seeing live football. He misses watching Arbil, and the team, he believes, misses its supporters. 'The fans are the twelfth player in the side,' he says. 'Arbil haven't their support and it affects their play. The fans are unhappy. They feel rejected.' Gichka helped organise a petition bemoaning their plight which has been sent to the Kurdish parliament elected last year; he is not confident that the politicians will be able to help.

Samir Abdullah also wants to meet the journalist from Britain. Mr Samir is an earnest 40-year-old, clipboard-toting administrator in charge of the local football leagues. With the gently severe air of a scoutmaster, he points out matter-of-factly that Western aid (which prevented starvation last winter, if not the one before) has not included help for football. Sport, he says, is important for the education of young people and for the morale of everyone. Understandably, the Kurds have developed great skills in making things last – football kit, corner flags and referees' whistles, as much as tyres, cisterns or UNICEF tents. But a pair of boots costs about 800 dinas ($30) – perhaps a month's wages for the few Kurds in gainful employment. And shin pads are like gold dust. Can I make sure, Mr Samir asks, that John Major is told?

Mr Samir is nonetheless delighted that Arbil's manager, Mohammed Khalil, is scouting at the knockout competition for local teams which he has organised at Arbil's ground. The tournament commemorates the fourteenth anniversary of the death of Mullah Mustapha Barzani, the legendary Kurdish guerrilla leader who defied Baghdad in the Sixties and early Seventies. But the spring rains have given way to soaring summer temperatures.

The pitch is dry, and suddenly, tempers flare. A game between

Asir and Seka ends with a pitch invasion and general punch-up after Asiri players, two-one down, dispute a close decision and then assault the hapless referee. Watching with me from behind the goalposts, Gichka tut-tuts and shakes his head: it all brings back unpleasant memories of a near riot in 1987, when Arbil had a goal disallowed in a match against Zaura in Baghdad.

Gichka decides he must return to his office to write a column for tomorrow's newspaper deploring such hooliganism. Just before he scampers off past the painting of the Football Martyr, his shadow lengthening in the twilight, I can't resist asking him if the Kurds use the expressions, 'it's a game of two halves' and 'the game's not over until the final whistle blows'. Of course, Gichka replies, his smile restored. I dare not ask him if the Kurds also say that football is more serious than life or death.

COMPLETELY PUCKED

Alex Kershaw

May, 1993

It took nine policemen to subdue John Kordic, the 6'2", 27-year-old heavyweight champ of the National Hockey League, as he struggled in a Quebec motel room last August. Finally strapped onto a stretcher, with yellow rope around his feet and double handcuffs restraining his bulging arms, his face bloated by steroids, Kordic was still conscious and swearing as he was carried out.

An hour later, the NHL's most notorious 'goon' – or 'enforcer' – was dead. His final days had been short on glory, long on desperation and capped years of famous drug and alcohol abuse. Sent packing by four NHL teams, the John Belushi of hockey had racked up 997 penalty minutes in 245 games, averaging nearly 30 minutes in the sin-bin for every point he scored.

'Kordic's real battle was not with fellow enforcers on the ice but with himself,' says Claude Bédard, the sports editor of the *Journal de Québec*. It was no coincidence, Bédard adds, that at the time of his death, Kordic's golden years had faded into rejection and despair. As one of the many coaches Kordic played for put it: 'John always had a time bomb inside him, a time bomb set to explode.'

Indeed, few were surprised that the NHL's most feared prize-fighter had finally gone down to defeat in the long struggle with himself. The fastest, most violent professional team sport in the world had, after all, flipped the switch that turned on Kordic, the fighting machine who left blood on the ice all over North America. But no one, least of all Kordic himself, knew how to turn the switch off.

*

John Kordic wasn't always a goon. As a schoolboy, he was coached in the finer techniques of hockey by his father, Ivan, a Croatian immigrant who settled in Edmonton in the early Sixties. Kordic dreamt of playing defense. And yet, by 1986, the year he picked up a winner's medal in hockey's equivalent of the FA Cup, the Stanley Cup, his father's pride was already tinged with remorse. He hadn't raised his eldest son to be a hockey star paid a reputed $200,000 for his right hook as much as his ability to skate.

'John wanted to be seen as a hockey player, not just a fighter,' says Claude Bédard. We are seated in the press gallery overlooking the ice in the Coliseum, the Québec Nordiques' cavernous stadium. A game against the New York Islanders is in its third quarter. 'John was very frustrated. Two months before he died, he told me he sometimes cried himself to sleep at night. He wanted to stay in hockey, but the only way he thought he could do that was by continuing to fight. He felt trapped.'

Hockey requires superlative skill, reactions and agility. It also demands almost superhuman stamina and strength. A fight breaks out below us as a New York Islanders enforcer smashes a Nordiques player against the perimeter wall and then mercilessly cuffs him. 'Hockey,' says an indifferent Bédard, 'is probably the toughest game in sport. The average player's lifespan at the top is five years. You either play well, deal with the pressure, or you fall by the wayside. At the top, it's a hard, hard game.'

Given such demands, Kordic struggled doubly hard with the role in which hockey cast him. After joining the Montreal Canadiens in 1985, he confided: 'Everyone pretty well knows my role and it's no secret what I have to do.' Kordic had been hired to be an obstructer, an enforcer, a goon, a 'bare-knuckled caricature of a professional athlete', as *Sports Illustrated* later described him.

Right to the end, Kordic complained to family and friends that he didn't want to fight. But he was afraid his career might end all too soon if he did not. And yet, in public, he appeared to revel in the violence. Playing for Sherbrooke in the American Hockey League in 1985–6, Kordic littered the ice with the bloodied and beaten. After beating up Gord Donnelly of the Nordiques in 1986, Kordic skated off the ice, kissed his fist and raised it in gladiator style before the baying crowd.

Nobody could 'take' Kordic. According to a former coach, Kordic 'beat the shit out of everyone', becoming a figure on *Hockey Night in Canada* highlight tapes. In the NHL's bad boy Hall of Fame, he will always rank with the greats alongside Stu 'The Grim Reaper' Grimson and Dave 'The Hammer' Schultz, the all-time top goon with 472 penalty minutes in one season.

Already a cult figure with Montreal Canadiens by Christmas 1986, off the ice Kordic was beginning to crack up. To lighten up after matches, to while away the long, lonely hours in hotel rooms, Kordic began snorting cocaine, the fans' boozy mantra – 'Kordic! Kordic! Kordic!' – still ringing in his ears. But there was another ingredient to the drug cocktail which was to kill him six years later. In the autumn of 1986, when he had reported to training camp for the Montreal Canadiens, Kordic did so looking like the Incredible Bulk, having added fifteen pounds of synthetic muscle over the summer.

The first NHL player to get seriously into steroids, Kordic always knew the NHL's punishment for drug abuse would be severe. Found with a rolled-up $50 bill and a line of coke, he could expect to be banned for at least half a season. Then again, faced with losing a Cup-winning player, a coach might well turn a blind eye. Found injecting steroids, Kordic could simply shrug his bulky shoulders, smug in the knowledge that steroid use in the NHL is legal if prescribed by a doctor.

As Kordic battered his way through the crowded ranks of NHL tough guys, it was not only the anabolics and cocaine that began to take their toll. On the outside, Kordic was an imposing wall of taut meat. Inside, his psyche was all flab. His father had begun to beg him to quit hockey rather than fight on. Montreal players and coaches increasingly saw a red-eyed Kordic during post-game conversations with his father, even when the Canadiens had won. Kordic later admitted that his father's disapproval prompted him to drown his anguish in Bloody Marys.

In the autumn of 1988, Montreal traded Kordic to the Toronto

Maple Leafs. The Stanley Cup hero of just two seasons before would not be missed behind the scenes. He had become a liability, his life off the ice a gathering shadow of the unpredictable aggression he showed on it. There was the time Kordic's landlady called Montreal coach Pat Burns in the middle of the night to get her spaced-out tenant off the roof. (His teammates had long called him Sniffy.) An incident in which Kordic was said to have thrown an ashtray at Burns only hastened his exit.

In Toronto, Kordic's descent, already fast gaining fatal momentum, became a nosedive. Within months, by December 1988, he was suspended for ten games for 'highsticking' Edmonton Oiler Keith Acton, cynically breaking his nose. While Kordic was serving his suspension, the then general manager of the Leafs, Gord Stellick, was told by a senior Toronto police officer that Kordic 'was hanging around with hookers and druggies'. Kordic protested his innocence. But there was no denying he was already a late-night celebrity with the Toronto police. There were also stories of dressing-room scuffles with fellow players.

Then, in October 1989, Ivan Kordic suddenly died, aged 54, of liver cancer. Father and son's differences remained unresolved. Kordic started missing games. His cocaine habit snowballed, and his mood swings became more extreme. He appeared desperately short of cash. At least twice he asked for a salary advance. His father's death, all those who knew him now agree, removed the last brake on Kordic's escalating drug abuse and vodka binges. Kordic totalled a $40,000 Corvette roadster in a crash.

In the summer of 1990, the Maple Leafs' management encouraged Kordic to enter a drug rehabilitation clinic. The stay was short-lived and, by February 1991, Kordic had moved on yet again, to the Washington Capitals. In Washington, Kordic played just seven games. By now downing a bottle of vodka a day, he was suspended twice for alcohol-related offences before finally being dispatched to yet another substance abuse centre, this time in Minneapolis.

While in Minneapolis, Kordic found a soul-mate in rehab clinic companion Bryan Fogarty, a former Québec Nordiques defenseman. At Fogarty's suggestion, Kordic approached the Nordiques' manager, Pierre Pagé, for a job. Acutely aware of what they would be taking on, the Nordiques set stringent terms before signing Kordic in August 1991. Pagé agreed to give Kordic 'one last chance in the NHL' on condition he did not drink and would be tested regularly for drugs. Yet, only a month before signing for the Nordiques, Kordic had been involved in what the *Journal de Québec* described as a 'racial incident in East Montreal'. Kordic said he had tried to help a young white youth who was being chased by several blacks. He had used a baseball bat to fend off the assailants.

Kordic's addiction had a pattern – he would spend months clean between binges – and it soon reasserted itself in Quebec. The perennial loner soon became a fixture at bars and strip joints along the Boulevard Hamel, a neon-lit motel strip in a suburb of the French-speaking city. Late one night, two weeks after arriving in Quebec, while he sat sipping soft drinks with Fogarty in a strip club, Kordic met Nancy Massé. A former *Penthouse* model, 23-year-old Massé did not recognise Kordic. Painfully shy, he finally summoned up courage to ask her to a game.

Miss Budweiser X 1992 sits flicking through a scrapbook of cuttings and pictures of John Kordic, her centrefold figure snug in tight leggings and breast-hugging top. It is four months after Kordic's death and three days before Christmas 1992. Outside, the temperature is rising from the previous night's twenty degrees below. A foot of ice-crusted snow muffles the cries of children on sledges.

As Massé turns the pages of the scrapbook, past 'Death of a Goon' and 'Death Trap' headlines, a picture of Kordic's last months develops. His expressions grow wearier, his face grows more bloated and his body more oversized in each snapshot. 'John wasn't the tough guy everybody thought,' says Massé wistfully in a thick French accent. 'He was a little boy in a big body, a gentle giant. He was a good guy. He had to fight. He had no choice.'

The Kordic whom Massé loved, she swears, was the very opposite of his public persona. When Kordic was straight, he was 'cute', human, insecure and touchingly vain. She remembers plucking his eyebrows, and his habit of constantly running his fingers through his mousy brown, gelled hair. She recalls, a smile fluttering across her tanned features, the nightly *pssss* of hairspray before John came to bed. 'John was a big "Mou". He used to cry during movies. Every time he watched the video of "November Rain" by Guns 'n' Roses, he'd start crying. He used to say, "Don't you ever tell anybody I cry." He hid his problems very well.'

Massé remembers the first meal she cooked for Kordic. He wouldn't touch the wine-laced beef bourguignon she had slaved over. He said he'd quit drinking. And for the first two weeks of their relationship, adds Massé, although they slept together, she and Kordic simply cuddled. For some things Kordic could wait.

But time was fast slipping away for Kordic on the ice. His stay with the Québec side that had finished bottom of its division for the five previous seasons was to last just five months. Kordic had played nineteen games, scored two points and spent 115 minutes in the sin-bin when, in January 1992, the Nordiques released him after he failed a blood test. Kordic had not stopped drinking, snorting or shooting up. Although Nordiques manager Pagé denied Kordic had tested positive for cocaine, Massé admits Kordic was using the drug at the time.

'When we signed Kordic, we knew it was his last chance,' says Nordiques vice-president Jean Legaut, as we sit in a brasserie popular with Québeçois power-brokers. An amiable, bluff character, Legaut has long been respected in the NHL for his frank, passionate views. He agrees Kordic's death has stirred a long-overdue debate about the violence in his beloved sport.

'There has been too much fighting,' concedes Legaut. 'An emphasis on strength rather than skill was killing the game. But I still think one good fight, as far as most Canadian fans are concerned, is acceptable. At the end of the day, hockey's like boxing. Once the bell rings, the bullshit stops. All the fighters in hockey have the same fear – the day they lose a fight, they lose their career.'

No one can recall Kordic losing a fight on the Coliseum's ice. Then again, Kordic wasn't just a bare-knuckle pugilist. Throughout his career, he broke the honourable goon's rule by using his stick.

'He was living on the edge of a precipice,' says Jean Martineau, the Nordiques' press manager. 'You can't do that every day. Eventually, you fall off.'

In the weeks after he was 'released' from the Québec Nordiques, John Kordic began to disappear for days at a time. And then, one freezing morning in late January, Massé received a 6am wake-up call.

'I'm calling to say goodbye,' said Kordic.

'Why don't you say hi?' replied Massé.

After frantically calling 'every damn hotel in Quebec', Massé tracked Kordic later that morning to a motel in the suburbs. He was still conscious. The sleeping pills had not yet taken effect. She took him home in an ambulance, poured coffee down his throat, kept him awake. 'When I look back,' says Massé, 'I realise John was just crying wolf. He wanted attention. The suicide attempt wasn't serious. It was a cry for help.'

In March 1992, Kordic signed a minor league contract with the Edmonton Oilers, finishing the season with a different team, Edmonton's American Hockey League farm team in Cape Breton. Despite again spending most games on his backside in the sin-bin, according to coach Don MacAdam, Kordic performed well in Nova Scotia. 'When he went to Cape Breton,' recalls Massé, 'MacAdam tried him in a different position. John was a changed man. I never saw him so happy.'

By early spring, the season over, Kordic was back on the thawing, muddy backstreets of Quebec. He moved in with Massé. On July 7, she woke to red roses, marmalade on soggy toast, coffee and a marriage proposal. When she agreed, Kordic sobbed with relief. They spent the afternoon driving round Old Quebec in a horse-drawn carriage, planning the rest of their lives together. She still wears the diamond-encrusted ring.

In the autumn, they would return to Edmonton, settle down, start afresh. Kordic said he was 27, that he had to stay a goon to make his last chance with the Edmonton Oilers work. He was even beginning to contemplate his first meeting on ice with his 22-year-old brother, Danny. A 6'5" defenseman for the Philadelphia Fliers, Danny now shows signs of becoming the skilful all-round player John Kordic had always longed to be.

Kordic told Massé he wanted to start a family. On the surface, she remembers, he appeared happy, forever bellowing the line 'Me Tarzan, you Jane' from the song 'Superman' by his favourite Edmonton band, The Crash Test Dummies. 'He was always singing that fucking song,' smiles Massé. 'In the car, everywhere. I guess he related to the words. He'd beat his chest like Tarzan. He used to say the guy on the album cover looked like him, only with wings and a cape.'

There was just one problem. Massé was engaged to a serious drug addict. Kordic was still snorting cocaine when he thought she wasn't looking and openly injecting steroids when she was, usually in his fleshy left buttock. 'He hated needles,' says Massé. 'He would tremble when injecting himself. Sometimes the needle would snap off and he'd shout, "Nancy! Nancy!"'

At 3.30am on July 16, Quebec police responded to a noise complaint at the Kordic-Massé house. After a minor scuffle with the officers, Kordic was charged with assaulting Massé and later barred from living with her pending a hearing in court on August 11. The charge was to weigh heavily on Kordic, despite his lawyer Serge Goulet's confidence that he would be found not guilty.

'John didn't beat me up – he just pushed me up against the wall,' Massé now says, pointing to the wall which Kordic then punched. 'I was saying, "You don't touch me, you're high." You see, John never wanted to admit he was high. Then, at 1am, my ex-boyfriend Eric arrived at the front door. John told him: "If you're still there in five minutes, I'm going to kill you." So Eric called the cops.'

Despite the court order, the couple continued to see each other. Kordic would pick Massé up at the Cabaret Folichon, an 'up-market' strip club on the outskirts of Quebec, when her shift ended around 2am. Staff there remember him variously as a fast drinker, fond of Bloody Marys and Caesars, but also as a quiet, shy young man who didn't appear to get drunk and who, when harassed, would signal for them to sort out the problem.

Pending his hearing, Kordic stayed for three weeks with Bruce Cashman, the manager of the World Gym, a Quebec establishment popular with Nordiques players. 'John was a great guy,' recalls Cashman. 'Sometimes he was OK. But then you'd lose him for a few days and he'd come back in a bad way.'

Ten days before his death, Kordic called James Fearing, who had been his drug and alcohol counsellor during his stay in Minneapolis the previous summer. Fearing scheduled a visit to Quebec for two weeks later. By then, it would be too late.

There were other, muted calls for help. 'The week before he died,' recalls Massé, 'John told me: "Never mind what happens. I will always love you, even to my grave." He was crying. He said: "Just don't ask questions – don't doubt that I love you." He told me he had always dreamed about being a star when he was a kid. He said the only thing he wanted now was to be unknown.'

According to evidence presented during the inquest on his death, John Kordic blew $12,000 in the fortnight before he died. More than enough for the new mountain bike Massé remembers him buying. Certainly enough, during the last week of his life, for the four grams of cocaine he was allegedly snorting each day as he wandered in a daze around the suburb of Ancienne-Lorett.

At 2.45am on Thursday August 6, 1992, John Kordic showed up briefly at the Cabaret Folichon. It was just before closing time, and he was carrying luggage. Kordic spoke with Massé and appeared to one eyewitness to have breathing problems. 'He told me he loved me,' recalls Massé, 'that we would spend Sunday together, that the court case the following Tuesday would soon be over.'

On Friday August 7, according to the *Toronto Globe and Mail*, an English-speaking man checked into the Maxim motel less than a kilometre from the Cabaret Folichon and its gaggle of tanned strippers. No one saw Kordic arrive at the spruce, family-run establishment. But staff there say he stayed in the English-speaking man's room and left twice during the night, at 2am and 5am on Saturday morning. The second time he did not return. A cab driver reportedly took Kordic to a house where he could buy 'some chips –

some very strong chips' – making it clear he was referring to cocaine.

At 4.30pm the next afternoon, bloody and bruised, Kordic staggered back to the four-star Maxim, slapped a $100 bill on the counter and ordered a room. Co-owner Marlene Bouchard, a chic middle-aged woman with a mass of blonde hair, reluctantly obliged. 'He looked like he'd been in a fight,' she recalls, as she sits near the polished counter in the Maxim's airy reception. 'He had a big bruise on his face, blood on his hands. He could hardly breathe and he was leaning on the counter for support. He said: "Don't you know who I am?" I asked him if he wanted to go to hospital, but he said he wanted to sleep. He asked me to give him a wake-up call at 11pm.'

At 8pm, Massé claims a sober Kordic called her. She had just been crowned Miss Budweiser X. 'He told me he'd seen my picture in the paper and liked it. He said he'd been playing baseball with some guys and that he was going for a nap. He wanted me to call him back later. I never got the chance.'

At about 9pm, Kordic began to ring the Maxim's reception desk. 'It was fuck this, fuck that,' recalled Bouchard. 'He kept calling, for about twenty minutes. We tried to reach his girlfriend at the Folichon. Residents began to complain. Around ten, we called the police.'

In an attempt to calm Kordic down, Bouchard's brother and Michel Marcoux, the Maxim's assistant manager, ventured to room 205 and knocked. 'The place was a mess,' remembers Marcoux, standing in the room's doorway and pointing to the room's queen-size bed. 'Two suitcases of clothes were everywhere. The furniture was damaged. There was blood on the bed, just there. Kordic looked really paranoid. He had big problems breathing. He was thumping himself in the chest all the time, like Tarzan. He kept running his hands through his hair.'

Shortly after 10pm, two local police officers arrived. A few minutes later, they were joined by seven others. All nine unbelted their guns, leaving them in the hall outside room 205 before entering. For a few minutes, they struggled to restrain the massive,

238-pound NHL heavyweight champion as he ranted, swore, pounded on the walls and sweated from the steroids he had almost certainly injected earlier. At 11.11pm, seven minutes into the journey to Université Laval Hospital, Kordic's final fight, this time for life, was over. A paramedic attempted mouth-to-mouth. A policeman massaged his heart.

Kordic's autopsy report showed heart failure and a build-up of fluid on the lungs – consistent, experts say, with steroid abuse, as was Kordic's aggressive psychological state, dubbed 'steroid rage'. Several vials of the drug were, in fact, later found in his motel room, along with dozens of unused syringes. Needle tracks scarred one unnaturally muscular arm. At the time of his death, Kordic was 28 pounds over his normal weight. He looked more of a goon than ever.

Near the end of her well-thumbed scrapbook, Nancy Massé has glued a black and white picture of Ivan Kordic embracing his son. John Kordic is holding the Stanley Cup aloft. 'John never accepted his father's death,' says Massé. 'He told me: "Nancy, everything I've done in my life – it was for my father. Now he's gone. And he was not proud of me."'

As she closes the scrapbook of their life together, Massé says she can still hear Kordic's playful shouts; his disguised screams for help, 'Nancy! Nancy!', still echo inside her head. Almost a year to the day after she first met Kordic, Nancy Massé recalls, she threw a single, dead engagement rose onto his coffin.

John Kordic was buried on a windswept hillside overlooking Edmonton. His grave is a yard from his father's.

MANSLAUGHTER UNITED

Chris Hulme

April, 1995

The players of HMP Kingston's football team have signed on for life. But, for 90 minutes every Saturday, they're free to escape into a world where the only penalty for foul play is a red card.

Eighteen or so footballers are listening to their coach explain the rudiments of defending corner-kicks. 'One of the few things England got right under Graham Taylor was that we didn't concede goals from corners,' barks Nigel Wheeler, a physical education instructor. 'That's because we were organised.' Wheeler orders players into the goal mouth, assigning five positions to be defended as surely as if they were in the Alamo.

Practice corner-kicks are fired over. On cue, the goalkeeper screams 'out' and the players charge after the ball, hoping to catch imaginary opponents in an off-side position. The drill works well for the first few corners but breaks down as they lose concentration. They are called into a huddle. In these moments, it is just possible to forget whom Nigel Wheeler, fresh-faced and 32, is coaching. The players listen with the same desire to get things right for match day that you'd expect of internationals or, for that matter, local league players. Football – the great leveller among men – is shutting out the rest of the universe.

The illusion soon fades. A 50-foot-high wall that towers over much of the pitch, and a security guard patrolling on the distant touchline, bring reality back into focus. This is a unique football team. It will never play an away match, never have a post-match drink with the opposition, never have a Cup run, never invite along dads, brothers and friends to watch, and never get drunk the night before a game. Wheeler is a prison officer and the players are convicts doing life sentences. They are murderers, rapists, arsonists and child abductors to a man.

Her Majesty's Prison Kingston has been locking up lifers for over a century. Like many British jails, its name tells you nothing about its location. Kingston Prison is in Portsmouth, Hampshire. It stands about one mile across flat, industrial hinterland from Fratton Park, the home of the town's Endsleigh First Division club. Kingston is a category B jail – only terrorists and mass murderers are considered a greater risk to the public. The prison resembles a small castle, complete with turrets. Only the characteristically small cell windows suggest that its true function is not to defend the old port from foreign invaders, but to lock up the enemy within. The main cell block has three corridors stretching out from one central area – a spot occupied by a snooker table. There is a second level, with a balcony. The guards prefer this radial design to what you might find in a more modern prison. They can get a good view of what is going on by simply looking in three directions. There are no hidden corners.

The jail has had a football team for as long as anyone can remember. It is a member of the Portsmouth North End league. Special dispensations allow Kingston to play an entire season at home and also permit blue goal posts. They need to be this colour to stand out against the security wall that runs behind both goals and along one side of the pitch. It has a white strip painted from ground to well above eye-level, interspersed with giant red numbers – all designed to aid capture in the event of an escape attempt. (There has been one in ten years: the prisoner got away only to be recaptured during a bank raid two weeks later.)

Wheeler has managed the team since moving from London's Wormwood Scrubs eight years ago. A father of two young children, he looks like a sportsman. He's about 5ft 7in, has neatly slicked-back dark hair and a well-developed physique.

He shares a cluttered office with another instructor and Kingston's head of physical education. Two desks and five cabinets prop up assorted files, books and papers. Sports gear litters the floor. On a pinboard, a photograph of Kingston's 1988 championship-winning team stands out from the Home Office memos. It's a relaxed room.

Wheeler plays in the team, as does another prison officer, Kevin Pratt. 'There's no real problem us being staff,' he says, searching out his boots ahead of training. 'The prisoners would create if we didn't deserve our place. But they voted Kevin player of the year last season. They appreciate what he does for the side.'

The lifers have a football session on Tuesdays, open to all inmates, squad training on Thursdays, and league games on Saturday afternoons. If they're lucky, they sometimes get a Sunday friendly. The prison supplies their boots and kit, but many players have their own. A handful of inmates watch on match days.

Running the team is clearly a labour of love. Wheeler is training to become a fully qualified FA coach and obviously enjoys taking a call from a PEI at another jail, who wants to chat about a convict. The man has just been transferred from Kingston, having been downgraded to security category C. He was Kingston's captain. 'He's a great sweeper. A bit unorthodox,' chortles Wheeler, 'but he'll stick his boot in there for you. By the way, if you see him with a pair of red Spall shorts, they're ours. I want them back.'

As we walk to collect the players, unlocking and locking a monotonous number of iron bar gates, he mentions that they'll be keen to get going as the last two matches were postponed. The players are waiting by the snooker table. They wear an assortment of old T-shirts, shorts and track suits, and carry their boots. Most are between about 25 and 35, though there is a grey-haired man, probably in his fifties. They look like a gang of builders. Going through three sets of locked doors, we leave the bright artificial light and surprising warmth of the prison for the great outdoors. Beneath a blanket of grey clouds the players start warming up and knocking passes around.

The postponements have created some antagonism. Wheeler knows the players are frustrated because one, it transpires, complained to the Governor. He calls a team meeting and spells out the facts of life: 'Look, the Governor was never going to change our decision, so it's no good complaining to him. In future, you should just accept that when a match is called off the PEI's decision isn't going to be reversed. We've just re-laid the pitch. It would be ripped up if we'd played in those conditions.'

The session gets going. After working on corner-kicks, the team splits into groups for games of two-touch possession. To save the turf, the squad then moves to the other end of the pitch for passing shuttles. Then it's a full-scale practice match. Two captains are chosen to pick the sides. 'Dobbo, you've got a lot to say for yourself – you pick one team. Phil, you do the other.'

Joining in, it seems sensible to be alert to the possibility of heavy tackles, maybe worse. The thought that any one of these prisoners could have been given a hard time by the Great British Press during their trials comes to mind. The paranoia is not helped by two prisoners taking the first opportunity to chat. It's hard not to clam up.

Soon, though, the great leveller takes over. The prisoners and the prison officers simply become players in the beautiful game. Well, an unremarkable football match anyway. The only thought that stays in the mind is that if somebody knocks you over on this pitch you don't call him a fucking psycho. They troop off afterwards, disappointed the session has come to an end.

The afternoon is locked out for another day. Showered and changed, the Kingston captain, Phil Sussex, is happy to talk. He sits down in the empty cell where we meet and rolls a cigarette. Wearing blue jeans and a sweatshirt with 'The Gunners' written across the chest, he looks older than he did in the game. Then, his fair red hair flopped forward, showing his fringe. Now it is combed back, revealing a receding hair line. He has slightly bulging eyes and a stubbly beard. You imagine he could affect a good stare.

His London accent reminds me of Glenn Hoddle. 'I dunno about that,' he laughs, 'but I used to love to watch him play.'

Sussex is a friendly, world-weary captain. If you were sent to

Kingston and wanted to join the football team, he would be the man to ask for advice. But what would he say? 'The first thing you'll come up against is that if you can actually play, you're an immediate threat to one of the lads in the team,' he says, puffing out smoke. 'Maybe he's a tryer, someone who does his best for 90 minutes. You could take his place. So you'd get little niggles. Nothing physical – but people would say to me, the captain, "Cor, I don't think he's any good."

'Everyone gets it. Trevor, the tall black guy who plays up front with me, got a lot of stick when he came here. He was too flash. He'd say to me and Nigel, "They're all saying I'm fucking rubbish". All I could tell him was "keep trying". Outside, if you can't get in a team or if you fall out with someone, you can join another side. In here, you can't.

'It's also different because outside, if you call your goalkeeper a prat during a game you can have a joke about it with him in the pub. Here, you might stare at each other across the landing for two days.' He chuckles at how childish it sounds. 'It has happened.'

The prison thing, as he calls it, affects all aspects of Kingston FC. Team talks are rarely open discussions. 'The lads are reluctant to criticise each other. The last thing you need in here is another enemy.'

He is suitably circumspect about team-mates. 'We're OK when we all work hard. We've got a lot of lads who've been in jail since they were fifteen. They've only ever played jail football. Jail football in young offenders' institutions is murder-ball. They just kick anything that moves. They have to adjust.'

Being captain means that he gets a steady flow of visitors to his cell. 'We talk about who is and isn't playing well. Before our last game, I was handed about five team sheets to give to Nigel. The lads are very keen.'

Match day is the highlight of the week. Sussex wakes up at 7am when his cell light is switched on by officers performing a security check, via the door spy-hole. He then has a coffee from a flask he is allowed to keep in his room and listens to his battery-powered radio. His door opens at 7.45am. Breakfast is always a fry-up at weekends. On most week days he'd then go to work in the prison print shop – earning £7, which pays for tobacco, batteries, phone cards, and a few extras. At 9.30am on Saturdays, however, he's one of a small group of players allowed out on to the pitch. They set up the nets and corner flags, then knock a ball around until Wheeler calls a team talk at 11.30am. An hour later they are 'banged up' again. On the stroke of 1.30pm, their doors open and they stand, kitted out and ready for action.

'We normally have good, physical games,' says Sussex. 'Some visiting players and referees are a bit intimidated about coming into the jail – especially if it's their first time. But a lot of them we see year-in, year-out. You don't generally have a lot of time for a chat. When the match is finished by about 3.45pm we have to go inside for our tea.' They are locked in their cells again at 9pm.

Opposing teams are not above taunting the Kingston players. 'Sometimes if we're winning, you'll hear one say to another, "I'm finding those three pints hard to digest".' Sussex laughs off the irritation through gritted teeth. 'I always think, "Cor mate, I've been in here seven years; I dunno how long I'm gonna be in here, and you reckon all I'm thinking about is fucking drink." It's the last thing on your mind.'

Having consecutive games postponed was nevertheless an aching hardship. 'I have a right downer if the game is cancelled. Weekends are the longest days. You can only play so many games of snooker. Boredom is a major problem in prison. I often bury my head in my chess computer.'

Most prisoners doing long sentences have what you might call a resigned temperament. The prison officers describe them as being 'settled into their sentence'. To anyone else, they can come across as defeated men. It's hard to imagine them pulling together in a team. Sussex understands the impression. 'It does feel good when you win – but it's only recently that I made any sort of fuss when I scored a goal. You'd sort of creep to the half-way line thinking, is it OK to celebrate? Being a lifer, you've got this shadow over you all the time. You can't really forget it when you play football. Your sentence is different to everyone else's in the prison system. You're on your own. Prison is a competitive society. You know that if you don't look after number one nobody else will. I even do it on the football pitch. I might make a comment, trying to encourage someone, and I'll think, "I hope the screws fucking heard that".'

The regime at Kingston, he says, places a great deal of emphasis on behaviour. A fight between players might be glossed over at a jail like Swaleside in Kent, where he did an earlier part of his sentence. At Kingston, though, it's the nightmare scenario. The players know it could add time to their sentences. They are, consequently, one of the best behaved football teams. Kingston once went three seasons without picking up a single booking. The irony is lost on Sussex, who for the first time loses his genial tone. An edge of anxiety enters his voice. 'There are staff who think I get too aggressive during football. So I've gone for 50–50 balls and pulled out. Nigel, the manager, will ask me, "Why did you pull out?" But there might be other officers watching on the side-lines. They could write a report about you and you wouldn't even know about it. They could add years to your time. It's my future.'

Phil Sussex can't remember what started the fight. But he was one of three men who killed a man outside a London pub in 1987. The court was told that one of many blows, a kick to the head above one eye, caused the victim to lose consciousness. He died 73 days later in hospital.

Sussex was a builder, working in and around Islington, where he grew up. The son of an engineer, he had a girlfriend and a baby daughter. He spent too much money on drink. Sussex led the kind of life that could have got him dubbed Mad Phil. Nobody said it to his face. He'd done two stretches inside for burglary.

To protest your innocence during a life sentence would prolong your incarceration indefinitely. The prison service says you have to admit guilt to come to terms with your crime. So Sussex makes no bones about the fact that he is guilty. You are, however, left with the understanding that he has swallowed the bitterest pill of the three men who were convicted of murder.

'It was just a poxy pub fight,' he says. 'I broke it up once, and took one of my co-defendants back inside the pub. He went outside again and carried on leathering this fella. In court, they tried to say that all three of us had planned it.' He smiles an empty smile, as if to say he has no right to complain. 'A geezer died. He was 35 and had two sons. I was there.'

The subject won't go away so easily. 'I don't feel guilty of murder,' he says spontaneously. 'It's something I've tried to get across to these people. I mean, they ask about remorse. I'm remorseful, of course I am. But I'm remorseful every time I read in a newspaper that someone's been killed. I can't connect it to me personally. I know that I didn't hit him.'

He would be annoyed if you told him Britain was soft on criminals. Or that lifers get off lightly because they have their own cells, TV rooms and access to telephones, and that many, like Phil, do GCSEs while they are banged up.

'I don't see the sense in giving a man fifteen or twenty years in jail. After five years, you know if that man is going to be a threat again,' he says, frowning. 'You couldn't not know. You can watch him all day, every day. There are evil people in here, people who you think should never be let out. But 99 per cent of the murderers I've ever spoken to . . . it was down to five seconds of sheer madness. Even the big tough guys. They can't believe they did it. Guys who've killed their wives or turned around and hit someone with a glass.' He shakes his head. 'You can't take some mistakes back.'

He feels sad that some convicts are treated as lepers. 'There was one time when I was one of two captains picking five-a-side teams. This bloke, who I knew had killed his baby daughter, was standing behind us. We didn't see him. We picked the teams and he was left out. So he says to me [Phil puts on a generic northern accent], "You'll have to fucking have me. Hard luck." I let it go, but I said to him afterwards, "There's no need to be like that – I've given you no trouble whatsoever. It's silly to say that. I didn't see you." And then he said to me, "You know what I'm in here for, don't you?" I said, "Yeah, I do know." Then he started telling me about how it happened. The child was crying and wouldn't stop. He threw her at the wall. It was terrible, inexcusable. But he's not going to go out of here and throw children at the wall. He was a young man, trying to be a father, trying to run a household, on the dole. And it all got to him. There's no excuse for what he's done – there's no excuse for violence – but he's not an animal.'

Sussex's dream is to be released in 1999, by which time he'll have served twelve years. 'I just want a job where I earn enough to support myself. That's it. I won't need anything else.' Avoiding eye contact, he adds, 'I'll be 37 if I get out then. Which, luckily, is still, you know, fairly young.' He would then be on indefinite probation. Like all lifers, one mistake could see him hauled back to jail.

The football team gives him some kind of mental release from confinement. But the frustration of being deprived of freedom is written all over his face as he tells the story of how Kingston were deprived of a fixture. 'We used to have a team travel from London every year, blokes who all worked for the same firm. The last time they were here, some prat broke into their changing room and stole all their money. That was bloody annoying. It's petty shit like that which makes people think, "Tie them to the wall. Put fucking balls and chains on them." Things like that ruin it. We haven't seen that team again and we don't expect to. That's sad. They were a nice bunch of lads – we had a good game of football and a laugh. The result didn't matter.' Cupping his mouth with one hand, he sighs, 'We never found out who took the money.'

At least Phil Sussex knows he is the first name on the Kingston team sheet. Craig Dobson, a 28-year-old Mancunian of the United variety, wishes he was so lucky. Dobson was recently relegated to the substitutes' bench – something he finds hard to accept. 'You'll have to ask Nigel why. I like to think I always give 100 per cent.'

Dobson is a younger and more nervous presence in the cell than the Kingston captain. He answers questions in the clipped style of a media-wary footballer. He'd fit in well at Dalglish's Blackburn Rovers.

Dobson, it turns out, is the player who complained to the Governor about the postponements. 'Most of us would play if the pitch was under two foot of water,' he says. 'There's nowt else to do.'

Television helps. 'I'll watch Halifax v Runcorn. I don't care as long as it's football.' The prison has Sky Sport, but he only sees the first half of Monday and Wednesday night matches as they get banged up at half-time. Dobson listens to the rest of the matches on the radio.

During Italia '90, he spent a month in hospital recovering from an operation. 'I saw every game,' he says cheerfully. USA '94 was more difficult because so many matches started after 9pm. Mexico '86 was the last World Cup Dobson watched at home. The following year he broke into his grandmother's house to steal valuables and beat her to death when she confronted him. The crime seems all the more shocking for absurd reasons: Dobson has blond, stylishly cut hair and seems too clean-cut for this environment.

'It was a domestic,' he says, pausing uncomfortably before blurting out the word 'murder'. 'It's past now. I've got to get on with it.' Dobson has no hope of release until 2001. How does he cope with the gravity of his crime, and with missing the best years of his life? 'I've always said you do your jail or you swing. I'm not one for swinging,' he shrugs.

Family support is important. 'I get visits from me Dad and Mum – though they're split up now. My brother sometimes comes, too, but he's got commitments – a wife, child and job.'

Despite everything that's happened, Dobson's father is still proud of him. Last year Mr Dobson donated a new kit to the team. It was a gesture of support for Kingston prison football club. In some small way, it was probably also a means of exercising his love for his son. It's a melancholy thought that he'll never see him wear it.

RED HOT PROPERTY

Jim White

October, 1994

You get a whiff of it the moment you step off the tram at Old Trafford station. Wafting down the Warwick Road, over the heads of the thousands making their way to Old Trafford stadium to worship Manchester United, striking nostrils with even more force than that rich aromatic match-day combination of hot dogs, police-horse manure and beery farts, is an unmistakable smell: money.

The whiff is everywhere. Once a fortnight this quarter of a Manchester industrial estate hosts more than just a football match. It transmogrifies into a bazaar, as teeming, colourful and chaotic as anything in Istanbul. Every centimetre of pavement within half a mile of the ground is occupied by commerce. Fast-food wagons churn out cholesterol by the coronary load; stalls sell souvenir scarves, hats, badges and posters; a man trades in rare match programmes; boys with bin-liners jammed with T-shirts yell: 'Get your Cantona, only a fiver'; youths by the dozen off-load piles of magazines, newspaper supplements, lottery tickets; a woman under a golf umbrella paints adolescent complexions red, white, yellow or green; and men with shifty faces move against the tidal flow calling out their mantra: 'Anyone need tickets? I'll buy or sell.'

But the most extraordinary sight comes once you have fought your way into the shadow of the ground itself. There, snaking round crush barriers cemented into the forecourt, is the queue for the Manchester United superstore. People already burdened by United apparel – shirts, sweaters, jackets, earrings – line up for at least an hour behind at least 2,000 others for the privilege of buying yet more stuff: 3-D posters of Giggsie (£5.99), Peter Schmeichel souvenir drinking mugs (£9.99), Lee Sharpe duvet covers (£25.99). Also goat-skin leather purses with embossed club crest (£12.99), and embroidered away colours toddlers' romper suits (£14.99). A range of 1,500 items of United memorabilia is available to empty the pockets of the faithful.

'Sometimes on a match day,' says Edward Freedman, United's merchandising manager, whose office overlooks the superstore, 'the chairman comes here, and we both stand and look out over the queue. Then we smile at each other.'

Manchester United are not simply the most successful football team in the country, they are also the most successful footballing business. In a financial sector which traditionally involved about as much chance of a good return on investment as opening your wallet over a drain, at United they have introduced a new word to the football vocabulary: profit. A projected £10 million worth of it last season.

'If we were asked to recommend the shares of a football club,' said a City analyst when United's interim results were published in April, 'these are the only ones we would feel comfortable about.'

It has not always been like this. For years the club's only source of income was from the click of the turnstile, with the odd bit of loose change accruing from television fees, sales of programmes, and profits from the dodgy pies supplied by the chairman Louis Edwards' meat company. Then fifteen years ago, Martin Edwards succeeded his father and diversification became the goal.

'We took a look round and realised the potential of the place,' explains Danny McGregor, United's commercial manager and a long-time Edwards' associate. 'And, I suppose you could say we set about exploiting it. In the best sense of the word.'

Under Edwards' leadership, the numbers of executive boxes were increased, facilities upgraded, the rich middle-class of Manchester encouraged to attend, sponsorship deals signed. The tills began to ring. Not everyone, though, was happy about it. Disappointed by a team failing to match the standards set by Sir Matt Busby, the club's guiding light for 40 years, many of Manchester's die-hard fans believed that the chairman's commercial assiduousness was motivated less by an effort to make United the top side in the land, than by a desire to fatten up the enterprise in order to maximise his stake. Such suspicions were hardly allayed when twice in the Eighties he tried to sell out – first in 1987 to Robert Maxwell for a reported £10 million, and then again in 1989 to a consortium headed by a Manx businessman called Michael Knighton for more than £20 million.

Four years on, Edwards remains in his grand offices with a sweeping view of the stadium. How glad he must be he failed to sell. In 1994 the club is worth, at a conservative estimate, eight times more than it was when Robert Maxwell's frame was in the picture. Edwards' own shares in the club – he holds 3.38 million – are valued at more than £20 million. More pertinently, in the last published accounts in 1993, it was shown that the Edwards bank account was improved by £174,500 in salary and over £600,000 in share dividend payments.

Three important things have happened since Edwards tried to sell. First, the club was floated on the stock exchange, and a host of professional expertise was brought in to ensure that the shareholders had a regular dividend fix. Second, United and other top clubs broke away from the Football League and negotiated an astral-sized television deal of their own; an arrangement in which, unlike the past, the gargantuan fees were not shared with the poorer, lower-division clubs. And third, a team emerged under Alex Ferguson, the manager, which started playing the most beautiful football seen in this country for 25 years. Even better, this was a team stuffed with photogenic teen idols and newsworthy foreign geniuses. They were a running, shooting advertisement for Martin Edwards' brand.

'Winning things is great business,' says Danny McGregor. 'Hey, when you've got a great team, all of a sudden people don't complain if the rolls in the hospitality restaurants are stale.' Indeed, such is the aura surrounding Ferguson's team that people travel from Norway, from Ireland, from Malta to watch them play: all, inevitably, on the club's own 'see a match meet a player and have supper at Harry Ramsden's fish shop only £270 for the weekend' package trips. They even fetch up at Old Trafford when there isn't a game on. But not to worry, they can spend money. Every day, bar match days, you can go on a guided tour of the stadium and last season more than 100,000 people took the opportunity. At £4.95 for an adult, £2.95 for children, the tour alone generated more income than a third division club might make in half a season.

All this makes Edward Freedman a very happy merchandising manager indeed. He sits in his office reeling off the financial superlatives.

'We have the best-selling replica football shirts in the country. We have seven titles in the top-selling videos in the country, including the number one. Our Manchester United magazine sells more than 100,000 copies a month, making it the biggest-selling football title. More than 10 per cent of Great Universal Stores mail-order business involves Manchester United merchandise. We . . .'

So it goes on. In the two years since Freedman arrived from Tottenham Hotspur he has set about marketing United with the unabashed enthusiasm of a McDonald's executive. And the McDonald's of football is what United have become – the universal cultural imperialists. Go into a sports shop in Bristol, for instance, a city with two long-established clubs of its own, and you will find the biggest-selling line is not Rovers or City, but the United kit in all its vulgar permutations.

'Manchester United is a unique brand,' says Freedman. 'Arsenal, for instance, despite all their huge success on the pitch, are big only in north London. United, however, are national, international, global. So, with skilful marketing you can achieve anything.'

As well as a huge mail-order operation, Freedman has opened up United superstores in the high streets of Belfast, Dublin, Plymouth and Manchester. By 1996, long-suffering parents will be able to finance their offspring's requirements for red paraphernalia in Sydney and Tokyo, too.

Such entrepreneurial vigour has pushed the contribution of merchandising to the United plc balance sheet from the barely noticeable in 1991, to nearly 30 per cent of turnover last season. Propelled by an advertising campaign worth billions provided gratis by the media, the average spend in the souvenir shop by match-goers is now £2 per head per game. There are, it seems, no limits.

'Yes there are limits,' insists Freedman. 'We will not sanction anything which diminishes the good name of our club. That is why we need to sort that lot out.'

He points out of his office window, down on to Sir Matt Busby Way, where the match-day open market sites itself. There the freelance salesmen act with extraordinary dispatch to exploit an opportunity. The game after Sir Matt Busby died there was a man selling red and white carnations to lay on the impromptu shrine which had developed on the stadium forecourt; a week after Leeds fans – despite their team's urgent appeals not to – chanted throughout a pre-match minute's silence in Busby's memory, T-shirts saying 'Leeds Scum, even your players are ashamed of you' were moving swiftly at a tenner a throw. And every game, the same band of touts ply their trade, supplying tickets on demand to anyone with pockets deep enough.

'Where d'you think we get 'em?' said one of the touts, a man with an angry scar linking nose to ear, when asked how he managed to have a fistful of tickets for every game in United's calendar. 'The system's corrupt from top to bottom. We're just the corruption you can see, mate, selling them for those what prefer not to have their faces known. Want tickets for Wembley, by the way? I got best views.'

Officially, such activity makes the club officials apoplectic. 'We cannot allow that sort of thing within sight of our ground,' says Edward Freedman. 'For two reasons: one, it is not the image we want associated with our club. And two: these are poor-quality goods and over-priced tickets that rip off our supporters.'

But, unofficially, they accept it is not so easy stopping those who seek to jump aboard United's financial juggernaut.

'We are trying,' Freedman says. 'What we have done is to bring those who were keen to play by our rules into the fold, by supplying them with goods. About 90 per cent of those merchandisers you see out there are supplied by us. As for the ticket touts and other parasites, we have taken steps to discourage them.'

United's steps include employing a security firm headed by a man called Ned Kelly, a bruiser who bears the aggrieved look and fearsome sandy moustache of an Afrikaner resistance fighter. Kelly and his men patrol the streets round the stadium encouraging freelancers to pack their stalls and scalpers to disappear. He also co-ordinates undercover teams ('hush-hush, sorry, can't talk about it') which have infiltrated Manchester's unofficial souvenir trade with an eye to prosecution.

'We have also copyrighted the club emblem and the club name,' says Freedman. 'It is now a criminal offence to pass off merchandise as genuine. If you want to make money from this club, you come through us. You need a licence.'

'Licence?' laughs Steve, a jack-the-lad entrepreneur who runs a T-shirt business called Barney's Football Chic and was not keen to have his surname advertised. 'Don't make me laugh. A licence from them? If you want decent United clobber you come to me. It's them what should be paying me for giving them some cool.'

Steve's shirts cater to a different palate than that favoured by the mass of trippers who pour into Freedman's shops. He offers clever parodies of designer sportswear labels with United themes; the big mover is the L'Eric Sportif, a twist on the Le Coq Sportif logo incorporating a cartoon of Cantona. His shirts are both very expensive and tricky to track down.

'It's like finding a new night club,' said Steve. 'You want to keep it to yourself, don't want everyone coming, do you? So I don't want everyone wearing my stuff, otherwise it's no longer cool. I've sold 500 L'Erics so far; I could sell ten times that.' Steve, who like most of his mates in the cool parts of Old Trafford is decked out top to toe in American sports labels – Ralph Lauren, Timberland –

prints his sight gags on T-shirts bought from the Champion company, an expensive source.

'I resent this idea put about by the club that anything unofficial is a poor-quality rip-off,' he says. 'Sure, some of the stuff for sale outside the ground will fall apart. But the lads I want to sell to are too sharp to buy that anyway. I would rather die than see a Barney T with a baggy neck.'

You can buy Barney shirts only by mail order through the United fanzines. Like Barney, these publications are aimed at those in the know. There are four of them, sold by their editors outside the ground, on trains, on coaches, anywhere that United fans congregate. Rude, opinionated and acidic, all used to be stocked in the souvenir shop. But when Alex Ferguson discovered quite how rude, opinionated and acidic they were about some of his players, he had them banned. Now their relationship with the club remains distant. Which is how their editors would prefer it.

All four were founded in the dark days of the late Eighties and still view the money-making operations co-ordinated by Our Martin (as they call him) with suspicion; they see United as *their* club, and not a property to finance the expensive Edwards lifestyle. But with a nice piece of irony, as interest in the club has reached boiling point, they too, all four of them, have started to make money. Andy Mitten, for instance, a 20-year-old journalism student who runs the title *United We Stand*, found himself selling over 1,500 copies at the game against Wimbledon in south London last season.

'It was unbelievable. I don't know where these people came from,' he remembers. 'They came decked out in all the souvenirs; they just hoovered up anything to do with United.'

But what has made all four titles much more cheerful publications is not making money, but the fact that United have started winning again on the field. 'In the end, what we care about is what happens there. Of course we all whinge and moan about the commercialisation,' says 'Red Eye', a contributor to *Red Issue*. 'But if a kid buying a United shirt in Portsmouth means the club has enough money to buy a Roy Keane or two and it keeps admission prices down, then who are we to worry? Anyway, you've got to admit they've got their act together to make the most of their success. I mean Liverpool didn't. They could have been making millions in the Eighties. One good thing about greed: it certainly helps you get your act together.'

Over the close season, while Alex Ferguson was busy strengthening thighs and hamstrings on the training pitch, Edward Freedman was busy getting his act together off it. Last spring he took over the lease on a 57,000-square-foot car spares warehouse abutting Old Trafford stadium, a place the size of a fringe-of-town megastore, which has been converted into a souvenir supermarket. Opened for the new buying season, it is a monster shop, where United stuff can be bought by the trolley load: Reds 'R' Us.

'When I looked at those queues on a match day and the fact that it took an hour to get into the shop and I thought of how many people must be put off from coming in, I realised something had to be done,' says Freedman. 'Our critics may complain about exploitation. Not true. No other club, no other chairman, pumps as much back into the organisation as ours does. No, no, no. We are satisfying a demand, no more than that. And I tell you, the way we are going, football will be the growth business of the Nineties.'

It was on the final day of last season that the growth business of the Nineties took another spurt. Old Trafford was in carnival, the championship won again, the celebrations tumbling from the stands. It seemed, the United merchandising department thought, the perfect opportunity to unveil their 'new concept in sports marketing'.

Just before kick-off, four girls walked on to the pitch carrying an airship load of red balloons. At the count of three conducted over the Old Trafford public address system, the balloons were released. And there in the centre circle usually graced by Hughes, Cantona and Giggs was a man in a big fluffy comedy devil's outfit. He was, the frantic public address system announcer said, Fred the Red: 'The new Manchester United character mascot', the Ronald

McDonald of Old Trafford. To celebrate his arrival, the crowd's attention was drawn to the Fred the Red catalogue, stapled into the centre of the match programme, just before the news of ticket price rises for the new season. Merchandise of a range and quantity that would need a superstore of its own were on offer: Fred pens, Fred shirts, Fred India rubbers; a Fred TV cartoon is planned. For a moment, as Fred waved to the crowd, you wondered what United were more proud of here – the finest set of footballers assembled in a generation, or the invention of a new way to satisfy demand.

At the end of the game, when the team received the Premiership trophy and squatted on their haunches for the traditional winners' photographs, Fred was still there, bouncing around waving as if he was the main attraction. Suddenly, on a signal prearranged amongst themselves, the players charged at him, downed him and, with a roar of encouragement from the crowd you could have heard in Liverpool, tore his monster suit off.

Footballers 1, Commercial Activity 0. It could be the last victory for a very long time.

MEXICAN RAVE

Andrew Downie

December, 1995

It's a hot, dry Sunday afternoon in northern Mexico and 20,000 football fans are packed into Torreón's Corona Stadium, a squat, low-slung ground that is buzzing with noise and anticipation. The fanatical supporters of the local Santos Laguna team are on their feet and the atmosphere is almost as overwhelming as the 90-degree heat that smothers this arid industrial city and the barren hills around it.

On one side of the ground, a grey plume of smoke billows from a flare on the pitch, while in the stand opposite two men hammer out a war dance on oversize tom-tom drums. One row behind, a chorus of ten buglers trumpet a charge worthy of a team nicknamed 'The Warriors'.

The fans are here for Santos' first home game of the season, a match that should see them take two comfortable points from the Tigres, a team from nearby Monterrey. The boys in green and white hoops need a win today to make up for last week's opening-day loss against Atlas, and just seventeen minutes into the game the fans get the start they so desperately want. A nod across goal is met perfectly by the head of centre forward Carlos Juarez and the ball flies into the back of the net.

A roar spews from the terraces and within seconds a chant rings around the ground: 'SAN-TOS, SAN-TOS, SAN-TOS.' Yet in the top corner of the main stand, the exultant cries are not sung with a Mexican accent. 'Worra team,' says a voice in an unmistakable

Lancashire brogue. 'Aye,' agrees his friend, speaking in thick Glaswegian. 'Pure magic.'

Graham Cruickshank and Neil Crowther clap furiously and wave their Santos flags before settling down to watch their heroes stroke the ball about the green turf below. The two men – football fanatics, British eccentrics, Santos devotees – raise a cold beer to their lips and smile once more at the sheer improbability of it all.

In 1986, Graham and Neil were like any other football-mad Brits desperate to see their countries play in the World Cup Finals in Mexico. Graham, a Partick Thistle fan from Glasgow, and Neil, a Manchester City supporter from Middleton in Lancashire, joined tens of thousands of Scots and English supporters who came to Mexico in search of sun, sea, cheap booze and maybe even a half-decent game of football.

The two young men drank bottles of tequila, ate platefuls of tacos and flirted with the local women. They liked Mexico. In fact, they liked it so much they stayed, married, and got jobs in Mexico City. Life was good to them: they bought attractive houses and new cars. The climate was favourable and daily life a little less structured than at home.

But of all the things they missed – Heinz baked beans, fish and chips and *Coronation Street* – one thing topped the list: a good football match. Ever since they arrived in Mexico, the lads had been regulars at first division matches. They had seen every team in the country at one time or another, although when they could get tickets they preferred to go to the big games, the Mexican equivalent of Manchester United v Liverpool or Rangers v Celtic.

Then, in 1993, after years of having their soccer wanderlust satisfied by attending a dozen or so uninvolving encounters a year, the two friends decided they wanted something a bit more intense, a team to remind them of Manchester City or Partick Thistle. 'We were fed up watching the same crap,' says Graham. 'So we decided to pick a team and follow them.'

It was not a difficult decision. Their strict criteria ruled out the five clubs in Mexico City (too close to home), the three teams allied to universities ('too poofy and full of students,' according to Graham) and three of the most wealthy provincial sides (too successful). That left seven teams. In the end, of course, they opted to support a side as ordinary as it was obscure. Or, as Graham explains: 'We went for a team that didnae have any supporters.'

The Santos Barmy Army was born.

Why anyone not raised in the dusty, soulless city of Torreón would want to support Santos is a mystery; it's like a couple of lads from north London deciding to follow Grimsby. Formed just twelve years ago as the local social security works side, the team of journeymen have spent most of their seven years in the first division fighting to avoid relegation. They have few class players and no need to waste money paying someone to polish silverware.

But still, within a short time, Neil and Graham became Santos experts. By reading newspaper reports, watching television and consulting Mexican in-laws, they memorised the personal details of each team member. They bought green and white hooped jerseys, Santos T-shirts and flags and, just like fanatical six-year-olds, scribbled the name Santos all over the football they used for a kickabout. They took to their role with gusto.

According to the blokeish logic adopted by the pair, the complete absence of glamour, flair or anything resembling success made Santos even more appealing. 'That's why we went to support them,' explains Graham. 'They were rubbish.'

There aren't many sports stadiums in the word named after a beer. There is no Newcastle Brown Park in the north-east, no Tartan Special Stadium in Scotland. Even in America, Adland itself, the Budweiser Dome or the Miller Lite Field has yet to catch on.

Completed in 1970, Torreón's Estadio Corona is not the most impressive of grounds. A throwback to the days before such disasters as Hillsborough and Bradford made football authorities radically rethink football stadium design, the ground is terraced and has a very conspicuous lack of executive boxes. The poor buy tickets at windows marked 'sun'; the rich take their seats in the area called 'shade'.

But despite the flamboyance of Santos fans, it's unlikely the concrete bowl has ever seen anything like Neil and Graham. But then again neither have Graham and Neil ever seen anything like the Estadio Corona. Although they have followed Santos religiously for more than two years, neither of them has ever got to see Santos play at home – until now. 'We cannae get tickets,' moaned Graham last season. 'The fans up there are mental.'

Indeed, the vast majority of the 20,000 seats at the compact ground are full on match day. Santos supporters are famous for their devotion – they are the best in Mexico, according to one newspaper poll. Both parts of the ground – sun and shade – are full long before kick-off.

Santos home games don't start until 4pm, but that doesn't stop the Santos Barmy Army marching to the ground at 1.30pm. There are things to buy: Neil stocks up on T-shirts and car stickers; Graham buys presents for his family. 'Ah've got tae get a strip for the wee man,' says Graham, referring to his five-year-old son Norman Alonso. 'And my daughter Claudia watches the games with me on the telly, so ah've tae get a shirt for her too.' Claudia is three.

The sight of two fair-skinned foreigners shopping for Santos shirts puzzles the home fans. A row of pre-pubescent girls – Santos cheerleaders – point and snigger and self-consciously try to avoid revealing their silver and green pompoms hidden among the pile of clothes that surround their spangly tights. The pompoms do make an appearance at half-time, but the crowd isn't watching; they are too busy discussing Juarez's header and asking themselves why Santos aren't pushing forward in search of a match-clinching goal.

It's a question that is aired more and more in the second half as Santos let the Tigres back into the game. After having a penalty claim turned down by the referee – while the home fans are chanting the traditional Mexican '*¡ratero, ratero!*' ('robber, robber!') at the man in black, Neil is screaming, 'The referee's a wanker' – Santos lose control and when Tigres' American international, Tab Ramos, is sent off sixteen minutes from time, the away side really begin to battle. With ten minutes to go, there is a goal-mouth scramble and Tigres are level.

Across the stadium faces drop as orange peel and beer-filled plastic cups fly onto the pitch. Neil and Graham cannot believe it. They don't know what to do – roar the boys on for the last ten minutes or cry because their heroes have let them down.

A jovial Scot with a face almost as red as his hair, Señor Cruickshank is not the kind of Glaswegian to whom the word dour could ever be applied. The former head of the Mexican-Scottish Society and a well-known member of the country's 3,500-strong British community, 33-year-old Graham is a fairly decent chap when he's away from the soccer field. A warehouse manager before Mexico '86, he left his job to join forces with his new wife at her Mexico City travel agency, now renamed Caledonian Travel.

Neil, meanwhile, is a slightly built 34-year-old with keen eyes and a curly moustache whose occasional outbursts on the football field have earned him the nickname 'Mad Dog'. Off the pitch he is a smartly dressed teacher who runs his own company teaching English to Mexican executives. A former marketing man for ITV, Neil met his wife Carmen in a city-centre bar just before the England v Paraguay match in 1986. The two hit it off so well that he took her home to England, where they lived for several years before returning to Mexico City in 1991.

The two Brits met later that year when they turned out for a UK expat team that had entered the annual 'Little World Cup' organised by other exiled football fanatics living in Mexico. The British team had a mixed tournament – they beat Switzerland and lost to Argentina – but the two lads clicked and, as Neil puts it, 'have been drinking together ever since'.

Graham is the more social of the two, and also the more rambunctious. Neil is a little more sensible and circumspect, especially among strangers. Together, though, they are like teenagers, forever swapping obscure and exclusive references to subjects such as Seventies footballers, Eighties singers and Nineties acquaintances. The string of invariably unfunny and personal jokes are inevitably followed by a grin from Graham and a cackle from Neil.

And to hear them tell it, their footballing escapades are rivalled only by their drinking sessions, which can last hours – or even days in exceptional circumstances like World Cups and local tournaments. The two can drink so much Corona beer that they like to be referred to as the 'crate twins'. At games, they regale the opposition and their bewildered fans with the theme from *It Ain't Half Hot Mum*. Another terrace favourite is the chant: 'Steve Wright, Steve Wright, 275 and 285, Steve Wright, Steve Wright, National Radio One.' Jimmy Hill comes in for frequent abuse, as do Manchester United, Rangers, Celtic and a host of others. Of course, no one in Mexico has a clue what they are on about.

And the exuberance goes beyond football stadiums. Graham, for example, narrowly avoided arrest during the run-up to last August's presidential election when he threatened to scale a flagpole and steal a campaign banner emblazoned with the initials of the *Partido Trabajadores* (Workers Party). The huge, red and yellow flags that waved above the city's main thoroughfare were perfect for Glasgow's Firhill, the home of Partick Thistle, says Graham. 'PT – Partick Thistle – the boys would've loved that back home,' he says, laughing. Partick Thistle (Billy Connolly once said that when he was growing up he thought the team was called 'Partick Thistle Nil') play in red and yellow.

Graham and Neil's friends and family have become accustomed to their obsessive undertakings and even Neil's father has got in on the fun. On his most recent trip to Mexico earlier this year, the retired British Gas technician went to see Santos play twice. They won both times. 'He thought they were brilliant,' says Neil. 'He's never seen them lose.'

The Cruickshank clan is equally enthusiastic about Graham's compulsions, although his wife, Eugenia Burgos de Cruickshank, is by now resigned to her husband's fanaticisms: if it's not Santos, it's Partick Thistle; if it's not Partick Thistle, it's Scotland; if it's not Scotland, it's one of the four teams her husband regularly plays for in his new home. 'Ooooooh,' she sighs, rolling her eyes skywards and dismissing her chuckling hubby with a flick of the wrist. 'He's *loco.*'

Graham and Neil are not the only football supporters in Mexico who are '*loco*' – the country is full of fans who take their devotion to extremes. When the country's biggest team, Club America, was knocked out of the cup play-offs last summer by arch rivals Cruz Azul, two fans committed suicide. A Cruz Azul fan then strung himself to his lavatory cistern and jumped to his death when his team lost in the final a week later.

Fanatical supporters don't just die from hanging. Just weeks after the professional season ended, two teenagers were shot dead in the south-eastern suburbs of Mexico City after their team won a narrow victory over a rival squad. The first was targeted for no other reason than he had scored the winning goal. Then, within hours, another youth was murdered in the northern outskirts of the city when a fight over a disallowed goal led later to a gun battle between opposing players. The same weekend, a 16-year-old was killed in Ecatepec, an area just outside Mexico City, when he took a bullet in the head after an argument on the field.

The soccer psychosis spills over into the top-flight game, which is rife with indiscipline. Players routinely abuse their managers in public and feuding between players and officials is common. When Club America's star striker, Luis Garcia, disagreed with the tactics of his new manager last season he brazenly told reporters: 'A 10-year-old knows more about football than he does.' Mexican goalkeeper Jorge Campos said if the federation sacked national manager Miguel Mejia Baron, who played Campos at centre forward as well as in goal, then he wouldn't play for his country ever again.

Football crazy, indeed.

So Graham and Neil were in good company when two years ago the mighty Santos Laguna, who just a few months before narrowly avoided relegation, began just their sixth season in Division One. The Warriors made their usual inauspicious start to the new season with a few defeats, a few draws and an occasional win. They perked up a little as the campaign progressed and at the halfway stage had gained nineteen points from nineteen games – a respectable, if unspectacular, total.

But during the approach to the play-offs, Santos suddenly set the league alight. Over the next three months, they went fourteen games without defeat. For the first time they qualified as one of the eight teams to progress to the league's lucrative home-and-away knockout stage. From then on, as far as Neil and Graham were concerned, it was Fantasy Football. In the first round, Santos beat Atlas 3–2 on aggregate. In the semi-final, a 2–0 win at home to Toluca was enough to give them a place in the final, even after losing the second leg 1–0 away from home.

The final showdown was in May last year against the Autonomous University of Guadalajara (more commonly known as Tecos), a team that had led the league for most of the season and proved themselves the best in the country. It was an unlikely showdown: Tecos, the toast of the year, versus Santos, the perennial no-hopers. The first game of the home-and-away final took place in Torreón with Santos grabbing a vital 1–0 victory to take to the return leg a few days later. Despite their exhaustive efforts to get a ticket, neither Neil nor Graham had managed to see any of Santos' play-off matches live. Instead, they were forced to don their strips and wave their flags at local bars that carried the games live on television.

Then, on the eve of the final match, Neil got an unexpected phone call from a business contact in Guadalajara, a director who had taken language classes from the Englishman. He had one spare ticket for the game. Neil flew to the city, 250 miles north-west of the capital, the next morning. The game was finely balanced and went to extra time after Tecos won 1–0 to leave the aggregate score level. However, within a few minutes of the restart, Tecos scored again, and 25 minutes later the Santos football fairy tale was over.

Needless to say, the less than bashful Brits are convinced that the side's sudden charge up the league was down to one thing, their generous patronage. 'They were rubbish and then we started supporting them and look what happened,' says Neil. 'Aye,' agrees Graham. 'The home team doesnae know what's come over them when we're in the stadium. A few choruses from *It Ain't Half Hot Mum* and they're intimidated. It's us, man. We're magic.'

At the final whistle in the Corona Stadium, Neil and Graham get onto the pitch and seize the opportunity to meet their idols. Neil tells Tigres' best player and recent signing Martin Ubaldi he should have stayed with his old club Atlas. Graham greets dejected goal-scorer Carlos Juarez with a comforting, 'That's the way these things go, eh?'

About 45 minutes later, the players wearily leave the stadium and head for the team bus, the mood much calmer than the hostile wrath that erupted at the end of the match. Neil and Graham are no longer dispirited; they are content to have a beer in their hands and to have had the chance to see their heroes perform on their home turf. When a friendly steward allows them to greet the players in the tunnel, the remnants of the black mood disappear totally.

Graham even takes the manager aside to offer a piece of advice. 'Listen,' he says, resting his hand on Patricio Hernandez's shoulder like a father sharing years of experience with his young son, 'give it a few weeks and they'll be winning. Nae bother.'

The players are also a little happier – despite dropping a vital point at home. But they are not as happy as Neil, who is at that moment having his picture taken with the players. 'This is it,' he beams, wrapping an arm around the neck of defender Hector Esparza. 'This is a dream.'

CREASE LIGHTNING

Mick Imlah

May, 1993

There are fast bowlers and *fast* bowlers, and England has two of the latter. In the heat and dust of Calcutta, Devon Malcolm is steaming in to bowl to Sachin Tendulkar, while in the dead of the English winter, in the whitewashed indoor net at the County Ground in Bristol, David 'Syd' Lawrence is shaping up off six or seven paces to bowl to me.

Lawrence knows this won't be quick, in his terms; he is still feeling his way back into bowling after a dreadful injury, and, as he's said, he doesn't want to harm me. But the trick of fast bowling is not in the bowler's mind; it's in what he puts into the mind of the batsman. Syd describes this acutely: 'You know it might bowl you, or get you caught. But, as well as your wicket, there's yourself to protect. You know it could hit you in the face. It could break your arm. It could smash your fingers. It could smack you in the ribs, or in the groin. And, you know, this will *hurt.*' (He reminded me of these uncertainties as I was strapping on my pads under a noticeboard on which a number of medical emergency numbers were prominent, as well as an advert for something called a 'Batting Clinic'.) Syd is boisterous, cheerful, all (I'm afraid) bounce. His seventeen stones are compressed into bulgy muscles; if there hadn't been cricket, he'd have been a heavyweight boxer, and from 22 yards, as he leaps and coils up his arms to bowl, he looks huge.

The first ball is full length; I get more or less into position, and it squirts away off a thick outside edge towards point. Bold for an instant, I nearly make a joke about scampering a single, but think better of it, remembering Syd's earlier remark: 'I've met a lot of good people through cricket – but I've also met a lot of wankers through cricket.' Besides, any notion that batting against him is *not impossible* is premature. I have a sense of where the second ball's gone, but I can't say I've seen it. It didn't seem short-pitched, but it's whammed into the rear netting at something above waist height, and I reconstruct a flight path that takes the ball through the narrow gap between my gloves and my box. 'Let me know,' calls Syd, 'when you want me to step up the pace.' 'Ready when you are.'

Now I know the thing to do is to get into line – to get my feet across so that my head is over the ball. *So that my head is over the ball.* But some other instinct intervenes, and when I think Syd might be putting his back into it, I'm backing out of it – the two little steps to leg that are the signature shuffle of the batting coward. My bat, meanwhile, is completing a slow, horizontal curve at something that fizzed by long ago. I have given the bowler my measure (about an inch and a half), and Syd settles into a patient, scornful groove of what – to him – are little outswingers. I can't even lay my heavy, stupid bat on these. It's as if we dwell in different time scales, like a fly and human swatter. I wanted to ask him to bowl a bouncer at me, but I'd have to lie down before he delivered it.

These horrible symptoms begin to afflict the club batsman at around 60 miles an hour. At full fitness, off his full run, Lawrence comes through about 90. The fact is that Derek Pringle would be a bit sharp for us. A friend of mine, a good club cricketer, remembers being embarrassed by the *pace* of Derek *Underwood*. But is it always so much easier for the really good players?

A left-handed county opener, in the middle of a reasonably successful season, describes the exhilarating effect of two overs from Warwickshire's Allan Donald – currently the fastest bowler in the world – just before lunch. (He'd survived somehow, and could look forward to facing Donald again after the interval.) 'Lunch was chicken salad, but I didn't know I was eating it until I'd had about two thirds. I went to the loo, and sat down with my pants on. It was like being concussed.' Herbert Sutcliffe, one of the greatest opening batsmen, put it this way: that some can play fast bowling and some cannot, but if they all told the truth, none of them like it.

And top-flight batsmen have been lumping it a lot of late. From the mid-Seventies until the end of the Eighties, Test cricket was dominated by the West Indies; not because they had batsmen of the quality of Gordon Greenidge, Desmond Haynes, Clive Lloyd and Viv Richards, but because they could regularly field four bowlers of the highest pace in the same side, choosing over that period from Roberts, Daniel, Garner, Holding, Marshall, Croft, Clarke, Walsh, Patterson, any of three Benjamins, Davis, Gray, Ambrose, Bishop and Moseley. Meanwhile, England had only Bob Willis (and Graham Dilley on occasions) of comparable pace – and when Willis retired in 1984, they had no one. If there had ever been any truth in the myth of whistling down the pit for your new pace man – and of Test-opening bowlers only Harold Larwood and the twice-capped Les Jackson were ever miners (Fred Trueman worked in a colliery office) – then the seam was long since exhausted. But a new fast-bowling stereotype had replaced it in the leagues – a big, black stereotype. And it was from this new resource of England-qualified black players that two real candidates emerged.

Devon Malcolm – distinguished at the time by thick spectacles – came first, making his debut in 1989 against Australia. He can recall it now with a smile. 'I had Geoff Marsh lbw before he'd made ten – he was dead, man. Even the non-striking batsman was shaking his head . . .' Then the umpire shook his, and, at the end of the day, Australia were 301 for no wicket. Malcolm went on to concede more runs (166) in an innings than any Test debutant since 1954; and the chairman of the selectors' consolatory praise was all the fainter for getting his name wrong ('I think we saw some promise from Malcolm Devon').

In the first Test in the West Indies the following winter, things didn't seem to be getting any better. On a boiling-hot Jamaican morning, Greenidge and Haynes were making leisurely progress;

Malcolm's bowling was wayward, and he'd begun to blunder in the field. 'I was at long leg, Greenidge flicked it down towards me, and put pressure on me by shouting for two. It went straight through my legs for four. I said to myself, whatever else you do in this game, you do that again, and you're knackered.' Two overs later, Malcolm very nearly did do it again; only this time the ball struck his knee, and he was able to recover and throw instantly. The throw was hard and flat and straight. Greenidge was out by a yard. ('That was *so sweet.*')

England had entered the series, and Malcolm had made his first mark. Some overs later, he had the great Viv Richards lbw, and the foundations were laid for a famous victory. In the second innings, his victims were Greenidge, Haynes, Richards again, and Jeff Dujon – three of them clean bowled. In the next Test, at Trinidad, he took ten wickets and set up what would have been a second win but for the rain that fell on the fifth afternoon. England were transformed from the side that had suffered fourteen defeats in fifteen games against the West Indies; and the difference was Malcolm. The difference was pace.

Malcolm had another good tour in Australia in 1990–91, but the next summer saw him dropped to make way for Lawrence. Fast bowlers have traditionally been most destructive in pairs, but the fact that Malcolm and Lawrence are so similar in style has combined with the natural conservatism of the England selectors to prevent them playing together in Tests. Hence they've had, in effect, only one international career between them, and are yet to achieve a joint total of 100 Test wickets.

But while the selectors regard them as the same bowler, and while they are equally popular in the changing room, they're quite different in temperament. Lawrence, born and raised in Gloucester, is ebullient and energetic in everything he does, emphatically one of the lads. Malcolm, born and raised in Jamaica, is 'the sort of bloke who takes four-and-a-half hours to put on his shoes', according to Mickey Stewart, the former England manager. Both on and off the field he sometimes gives the impression of remembering warmer days.

I met him at Lilleshall, where the England players, preparing for the winter tour of India, were examining their individual shortcomings. (Mike Gatting, for example, batting in the net, to self: 'HOW DID YOU MISS THAT YOU FAT C***?') Malcolm was comparing videos of his action before and after his coaches' adjustments. He is more technically minded than you might expect, especially to judge from his batting. Indeed, it was the sight, not of fear, but of sound technique in an opposition batsman that made him want to be a professional cricketer.

At eighteen, the game was a matter of 'scaring guys' in the Yorkshire leagues ('six for twenty, seven for fifteen and so on') until, in a game against a Yorkshire Schools XI, he bowled to Ashley Metcalfe, now an opening batsman for the county. 'And it was just like watching Boycott on TV. Everything was so correct and solid – not stepping away and giving it this business.' He sweeps his arms contemptuously in a sideways swish. 'That was the day I knew I loved cricket.' The wicket of Boycott himself, yorked in the only recorded victory of the Yorkshire League XI over the county side, provided Malcolm with his route into the first-class game. The Derbyshire coach Phil Russell saw the headlines ('Yorkshire Devon Creamed'), gave him a net, offered him a contract, and that was the end of a career in accountancy.

We love our fast bowlers, but we don't like theirs. The only cricketers with the power to injure others, they can make proper villains of themselves. Of course, the ball which hits one batsman in the temple is exactly the same as the ball which another batsman gloves to the keeper, but some bowlers have not seemed to prefer the second outcome enough. Jeff Thompson, the fastest of all measured bowlers at just under 100mph, ruffled a few feathers with his talk of English 'stiff upper lips' and his love of splitting them; still, it was the English who invented the angle of attack known as Bodyline. But black fast bowlers, which until the Eighties meant West Indian fast bowlers, have usually seemed the most physically threatening.

In the early days of West Indian Test cricket, quick bowling was even seen as an instrument of voodoo. On the eve of the Test match in Georgetown in 1935, England's opener and captain, Bob Wyatt, was approached by a Guyanan carrying a beautifully carved miniature coffin, which he opened to reveal the model of a corpse, as he hissed: 'This is what Martindale do to you.' The next morning, a short ball from the Bajan Manny Martindale reared and broke Wyatt's jaw in three places. The injury was so bad that there was indeed fear for his life. Two later West Indians, Roy Gilchrist and Charlie Griffith, sometimes seemed intent on murder at twenty paces. The controversial Griffith, before his fearsome bouncer was finally denounced as a chuck, very nearly killed the Indian captain, Nari Contractor, in a game in Barbados; a brain operation saved the batsman's life, but he never played again.

Accidents will happen, but some bowlers encourage batsmen to think that accidents are part of their plan. Verbal intimidation – what Lawrence derides as 'yapping' – has been in use since the prime of 'Old' Clarke two centuries ago: Clarke's custom was to 'prey upon the terrors of his victims by making caustic and cocksure remarks about what he would do with them when he had them in front of him'. (Anyone who doubts that the underarm bowling of Clarke could fulfil these threats is referred to the case of 'Long' Robinson, who had two fingers of his right hand 'struck off by the violence of the ball'.)

The arch-aggressor Trueman was in Clarke's 'cocksure' tradition: at the age of sixteen, he greeted a hard-faced veteran, arriving at the crease, with the news he'd let him have one off the mark, but after that he was going to 'pin' him 'to the fucking sightscreen'. These days yapping is more an Australian speciality. Both Malcolm and Lawrence prefer, as the latter puts it, to 'let the ball do the talking'.

Violent, abusive or, worst of all, successful fast bowlers make things harder for those who follow. The recent legislation limiting bowlers to one bouncer per batsman per over is a response to what had become the standard West Indies practice of three bouncers an over all day. But the ruling dismays both Malcolm and Lawrence, neither of whom used to bowl an excessive number of short balls. For Malcolm, it's a 'crap rule'. For Lawrence, it's another instance of how the game is constantly being redesigned for the benefit of batsmen. 'Can you imagine them ever saying that a batter is only allowed to play one cover drive or one pull shot per over? But it's been the same every time bowlers have gained an advantage – they change the rules to hamper them. What they're after, in effect, is for you to bowl the ball the batsman wants. Sometimes you think they'd be happier with a bowling machine at either end to serve batters. I think it's very strange...'

Complaints like this intensify when fast bowlers consider what the wear and tear of their occupation tends to inflict on them. Freddie Trueman's boast is 'I bowled for twenty years and I never pulled a muscle.' But for most fast bowlers, physical breakdown – hamstring, shin splints, back strains, knee damage – comes with, and jeopardises, the job. Lawrence talks of fellow bowlers – Lillee, Foster, Fraser, Bishop – who have lost a year or more to serious structural damage; and of others – such as the ill-fated Ricky Ellcock of Middlesex – who will never bowl again: all crippled by doing what the body is not built to do. As Lawrence says: 'No other sport asks you to go repeatedly through such unnatural movement – to run 40 yards, to leap sideways, to set yourself like a catapult, to fling it down, and at the moment of delivery all the pressure comes down on your braced left leg, and it's all absorbed by your left knee...'

At this he looks rueful. For if Lawrence never takes another Test wicket, he will always be remembered for one of the most spectacular injuries in the history of televised sport. In Wellington, fifteen months ago, he was bowling with characteristic whole-heartedness in a Test match that was yawning towards a draw, when his knee snapped in two with a noise louder than the crack of a Robin Smith square cut. It was nine months before Lawrence was able to bowl again, and even now there is stiffness around the repaired kneecap. But he manfully accepts his ration of serious injury and looks forward with a visible appetite to the new season and several beyond. At 29, he wants to emulate Lillee, Willis and

Hadlee, all opening the bowling in Tests when they were 35.

These great names apart, the omens are against him. Among English bowlers, it's not so much the ability that fades as the will. It's one thing for Devon Malcolm, say, to run in on a bouncy wicket in Perth in front of 30,000 people; another to trudge back to his mark with all his sweaters on at half past five on a blustery May afternoon at Derby. Frank Tyson, the fastest bowler in the world for two winters during the Fifties, has described how his will was nobbled by bowling on the notoriously dead wicket at his county ground at Northampton. What Tyson lost was that motor of optimism and self-belief, without which there would be no fast bowling: the conviction that he could take a wicket with every ball, the prejudice in favour of himself that had a bowler like Trueman sensing movement off the pitch and errors in the stroke where none existed.

English county cricket is unique in asking men to bowl fast nearly every day for four consecutive months. And even those days when the body is willing, the feel for the job can be fickle. Malcolm summarises the feeling: 'Sometimes you pick up the ball, and it feels *nice*, and you know you're going to take wickets. Other mornings – Jesus, it feels like a football, and you know, damn, you're going to struggle all day.' But Malcolm will never compromise his bowling nature. 'I'm a strike bowler,' he insists. 'I'll go for four runs an over, not two.' And if the rewards for absolute speed are intermittent, then they're high when they come; those enthralling phases when rhythm and fitness and pitch combine perfectly, and the world's best batsmen can only grope and fend as helplessly as me against David Lawrence at half pace. As Frank Tyson puts it: 'To those who have bowled quick, really quick, there is no comparable feeling in the world.'

SHE'S GOT BALLS

Ian Ridley

October, 1993

The sign on the door prepares you: 'Nudity required. Apply within.' In fact, the whole tatty block which houses the London office of the *Daily* and *Sunday Sport* on its third floor prepares you. It is located a few hundred yards from the City and the opulent, glassy headquarters of major companies, and another few hundred from Shoreditch and its inner-city graffiti of despair. The entrance is around the back. Welcome to the twilight zone of the British press.

In the open-plan *Sport* office – all grey carpet tiles and yellowing back issues – sales and marketing director Karren Brady is on the telephone to her boss, publisher David Sullivan.

'It's about five and half inches in height,' she is saying. 'They want to do an insert.' 'It' is an advertisement, but could just as easily be a suppository. Everything here seems to be an innuendo.

In such surroundings, it is difficult to take Brady as seriously as she deserves. For, at 25, she is both a linchpin of the *Sport* empire of sleaze and the managing director of Birmingham City, the only woman in charge of a professional football club. Inevitably, when Sullivan paid £25 million to acquire the club last March, it was said that Brady had been bought a plaything by her boyfriend. But she adamantly denies both allegations, just as she denies any amorous involvement with either the boxer Chris Pyatt, who lives in (and thus helps out with the mortgage on) her £150,000 flat looking out over Tower Bridge, or the Arsenal footballer Kevin Campbell.

For our interview, Brady chooses a rather different environment, an airy Italian restaurant in Knightsbridge. To get there she drives me through the West End in her Porsche Carrera. Such manifestations of style are in contrast with the tackiness of the *Sport.* But then, pretty and pretty tough – 'as nails', says Sullivan – Brady is a woman of contrasts, surprises even, almost daring people to judge her and, gratifyingly, not judging others herself.

This supposed soft-porn bimbo was in fact a convent and then a public schoolgirl, a captain of hockey, swimming and badminton who passed nine O-levels and four A-levels, in English, history, politics and economics, at the predominantly male Aldenham School in Hertfordshire. She has, though, no qualms about being associated with two men, Sullivan and Pyatt, whose colourful pasts include court appearances, at the end of which they were cleared, or about giving two-word answers to footballers who fancy themselves and their chances of making passes of the off-field variety. And she has no difficulty reconciling an interest in boxing with a delicate taste in shoes – more than 100 pairs at the last count – and £800 evening gowns. ('I bought it on holiday in Capri,' she says of one gown, 'and I was really pleased when I saw the same one in Harrods for £1,200.')

At sixteen, Brady was turned down for a job as a check-out girl in Waitrose for being too glamorous. 'I was really pissed off. I really wanted that job,' she says. 'I've never shopped there since.' At eighteen, spurning the chance of going to university because she didn't like what it had done to some friends, she joined ad agency Saatchi & Saatchi.

'I remember,' she says, 'being sent to supermarkets to check on the position of a cheese they were advertising and report back. I noticed that if you moved the cheese to a better position they sold better and nobody bothered to move them back. I thought that was what the aim was. I suppose it did show that I am a person who makes things happen.'

After a year of the three-year traineeship impatience took her to the ad sales department at the London radio station LBC. She first encountered Sullivan working there; he was impressed with her hard sales pitch. An initial £5,000 commission developed into £2 million worth of advertising. Soon Sullivan asked her to work for him full-time.

'I just thought it was really exciting,' she says, looking back on £32,000 a year and a Volkswagen Golf. (The Mercedes, given to her by a boyfriend, had gone back when they split.) Her parents – her father is a wealthy businessman who owns a printing business in north London and has an estate in Enfield – just thought it was 'weird'. Her mother, she says, simply told everyone at the tennis club that her daughter was 'in advertising'.

Brady describes the *Sport* as 'an adult publication for a young group who want a good laugh and a bit of sex thrown in'. And those telephone sex lines? 'Most of it is nonsense, drivel but harmless,' although she does check 'anything sensitive in there'.

'I think,' she says, 'it is good and important that people can see independents come into the market and find a niche, make a hole and dig away at that hole. Some pretend they are buying it for the sport coverage, but there will always be an image problem. The paper is unique because it accepts that it is different.' They can't take on the *Sun*, which she admires, and its 'investigations'. 'They are nasty to people and use them up. We don't. Mainly because we can't afford to.'

And when she meets men and the talk invariably gets around to what she does for a living? 'Some say, "What's that?" Others say, "Oh, that's the paper with big tits, isn't it?" Then you know that they are a raving punter and you just walk off.'

Brady is frank to a fault. And fruity. She is wearing a Wonder Bra, she reveals. 'I was called fried eggs and all that at school. Size does matter. It's just like men worrying about their willies, and some of them have good reason.' She smirks at the recent memory of her Jamaican holiday hotel with its adjacent naturist beach, where some American gentlemen had apparently over-inflated opinions of themselves.

As for Sullivan: 'I am not like his women, I'm not his type. I am probably too strong a character. We are very alike in that we both like people who get things done. I don't want to know how you get from A to B, I just want to know that you are at B. But we are unalike when it comes to money. I asked him to get me a Ralph Lauren blazer when he was on holiday in the States because it was cheaper over there, but he couldn't understand how anyone could spend £400 on a jacket. I think,' she adds, 'he chose me because I am honest and loyal.' Then she tells me off the record, so as not to cause any offence, the name of the broadsheet newspaper whose £63,000 a year (a third as much again as she gets now) she rejected because she likes the job and the people where she is.

'I am sure,' Brady says, 'David would have been successful in any business he chose to go into. He chose this one because he admired Hugh Hefner.' And Sullivan's background and reputation? 'All I would say is don't judge him without knowing him.' And the same, it seems, applies to her.

The graffiti prepares you: 'The Board Must Go'. In fact, the whole area surrounding Birmingham City Football Club in the once industrial suburb of Bordesley prepares you. 'Welcome to St Andrews', it says outside the ground, though the barbed wire crowning the fencing to deter would-be burglars suggests otherwise.

Around the stadium are a partly demolished warehouse and new housing estates, a bingo club and an evangelical church. The ground itself, with its carpeted bars, suites and boxes looking out on outmoded terracing, has for years been all gravelled car parks, weather-beaten corrugated roofing and peeling paint – though a £20,000 lick this summer helped. Welcome to the twilight zone of English football.

Second City and second-rate, the club has 118 years of underachievement behind it. The club did reach the Cup Final in 1931 and 1956, won the League Cup in 1963, and the Leyland Daf Cup for lower division teams two years ago. And there have been great players, notably Trevor Francis, who burst onto the scene as a 16-year-old. But mostly there haven't been. Mostly, the club has been a joke. 'You draw some, you lose some,' lamented their most famous supporter and former director, the comedian Jasper Carrott. 'After three games this season, I know my club Birmingham City are going to be relegated. Is this a record?' a fan once wondered in a Sunday newspaper. 'Keep Right on to the End of the Road' has been their theme song, and it has often seemed as if they were almost there.

Sullivan, a Welshman who supported Newport County as a boy, had been seeking a club and decided that Birmingham was ripe. Many thought it was just the latest joke. They would be called Bummingham Titty; the programme would have to go on the top shelf of paper shops; the *Sport* would carry fanciful stories like 'Football Found at St Andrews'.

But Sullivan and Brady assured the fans that the club would be separate from the newspaper, though a silly summer story that football's Madonna was seeking to bring football's Maradona to the club confirmed the link. More importantly, they invested £1.5 million in new players, who kept them out of the Second Division last season and suggested a Premier League promotion campaign this one, and they have also announced a £4.5 million plan to turn the ground over sixteen weeks into a 25,000-capacity all-seater by next summer. This, and the desperation of football supporters watching their club dying under previous regimes, led to them being warmly welcomed. For dying Birmingham most certainly was.

'I thought it would be bad,' Brady says, 'but I didn't realise how bad. In my first week I wondered what I had taken on. There wasn't an area of the club that was making money. If you asked how much money the shop had taken in the past year, no one could give you an answer because there was no paperwork. It took three months to find some. I saw two prongs on top of the floodlights and wondered what they were. Nobody knew. They turned out to be receivers for mobile phones, which we were paying for.'

Brady did not pretend to know anything about running a football club. She went to Arsenal – the club she had supported from her father's executive box at Highbury, not missing a game for six years – and asked the managing director Ken Friar for ten minutes of his time. When Arsenal's vice-chairman David Dein – one of football's new breed of aggressive marketeers – walked in, she closed the door behind both men and picked their brains for four hours. 'They told me not to let my heart rule my head, never to get involved, and to put everything out to tender.'

There were early moments of naivety. Soon after taking over, Brady was invited out to lunch by Doug Ellis, the chairman of Birmingham's big brother, Aston Villa, and known in the game as 'Deadly', and the club's manager Ron Atkinson, known as 'Big'. She took her own club's manager, Terry Cooper, 'for protection'. Flicking through a Villa programme, she read about a player called Dalian Atkinson. 'Is that your son?' she asked Big Ron. 'He said, "Yeah", and I said, "How nice". I could see everyone looking down and thought, I'm on a wind-up here. Then he told me that Dalian was black.'

What was her own players' reaction to her? 'They were very shy. They were the most polite, well-behaved bunch of individuals I had ever met.' You point out that the club were once known as the Brummie Bashers. 'Well, they are not like that now. The first time I went to a pre-match meal you could have heard a pin drop. And when I asked them if there were any questions, there was just quiet.' And the players' wives? She does not worry what they think of her.

'I feel sisterly towards the players,' Brady says, 'and the whole place lights up when they are around. You see kids playing outside the gates and when they see a player it makes their day. I do see what a club means in people's lives.' Thus Brady has quickly learnt what all associated with football come to know: that it is unlike other businesses, that it is hard not to let heart rule head. 'I just loved being back,' she said after returning from a summer break. 'I just wanted to stay there 'til ten o'clock at night.' At first she was going to run the club two days a week; but now she prefers to base herself there.

Inevitably, Brady has had to put up with being patronised. When Birmingham played at Watford, she was shown to a room for directors' wives before persuading the jobsworth of her status. 'But I don't mind,' she says. 'Only people full of themselves would be offended.' What she does hate is anyone calling her 'babe', 'love' or 'darling', as anyone who has done could tell you. And she would suspend any of her players who wolf-whistled at her.

Brady thinks the fact that she was one of only a few girls at a mostly male public school has helped her cope with masculine occasions. At the Midland Football Writers' Dinner one well-known player was touching her elbow. When drunk enough, he propositioned her. 'I told him to piss off,' she says. She thinks that the eight-foot lilies sent anonymously and which she gave away to the secretaries came from the same player, out to win a bet. She would like, she says, to go out for lunch with Ron Atkinson, 'just by myself to hear his views on football and my players, but I know everyone would then ask him, "Oh Ron, did you get your leg over, then?"'

She has her favourite players, she admits, but she wouldn't want to marry a footballer. 'I would just worry about the injuries. Besides, I don't think I'm a footballer's wife.' Nor a boxer's. 'I was at a Frank Bruno fight sitting behind his wife and she was shouting and crying when he was being hit. I just couldn't go through all that.'

Brady first went to a fight with Sullivan to entertain business clients, and then when the *Sport* sponsored bills. 'What is the appeal? Well, it's not the sight of men's bodies. I prefer my men slightly overweight. Having said that, my ultimate dream man is Jimmy Nail and he's skinny. Actually, there's not a lot of appeal to boxing when I think about it. I had a boxer fall on me at ringside about a year ago. I hate sitting at ringside. All that sweat and blood.'

She was at the Michael Watson-Chris Eubank fight. Watson had been staying in a cottage on her father's estate as he trained, doing his running about the grounds. On that night when he didn't get up, Brady thought he was just suffering from exhaustion. 'Then when I knew Michael was having brain surgery, I just thought, "I have never known anyone who has died in my life. I am going to know somebody who is going to die."' She's relieved, of course, that she still doesn't.

'I suppose the appeal of boxing for me is seeing people do well when they have worked really hard. I see all the effort that Chris has put in just for that moment and know he deserves it. And he has status and money when he might so easily have been on the street.'

As for her own status and success, Brady is all too aware of the problem. 'People who see successful young women think that there must be an angle there,' she says. 'It's too good to be true that a woman from a good upbringing can walk into a good job and be a director. They think, "Oh well, she's bonking the boss."'

Yes, such attitudes die hard. A photograph in Brady's St Andrews office shows her at a lunch, meeting Prince Edward. 'This is Karren Brady,' he was told. 'She's taking Birmingham City Football Club by storm.' 'I bet she is,' he replied.

SPOT THE BRAWL

David Cohen

April, 1996

Sergeant Ray Whitworth, in his hard hat and luminous yellow bib, stands between the dugouts of managers Bruce Rioch and Alex Ferguson and surveys his beat: the high-tension cauldron that is Fortress Highbury. He has the best vantage point in the stadium but, unlike the 38,000 baying supporters viscerally connected to the ball being kicked around the pitch, he is calmly and rationally not watching the football.

Whitworth doesn't see Dennis Bergkamp's opportunist goal (roooooaaaaar) nor Peter Schmeichel's save from Ian Wright's spectacular diving header (a torrent of applause). Instead his eyes are trained dispassionately a couple of degrees above the fray, trying to assess, as he puts it, 'the mood, the density, the stress'. As the game gallops towards the final whistle, he focuses attention on the south-west corner where the 2,700 away fans exchange verbals and posture with the adjacent Arsenal supporters.

'Oi! Oi you! That's enough. Sit down and shut up!' he commands an over-excited spectator who has left his seat (in the disabled section, no less) to hurl insults ('You ponce! You ponce!') at Roy Keane on the near touch line. 'I'm an epileptic. I felt a fit coming on and shouting is the only way to stop it,' the man explains. 'That's the most novel excuse I've ever heard,' mutters Whitworth.

With seconds remaining on the clock, hundreds of orange-bibbed stewards form a chain around the perimeter of the pitch. 'We have to be prepared for a pitch invasion as a matter of course,' Whitworth explains, tuned into the police radio, digesting last-minute tactics and deployments. 'By taking possession, we're sending out a high-profile statement that the pitch is ours. We're saying: "Don't even think about it, mate."'

But the flashpoint is expected after the game when, according to Whitworth's intelligence, the Arsenal and Manchester United hooligans, whom he refers to as 'the hardcore', have planned to meet outside the stadium for 'an off' – slang for a violent confrontation. In the hooligan league table, Arsenal's lot ('the Gooners'), who are about 200-strong, rank about middle. 'Our hooligans weigh up the opposition before wading in, whereas there are some groups who will take on anybody,' says Whitworth. 'The Millwall hardcore walk down the road and give you a slap just for being there. But our hooligans are discriminating.'

Sergeant Whitworth and his partner Police Constable Billy Miller ('Just call us Billy and Ray') are Arsenal's football intelligence officers. Together with their boss, match commander Paul Mathias, who has presided over 150 matches and is also the chief superintendent of the nearby Holloway police station, they form the most experienced football intelligence unit in the country. Foreign dignitaries and police officers from all over Europe – most recently France, Russia and Norway – come to observe the Highbury operation first-hand. Their expertise is much appreciated by Arsenal too, so much so that when the Gunners won the European Cup Winners Cup in 1994, George Graham had them photographed with the trophy, insisting: 'Billy and Ray are part of the team.' Never mind that Ray is an ardent Blackpool supporter.

There are more than 92 football intelligence officers (FIOs) countrywide, at least one for each professional football club, though not all are full-time like Miller and Whitworth. Their intelligence is co-ordinated by the Football Unit at NICS (National Criminal Intelligence Service), which maintains a database of some 5,000 known hooligans. On their combined shoulders rests the safety of hundreds of thousands of supporters every week, not to mention the worldwide reputation of English football. In the run-up to Euro '96, the biggest event to be held in this country since the 1966 World Cup, the work of FIOs has gained heightened significance.

Since FIOs were introduced in the late Eighties, public disorder at domestic matches – once so chronic it was tagged 'the English Disease' – has become the exception rather than the rule. The advent of all-seater stadiums, closed-circuit television inside grounds and better-trained stewards, has helped too, and it is now increasingly difficult for hooligans to wreak chaos during the game. But the hooligans have not gone away, says Chief Superintendent Mathias, they have merely changed their strategy: 'They are most likely to riot when England play away because they perceive that surveillance abroad is weaker [hence the mayhem at Dublin's Lansdowne Road in February 1995 when the England-Ireland friendly had to be abandoned]. Also, they have become more sophisticated on the domestic scene, preferring to meet before or after a game. These aren't chance meetings. They call each other on mobile phones and set up where and when. It's Billy's and Ray's job to find out their plans. The nitty gritty of how they do it is secret. But every time a confrontation is headed off, it is because their intelligence has enabled our men to be in the right place at the right time.'

At 8am on the morning of the Manchester United match, Whitworth and Miller arrive at the 'Football Office' at Highbury Vale Police Station, less than a mile from the ground, to begin preparations. Their office – like a *Boy's Own* den – is festooned with framed Arsenal jerseys, programmes, scarves and press cuttings. In one corner, alongside joke banknotes printed with the head of Bruce Grobbelaar ('Bank of Grobbland – promise to let in one goal in return for £50'), there are photographs of the Arsenal hardcore. These include the back view of one of the infamous Gooner 'generals' known as 'Fatman' (a massive character with a torso like a hippo), shots of smashed-up latrines and close-ups of various weapons – flick-knives disguised as pens, CS gas canisters and truncheons. Below the display is a stick of rock, still in its wrapper, with the message 'Just for you' on the label. The rock, says Miller, is 'a gift' from one of the Arsenal hooligans: 'I daren't eat it in case he stuck it up his arse.'

Whitworth and Miller are both in their late thirties but could not be more different: Ray is ginger-haired, tubby, dour and phlegmatic like a bulldog, while Billy is a lithe and exuberant puppy. Whitworth refuses to talk about hooligans, but Miller can't help himself. He opens a cupboard to reveal about a hundred neatly stacked videos – 'the Hooligan File' – and grins broadly. 'The real juicy bits, you'll never see. We're not trying to be difficult, it's just that we have a rapport with these people. They hate to be misrepresented. Every time an inaccurate report is published, they're on the phone to me letting off steam, "Look at what this fat-cunt-wanker wrote. We'll show you fucking pussyfoots!"'

Miller points to a cutting alleging that one of the Arsenal hooligan leaders – by the name of Charlie – has National Front connections. 'Our boys aren't racists. Won't tolerate it. Some of them are black and that really wound them up. The whole National Front/Combat 18 angle on hooligans is overdone, inaccurate and out of date. It might apply to the chaps from Chelsea. But if Charlie comes back to Highbury [he hasn't been for five years], he'll be slaughtered.'

On match days, Whitworth and Miller divide their duties as follows: Miller is confined to tracking the movements and intentions of the two sets of hooligans; Whitworth is in charge of Miller and is also responsible for every other piece of the complex puzzle – a logistical headache which involves the deployment of more than 130 serials (policemen).

'One fast ball I haven't thought of and I'm in the shit,' says Whitworth, as he puts together the intelligence briefing sheet headlined 'For Police Eyes Only'.

'You mean *we're* in the shit,' responds Miller. 'We're a team. Remember?'

'We are?' muses Whitworth. 'How come I deal with all the shit parts then?'

'Aaah . . .' says Miller, 'because you're that part of the team.'

The Manchester United FIO, Steve Barnes, arrives mid-morning.

There have been reports of a death threat against Eric Cantona, but no special arrangements have been made. 'Players like Cantona and Ince get death threats all the time,' says Barnes. 'We don't regard this one as serious.'

'Hurrummppph,' says Whitworth. 'Footballers like nothing better than to be treated like superstars. I take the view of the chief superintendent of Copenhagen who, when asked to provide a police escort, replied: "May I remind you that you are just football players. Not even Pavarotti got an escort."'

Whitworth and Barnes swap intelligence. Before the season starts, every game is graded – A, B or C – and police manning levels are set accordingly. The bitter London derbies against Tottenham and Chelsea are 'high-risk' Cs, but the Manchester United game is a 'medium-risk' B. The grading is determined by a combination of factors such as: the anticipated crowd (the game was sold out seven weeks ago, although, as Whitworth says, 'some without tickets will be full of determination to get into the ground and may even charge the turnstiles or march through someone's house believing their back garden leads to the football ground'); the reputation of the visiting supporters ('United can turn out 400 hooligans; I'd expect at least one clash,' says Miller); and 'bad blood' between teams (United's Alex Ferguson has been on the radio appealing for a truce – in 1991, a fracas between the players resulted in steep fines and Arsenal being docked two points in the league).

Manchester United and Arsenal have the worst tout problem in the country. Today, Whitworth is running a special undercover tout sting, codenamed 'Box Office Six'. The officers on the sting include two skinheads in denim jackets and two women in tall leather boots, one with 'Gunners' emblazoned on her jumper. While Whitworth briefs the serial in charge of traffic and skip removals ('the shite-est job of them all'), Miller and the others indulge in typical non-PC gag-swapping: 'Why is Will Carling's willy all different colours?' asks one. 'Because he dips it in Di,' they answer in unison. 'Apparently they found the murder weapon for the OJ Simpson case,' tries another. 'It's a six-foot-two spade.' They hoot.

There used to be 60 touts working Highbury but their numbers have halved since the Criminal Justice Act of 1994 made touting at football matches a criminal and arrestable offence (fines vary from £50 to £500). 'We have a couple of Mr Bigs who are extremely rich,' says Miller. 'Then you've got "the needy and the greedy", runners and old men supplementing their benefit.'

Whitworth hands out identikit photographs of half a dozen touts arrested in the previous operation and assigns the beats: Gillespie Road to the skinheads, Avenell Road to the female officers. 'We estimate that with tickets going at four times the cover price [£80], the touts will be out in force,' says Whitworth. 'There is also intelligence that they will sell a programme for £50 with a free ticket inside. We know of two safe houses being used to store tickets. Their addresses are disclosed in your package. Happy hunting.'

Miller offers some last-minute advice. 'The touts are like a union. Once they know you're there, they'll organise a sacrificial lamb. He'll be the one shouting: "Tickets! Tickets!" He's actually saying: "Woo-woo, come and get me, lads!" Because as soon as you arrest him, your cover is blown. And while you're in the charge room filling out the paperwork, it'll be, "Let's nip out and do some business." Leave the loudmouth to the officer in uniform.'

At 11.45am, match commander Mathias (code-name 'Gold') strides in for the main briefing. Until now, Whitworth has been running the show, nervously ticking off in his mind every detail needed to keep the operation on track. Mathias welcomes the officers to Highbury and asks Miller to outline the latest intelligence. 'Today's information is coming in thick and fast and is changing by the minute. We now have two definite locations where the hooligans intend to meet. The feeling is that if both groups are found, they can be herded to the ground quite happily. They do not want a confrontation before the match because they wish to see it. We feel the main danger will come after the final whistle.'

With 40 minutes to kick-off, Miller and five serials are parked outside the Highbury Arms where the Arsenal hardcore are drinking. The stereotype of the football thug being a young, unemployed skinhead in bovver boots with 'Arsenal' tattooed on his forehead is long out of date, claims Miller. 'Some are professional types, solicitors even.' From inside the van, on Miller's instructions, a cameraman aims the lens at various 'known' hooligans. 'We're starting to photograph them in preparation for Euro '96,' says Miller, who alternates between wielding a massive £18,000 video camera and mingling, in full uniform, with the hardcore.

The hardcore spill down the hill in an untidy band across the road and proceed menacingly towards the ground. Miller and his men attach themselves like limpets to the side of the moving mass. Miller talks covertly into his radio, tension etched across his brow for the first time. Mounted police and two 'furry crocodiles' (police dogs) appear out of nowhere and keep station alongside. The hardcore turn sharp right and head, briskly now, some still with drinks in hand, for the away supporters' gate. 'Head them off!' bellows a serial on horseback.

Miller appears to be keeping certain individuals, the leaders, in his sights. 'They are saying, "We are here. Where are you?"' he explains. 'It's all about not losing face.' Their way barred, the hooligans make a U-turn and head for the turnstiles.

Inside the stadium, Whitworth takes up his position between the dugouts. In the glass-fronted police control room high above the south-west corner, Mathias shifts his gaze between the crowd and the banks of television screens.

With a single lever, the video operator manipulates an externally mounted camera and scans the whole ground, going in tight or pulling back for an overview, looking for booze under the seats, infiltration of Manchester United supporters into the Arsenal part of the ground, whatever is required. It costs Mathias £100,000 a year to police Arsenal, excluding the £55,000 he pays in salaries to Whitworth and Miller. Prior to joining the police, Whitworth was a quartermaster in the army and Miller, who left school at fifteen, a community officer 'with a talent for getting on with ordinary people'. 'These years as FIO have been the best of my life,' he says. 'I can't believe they pay me for what I do.'

The game passes without incident, but afterwards, as the police intelligence indicated, a fracas develops outside the ground as 60 of the opposing hardcores come face to face. Punches fly. There's a flurry of kicks. 'Get between them! Get between them!' Mathias shouts at his men over the radio, watching the mêlée unfold on the video monitor. Police sirens blare. Within seconds it's snuffed out, the fighters separated and dispersed.

This is football's equivalent of safe sex: the hooligans get to offload some testosterone, the police maintain order (without having to resort to water cannons and the like) and the virginity of the average football fan is left intact.

I catch up with Miller and ask him how he does it. 'You saw things today that you don't know you saw. I'm like a magician; you can observe what I do but you won't know how I do it. I've got to know who to talk to and when, who I can't go near. It's like dealing with dangerous dogs – pat the wrong one and it bites your hand off. There are those within the hardcore who wouldn't piss on me if I was on fire, who call those who speak to me turncoats. I have friends ... wrong word ... I have contacts with people who are the front-runners in the firm. If they got overturned, I'd lose my influence.'

Some European clubs such as Paris St Germain actually employ ex-hooligans to control their hooligans. 'This poacher-turned-gamekeeper model is quite possibly the way forward,' says Miller. 'I've learned that they have their own hierarchy and that to police them successfully you have to respect that. Football hooliganism is a club that you join for life. Once you're a Gooner, once you're in the firm, you don't leave. If they say, "We want to see your arse at Arsenal on Saturday," and you don't pitch, you lose the protection of the group.'

Back at the nick, Whitworth confirms eight arrests in total: three for public disorder, two hapless touts, one drugs bust and two drunks, all bailed and released. There is a message on the answering machine from a local resident complaining about fans urinating against his garage door. It's 7pm, ten hours since Whitworth last ate anything, and he looks exhausted. He works 60 to 70 hours a week, significantly longer than the average sergeant's 40-hour lot. 'No complaints,' he says, sipping his Perrier and burping appreciatively.

This season is Whitworth's last in the job (it is a highly sought after, high-profile position and there is a three-year rotation), but he will go out in a blaze of glory, tipped as he is to be the England football liaison officer for Euro '96. He stuffs a pile of paperwork into his briefcase and mumbles something about 'the job never being over' and having 'post-match reports to compile'. But for tonight, he's off for a bath, to bed, 'and if I can keep my eyes open, *Match of the Day*'. A good game. The first chance he'll have had to watch the football.

RETURN TO SENNA

Russell Bulgin

June, 1994

Estoril, Portugal, January 18, 1994. This is Ayrton Senna's first day with the Williams Grand Prix team, and the significance of the moment isn't lost on the attendant press circus: the world's fastest racing driver is about to step into Formula One's fastest car. This is the consummation of one of motor racing's longest courtships. Team boss Frank Williams has been trying to get Senna into one of his cars for almost ten years. Senna has been trying to get himself into a Williams for at least two. But now it's confirmed, official, and everywhere Senna walks, pit-to-motor-home-to-car, someone from Williams sidles three paces behind. To carry his Rothmans jacket. To hold his yellow helmet. Just, it seems, to be there.

And when Senna finally wriggles into the car, he has to endure four laps trailing a Renault Espace laden with photographers at 40mph: PR counts for more than powerslides. Motordrives whirr as Senna dawdles with nearly 800 horsepower keening under his right foot. This is media-pleasing, pure and simple, and, to the average racing driver, dull, a distraction.

But Senna is not the average driver, never has been. I remember when I first saw him, a callow 21-year-old, at Brands Hatch in 1981. The occasion was a Formula Ford race, low-key but important to a gridful of racing drivers. Ayrton Senna da Silva – as he was then known – led but, close to the chequered flag, got chopped by a backmarker. The cars collided and a coolant pipe was ripped from Senna's car, sluicing the rear tyres. Senna indulged in a quick spin, then continued, green fluid swooshing from the spindly yellow-and-black car. Kept going to finish the race in the top six.

Thirteen years and three World Championships later, Senna is just as determined, if not more so. For his dominance of Formula One has been thwarted in recent years: he could only look on as Williams provided title-winning cars for Nigel Mansell in 1992 and Alain Prost in 1993. But now he is in the car he most wants to drive – the car which should take him to his fourth championship. And he's here in Estoril to work, even when trailing the Espace.

On the pitwall, headphones crackle. Senna is doing his set-up laps right now, eager to work, eager to drive.

'I see 11,000 revs, second gear,' he says on the radio, over the nagging whine of the Renault engine. 'I see one-six-four on the dashboard – I don't know what this means.'

'It means,' comes a reply, English, downbeat, almost sardonic, 'that you've got plenty of fuel, Ayrton ...' The Espace peels off. Senna floors the throttle, goes third-fourth-fifth gear, the V10 engine barking thrash-metal ugly and, amid a flowery cascade of titanium twinkles as the chassis repeatedly smites the road surface – 164 litres of race-blend Elf is a heavy fuel load – begins a new career in a new team.

Later, in the dusty pit garage, Senna is thinking about speed. About the nub of his job. Car change, season to season. Technical regulations alter: last year computerised active suspension was permitted, but for 1994 it's banned. This makes it difficult, year on year, to judge pure pace.

So is Senna getting faster? The question doesn't throw him. He just does what he does: places his chin in hand, squeezes his cheeks between thumb and forefinger and says nothing at all. For twelve seconds. Then he looks up. 'Maybe not. But I am getting wiser...

'There is a limit,' he continues in his excellent but formal English. 'There is only so much you can do. What you can get is more consistent, or precise, or quick with the decisions – the correct decisions. That is what I think. In fact, where I can pick up speed is difficult to say, because my limit is as fast as I can go.'

'As fast as I can go.' There, in a phrase, is the id of Senna.

Tom Walkinshaw, mastermind of the Benetton Formula One team, suggested that there were three drivers in Grand Prix racing who could give a team a win when, on the day, it didn't deserve victory. They were his driver, German Michael Schumacher; four-time World Champion Alain Prost, now retired; and Ayrton Senna, with 41 Grand Prix wins, a record 62 pole positions, nineteen fastest laps and 614 championship points from 158 races.

There's another pause from Senna. Ten seconds. 'I have been going faster,' the Brazilian says. 'Over these last ten years, the results speak for themselves. Perhaps I am understanding better where the limits are to going faster, where to go faster, more consistency.'

Senna began racing at the age of four. His São Paulo family was well-to-do: his father hired a driver to take Senna to the kart track each day, after school. He raced karts in Brazil and Europe and began car racing in Britain in 1981. He won in Formula Ford, the learning category. By 1983, he was on the shopping lists of Grand Prix team owners.

McLaren boss Ron Dennis offered to fund Senna in Formula Three in return for an option on his future services. Senna demurred: he wanted control and won the Formula Three championship with funds he found from Brazil. Frank Williams gave him his first taste of Grand Prix power, in a private test at Donington Park in June 1983. But Williams and Senna couldn't agree terms, and Williams would have to wait until January 1994 for Ayrton Senna to drive one of his cars again.

Senna joined Toleman for the 1984 season and was a lap away from winning the Monaco Grand Prix when the rain-lashed race was abandoned. Joining Lotus, he won his first Grand Prix in Portugal the following year. Then came McLaren. Six years, three World Championships. Super-success. And its price.

A friend called me in 1988. He had dined, he said, with Senna on the evening he clinched his first World Championship in Japan. Their conversation was in Portuguese – low-key, sentimental. About the old days: racing in São Paulo's Parque Anhembi as kids, in go-karts. About time past. Senna, said the voice on the phone, had everything and nothing at all. He seemed the loneliest man in the world.

Senna is regarded by his peers in Formula One as many things: aloof, difficult, infuriating, slightly petulant, overly obsessive ... Yet he understands the value of psychology better than any other driver, knows full well that he is, quite simply, the fastest – which is why he demands respect and will take umbrage when he is baulked by a young driver; which is why he will negotiate his contracts interminably until he wins the terms he considers his due.

As Ron Dennis of McLaren once remarked: 'With Senna, we deal in units of $1 million.' In Formula One, they say that Senna is worth $70 million. That the Banco Nacional sash slathered across the midriff of his overalls, and the similarly logo'd cap he always wears out of the cockpit, earn him $6 million per year. His Williams pay-packet for 1994 is estimated to be $13 million. The contract with Williams, it is rumoured, consists of three documents, each around an inch thick: management, promotions and the tax plan.

He has his own London office, with an ex-International Management Group financial expert looking after his affairs. He has a private jet. A helicopter. Seven floors of an office block in São Paulo are devoted to his business operations. His payroll, he says, 'is over 50 people right now, easily. I think between 50 and 100 people.' In Brazil, Senna is the official importer for Audi cars and DeLonghi heaters.

He has invested over $1 million in an educational comic detailing his racing exploits for children in Brazil. He is religious, reading the Bible when going long-haul first class. He has homes in Brazil, Portugal and who knows where else. He has ordered a £530,000 McLaren F1 road car for delivery in 1995. He is reputed to have made $1 million last year just for three days' filming television advertisements for a German company.

That was a bonus, as 1993 was a critical year for Ayrton Senna, racing driver. McLaren's long-term masterplan had combined Senna's skills with the R&D of Honda to take three World Championships. Then Honda pulled out. McLaren had to make do with customer Ford engines, less advanced than the latest versions supplied by the Benetton team. For once, McLaren was at a competitive disadvantage. Senna wasn't used to that.

There was a quote attributed to him: 'I am programmed to win.' Senna looks up, answers: 'I never said that.' Yet can he get any satisfaction from finishing seventh in a race, if he drove to the limit of the car and the track? The reply, for once, is instant. 'No.'

So what is success? Senna is insistent: 'It is to do it right. To be competitive as long as I can. Which means to be well physically, and in my mind, to perform and exploit my potential, and learn through this as well. To be in the right place, so I can develop my potential and be competitive.'

The right place, the right team, for Senna in 1993 was Williams. Williams had the technical depth in designer Patrick Head and avant-garde aerodynamicist Adrian Newey; it had powerful Renault engines and its cars bristled with clever-clever hypertechnology. Williams also had Alain Prost. Prost and Senna had been team-mates at McLaren, but their relationship deteriorated quickly. At Suzuka in 1989 the two McLarens collided in the penultimate round of the World Championship, giving the title to Prost.

Senna was cast as the bad guy. Aggressive, unyielding, he was heavily criticised after the collision. But the rarely seen helicopter film of the incident, motor racing's equivalent of the Zapruder footage of Kennedy's assassination, clearly shows Prost moving over on Senna, wheels banging wheels, nudging him off. A year later, Senna and Prost, by now with Ferrari, collided again at Suzuka. This time, Prost lost his championship chance as a result. Some saw it as Senna's revenge.

So Prost didn't want Senna at Williams and had power of veto over his team-mate. Damon Hill, untried but amenable, got the drive. Senna offered to race the Williams for nothing: a bold gesture, albeit one which would have been tempered somewhat by his retention of the Banco Nacional millions. Prost refused. Senna stayed at McLaren. With Ford engines, a power disadvantage and, perhaps, a point to prove.

So he tested an IndyCar early last year. 'Well, I wanted to see what it was like.' Would he have followed Nigel Mansell and raced in America? 'Yes. I was not happy about the situation in Formula One, and I was looking for alternatives.' A pause. 'Driving, or not driving. Or driving something else.'

But could Senna actually stop racing? More than most drivers, his life is racing: his whole philosophy of self-improvement is centred on going faster and learning more. 'At that time, for a period of time, yes. But as it turned out I did not, and I decided the best thing was really to try and recoup. I decided the best thing was to drive for McLaren, and it was the right thing to do.'

He negotiated with McLaren race by race, winning as he went in South Africa and at Britain's Donington circuit: in fact, he would win five Grands Prix through the year, further cementing his reputation. The contract was eventually signed after seven races. And it was Senna who buckled. 'I said, "I cannot take [this] anymore – it does not work. Now, somehow, we have to make a deal, a decision, or I will not compete anymore."' In other words, Senna the driver got the better of Senna the formidable businessman.

But Prost announced his retirement in late 1993, and Senna signed with Williams and Renault for 1994. Leaving McLaren seemed hard. 'It was and it is. I have friends there. We worked together, occasionally we had our differences, but we worked together for six years; nothing can change that. We are friends, and it is tough to change that. Because for me it was not only racing or business, it was a big part of my life.'

And what motivates Senna today? He has three World Championships: Alain Prost had four, and Juan Manuel Fangio won a record five in the Fifties. Senna, say the whisperers, is shooting for six. There's an edge to his voice now. 'I will tell you one thing: it took me ten years of Formula One to win three championships. I will not be driving another ten years to win another three championships. It would not be easy – and I know how hard it is because I did it.'

Yet when Senna mentions Fangio – now 82 and in ill-health – his toughness drops away. The Brazilian seems awed by the

Argentinian. 'I had admired Fangio so much,' he says, 'because his attitude is the way to behave as a sportsman, as a man. His conduct, and his clear understanding of what racing is about, even now though he has been retired for a long time, his understanding is very good. It is simple, not complicated, but very precise.

'And I am sure,' Senna adds, 'if Fangio was 30 years old, with the knowledge that he has, driving an ordinary Grand Prix car, he would be just as competitive as he was in his day, because he has got the mentality and, for sure, the skills, otherwise he would not have done so well.'

Senna's life – fast, ardent and acute – has given him everything. Does it ever seem like a dream? One decade: from a rented house in Reading to becoming a global synonym for going into corners deeper, braking later, pushing the throttle earlier, lap after endless lap. 'No, because it has not happened one day to the next. It has happened fast, but it has always been growing, one on top of the other.'

Senna, dark eyes bright beneath the blue baseball cap, warms slowly. 'I was given the opportunity to learn and mature in the situation as it developed.' But does he ever wonder about it all, the money and the madness? 'Sometimes I am jogging, and I am thinking while I am jogging, *"I won three World Championships!"*' Senna becomes a little more animated, more Latin. The words rush: the pauses, the chin-stroking, seem an age away. 'Then it sounds like [much quieter], "I won three World Championships." And then five seconds, ten seconds later, it sounds like [almost whispering], "I won three championships." Half a minute later, it's [laid-back], "Yeah, I won three championships."'

This is Senna putting his career, his life, in perspective. 'Do you understand? I know how good, how important it was for me, but I have absorbed it in a healthy way. It is not like I say, "Yeah, I am three times World Champion, I am the best". So I am very aware ... It is a great achievement, but at the same time it has a lot of logic, a lot of work. Time after time, day after day, week after week, year after year, for 30 years. It's not just a headline.'

Senna won last season's Japanese Grand Prix. The track was wet-dry, the conditions taxing. During the race, rookie Eddie Irvine, racing for Jordan, repassed Senna after being lapped. This was a minor breach of racing etiquette. After the race, Senna visited the Jordan team office. Discussion disintegrated into scuffle. Senna hit Irvine, and a journalist had a C90 cassette rolling.

Which is why Senna begins the 1994 season with a six-month suspended ban from FISA, the sport's governing body. Another transgression and he will miss races. When asked about the downside of Formula One, Senna hits the pause button. For ten seconds. Then for a further 27 seconds of silence.

'The decisions,' he says, 'that are made on the political side of Formula One are not always the correct ones, or the fair ones, for different reasons. But no matter what they are, you have to accept them if you want to be a Formula One driver. Because you have no choice, no matter how good or bad you feel about them. The only alternative you have is to accept, or not to drive. And because I love driving so much I have to accept, in different moments of my career, situations which in ordinary life, no one would be able to impose, or enforce. But it is part of Formula One.'

Politics, then, is an irritation, a background noise. Containable, at a price. But what frightens Senna? I recall sitting with him in a Welsh café, miles from anywhere, in August 1986 after a day spent testing rally cars. A stream burbled outside as the rhythm of the day faded, the stories of what was happening in Formula One fizzled out. And Senna started to discuss risk, the possibility of getting hurt. He did so as if he were talking about an old friend, and his tone remained absolutely level, cool, as he rationalised the dangers of his job, the downside of going wheel-to-wheel at 200mph. Risk was to be teased, he suggested, but never trivialised.

And now? 'Well,' Senna says, 'if I ever happen to have an accident that eventually costs my life, I hope it is in one go. I would not like to be in a hospital suffering from whatever injury it was. If I am going to live, I like to live fully. Very intensely, because I am an intense person. It would ruin my life if I had to live partially. So my fear is really to get injured, to get badly hurt.'

Eight years ago, Ayrton Senna described his perfect day as

follows: 'A sunny day, no wind, not too hot ... Silverstone is nice. Quick car, competitive car, easy with the mechanics, everybody relaxed. And just drive it. Drive it very quick, on the limit. And then, at the end of the day, transfer myself to Brazil, go to the disco, go to the cinema – all in 24 hours.'

Ask the question today, and the answer is immediate: 'I want to wake up at home in Brazil, near the park, or the beach house, with my family and my friends there. Go to the race track, race. Maybe have half an hour just to get used to everything, then have the race in the afternoon. Go back home.'

For Ayrton Senna, then, everything and nothing changes. More money, more success, more intensity: but still, at his core, he remains the kid racing karts, the guy defining himself by finding new ways of going faster. Except that now there's a difference: an advantage of a thousandth of a second can be repaid in millions of dollars. Reminded of his answer back in 1985, Ayrton Senna beams. 'Yes,' he says slowly, 'I am still looking for the same things.' At 200mph, then, a life so simple. And so complex.

Unsung Heroes

BACK ON BOARD

Clive Gammon

July, 1993

This is Kilcummin beach in County Kerry, south-west Ireland. Long lines of rollers cream in from the Atlantic Ocean and a man sits in the dunes above it pulling on a wetsuit. A wet, cold wetsuit. 'Like putting on a used condom that's been lying out in the grass all night,' he says. When he's done, he tucks his surfboard under his arm and walks towards the water.

Nobody is going to mistake him for one of those blond, clean-cut, innocently hedonistic characters out of *Baywatch*. He's about nine stone and built, as he says himself, like a water biscuit. He's so frail-looking that, when you first meet him, you feel a strong urge to get him a bowl of hot soup. His face is mobile, flickering with constant mood changes, a tad slant-eyed, a touch other-worldly. It is one of those magician's faces that the poet WH Auden noticed as characteristic of the Welsh.

Don't be fooled by his appearance. Twenty-seven-year-old Carwyn Williams is as terrier-tough, as instinctively balanced, as Welsh fly halves used to be. And he has the right bloodline: his father was a miner from Seven Sisters in the Neath Valley and he grew up speaking the old language.

But it was in a different sport that, almost five years ago, Williams made an astonishing breakthrough. In a tournament at Hossegor, on the Atlantic coast of France, in August 1988, he beat Damien Harriman, the Australian world surfing champion. Other spectacular wins followed and, the following year, he became the first European in the sport's history to be invited to join pro-surfing's world circuit, hitherto a monopoly of about 32 boardriders, mainly Australian and American, but joined latterly by one or two Brazilians.

The rules of the pro-surfing circuit vary somewhat from year to year, but its basic structure is comparable with that of Formula One motor racing. Each year there are ten major events, and points won at them count towards the World Championship. As in Formula One, the venues change occasionally, but typically, one would be in Australia, two in Japan (mainly because they're big fans and big bankrollers of the sport) and others in France, South Africa and Brazil.

Individual surfers fight their way up through the lower formulae to the top. For a European, let alone a boy from industrial South Wales, to make it to the top tier is the equivalent of the Oakland Raiders recruiting a wide receiver from Holland Park Comprehensive.

'All of a sudden the whole world wanted to know who I was,' says Williams. 'Nobody from Europe had done this before.'

Williams' life started turning into a rosy dream. *Surfer* magazine, the bible of the sport, commented: 'At this point, Carwyn is a blitz-or-bomb performer: a walkover when he's out of synch, a world-beater when he's firing. [But] he may have the pure talent of a top sixteen performer . . .'

'My car was full of prize money,' he remembers. 'I hid different currencies under the mats – francs, escudos, pesetas. Where else would I keep it? I lived in my car.'

Lucrative sponsorship offers also flooded in. 'I didn't know what to do,' he says. 'I even went home to Wales to barter one company off against another.' Finally, he decided on a French firm called Quiksilver, and dyed his hair red to celebrate.

Williams had arrived: he had a sponsor, a manager, coaches, sports psychiatrists and a bright future. Less than a year later, however, just days after he'd been offered a 25 per cent increase on his Quiksilver contract (but was pressing for 50), the dream was over. It came to an end at the side of a French motorway.

'A crowd of us were driving up from Spain,' says Williams, 'and

I was planning to stop in on this French competition, just to win some spending money before going to South Africa. I was sort of drowsing in the back of the car when we hit. We were doing 100-plus in a Mercedes, and the driver didn't see this caravan. It exploded when we hit it, and we hurtled off the road into a tree.'

Williams snapped every ligament holding his right leg together. He was told he would never surf again.

'It went straight by me the first time,' he says. 'Then I started freaking, shouting, telling the doctor what a stupid man he was. I was crazy for a couple of weeks. I didn't really start believing it for a few months.'

But now, astonishingly, after a four-year struggle, Williams is here, working the Irish surf. It has a special significance for him. 'I remember,' he'd told me the previous evening, as we sat over a couple of pints at Dick Mack's in Dingle, 'lying in the hospital bed and thinking, "I never surfed Ireland. And maybe I never will now."'

And so we'd come to the west of Ireland, almost as a psychological part of Carwyn Williams' fight back. 'Know something?' he says. 'I used to want to blow Ireland up, right off the map. Nothing to do with politics, of course. But because it gets in the way of the waves coming across the Atlantic Ocean to Wales, see? Our waves.'

Now, at Kilcummin, he puts on a bravura performance, making the most of waves that aren't really living up to Ireland's reputation as surfing's last frontier; unvisited, as yet, by the pro circuit. (Although it is very much on the future agenda: according to Dr Paul Russell, doctor of wave physics at Plymouth Polytechnic, Ireland has the best and biggest wave pattern outside of Hawaii.)

Meanwhile, Williams is making the most of what's there. And what comes through at Kilcummin beach is the special elegance of his style as, at speed, he puts on a performance which almost requires the jargon of the sport to be described. One that features his 'cutbacks' (or 're-entries') as he turns figures-of-eight in white water, his '360s' (which should be self-explanatory), his 'floaters', as he works horizontally along a wave, then free falls to the bottom of it, still standing. And, above all, his 'airings out', when he actually seems to move in the air, flipping, changing direction like a water sprite.

Williams, you learn very quickly, is something of a paradox. He's travelled the world since he was a teenager, hunting the great, classic surf breaks of Hawaii and Australia. But his passion for waves stems from somewhere very different.

He'll put it simply enough. 'In Swansea, where I was brought up, you get a lot of respect if you surf.' It's inner-city surfing he's talking about. Well, almost. The little beach called Langland, where he surfs, is actually a three-mile bus trip from Swansea city centre. Scenically, it's not in the same class as the magnificent beaches further west on the Gower Peninsula, and a lot less classy than it once was. In summer, it's jammed with day-trippers from the Valleys. But in winter, it belongs to arguably the toughest bunch of surfers in the world.

Winter surfing in Langland means howling offshore winds, helmets and gloves, and not being able to feel your feet for cold. 'Langland is hardcore,' says Williams. 'I started out surfing in shorts and a rugby jersey. It was six months before I stood up on a surfboard, probably because I was so cold. I could only stay in the sea for twenty minutes at a time. I used to go blue and orange and stuff.'

Langland may be a world away from the Beach Boys, but it was here that Williams laid down the basis of his skills, learning them well. In one year, aged seventeen, he won the Welsh, British and European titles. And by the time he was nineteen, he'd picked up enough prize money to start on the road that would, in the end, take him to the top of his sport.

With £1,500, he had enough money for a six-month trip to Australia. Half of it went on an air ticket, and much of the rest on an ancient Morris 1100, in which he slept. 'I travelled thousands of miles in that 1100, all for competitions,' he says. 'Most of the time, I kept the ocean on my left, and every time I saw some surf I'd stop a while. I'd thought I was something when I left Europe. I'd won all this stuff, hadn't I? But when I got there I found I was just a beginner. "Talented but immature," they said. I realised then I'd have to go to Australia year after year.'

There are also professional reasons for his travels abroad. 'See,' he says, 'in Wales, we don't get quality big surf. If the surf sets big, it's got a lot of wind behind it, gale force sou'westerly. It makes them easier. They've got a lot of gradual slope to them. So you have to go to the other side of the world to get the big swells coming through with no wind on them – just marching walls of water that hit a rock bottom under the sea and break fantastically. When I first got to see waves like that in the Pacific, I couldn't handle them. I was hanging on like death.'

Williams arrived in Honolulu when he was just out of his teens and once again adopted his normal hobo lifestyle. 'I checked all my stuff into an airport locker,' he says, 'slept on a bench, caught the bus to Waikiki, and got up onto the roof of the Hyatt Hotel to figure out where I was.'

Buying a rotting old '76 Chevy, in which, again, he lived, he took to touring the north side of the island.

'Hawaii is the testing ground to see if you've got it or not. And at the end of two months, I'd surfed the best they'd got, the heaviest two waves. I was six weeks on Sunset. During the second week, I had a twenty-foot wave break in front of me and I just ... my body just stopped, and I watched the wave march, twenty foot of white water going fast. And I thought, "You twat! What do you do it for? You're gonna die!" I lost my brains. My body was all limp. And the wave marched over me. But I lived. It was a mighty boost to my inner strength.'

It was not only the waves that he had to contend with. 'Hawaiians are very fierce about their territory, and you see some terrible things at the Pipeline [the place where the largest waves break]. Look at a guy the wrong way and he'll either paddle over and hit you, or give you a choice: your face or your fin? Then they punch out your choice. They are very tough. In the summer there's no waves, so they train all the time. Big guys!'

So Williams trained and trained all that winter in Hawaii, survived the injuries, and beat the Pipeline. He went to Australia again to start his first season on the big pro circuit – which ended up against that tree in France. He was shipped home to hospital in Swansea, where, during a long, hot summer, he went so low he was constantly crying.

'I kept catching myself thinking, hey, in six weeks' time the circuit is going to start over again, and I was still kidding myself that I would be there. I didn't sleep at all, even after they let me out of the hospital, all the rest of that year. The pain was one thing, but also my brain was chanting, "You're not going to surf again." I was in a deep hole. I went down for nearly a year and a half.'

Williams drank heavily through most of the injury, and was in serious danger of becoming an alcoholic. Then, on St David's Day, 1991, he had an operation in Cardiff to try to rebuild his knee.

'Part of me started to think I might get better,' he says. 'But I'd been out of the sea for a year and a half. I was thinking of other ways of life, but I didn't have any qualifications. I was spinning out. Then I thought, "Bollocks to that." I had to get back to surfing, pure surfing, as a start, never mind the circuit and the competitions.'

Even though he'd lost two stone, he kept working himself, cycling and swimming. And one day last spring, he walked down to Langland with his board and got back in the water.

'God, it was as easy as riding a bike. I got up on the first wave and felt the wind coming into my face like it used to. I was knackered all the time. But after I'd got in the water I started sleeping and eating properly again.'

And then, in the summer, he somehow raised £1,000, bought another old vehicle (this time a Renault van), and took off. 'I surfed three times a day – with leg braces on,' he says. 'I ran up and down sand dunes. I got healthier and healthier.'

It was no coincidence that during that summer the big tournament at Hossegor would take place, the one in which, two years earlier, he'd beaten Damien Harriman, the world champion. Harriman still held the title and would be surfing in this French event.

'The day before it started, I went down there to ask if I could judge maybe, or commentate, or even work with the night security. And then the organiser told me, "There are two spots left in the qualifying round." I was scared, but, my God, I was there on the beach again, in a competition situation. I had to borrow this big old board. And, oh God, I came second out of 80 people in the water.

'I was on the podium that evening, thousands of people there – they get huge crowds in France. I threw my arms up in the air. I'd won a thousand quid and it was all on again.' And as he came out of the water, French television was waiting for him. 'I was almost a legend again,' he laughs.

In a better world, there would be a perfect ending at this point. But that night Williams couldn't sleep for the pain in his leg. He couldn't even run properly; his leg wasn't good enough yet.

Yet now, here in Ireland, he pulls off his wetsuit and frees himself from the braces he wears beneath it. 'There's been loads of pressure since to make me compete again,' he says. 'But my leg still hurts – I can't disguise it. Still, I'm training really hard and getting strong with it, even though I'll have to use two leg braces for ever.'

He looks around for them to pack them away because it's time for us to be heading back across Ireland to catch the ferry to Wales. But a wild-looking County Kerry bullock is galloping away with one of the braces in its jaws. We go in pursuit of it, without success. Williams takes the loss as a sign: 'Maybe Ireland's telling me that I won't need to wear the brace one day.'

And Ireland delivers a last message, too. We've been unlucky with her fabled surf, but now, and just too late, as we drive back along the coast, a big sou'westerly swell, born out in the Atlantic Ocean somewhere, starts putting a perfect wave onto a surfing spot called Inch Point.

We pull over, and Williams, I can see, is itching to drag his wetsuit on. 'But we'll miss the last ferry,' I tell him sternly. 'We'll only just make it as it is.' He takes the point. 'I'll be coming back to Ireland, though,' he says, 'now I've seen the potential.'

That may be some time off. This month he is working on his

comeback in Australia, riding the great winter waves they have there. And that perfect ending is still possible – so long as his right knee starts to match up with his courage.

CRASH COURSE

Russell Bulgin

April, 1994

Johnny Herbert is talking about the shunt, the immediate aftermath, the blurry seconds when he knew, if nothing else, that he was still alive. Still strapped in the car, still conscious, still aware. 'And then,' he says, 'eventually when I stopped and I looked down, my first thought was that I had lost everything from the left knee down. That was the first thing.'

August 21, 1988 was the day Herbert's dreams were put on hold. The occasion was an international Formula 3000 race at Brands Hatch, his home circuit: the seventh round of an eleven-race championship designed to mould future Grand Prix drivers.

Autosport magazine reported events with dour understatement: 'Herbert and [Gregor] Foitek collided at around 150mph, their cars cannoning violently left into the bridge, whereupon the GA machine [belonging to Foitek] cartwheeled sickeningly down the guardrail. Johnny's car rebounded into the path of Grouillard, who had no alternative but to ram him hard, while Blundell, amazingly, got through.'

This was a bloody, gothic accident, littering a daisy chain of shattered carbon fibre across tarmac streaked with trails of locked-up rubber. Before the race, Herbert was perhaps half a year away from becoming a Grand Prix driver: eleven months previously, the Benetton Formula One team had tested him, at Brands Hatch, and he had coolly outpaced regular driver Thierry Boutsen. Herbert hadn't sat in a Grand Prix car before, but in less than twenty miles he was driving the 800bhp Formula One Benetton with the same smooth, deep turn-in style he used in his 170bhp Reynard Formula Three car.

On the day of the shunt, Frank Williams of the Williams Grand Prix team was supposed to be at Brands Hatch with a Formula One contract in his pocket for Herbert. Nigel Mansell was leaving Williams for Ferrari, and it seemed a strong possibility that Herbert, just 24, the son of an electrician from Romford, Essex, and ex-pupil of Forest Lodge Comprehensive, would replace him.

As ever, Herbert had done his stuff. He felt good, relaxed, confident. He had already won one race in the Formula 3000 series, at Jerez, Spain. The previous season he had dominated the British Formula Three Championship. Eight years of karting had taught him to race hard, drive smoothly, think ahead. Brands Hatch began as business as usual. Herbert qualified on pole position in his Eddie Jordan Racing Reynard-Cosworth. Led from the start. Dropped his lap times into the one minute sixteen seconds bracket. Controlled the race. Then two cars collided. Red flag. Restart.

Herbert got too much wheelspin, which happens on the sloping start line at Brands. No problem. Team-mate Martin Donnelly led through the first corner. As Herbert chased, so Swiss driver Gregor Foitek banged wheels with him. Foitek and Herbert had already had a coming together at Vallelunga in Italy, back in April. It had been a somewhat silly, low-speed collision. Slightly concussed, Herbert was forced to miss a race, but bounced back to take seventh place at Silverstone and then a third at Monza, Italy. Now he was ready to win again. But at the second turn, Foitek pushed Herbert's Reynard-Cosworth.

A little tap, nose to gearbox. Two more corners, and on to the long straight. Foitek moved to overtake. *Autosport* described what followed as 'the biggest British racing accident for a decade or more'.

'I remember that there was a tiny knock and then it just went very sideways,' says Herbert, in a chillingly matter-of-fact way. 'I remember going along sideways as if I was being pushed for a while, and then it went left. I remember hitting the first barrier and the car spinning, then I hit the second one and kept spinning a lot, and then stopping and looking down and seeing this big hole at the front of the car.'

There was, in fact, no front to the car. It had been ripped off in the initial impact: Herbert had hit the barrier, quite literally, feet-first at around 100mph. His description of what happened is flat, rational, studied. No talk of impact, of dry fear, of self-doubt. No mention of Foitek. No recriminations. Just one of those things.

Herbert talks about his accident – his smashed ankles, his crushed heels, his pain – as if it happened to someone else: someone he didn't know too well. Does replaying the accident in his mind bother him? 'No, not at all,' he says, sounding slightly bored. Why not? 'Well, I don't see why it should. The way I look at it, even if I had lost my legs I had to get on with the rest of my life, so it did not really matter. Some people might go hysterical and scream, but that does not really do anything. It does not bring them back. Why get hysterical over something you have lost and will not come back?'

Herbert is short and blond, disconcertingly pink-cheeked, blue-eyed, almost impish. His conversation is straight and easy-going. Dyslexia makes him struggle for the odd word: he says he works on his vocabulary, checks the thesaurus program on his computer. Often he will throw his head back and wriggle out a deep, rib-shaking giggle, a loud guffaw which seems at odds with his compact, thick-necked build. In Formula One, they say Herbert likes a laugh. He's a bloke rather than blokey; talented in the car, ordinary out of it. To be ordinary amid the hype of Grand Prix racing is to be extraordinary. And that – along with a sublime ability to drive – could be Herbert's secret.

But it is not enough to explain how Herbert came back to racing after a vicious accident, finally got into Formula One with first Benetton and then Team Lotus. Herbert, always laid-back, can be stubborn too. 'At school,' says his former manager Mike Thompson, 'he had some sort of argument with the teacher and they told him to go to the headmaster, and he refused. So they eventually dragged him up to his headmaster still clutching his desk.'

Thompson was there after the crash, in Sidcup General Hospital, with Herbert's parents. The left ankle was badly smashed. It could not be screwed together because, as Herbert explains, 'it was all mushy. They were always moaning that I would have to have the thing cut off, but I think that was just the doctors giving the worst scenario you could have. Because it was full up with dirt, basically, with tyres and flags and marshals and most of Brands Hatch.'

Herbert smiles. The joke is weak, mistimed. He's bored with telling the story. 'The way the body is,' he continues, 'they just get as much as they can out quickly, then sew it together and see what happens. And the body will take care of all the shit in there. I think the last time I had something come out was 1991 or 1992, and it was a blade of grass.'

Benetton team manager Peter Collins kept close contact with Herbert in hospital. Collins is one of racing's finest talent-spotters; he had championed a young British driver named Nigel Mansell at Lotus back in 1981, and he felt the same way about Herbert. Quick, tough, aggressive and down-to-earth.

Collins recalls: 'On the Thursday after the accident when I saw him I said, "How are you feeling? I just cannot believe what went wrong; it was a terrible accident." And Johnny said, "No, it's not a problem." And I said, "Why's that?" He said, "I have watched the video about 30 times – and I did not make a mistake." So the injuries were irrelevant. The only thing he was concerned about at the time was whether he'd made a mistake. And when Johnny had watched the video and convinced himself that he did not make a mistake as such – the accident happened because he was effectively pushed, or they tangled wheels – his mind was totally clear about where he was going.'

There were problems, though. 'We didn't have any insurance,' admits Mike Thompson. 'I thought Eddie Jordan was doing it; Eddie thought I was doing it. So in the event I put him in a private hospital.' Thompson raised money from racing car designer Adrian Reynard and team sponsor Q8. 'We found the rest,' he says, adding, 'it wasn't a big deal.' Actually, it was: the bill was £8,000 for the first month alone.

Morphine made the pain subside. Herbert says of his lost weeks: 'I could actually sit there and be talking normally, and then, if I closed my eyes, me and my wife would be under a waterfall with no clothes on. Then we started to cuddle each other, and then our skin fell off and these monsters appeared, and then I would eat her, and then another monster would come up and eat me, and there were all these monsters and they were just eating each other. But if I opened my eyes it would go.'

Barely a month after the accident, the monsters still real, Herbert was signed by Collins to drive for Benetton in the 1989 Formula One World Championship. This was an unprecedented show of faith in a driver who might not be able to walk again, let alone drive a stiff, truculently vibrating racing car. To Collins, it signalled the start of an estrangement with the Italian executives of the British-based Benetton team which would eventually see him leave to rebuild the Lotus Formula One operation. To Herbert, it was a lifeline. Benetton would fund a rehabilitation programme in an Austrian sports clinic, but more importantly, Herbert now had a target, a focus. In December 1988, less than four months after almost losing his left foot, he would once again be testing a Benetton Grand Prix car.

The Herberts were not a racing family. 'My dad was an electrician, but he used to play Sunday soccer. He was pretty useless at it. I always remember being there, but I do not remember watching him.' So what fired Herbert's imagination? 'My uncle Pete used to run this go-kart track in Cornwall, and every year we used to go on holiday for two weeks. I used to thrash about there every day. It started just from that: there was nothing in the family beforehand.'

Herbert is fuzzy on details and dates. Where most racing drivers can recount their times to two decimal places, he can't remember the make or colour of his first Formula Ford car. It's a side-effect of dyslexia, he says. 'But I don't get my words back-to-front, like I think [fellow dyslexic] Jackie Stewart does,' he adds with a firmness that suggests this distinction is important to him.

Karting is where kids prove that they can race: Ayrton Senna, Alain Prost and Nigel Mansell all karted. To become a Grand Prix driver without a past life in karting is not impossible, but karting makes racing intuitive and overtaking instinctive. Herbert's first kart was old and heavy. The first race was at Tilbury Docks. Herbert was short, light, quick of reflex and utterly absorbed by his new sport. He was ten years old.

'I took it seriously,' he says now. 'I was disappointed if I did not win, and I always pushed myself – I wanted to win. But it was really just for enjoyment.' Herbert karted for eight years, winning the 1979 British Junior Championship at fifteen and then, three years later, the British 135 International Championship. In 1983, he switched from the nimble alacrity of a kart to a Formula Ford single-seater. He tested at Brands Hatch. 'I hated it because the thing slid everywhere. I was used to something that had grip, and the power was disappointing, and the gears. I remember the first time I drove I did not know anything about heel-and-toe; I spun at Paddock because I was just whacking it in gear and it locked up.'

He learned fast and raced in novice Formula Ford, but was sidelined by an accident at Oulton Park: a suspension arm pierced his calf. In 1985 he almost won the prestigious RAC Formula Ford 1600 Championship, scoring a superb victory in the 200-car knockout Formula Ford Festival driving the unfancied Quest, a car built by a company owned by Mike Thompson. Thompson became Herbert's first mentor; he found money to race with and built Herbert a Formula Ford 2000 car, which didn't work. So Herbert moved up to Formula Three, the toughest category for young drivers with an eye on Grand Prix racing. He finished fourth first time out. At the end-of-season Cellnet Superprix, he was third.

Peter Collins noticed him there: 'His body language after finishing third in the Superprix at Brands, where he was obviously displeased, said a lot. And his demeanour, which just exuded inner confidence without being cocky. Those things made him stand out as somebody who was a bit different.'

To enable Herbert to contest a full season of Formula Three in 1987, Thompson assembled a group of seven investors and guaranteed the £125,000 which Eddie Jordan Racing required: the money men would get their return if Herbert landed a paying drive in Formula One. 'He had an absolutely brilliant natural talent,' says Jordan, who now has his own Grand Prix team. 'If I was to be ultra-critical, I would say that sometimes his mind wandered from the callous, calculating style – there were often times that he wanted to dice for the sake of having fun. But you could see that overall there was never any doubt that he would come around. He was never a crasher. He was always very kind on the car. He could always get the most out of it when you wanted him to.'

Herbert won five races and secured the title before the end of the season. In September 1987 he duly tested a Benetton Formula One car at Brands Hatch. Collins remembers: 'He just adapted so quickly, and it all just happened so naturally. It was beyond belief. He went quicker than Boutsen on the day in 30 laps, and really never put a wheel wrong. But it was more than just going quick. It was the way he approached the whole thing. He made the odd mistake, and instead of rushing everything to try and keep up the image of good lap times, if he got it slightly wrong he would roll off the lap.'

Herbert tested twice more for Benetton, but lost out when the team came to selecting its number-two driver for 1988. Alessandro Nannini, an Italian, was chosen. The next time he drove a Formula One car, at Monza, tyre-testing for Lotus, he was third fastest among a field of Grand Prix regulars at one point. Herbert had made his mark. He was quick, consistent and on the up. It was just a matter of time. He was racing hard in Formula 3000 – he won his debut race in the series, as he had in Formula Three – and Formula One looked a foregone conclusion. Then came Brands Hatch. And the accident.

'What got Johnny through that was sheer determination,' says Mike Thompson. 'At the end of November we went up to Buckmore Park, me and him, with a couple of 100cc karts, and we just went round and round and round. For about a month we were up there every week for two or three days, just pounding round. Because we knew he had that drive, that test in the Benetton at Silverstone, so we had to get him a bit brain-fit, and while he was going round we put lead on his helmet to build up his neck muscles.'

Herbert's crushed heels meant that he was now one inch shorter. He had a permanent limp and his right foot – his throttle foot – had lost 15 per cent of its articulation. The training was tough. 'We used to wrap all this foam round his leg, but at that stage the foot was still bleeding,' says Thompson quietly. 'It was healed up, but there were still cuts and so on that had not cleared up. But we were talking about weeks before he had to get in the Formula One car, so he had to get used to using his foot. The first day was a bit fraught, but thereafter he was actually doing bloody good times.'

Herbert had to be helped into the cockpit of the Benetton at Silverstone. He still couldn't walk. Did he have any apprehensions about driving again? 'None really. I got back in it just the same.' He drove it just the same, too, even though he was in considerable pain. He was fast in the test – both fast and consistent enough to secure a Grand Prix drive for the following year.

Today, Herbert still can't run and he strolls with a slight deliberation in his thick-soled Reeboks. When he took part in his first Grand Prix at Rio de Janeiro in March 1989, he used a bicycle to commute the few hundred yards from motorhome to pit-lane. In the car, however, he was supreme. He qualified tenth. In 106-degree heat, he finished the race fourth – the best Grand Prix debut performance since 1970. At Imola, a month later, he qualified 22nd and finished tenth. Although he qualified and finished at Monaco, he was off the pace. In Canada he finished fifth, but failed to qualify in Detroit.

'I thought it would all just come back,' he says now, with no trace of emotion in his voice. 'I did not realise that I did not have any strength at the time. When I did Rio, it was good, but the circuit hid the problem I had.' Herbert's problem was physical: he couldn't summon up the huge effort – the 150lb of pressure – required to press a Formula One car's brake pedal. At Rio this didn't matter: the circuit was flat, with constant radius corners placing a premium on line, smoothness and dab-braking. But at most other circuits, it did.

There was another problem, too: how Herbert was perceived by a Grand Prix pit-lane obsessed with the superficial. In Europe, Formula One drivers are regarded as athletes, and the sight of Herbert having to be helped in and out of the car proved too much for some of the Benetton hierarchy. 'There was Rick Mears in the States with crushed feet, racing at Indy,' says Peter Collins, 'and people saying, "God, what a guy, isn't he fantastic?" So it depends how you want to present things.'

Herbert was replaced by Italian Emanuele Pirro. 'Johnny understood,' said Collins. 'I think in some respects he was relieved. The right thing to do would have been for Johnny to have stood down after Monaco, or even Imola maybe, and to have given him six races off. But I knew because of the politics of the place that the moment I said, "Let's give him a rest," you would never see him in a Benetton again.'

Herbert continued to test for the Benetton team and drove for Tyrrell in the Belgian and Portuguese Grands Prix, when its regular driver Jean Alesi had clashing Formula 3000 commitments. He qualified strongly at Spa in Belgium, but food poisoning – 'I still don't know why I ate lobster' – kept him from racing at Estoril.

Formula One had seen Johnny Herbert and had delivered its verdict: he had lost it. He was physically incapable of driving to that standard. He was history. So Herbert did what the also-rans and never-weres did: in 1990 he went to race in Japan's domestic championships. The hardware was good, the testing seemingly limitless, and the team budgets were generous. Herbert spent his life commuting from Heathrow to Narita, but he kept racing: he earned an estimated £200,000 per year. If his career was about to fold, at least he would have some money in the bank.

Herbert had raced Mazda sports cars for some time and, in 1991, drove one in the Le Mans 24 Hours, accompanied by German Volker Weidler and Belgian Bertrand Gachot. Unfancied at the outset, the three won the race and gave a delighted manufacturer its – and Japan's – first victory at the French classic. The success proved vital for Herbert: suddenly, he was making news in Europe again. His recollections of the Le Mans endurance epic highlight two things – that it was an important step in his career, and that he does not think of himself as a long-distance sports car racer. 'I like my sleep,' he says, smiling, 'so I wasn't very good in the morning.' But what he doesn't say is that he had to drive the final two one-and-a-half-hour stints, thus proving that he was, at last, fully race-fit again.

In mid-1991, Herbert rejoined Peter Collins, who was now back at Lotus. He was a Grand Prix regular, even if three years later than he expected, and integral to the future of his team. Where Benetton had thought big following Collins' departure, hiring three-time World Champion Nelson Piquet, Lotus was small and Collins invested in technology rather than a superstar racer. The 1991 Lotus, an update of an older design, was neither fast nor reliable. But a new car for 1992 saw Herbert take two sixth places, and 1993's Lotus 107B allowed him to race wheel-to-wheel with Michael Schumacher's Benetton in the Brazilian Grand Prix, finishing fourth after a duel which had all the insolent ferocity of a kart race.

But then Herbert's hopes faded. Lotus had decided upon a hi-tech solution to finding Formula One speed, but the team's active suspension system was overly complex, difficult to optimise on a race weekend. The Lotus 107B was a quick-corner car, and Monza, home to the Italian Grand Prix, is a fast circuit. Herbert qualified seventh and then battled with the Ferrari of Gerhard Berger in the race. He passed the Austrian, ran wide and cannoned into the barrier. This was a 150mph shunt. And, typically, Herbert got out of the car, shaken and bruised, and talked to commentator Murray Walker on BBC television. It looked like a big accident, suggested Walker. 'I've only had one that was bigger,' replied Herbert.

A total of three fourth places and one fifth gave Herbert eleventh place in the 1993 World Championships, and for 1994 he has re-signed with Lotus and Peter Collins. He has finally made it. He earns a reasonable living. 'I do not want to be an absolute multi-millionaire,' he says, perhaps referring to Ayrton Senna's reputed $1 million-a-race pay cheque in 1993. 'I probably want to be comfortable. I do not see why I should be earning $20 million per year – that is just a joke.' He lives not in a Monaco apartment but in a Warwickshire village with his wife and his two young daughters. 'I am just a normal guy at home, really. I go to Tesco and do some shopping, then I might go to B&Q for a bit of paint. My first job when I get home is to get out the pooper scooper and cut the grass.' Herbert laughs. It might be a wind-up. But it's probably true.

Peter Collins has one story which he believes best illustrates Herbert's character. Rewind to the critical second Benetton test in December 1988. Herbert hasn't driven a racing car since his accident: if he performs poorly, the Benetton management will veto Collins' decision and Herbert will not race a Grand Prix car the following season. Herbert, still unable to walk properly, has to lap Silverstone competitively, and that means in a time of one minute and twelve seconds.

'He was still in quite a lot of pain,' Collins recalls. 'He went out and was doing seventeens on a damp track, and he came into the pits. We rolled the car back into the garage, and he flicked the visor up and looked up at me and said, with a really worried look in his eyes, "I don't think I can do it."' Collins pauses. 'Then he looked at me, and his eyes glistened. And he just burst into a big grin and went out and did twelves. That just sums him up.'

RING TRUE

Alex Kershaw

July, 1993

He belongs to an age of Zeppelins, Marlene Dietrich and four-ounce gloves. At his best, before Cassius Clay was even born, he'd have made Bratwurst of Frank Bruno. For those who are old enough to remember, he will forever be the greatest German fighter, the only mortal to knock out the best boxer of all time.

The high point of Max Schmeling's boxing career – when he laid out the legendary Joe Louis one muggy evening in 1936 in New York's Yankee Stadium before 40,000 baying fans – was to prove a bittersweet victory. Indeed, it has always been Schmeling's misfortune that by the late Thirties, as the shadow of National Socialism gathered across Europe, boxing had become politicised and its stars cast as representatives of rival ideologies. In 1938, when Schmeling, seen as a model Nazi, lost a return bout against Louis, it was as if the entire 'free world' rejoiced. Today, it is still said that Schmeling was 'Hitler's heavyweight', that in knocking out Louis in 1936 he was adding grist to Hitler's fantasies of Aryan superiority. As recently as October 1991, an article in *American Heritage*, a popular history magazine, described Schmeling as 'vehemently pro-Hitler'.

Max Schmeling deserves better. That he was manipulated by Nazi propaganda chief Joseph Goebbels is in little doubt. But the man who once boasted the likes of Greta Garbo and Marlene Dietrich among his admirers was never a Nazi. Schmeling not only openly consorted with his Jewish friends in the Thirties, he also risked his life to save others from Nazi persecution.

Schmeling has never spoken about this remarkable chapter in his life. Nor of his generosity to Joe Louis, who died, broke and broken, in Las Vegas in 1981 after years of mental decline.

Such is Max Schmeling's humility that even in his autobiography, *Memories*, he plays down other episodes which make him, as one Jewish émigré from Nazi Germany puts it, 'a truly great German'.

Max Schmeling sits in his neat office on the outskirts of Hamburg where, since hanging up his boxing gloves in 1948, he has worked for Coca-Cola. He now owns a part-share in a bottling plant and distribution company, Max Schmeling & Co. He is not rich, but certainly well-off.

It was with some reluctance that he agreed to this interview; years earlier he had granted what he hoped would be his last. Nonetheless, he was welcoming. His eyebrows are as bushy, his nose as flat as in the sepia-faded photographs of him weighing in with Joe Louis in the Thirties. His fleshy, speckled right hand, once the most feared in the world, is still a bone crusher.

'I don't think boxing's better than it was in my day,' says Schmeling. 'The sport is easier today. When I started boxing professionally, in 1924, we had to go twenty rounds. Can you imagine! We also used four-ounce gloves. Today you have six ounces and just twelve rounds.'

Born the son of a merchant seaman in 1905, by the mid-Twenties Schmeling had jabbed his way through the ranks of Europe's best boxers like no other Teuton before him, averaging a fight a month. He became German national champion in 1928. In the Thirties, his age and a lone 'negro' stood between Max Schmeling and world domination. He was already, at 30, past his physical best when he first saw Joe Louis fight against Paulino Uzcudun in December 1935 in Madison Square Garden.

There was no way, insisted reporters, that Schmeling could beat Louis, at 21 the most awesome boxer anyone had ever seen. Hadn't Schmeling seen Louis drive two of Uzcudun's teeth through his lower lip? Didn't he know Uzcudun had collapsed in his dressing room after the fight? Sure, said Schmeling, he knew all right. But he'd also seen something. Oh yeah? scoffed the press. Like what? Schmeling wasn't saying.

'I saw something which made me think I had a chance,' Schmeling now recalls. 'Joe had a wonderful straight hand, but he'd punch and then sometimes drop it.'

If Louis had a weakness, Schmeling had spotted it. He returned to Berlin armed with films of Louis in action. While an overconfident Louis slacked in his training, Schmeling took time out to lunch with Adolf Hitler in Munich. Why was Schmeling risking Germany's reputation, scolded Hitler, in a fight against a 'negro cotton-picker'? What made Schmeling think he'd last a round with the man tagged as the 'dark destroyer': the 'sepia slugger' who'd pulverised Primo Carnera (Mussolini's favourite), Kingfish Levinsky, Max Baer, Paulino Uzcudun and Charley Retzlaff in just sixteen rounds? Hadn't Schmeling already been humiliated in 1933 by Max Baer, of all things a Jew?

Hitler was not alone in writing Schmeling off. One of America's best sports writers, Paul Gallico, warned: 'Stay in Germany. Have no truck with this man [Louis]. He will do something to you from which you will never fully recover. You haven't a chance.' One cartoonist pictured Louis preparing for the Schmeling fight. 'Worry?' read the punchline issuing from Louis. 'Sure I worry – how to crack a hundred in mah golf.'

On June 19, 1936, Schmeling entered the ring in the Yankee Stadium first, his glistening hair greased back above bushy brows. Louis followed. For a few seconds the pair stood there motionless, staring at each other in the still heat. Did Schmeling really believe, deep down, that he could possibly win? 'Every boxer has to believe they can win when they go into the ring,' Schmeling says, smiling. 'Otherwise, you're done for.'

Within minutes, Schmeling showed that he had, after all, found Louis' Achilles' heel. In the fourth round, sure enough, Louis dropped his guard. Schmeling hit him smack in the face. Fear flickered across Louis' dazed features. A split second later, he hit the canvas for the first time in his professional career.

Six rounds later, Schmeling again caught Louis with a roundhouse right. Unbelievably, Louis sagged to his knees, cradled his head in his hands and fell backwards. The news-reels show Schmeling leaping into the air in victory, both arms above his head, his face bruised but ecstatic.

The left side of his jaw swollen like a softball, Louis skulked in his Harlem apartment for three days after his defeat, too ashamed to show his face. His ego was badly bruised, his 'jungle killer' reputation lay in tatters. 'This stuff about Louis and the "dead-pan killer",' scoffed one smug reporter, 'is so much bunk. This 22-year-old Negro is made of much the same stuff as any other boy of his age. He proved it in the dressing room when he wept unashamed.'

Black America wept with him. Schmeling still vividly recalls the 'hysteria and depression' he witnessed in Harlem as he drove to his mid-town hotel after the fight. As riots broke out in other American cities, some commentators even saw Louis' defeat as a blow to the nascent civil rights movement.

Hitler was beside himself. 'Most cordial felicitations on your splendid victory,' read his telegram. Goebbels went further: 'I know that you have fought for Germany. Your victory is a German victory. We are proud of you. Heil Hitler and hearty greetings.'

When, in July 1936, Schmeling arrived back in Frankfurt – on the ill-fated airship *Hindenburg* – to a hero's welcome, he gazed down at a landing area 'black with people'. A few days later, Hitler again requested Schmeling's presence. This time, Schmeling brought his wife and mother to lunch with the Führer in Berlin. Hitler insisted on replaying Schmeling's victory on film. In his memoirs, Schmeling remembers Hitler slapping his thigh whenever Louis caught a punch.

'Hitler was very interested in boxing,' says Schmeling. 'When we met, we did not speak about politics, only about the fight and the sporting situation. You have to remember the Berlin Olympic Games were due to start three weeks later. Hess was there, Goebbels – the whole government. Of course, he [Hitler] was a devil. No question about it. And the whole system was rotten. But I couldn't say Hitler was a beast when I met him. He was polite, charming.'

Legend has it that when Joe Louis beat James Braddock in 1937 to become world heavyweight champion, his first words were: 'Bring on Schmeling'. It was a challenge Schmeling gladly accepted. Within months, a rematch was scheduled for June 22, 1938. Schmeling would be 33, Louis still only 24.

Two years, says Schmeling, can seem a long time to a boxer in his thirties. In terms of the fast-changing political situation of that era, they were an aeon. In 1936, Max Schmeling had been lionised as boxing's white hope made good. But since then Hitler had forged the Axis pact with Italy and Japan, stepped up his persecution of the Jews and annexed Austria. In 1938, judging by American headlines, Schmeling had returned from hell as Nazism personified.

So hostile were the scenes that greeted Schmeling as he arrived in New York that police were forced to escort him through backstreets to his hotel where yet more demonstrators chanted 'Boycott Nazi Schmeling'. When he later strolled along Fifth Avenue, passers-by gave him the Nazi salute. Throughout his stay in Manhattan, Schmeling received sacks of hate-mail.

As the showdown between Nazism and democracy drew closer, the pre-fight atmosphere hissed with rumour: Hitler would make Schmeling minister of sport if he recaptured the title; Max Machon, Schmeling's American trainer, had a Nazi uniform in his closet; Schmeling had said no black man could beat a member of the master race.

There were also deeper-seated fears that Schmeling might take the title back to Germany. Not even the South's most rabid, extreme racists wanted to see the next heavyweight championship fight staged, as one journalist warned, 'in the land bossed by Hitler'. That the Louis-Schmeling fight was more than just another boxing match was underlined four days before the fight when eighteen American citizens were indicted on charges of spying for the Nazis –

by which time President Roosevelt had already invited Louis to the White House.

'The politicisation of sport which was pushed so hard by the Third Reich found a sort of echo on the other side of the Atlantic,' writes Schmeling. 'The one group came to emulate the other one, and this was bad for sport. At the time I was a young man with only the thought of a title fight in my head. I had tried in all honesty to persuade Hitler of the virtues of my Jewish manager, Joe Jacobs. Now I wanted to make clear to the Americans my right to a title fight ... The one attempt was as naive as the other.'

It is an unfair question, loaded with judgmental hindsight, but was Schmeling seduced by the Nazis? Did he knowingly let himself be exploited by Goebbels for propaganda?

He may have been guilty of naivety. 'We have no strikes in Germany,' he allegedly told one American journalist. 'Most everybody has a job. Times are good. We have only one union. We have only one party. Everybody agreeable. Everybody happy.'

But, unlike many of his peers, Schmeling never joined the Nazi party. 'The unfortunate thing during the Thirties was that every German was seen as a Nazi,' Schmeling says now. 'Even the people who were against Hitler.' As a public figure, it was never going to be easy for him to distance himself from Nazism. But his lingering in the Nazi limelight may be explained less by vanity than by the presence at his side of the glamorous Polish-born Anny Ondra (who would later become his wife), one of Goebbels' favourite celluloid Fräuleins.

Schmeling remained loyal to his Jewish friends and associates, even after the enactment of the Nuremberg Laws of 1935, which stripped Jews of German citizenship. Those friends included Dr Kurt Schindler, who accompanied him to New York for his first fight against Louis; and Paul Damski, a boxing promoter, who first introduced Schmeling to Anny.

'Nobody else would have their picture taken like this, but I didn't care,' says Schmeling as he pulls out a photograph taken of him with Jewish friends in 1937. 'When the photograph appeared, I had a call from the propaganda minister [Goebbels].'

quickly waved his arms over Schmeling. Official result: technical knock-out after 124 seconds of the first round.

Louis' victory sparked delirious street parties in ghettoes from Harlem to Oakland. The descendant of a slave had struck a blow not only for his race but also America – and democracy. In Chicago, crowds fired shots in the air. Former heavyweight champion 'Jersey Joe' Walcott, one of Louis' sparring partners, recalled years later how 'people came pouring out of their houses. They were so happy. It was like New Year's Eve.'

Heywood Broun, a journalist from the *New York World-Telegram*, summed up Louis' victory with remarkable prescience: 'One hundred years from now, some historian may theorise, in a footnote at least, that the decline of Nazi prestige began with a left hook delivered by a former unskilled automotive worker [Louis].'

There would be no be-bopping in the streets when Schmeling returned to Germany. Even before Schmeling had boarded the liner *Bremen* for the trip home, Goebbels was propagating the myth that Louis had been guilty of intentional fouling. Louis had used lead padding in his gloves, insisted the propaganda minister. In a fair fight, the cotton-picker wouldn't have stood a chance.

In his memoirs, Schmeling recalls that for Goebbels and Hitler he no longer existed after his loss. For several months, his name disappeared from the sports pages. And the film of his defeat was edited to emphasise Louis' bodypunches.

The coming Second World War would confirm the Louis-Schmeling fight in America's memory as Nazism's first defeat. 'Joe has a date for a return engagement with Max Schmeling,' trumpeted the *Chicago Tribune* when Louis later enlisted in the army in January 1942.

Schmeling had already seen action as a paratrooper by the time photographs of Louis taking his army medical put a lump in Uncle Sam's throat. He had been decorated for bravery as a Wehrmacht paratrooper and spent the summer of 1941 in hospital after a bad landing in Crete.

While recovering, Schmeling befriended a Welsh PoW who

shared the same ward. Schmeling offered the Welshman cigarettes and an orange, and chatted to him about Tommy Farr, the Welsh miner and British heavyweight champion whom Schmeling had beaten in the Thirties.

After later telling a journalist about the Welshman, Schmeling was severely reprimanded by a military tribunal for having said the British were 'fair fighters'.

Joe Louis' war was no less eventful. Fast mythologised as the 'first American to KO a Nazi', Louis twice risked his world title in charity bouts which raised millions of dollars for the war effort. After gracing a 1943 propaganda film, *This is the Army,* which also starred Ronald Reagan, Louis saw out the war touring American bases in Europe, boosting the morale of both black and white GIs.

When peace broke out, Schmeling and Louis briefly returned to the ring, retiring in 1948 and 1949 respectively. After spells as a tobacco farmer and boxing referee, Schmeling signed up for Coca-Cola and to this day promotes the brand in Germany. In the late Eighties, Schmeling set up a charitable trust. Ageing boxers, ailing sports writers, juvenile delinquents and his local church all now benefit from his generosity. Schmeling continues to enjoy his unique status as Germany's best-loved boxer.

Fate was not so kind to Joe Louis. His last decades were overshadowed by demeaning comebacks, a broken marriage, booze, drugs and mental illness.

To make matters worse, in the early Fifties, the taxman finally got wise to the Brown Bomber's high-spending ways. Not only had Louis somehow blown the millions of dollars he had made since turning professional in 1934 (his generosity was legendary in Harlem), he had also paid barely a cent in tax.

Had Las Vegas high-rollers not seen him all right, finding him a $50,000-a-year 'job' in 1971 greeting guests at Caesar's Palace, Joe Louis would almost certainly have spent his last decade shuffling in welfare queues. So destitute was Louis by the late Seventies that, in 1977, after he had been floored by a heart attack and was suffering from a cerebral haemorrhage which left him confined to a wheelchair and barely able to speak, Frank Sinatra had to pick up his medical bill. When he died in 1981, Louis owed the Internal Revenue Services millions.

One of Joe Louis' few comforts in his last years was his friendship with Max Schmeling. In 1954, haunted by memories of the animosity whipped up by the press in 1938, Schmeling had tracked Louis down to a Chicago golf club. He vividly remembers how embracing Louis for the first time outside a boxing ring meant far more to him than a third bout against the fighter even Muhammad Ali once called the 'greatest'.

'From that day, our friendship really started,' says Schmeling. 'We had never really been enemies. It was the press who created the rivalry. I visited Joe five or six times in Las Vegas before he died. His son [Joe Louis Barrow Jnr] visited me two years ago.'

It's December 1989, in Las Vegas. One-arm bandits all over town cough up nickels and dimes. Two thousand people, including Muhammad Ali, Larry Holmes, Sugar Ray Leonard, Don King and many others, pack the ballroom at the Sands Hotel. 'Schmeling! Schmeling! Schmeling!' they chant as an old man, his back straight, his head held upright, strides towards a banquet table. Mike Tyson enters, with a rolling swagger, and sits beside Schmeling. Henri Lewin, the president of the Sands Hotel, then crowns Schmeling and Tyson with diamond circlets.

'I'd decided to throw a special party to honour Mike Tyson and Max Schmeling, two of the greatest boxers ever,' recalls 70-year-old Lewin. 'Unfortunately, at one point during the evening, a former fighter stood up. He was half-drunk. He grabbed a microphone, pointed to Schmeling and said: 'Fucking arsehole. He's a Nazi."'

Lewin jumped to his feet, seething with rage, tears welling in his eyes, memories of being a 'Jew-boy' in Nazi Germany suddenly flooding back.

'I want you all to know,' Lewin stuttered, 'Max hasn't got that coming to him ... I'm now 70. I don't think I should wait any longer. I'm gonna tell you the real story.'

Schmeling's face crumpled with emotion.

'What the hell, Max,' said Lewin. 'Hitler can't arrest you any more. Why do you care about it?'

To stunned silence, Lewin told the boxing world how, during Krystallnacht, on November 9, 1938, Schmeling had saved his life.

While synagogues blazed and pogroms raged throughout Germany, for four days Schmeling had hidden Henri and his brother Werber Lewin in his own apartment in the bijou Excelsior Hotel in Berlin. Schmeling had left directions with staff that he was ill and should not be disturbed.

In 1939, the Lewin brothers fled Germany. After surviving the war in a PoW camp in Shanghai, they emigrated to the Golden State in 1947, where Henri Lewin worked as a waiter in San Francisco before becoming a highly successful hotel owner and occasional fight promoter.

'Max definitely risked his life,' insists Lewin now, the faint strain of a German accent still audible. 'Max ordered food for himself and then gave it to us. Hitler would have made chop suey of Max if he'd known. I wouldn't be alive today if it were not for Max – one helluva guy.'

Lewin did not tell the assembled glitterati in Las Vegas of another gesture from Schmeling, following Louis' death from a heart attack in 1981. 'When Joe died, Max called me from Germany and asked me to take some money to Joe Louis' widow,' recalls Lewin.

Lewin found Martha Louis seated beside her husband's coffin in the ballroom in Caesar's Palace. He handed over an envelope containing $5,000. 'Oh, Henri,' said Martha Louis. 'You don't know what this man has done for Joe and me for years and years. Nobody gave us anything. I mean, we were desperate. But Max was always Joe's friend. This man always helped us.'

Max Schmeling has turned a room adjoining his sunlit Hamburg office into an intimate archive. A black and white poster, taken in the Thirties, priced 30 pfennigs, covers one wall. It shows Max Schmeling embracing his stunning blonde wife, Anny Ondra, who died in 1978. On a facing wall hang the portraits of every pre-war heavyweight champion. As Max Schmeling gazes wistfully at Jack

Johnson, Bob Fitzsimmons, Jack Dempsey and Joe Louis, I recall a moving line from Joan Didion's latest book, *Sentimental Journeys*: 'You can't imagine how it is when everyone you know is gone.'

A box of red Everlast boxing gloves waits to be signed and returned to some American fans. Nearby, on a coffee table, sits a pocket bible bound in silver, a gift from a Jewish community in Israel. A dedication written on the bible's flyleaf reads: 'In the name of humanity and in honour of Israel, to a great German – Max Schmeling.'

THE SPOKESMEN

Russell Bulgin

January, 1994

Under the flat glare of the stadium lights, Chris Boardman's skin seemed the gloomy tint of putty: a hue exclusive to the terminally ill, rock veterans with a history of pharmacological experimentation and, ironically, the super-fit. Off the bike, a crisp arc of yellow-painted carbon fibre, the 24-year-old Boardman was trailed by video cameras stacked on shoulders and by preening men in blazers with clipboards. But when his conehead hat sank deep into his shoulder blades, when man and machine became one biomechanical blur around the Bordeaux velodrome, the bike's narrow tyres thwacking rhythmically against the pale track surface, Boardman smashed the world hour record. Alone out on the track, he travelled 52.27 kilometres in sixty minutes: 32.6 miles flat-out against a heart pounding at 185 beats per minute.

Boardman's approach on July 23, 1993, was rational, scientific, carbohydrate-loaded. He had already won an Olympic gold for Britain at Barcelona the year before. His bicycle would be fetishised in the cycling media: it weighed precisely 15.6 pounds and cost perhaps £30,000; it was stiff, long-slung and bespoke for its rider. Boardman's training was considered: his coach Peter Keen, a lecturer in physiology at Brighton University, seemed as interested in psychological conditioning as in conventional notions of muscle mass and anaerobic endurance. A trackside computer screen flashed Boardman his pace in monochrome, lap by lap: 52.21 kilometres per hour, 52.23, 52.30. His legs were muscled to circle the pedals: Boardman was as function-specific as a human being has ever been.

Boardman had trained in Bordeaux for two weeks. But after overnight rain, the summer morning of his attempt on the record smouldered warm and damp. And, for the first time, the lights in the stadium were turned on. This rise in humidity affected Boardman's pace as his grey pallor grew slick with sweat. On a stationary trainer, perfecting his pace, he had lost two kilograms in an hour; the core temperature of his body climbed four degrees at Bordeaux. (A six-degree increase is fatal.) He could have gone quicker still in cooler, drier conditions. And he might yet have to.

Just one week before, a 27-year-old Scotsman named Graeme Obree had attempted to break the world hour record, which had stood since 1984. Obree's training regime had been rather different to Boardman's: it had centred on blasting up and down a main road outside Ayr and fuelling up on cornflakes doused in UHT milk and marmalade sandwiches. And Obree's bike had been different, too: it was a home-built special which incorporated parts from a washing machine and a lump of steel found lying in the gutter of that same long, undulating stretch of Ayrshire dual carriageway. But Obree had broken the world hour record just the same.

The world hour record is the race to nowhere. This is, as cycling journalist Andy Sutcliffe says, 'crucifying yourself for 60 minutes'. That simple. That brutal. Traditionally, breaking this record serves as the finale to a successful road racing career. Fausto Coppi, Jacques Anquetil and Eddy Merckx won twelve Tours de France between them – and each man went on to hold the world hour record. The record, then, serves as a reminder of greatness, of cardiovascular superiority, of a job well done. It is cycling's ultimate haul of fame, a grand gesture signalling both pay-off and send-off.

To attempt the record and fail is to have an otherwise enviable reputation brought into question. Even three-time Tour de France winner Miguel Indurain has discussed tackling the hour record – but only when he no longer spends each July cranking through the Pyrenees and sprinting around Paris.

For Obree and Boardman, amateurs both, there were also risks.

Success would mean a chance of turning pro, of earning more than the odd hundred quid for humbling British club racers in early-morning time trials around the country. But failure in an hour record attempt would stall their careers.

Italian Francesco Moser took the hour record in Mexico City in 1984. Moser brought science and a calculated veneer of mythology to his challenge. His bike was aerodynamic – a sloping top tube, slippery disc wheels – and, thanks to his coach Francesco Conconi, his approach scientific. On January 24, 1984, Moser set a record of 51.151 kilometres at an altitude of 2,000 metres. Conconi even knew that air resistance – aerodynamic drag – increased by 1 per cent for every drop of three degrees Celsius. At 8.30am that January morning, the ambient temperature was just six degrees Celsius. The air itself was too slow, and so Moser had waited for the day to warm up. After Mexico, he tried again, in Milan and Stuttgart. He set a record at sea-level, but could not beat the Mexico marker. That pace seemed unsurpassable – and Moser merchandised the myth. His vineyard even produced wine branded with a '51.15' label.

Fifty-one-fifteen became an athletic benchmark, one of those cast-iron statistics which seem destined never to be beaten, if only because the chance of under-achievement was too great for an established professional to tolerate. But for Boardman and Obree, the hour record represented a chance to grow. Neither man is a traditional road racer, but a skilled time triallist, speeding individually against the clock for ten, 25 or 50 miles. The competition does not come against the cut and thrust of the pack or in thinking tactically, jostling for the final sprint head-down and elbows-out. Instead, time triallists spin. Turn big gears smoothly, powerfully, consistently, in a self-inflicted choreography of power, precision and pace. The world hour record is, simply, the ultimate time trial.

British cycling knew little about Obree. Merseysider Boardman, by contrast, was high-profile. He had taken the Olympic gold at Barcelona in the 4,000 metres pursuit, using an innovative LotusSport bicycle which matched the expensive constructional techniques and composite materials of a Grand Prix car with a radical look at the way the wind plays over a bicycle frame.

When a bicycle is travelling at over eighteen mph, the greatest single impediment it faces is aerodynamic drag. Streamlining becomes paramount. The LotusSport bike incorporated a number of ideas developed by Norfolk-based inventor Mike Burrows, including a single-sided front fork. Most bicycles secure the front wheel between two forkblades; Burrows, aiming to quell turbulence, dispensed with one blade and made the rear chainstays single-sided, too.

The resulting machine may have been intriguingly asymmetric, but it was undeniably effective. A stretched-out riding position gave Boardman a flat back and a low frontal area: the LotusSport bike teased air molecules with a hi-tech insouciance, clobbering a roster of design preconceptions – part art, part science, part mumbo-jumbo – which had seen mainstream bicycle development concentrate on tiny refinements over the past 40 years rather than massive design leaps. If, as Ludwig Mies van der Rohe suggested, God really is in the details, then modern bicycle design is nothing more than a slavish deification of established practice – and the LotusSport machine positively heretical.

The LotusSport bike had but one technical flaw – it was a couple of kilograms heavier than was ideal – yet came with a whole raft of offstage commercial complications. After the hype of the Barcelona Olympics, Lotus, Burrows and Boardman went their separate ways. Boardman continued to race and win for his club, the North Wirral Velo, and Burrows later began to work with a Scotsman. His name was Graeme Obree.

It was not Obree's physical conditioning which got him noticed. It was his bicycle. From a distance, it looked like a bastard cross between a kid's BMX racer and the kind of cruiser Harrison Ford might have thrown a leg over in *Blade Runner.* Tall where it should have been short, squat where it should have been long, Obree's bike was defiantly odd. Painted in a plain white finish, the fat downtube carried a bald notice in black block capitals: 'DESIGNED & BUILT X G. OBREE'. A homemade bike? Coming after the engineered sophistication of the Lotus bicycle, this ungainly machine looked funny. Funny-peculiar and, yes, funny-ha-ha.

The riding position was weird, too. This was not the fluid, graceful curve adopted by Boardman, but a hunched, crunched pose which rounded the shoulders, tucked the hands under the chest and snapped Obree's elbows back cleanly into his hips. The resulting stance may have had an aerodynamic benefit – it resembled, after all, the egg-like crouch adopted by a downhill skier – but at the cost of labouring the rider's breathing. And oxygen uptake and efficient air processing lay at the heart of surviving the aerobic excesses of the hour record.

Mike Burrows pronounced Obree's machine to have the most aerodynamic riding position he had seen. A drag saving of 6 per cent was suggested by various cycling experts: this was an estimate as the bike had never seen a wind tunnel, much less been scientifically tested. It represented Obree's intuition, nothing more.

But the design seemed to work. Obree took the British hour record at Herne Hill with it, managing a distance of 49.383 kilometres. He came head to head with Boardman at the National 25-Mile event: he would have beaten Boardman but for a puncture and subsequent bicycle change. He lost by just 58 seconds, despite the stoppage. Then, one weekend in late June 1993, Obree won a ten-mile time trial in Herne Bay in eighteen minutes 27 seconds against a strong wind, outpacing the opposition by one second short of two minutes. Eighteen hours later he broke the ten-year-old British 50-mile record by 50 seconds: he shattered the course record by an astonishing seventeen minutes and one second. The funny bike wasn't so funny any more.

And when Boardman announced that he would be attempting the world hour record in Bordeaux in late July, with two French custom-built Corima bikes, with his trainer Peter Keen, his logistics man Peter Woodworth and mechanics Paul Jennings and Dave O'Brien, Obree revealed that he, too, would be trying for the record. One week earlier, at the Hamar track in Norway.

Boardman would be tested at the Institute of Physiology in Chichester, confirming he would have to generate at least 410 watts of power for an hour – 740 watts equal one horsepower – and maintain a heart rate that could not fall below 180 beats per minute for the duration of the record attempt. He would train for two weeks at Bordeaux, taking eleven seconds off Moser's record in an unofficial run. Boardman was taper-training, reducing the volume of his training but increasing its intensity so he would peak precisely on the day of his record attempt. His warm-ups were metronomic, increasing his speed and his heartbeat in tiny increments: this was training as science, man as machine.

Obree, meanwhile, planned to fly from Glasgow to Oslo on Wednesday and go for the record on Friday. He would be accompanied by his wife Ann, his manager, some friends and the boss of a Surrey-based accountancy recruitment firm which was, unfathomably, sponsoring the record attempt. He would bring with him a loaf of Scottish bread, his marmalade and his cornflakes.

'To my mind, the design of the bike is more important than the materials used in it, or the quality of engineering in it,' says Obree. 'As long as the engineering is of a reasonable quality, the design is what makes it work.'

Obree, whispers the British cycling grapevine, is an eccentric. Quiet, slightly boyish. Unemployed, slightly odd. He does his own thing. He doesn't have a telephone. But, in conversation, Obree is bright and sharp. True, he can slide from enthusiastic schoolboy to deep thinker in the space of a sentence, but that's a quirk rather than a character defect. Each time his conversation pins him as dangerously naive, he immediately bounces back with a thought, an insight, that is plainly clever.

'You can make a biplane out of titanium – but it is still a biplane, isn't it?' Obree looks up. 'And you can make a jet out of the cheapest materials that you can make a jet out of, but it is going to go faster than the biplane, isn't it? So the design is what counts.'

Obree's grandfather's brother was a southern Scottish cycling champion in the late Thirties and his uncle a Royal Navy champion. But Obree started at the age of fifteen, turning up at his local cycling club 'in Doc Martens and a parka'. It was a tough baptism, he recalls. 'You sort of hang about and get cold. And the beginner will be soaking with sweat and you either hang on, or you go home. And if you do it long enough, you eventually stay with the bunch.'

He became a Scottish junior time trial champion. Broke his thigh when he was hit by a car out road training at night: dazzled by the headlights, he had nowhere to hide. Attended Glasgow University for two terms, travelling two hours each way each day by bus, to study design engineering. There wasn't enough time to train on his bike in the week – and he wanted to cycle. He was thinking about the big time.

He suspected he would be competitive. 'Because of the velocity I was travelling at on the road. Against the likes of, let us say, Chris Boardman in the national championship. I knew that I could go as fast as him in a straight line. With few hills, or few undulations, in terms of speed, I could go as fast, if not faster. So from that point of view I thought, well, I should really go for it.'

He trained. By himself. 'What I do,' Obree says, 'is train to how my body feels at the time. The hardest thing is not forcing yourself to train, but forcing yourself not to train. So I ride my bike every day whenever possible, and only once I am out on the bike do I make the decision – do I feel ready for training? Basically I make time for recuperation. It is the recuperation that makes you stronger – it is part of the training. Sometimes I can train as little as an hour in a week. On an average, though, without feeling tired, I would do about three hours of static training and about ten or eleven hours on my bike on the road.'

Because he was broke, Obree built his own bike. He had already discovered an unusual riding position which increased his speed. 'When you have got a strong headwind, if you go to the front of the race and crouch over the bars almost squirrel-style, with your hands quite close together on the handlebars, you can pull out an advantage. So that is how it started. But you can only hold that for about a mile or so.'

There are two other effects of the Obree position. It allows him to use the narrow, flat handlebars as a lever to push against and as a platform to support his body while he turns strength-sapping gears designed for speed. And, when viewed from head-on, his bicycle is exceptionally narrow in cross-section: when Obree is pedalling hard, his knees almost touch.

'If you lie on your back with your eyes closed and simulate a pedalling action in mid-air,' says Obree, smiling, 'you find your legs are very close together. It is the natural position to pedal in.' Critically, it also reduces the size of the hole Obree and his bike punch in the air, trimming drag.

Building the bike took 'four months in total. There was a lot of work. Each tube had to be manipulated under heat to give it that aerodynamic shape.' Obree scrounged parts. Design, after all, was paramount, the provenance of the components less important. Obree explains: 'I had an old washing machine outside the back door. The bearings that hold the washing machine have got to go at 1,200rpm and, with that weight in it, they have got to be good-quality bearings.' He is being serious. 'It was a reasonably new washing machine – it just wasn't working. I knew there was a good bearing system somewhere in there which, if it could be adapted, would be really durable.'

A piece of steel was required to make a crank arm. 'I was cycling along – I think it was the next day – and at the side of the dual carriageway there was a good piece of steel and I just picked it up. I had to cut it away and shape it, but it was a good-quality piece of steel.'

The rules of the UCI, cycle sport's governing body, demand that any rider attempting the world hour record must have two bicycles at their disposal. By the time that Obree was ready for Oslo, Mike Burrows was helping him out.

Burrows came up with a carbon-fibre monoblade fork for the original bike – now nicknamed Old Faithful – and helped design the second bike. This, although it looked similar to the original, was professionally made of steel, panelled in carbon fibre and carried a few one-off titanium components.

Obree decided to use the new bike for his record attempt in Oslo. He hadn't ridden it much and it pulled a much bigger top gear than he had used before: for each turn of the pedals he would travel 120 inches. On the old bike, he moved 116 inches per revolution. So in theory, he would be faster still – if he was strong enough.

The night before the hour attempt, a disco in the hotel meant he couldn't sleep properly. The way Obree works is up and at 'em: wake up, cornflakes, warm-up and ride. This morning he got hassled at the track – a video crew even followed him into the lavatory – and became increasingly nervous in the 90 minutes he had to hang around before the 11am start.

He tried. And failed. He covered 50.690 kilometres: 51.15 remained inviolate. Obree knew why: it was the new bike. 'It seemed OK just riding round, but once I started putting pressure on it I realised that my position was not quite right and it took its toll on the hour record. Plus, I did use too big a gear on it. I risked putting it up to a higher gear, and it was too big a gear.'

Obree then asked if he could try for the record again in the afternoon. The UCI officials thought he was joking: this was, after all, the toughest challenge in cycling. But Obree was serious, and the officials eventually allowed him another attempt at 9am the following morning. It had to be early because they had planes to catch. Obree would use Old Faithful. He says that 'stupidity and necessity' made him want to go again, immediately. 'Sometimes,' Obree says, 'I operate at my best when the chips are down and I am coming back from behind, against the odds to come back, because you just have to do it. I just had to do it.'

He got out of bed just after 8am, had his cornflakes, ate his marmalade sandwiches and got to the track. Did five or six warm-up laps. Didn't bother with embrocation oils or psychology or heartbeat monitors or computers. Just tucked his head down and rode. And he travelled further in an hour than any man had managed before: 51.596 kilometres. The record was his. Moser's reign, the myth of 51.15, was forgotten. 'Obree is strong, very strong,' said Moser. 'I'm surprised by what he did in Norway, but I don't think it was a product of chance.'

'The best moment was when the gun went off, before I finished.'

Obree's face lights up. 'Because the gun goes off when you have actually beaten the record, and that took about 59 and a half minutes. That was the best moment, because I had done it. And half a minute later I had finished.' Obree gives a big kid's grin. 'It felt brilliant.'

A week later, Boardman beat him in Bordeaux: he managed to travel 0.674 of a kilometre further in 60 minutes. Graeme Obree vowed to try again. For the time being, though, his recollections of breaking the world hour record will have to be enough.

DEATH OF A BOXER

Eamonn O'Neill

May, 1996

Scottish boxer James Murray was buried on a bleak, unforgiving autumn day last year. He had collapsed fighting for the British bantamweight title on Friday, October 13, 1995, while challenging the champion, fellow Scot Drew Docherty. Two days later, his life-support system was switched off by doctors in a Glasgow hospital. He was 25.

The funeral took place at the Coltness Parish Church in Cambusnethan, a grey, featureless town on the outskirts of Wishaw in the west of Scotland. A crowd of more than 1,500 had gathered; those who couldn't be accommodated in the church stood listening to the service being relayed on tinny loudspeakers. Reverend Graham Duffin's words echoed around the assembled: 'James Murray was a young man with so much to live for, so many hopes. There is pain, and a measure of disbelief – the dreams and hopes seem to have been stolen. James died doing what he loved; we hold on to that – the pride that he took in what he had achieved. Boxing was a sport that he loved and got so much from.'

At the end of the service, Murray's coffin was carried out of the church in silence. On top of the brass nameplate lay the dead boxer's Scottish bantamweight championship belt. People wept openly as the boxer's body was loaded into a hearse.

At the cemetery, expensive sports cars and four-wheel drives blocked the entrance; champions, ex-champions, promoters and managers had come to pay their respects. A strong wind caught the minister's vestments as he read prayers to the mourners. The crowd listened in coiled quiet. When the prayers ended, the lone figure of a Scottish piper stepped forward and played 'Scotland the Brave' and 'The Flower of Scotland'. Drew Docherty, standing a short distance from the graveside, stared in bewilderment as the coffin of James Murray was lowered carefully into the open earth. He was buried wearing his red robe.

Later, when the crowd had cleared, I stood at the side of James Murray's grave. Tattooed gravediggers milled around examining the floral tributes. One excitedly pointed out a delivery signed by Frank Bruno. A couple of displays were in the shape of boxing rings; another was in the shape of a glove. One wreath had been sent by the fight's co-promoter, Frank Warren; there was one from its televisers, Sky Sport. An Action Man figure adorned one tribute, dressed up as a boxer with his hands taped and raised in a victory salute.

Murray's grave was still open; the coffin was visible. I looked down and shuddered; the dead boxer was lying in the casket only feet from where I stood. I felt nauseous and uncomfortable. Behind me, two young girls walked away crying.

As I drove back to Glasgow through Wishaw I noticed the decay and creeping deprivation which has befallen the area since the nearby Ravenscraig Steelworks closed down four years ago. Shops were boarded up; only the amusement arcade appeared still to be doing business. When I got home I noticed there was mud from James Murray's graveside on my shoes.

James Murray fought Drew Docherty in the Grand Ballroom of the glitzy Hospitality Inn in Glasgow's city centre. There were six other bouts on the bill that night, but the British bantamweight title fight was the main attraction. About 700 people were in the room, those near the ring had paid £80 for their seats and a meal; further back were the £50-a-head tables; and, at the rear, the £30 'boxing-only' seats, where most of James Murray's fans were to be found . . .

Just before 10pm, the lights go down and the bagpipes start up. James Murray, hands up, eyes fixed, face tense, bouncing on the balls of his feet, moves through the audience towards the ring, accompanied by strains of 'Scotland the Brave'. Inside the ring he begins to dance, throwing short, stabbing jabs into the air. He's feeling the space of the ring, testing his reflexes and encouraging the blood to flow into his muscles. He looks ready to seize his big chance – the British title, the stepping stone to Europe and the World.

Within a minute of the first round, Murray floors Docherty with a left hook, his favourite punch. Docherty stumbles and falls through the ropes. But within seconds he's up, looking at the referee and shaking his head. By the end of the round, the bout has settled down into a hard, solid fight. Both boxers give and take good punches and look evenly matched.

In the fifth, Docherty snaps a left jab into Murray's face; the blow cracks into the challenger's chin but does not stop him from advancing. Murray's trainer, Dave Douglas, yells encouragement from his corner. The boxer suddenly drops his hands in a cheeky, show-off gesture of defiance and grins through his mouthguard at Docherty. He's feeling confident and wants everyone to know it.

But by the eleventh round, both boxers are looking weary. Their shorts are bloodstained, their faces puffy – Murray has cuts on his eyes and nose. As the fighters retreat to their corners, their chests heave up and down as they gulp in air. Murray's fans are chanting: 'There's only one Jim Murray! There's only one Jim Murray!'

'Jim, you'll need to win this round out of sight, out of fucking sight! Do you hear me?' shouts Douglas. Murray stares straight ahead and nods. Douglas pumps enthusiasm into the boxer and Murray mouths the words 'Right, Dave' through his gumshield.

With just 45 seconds of the twelfth and final round remaining, Docherty throws a couple of light punches. The first, a left jab, catches Murray on the top of his head. The second blow, a straight right, is aimed at his chest, but before it even lands it's clear something is wrong. Murray is beginning to buckle; his hands, which at all other times would automatically have been up in a defensive position, are hanging limply at his sides. He falls forward, as if in slow motion, onto the canvas. Murray has collapsed and is now lying, half on his knees, with his hands stretched out and his head bowed down.

As the referee frantically calls to the ringside doctor for attention and Docherty heads to a neutral corner, James Murray starts to die. He stares at the floor, blinking intensely and shaking his head. He looks vaguely as if he's trying to clear his mind of something that's bothering him. He is unaware that he's already been counted out.

From this point on, Murray's instinct is to survive, to live. He falls to one side and his cornermen take out his gumshield. As his bloodstained chest moves furiously up and down, Sky's ringside commentator screams into his microphone: 'Friday the thirteenth couldn't be more unlucky for James Murray!'

There is a stretched tension in the air; something has gone wrong. Suddenly, Murray's left leg begins to shake violently; it jerks and kicks backwards and forwards spontaneously. A cornerman stops it and holds it down. Then the boxer's whole torso starts to shake and convulse. He's clearly in severe agony. His mother, Margaret Murray, rushes out of her seat and starts screaming through the ropes: 'Jimmy, get up! Please Jimmy, get up!'

Panic erupts inside the ring. As the doctor attends to Murray, a riot among the fans catches everyone unawares. No one is sure what to do. Docherty stands up, sits down, then stands up again. Officials scream at the audience: 'Pack it in. There's a boxer in trouble in the ring!' Finally, a stretcher arrives and Murray is manhandled through the ropes. With Douglas at his side, he's carried off through the crowd towards paramedics who've arrived at the scene.

As the ambulance speeds through Glasgow, across the river Clyde towards the Southern General Hospital in Govan, the riot takes hold. Glasses, bottles and chairs fly through the air; innocent bystanders are caught in the mayhem. Punches are exchanged. The scenes are played out live on Sky, and police officers watching at the nearby Stewart Street station grab their jackets and race to the venue.

The arrests that follow, and the subsequent British Boxing Board of Control (BBBC) investigation, suggest that the majority of the trouble-makers come from the 'boxing-only' ticket area. The report states that the situation 'would appear to have been exacerbated by alcohol'. To date, police in Strathclyde have made over a dozen arrests in connection with the riot.

James Murray's death was the result of a massive subdural blood clot that formed on the left side of his brain at some point during the fight. A blow (or blows) caused the brain to move around; delicate veins and arteries were torn between the lining, called the *dura mater*, and the surface of the brain itself. As the blood flowed, it compressed the brain at the base of the skull causing vital functions such as breathing to be interrupted and threatened. Only immediate intensive care and a surgical operation could have saved him.

Nearly everyone agrees now that Murray was dying when he collapsed. 'I saw him drop his hands in the twelfth round,' says Kenny Murray, James' father. 'Jim would never normally do that – he wasn't protecting himself properly. Then he fell. I saw his leg twitch ... My son died in the ring.'

'When I saw his legs go, I knew something was wrong,' recalls Alex Morrison, Murray's manager. 'I thought it was maybe hypoglycaemia [lack of sugar in the blood], then I saw his legs shaking ... I can't remember much after that – I was in a daze.'

Only Dave Douglas believes Murray was still alive when he was carried out of the ring. 'When we were in the ambulance, I held his hand and kept telling him we were going to the hospital,' says Douglas. 'The paramedic told me he was going to be OK because he was breathing by himself. I wanted to keep talking to Jim to keep him tuned in. The last thing he did was squeeze my hand.'

In the early hours of Saturday morning, surgeons attempted to save Murray's life by removing the blood clot from his brain during a two-hour operation. Despite their desperate efforts, it was not successful. At 8.50am on Sunday, October 15, Garth Cruickshank, the hospital's consultant neurosurgeon, pronounced the boxer clinically brain dead and Murray's life-support system was switched off.

*

I'd known about Jim Murray the boxer before he died. While our paths had never crossed, I'd noted from newspaper reports that he'd boxed in the places I'd trained in as a teenager. (I also knew the place where he was buried – I'd been in Cambusnethan graveyard once before, to attend the funeral of a fellow schoolboy at high school in Wishaw. He'd been kicked to death by local thugs after a school disco. I think I was about sixteen at the time.)

Learning to box was not unusual – lots of boys I knew did it. Going to boxing training was like going to football practice; it was accepted and enjoyed. But even then I knew that boxers died; I can remember listening to the radio on the day in 1980 that the Welsh boxer Johnny Owen passed away after lying in a coma for over six weeks. My mother worried about me sparring that night.

The boxing club I trained at in Wishaw was where Jim Murray started his fighting career. The gym is housed inside a wooden building behind a large council house estate; it looks the same today. The whole place has a home-made appearance to it – it feels like a large garage. The trainers used to chain-smoke cigarettes and shout at the boxers. I was fourteen at the time and hit the bags until my knuckles bled. I was one of the lucky ones, though; at least I had proper bandages and decent boxing gloves. Some of the other boys wore hard industrial mitts stolen from Ravenscraig Steelworks. When they had finished hitting the bags their knuckles looked like raw mince. The showers were freezing and the roof leaked. The place reeked of sweat and faded glory. It was also the first rung of the ladder to something better. It was a ladder the young James Murray eagerly climbed.

James Murray was born in Newmains in Lanarkshire, twelve miles south-east of Glasgow. He had an older brother David, and a younger brother and sister, Roddy and Janie. Like many people in the area, he left school at sixteen. He had no great ambitions; his first jobs were in the building industry and in pubs with his father, but he liked neither. Slowly, he edged his way into the local boxing scene. He fitted the profile of the classic Scottish boxer: a wiry frame with dense muscle mass and a chiselled face that looked older than its owner's years. And like many diminutive Scottish boxers – most notably Thirties' world champion Benny Lynch – he soon discovered that he packed a formidable punch.

At nineteen, Murray got a job as a council gardener in Motherwell, but his first love remained boxing. His heroes were the Puerto Rican fighter Roberto 'Hands of Stone' Duran and American Sugar Ray Leonard, men who had risen from humble beginnings to be world champions. Murray dreamt of these men at night as he lay in bed. He dreamt of buying his family their council house and his sister a new car for her birthday. He made plans on the back of his fists.

Like many boxers, he held down a full-time job in addition to training and fighting. He went on a four-mile run every morning at 5.30am – whatever the weather. In the evenings, after work, he'd train in the gym and watch video tapes of his fights. He became fitter, and his body harder. His style became more assured and confident.

It was a dedication that paid off. Murray won the Scottish ABA bantamweight title in 1992 and turned professional in March, 1993. His first fight was against a boxer named LC Wilson, and he won it convincingly. In November, 1994 Murray won the vacant Scottish bantamweight title, defeating Shaun Anderson on points. In March, 1995 he retained it by beating Louis Veitch with a third-round technical knockout in front of hundreds of fans in Glasgow's SECC arena.

A couple of impressive victories followed, one of which involved a spot on the Frank Bruno bill in Glasgow's Kelvin Hall. By now he was getting attention from press and promoters alike; he was a boxer whose time had arrived. He had a record that any fighter would be proud of – sixteen fights; won fifteen; KOs in five; lost only one. James Murray was ready for a crack at the British title.

In January, I drove out to Newmains to meet James Murray's family. His parents, Margaret and Kenny Murray, are not wealthy people; they live in a former council house in a housing scheme in a town lying in the curious hinterland between Glasgow's suburbs and the countryside. The French photographer Robert Doisneau had a phrase for such an area; he called it 'the vague terrain'...

The first person I meet is James's mother. She sits, still grieving, in the family living room, underneath a huge photograph of James. The neighbours bought it for the Murray family instead of flowers. We talk briefly and quietly, but she can hardly bring herself to answer any of my questions. James had been the apple of her eye. 'The whole family is in pieces,' she says. 'It'll take God knows how long for all of us to be able to really talk about it.'

I am taken by James Murray's 26-year-old brother David to a pub nearby to meet his father. Kenny Murray is sitting in the deserted lounge drinking a pint of beer. He is suspicious and cautious at first, but after a while he opens up. 'I always knew Jim was special,' he says. 'I don't mind talking about him ... it gives me pride. His council workmates worshipped him, you know. They still have pictures of Jim on their walls.' I sit talking to Kenny Murray for hours. We are interrupted only by customers from the bar who insist on buying Kenny drinks. I ask him how he's been since his son died. 'I have a wee cry to myself sometimes,' he says in hushed tones. 'Sometimes when I go home at night, when I'm sitting in the house by myself with just that big photograph of Jim looking at me, I find myself wondering ...' He rubs his head as the words trail off.

'The dog still looks for him,' he continues. 'It used to sleep on the bed with him. Now he's gone, it wanders about whining for him; it's as if it knows he's dead.'

We sit listening for a minute or two to the noise from the television in the next room. Kenny Murray is like many men I know from this area: proud, decent and not given to putting words to his feelings. He nods in the direction of the crowd next door.

'I talk about our Jim a lot: they probably want me to talk about something else. I can understand that,' he says. His eyes fill with tears and he shakes his head. 'But it's hard, you know ...' We sit in silence.

*

James Murray's trainer was Dave 'Gypsy' Douglas. Douglas had been a boxer himself; between 1978 and 1987 he fought 48 professional contests, becoming welterweight champion of Scotland. He enjoyed the distinction of being the only boxer to win the title and successfully defend it. Although Murray had other coaches when he was an amateur, Douglas worked with him for three years and was very close to him.

'He was a gentleman,' says Dave, sitting in his house above the Clyde Valley in Lanarkshire. 'Like a second son to me, too.' Photographs of the dead boxer hang on the walls; another sits on top of the television. Douglas fetches a video of Murray fighting Louis Veitch last year and puts it in the VCR. Within minutes his daughter, Margaret-Ann, is in floods of tears and his wife is in despair.

'He was shadow boxing out there in the hall on the night he fought Drew Docherty,' says Helen Douglas.

Douglas drove Murray into Glasgow that night. Since he was Scottish champion and fighting at the top of the bill, he had been allocated his own private dressing room at the Hospitality Inn. Murray, however, insisted on changing with the other fighters, and Douglas says the atmosphere was good in the room before the fight. Murray had been lying on the bed cracking jokes; he was on good form.

'The day before the fight he bought new gear – boots and shorts,' says Douglas. 'Someone in the sports shop in Glasgow told me Jim had balked at the price, but the owner insisted that he take the best-quality gear for his big night.'

Like Kenny Murray, Dave Douglas seemed to enjoy talking about the boxer; only in the moments of silence that punctuated his conversation did he become sad and reflective. He tells me he had to take months off from training after Murray's death; the thought of going back to the dingy gym without his protégé hurt him too much. He'd briefly thought about giving up boxing, but he'd reconsidered. He's reconciled James Murray's death with the notion that death came from something other than a blow to the head from another boxer.

'Drew Docherty didn't kill Jim Murray,' he says. 'I think he had a weakness somewhere in his head – something that was there. He wasn't hit by any devastating punches.'

Alex and Katherine Morrison are the father and daughter who managed and promoted James Murray's fights. They operate from a workmanlike gym in a deserted area of Glasgow's East End. From the front it looks like just another brick-fronted garage, but inside, past the lorries and the mechanics, are the offices where the Morrisons run a profitable and successful boxing business.

The walls to their offices are lined with photographs and paintings of boxers. A life-size picture on the wall opposite me shows a young Muhammad Ali in his prime. Another photo shows a smiling Jim Murray standing with the Lord Provost of Glasgow and Drew Docherty at the pre-fight press conference.

'I'll never forget that fight,' says Katherine Morrison. She is small and pretty with big eyes and an earnest manner and is the only female boxing promoter in Scotland. 'I mean, I'm only 27 – I don't know many people who have died. It's hard when you're talking to a person one minute and they're dead the next.'

More than 500 boxers have died around the world since the Marquis of Queensbury Rules were introduced in 1884, including such recent casualties as American Gerald McClellan and 23-year-old Eastender Bradley Stone. I ask Katherine Morrison whether she considers boxing to be a brutal way to make a living.

'No, I don't,' she replies. 'If I promoted show jumping, it's still the same thing – it's a dangerous sport. I don't make anyone do it [boxing].' She wouldn't be drawn further.

Katherine's father, Alex, who managed James Murray, is well-known in Glasgow boxing circles. He's been in boxing – promoting, training and matchmaking – for the last sixteen years. When we begin talking about Murray, Morrison seems troubled and distant. He rubs his head and his gaze wanders around the room as he speaks.

'I had a premonition that something might happen in that fight,' says Morrison. He has a head of cropped silver hair, and wears a red jacket and matching waistcoat. 'I never felt good about it from start to finish. I'm not the same about boxing as before – I've lost heart.'

Outside, on an empty, silent Glasgow backstreet, a shaft of light from Morrison's office shines down on his prize possession: a Rolls-Royce. He opens the door and I dutifully look inside. I touch the seats, smelling the leather upholstery. 'Wearing a new suit, getting into one of these . . . there's nothing like it,' he says, softly. Anyone could see how a hungry young boxer like James Murray would have been impressed by a manager like Alex Morrison.

When the doctors at Southern General Hospital established that James Murray was technically dead, family members and close friends said goodbye to him in their own private ways. He lay in a hospital bed, linked up to medical equipment. Only a small medical swab on his head suggested he'd been through surgery.

One of the last to visit Murray was his trainer and friend Dave Douglas. 'I can't remember what I said,' says Douglas. 'I just kissed him and left him – he looked like he was sleeping.'

Alex and Katherine Morrison also went to see the boxer. 'When I went to say goodbye to him in the hospital he had never looked better,' recalls Alex Morrison. 'He had a great tan and the cuts he'd sustained had cleared up . . . he looked unbelievable. And yet it was the worst moment of my life.'

'His brother came out of the room where James was and threw himself at me saying, "He's dead, he's dead!"' says Katherine Morrison. 'We were in a room with his family. I can't forget the noises his sister was making; she couldn't say anything – they were all in shock.'

Shortly afterwards, Kenny Murray decided to donate his son's organs. It was, by his own admission, a spontaneous gesture. 'If a transplant could have helped Jim, we would have been grateful,' he says. 'I asked the family what they thought and they agreed. Several people benefited from Jim's organs.'

The family were paid the £5,000 fight fee and, in due course, will receive a £50,000 insurance fee Murray is entitled to under

BBBC insurance agreements for professional fighters who die through injuries sustained in boxing. Kenny Murray says he wishes now that he had also taken the *Sun*'s offer of 'tens of thousands of pounds' for exclusive rights to his son's story. 'Jim would have wanted us to have done it,' he says. 'He knew how hard money is to come by.'

Local people in Newmains have collected nearly £6,000 towards a £10,000 statue which they plan to erect in the town. The bronze memorial will show a life-sized James Murray in full boxing outfit and will be sited at the town's main crossroads. Murray's workmates in Motherwell have also raised £8,000 for medical equipment at the Southern General Hospital.

The week after Murray died, Drew Docherty visited the Murray house with his manager, Tommy Gilmour. It was an emotional visit. As he left, Kenny Murray shoved a poem into Docherty's pocket to encourage him; it was entitled 'Don't Quit'. The last verse reads:

> Success is failure turned inside out,
> the silver tint of the clouds of doubt.
> And you never can tell how close you are,
> it may be near when it seems afar.
> So stick to the fight when you're hardest hit;
> it's when things go wrong
> that you mustn't quit.

The words echoed the advice Kenny Murray had given to young boxers at a press conference a few days after his son died. 'Keep boxing and stay off drugs,' he urged. 'Remember: Jim Murray did not die with a needle in his arm. He did not die up a backstreet.'

Three months after James Murray's death, I am sitting with his parents in the living room of a family friend watching a televised fight. Drew Docherty is fighting for the WBO world bantamweight title against champion Daniel Jimenez from Puerto Rico. Docherty battles bravely over twelve rounds only to lose on a points decision. The Murrays are genuinely sad he hasn't won.

from the fight, Docherty is interviewed by a ringside commentator. 'I wasn't only fighting for myself tonight,' he says. 'I was fighting for ...' and then his voice breaks off. He starts to cry.

THE WILD ONE

Alex Kershaw

August, 1993

Asked recently on BBC's *A Question of Sport* to name the activity in which Gary Havelock is world champion, Ian Botham grinned inanely, shook his head and fired off the standard obscurities: bowls, shooting, archery ... What? Speedway? You must be joking.

In the Seventies, when speedway captured crowds matched only by football, David Coleman could have expected a snappier response. But that was a golden age, when speedway's 'powder-hall heroes' dashed off columns for tabloids, when 100,000 packed Wembley to watch four men slide around a dirt track at 70mph without brakes. Back then, Gary Havelock would have been a household name, a regular fixture on Weetabix packets, a serious contender for Sports Personality of the Year. Today, the pigtailed 24-year-old with a penchant for Buddhist symbolism dominates a forgotten sport.

Since winning the National League tournament with Middlesbrough in 1985 when he was sixteen, Havelock has both enthralled and exasperated the decimated ranks of speedway's die-hard fans. In 1986, he became British under-21 champion. A year later, he was European under-21 champion. Then, in 1988, he smoked a couple of joints at a party. He was banned for five years for failing a random test a week later, and his career looked to be over before it had barely begun. His sentence was suspended on appeal, but Havelock still spent 1989 in the stands.

Then, in August 1992, Havelock made a remarkable comeback,

becoming the first British rider since Michael Lee in 1980 to win the World Speedway Championship and the first to do so on his debut since Welshman Freddie Williams at Wembley in 1950. He mounted the winner's podium in Poland's Wroclaw Olympic Stadium with dreadlocks and beads in his hair. But there is more to the Gary Havelock saga than soft drugs, guts and gritty returns from speedway's wilderness. On the stooped shoulders of the young rider from Eaglescliffe, Cleveland, now rests the future, some insist, of a long-neglected sport as dangerous and compelling as IndyCar or Formula One.

Gary Havelock arrives to collect me from my hotel in a blue Escort festooned with ribbons. It's 5pm on a Saturday and he's fresh from his 26-year-old sister Lisa's wedding, sporting tails and a carnation. In three hours' time, he will captain Bradford's Coalite Dukes in the second leg of the 1993 Premiership Trophy against the Reading Racers.

Minutes later, I'm watching rugby league in Havelock's £73,000 Barratt-style home in Marton on the outskirts of Middlesbrough. A three-foot-high silver World Championship cup, engraved with names from speedway legend, takes pride of place near a carved wooden chair, a gift from Poland which Havelock calls his 'throne'. On the wall hangs a letter from John Major which praises Havelock for 'valiantly' overcoming an injury during the World Championship.

'There's the speed, the smell of the track, the characters,' says Havelock, explaining his 'life-long obsession' with speedway. 'There's no feeling like pelting round sideways at full-throttle, inches from the safety fence, with no brakes.'

Havelock has fractured more bones than he's had birthdays since his evenings as a dewy-eyed rider, fresh out of school with five O-levels on an Enterprise Allowance scheme, riding for Middlesbrough in the second division. Unlike his father, Brian, who first rode for the Newcastle Diamonds in 1971 at the age of 29, Havelock had barely finished teething when he first straddled a motorbike. 'As soon as I could walk,' he recalls, 'I was at speedway tracks with my father. I was three when I got my first bike.'

Waist-high, Havelock was winning grass-track events. But he was also crashing with alarming regularity. 'Mum was worried after I'd been in hospital a few times,' Havelock remembers. 'Dad had a word with me when I was eleven. He told me either I stay on the bike or stop racing.'

In 1984, at fifteen, Havelock applied for a speedway licence, saying his date of birth was September 4 rather than November 4, 1968, so he could qualify for the first full season with the Middlesbrough Tigers. Tim Swales, Havelock's first promoter and now chairman of the British Speedway Promoters' Association, remembers Havelock 'bursting onto the scene as a super-sub'. 'Gary was obviously special,' says Swales. 'He would play cat-and-mouse with other riders, sometimes waiting until the fourth lap to come from behind and win.'

After two seasons with the Tigers, Havelock signed for Bradford's Coalite Dukes, lured by the promise of first division purses and a wider, faster track – the size of arena he would need to master to become World Champion. 'I really struggled at first,' he says. 'The main difference were the starts and first corners. No one gave an inch.'

Just as 'Wonder Boy' Havelock began to scrape wins in top-flight speedway, in October 1988 he tested positive for drugs during the British League Riders' Championship. 'I'd had a couple of joints on the Monday before the Sunday race,' Havelock admits. 'I was nineteen. There were lots of people doing the same in speedway at the time. People said you could only trace it [marijuana] for three days. I didn't know it could stay in your blood for six to eight weeks.'

Attacked mercilessly by the *Speedway Star* as the embodiment of speedway's moral decline, and shunned by all but a handful of riders, Havelock was banned for the 1989 season. 'It was pretty bleak,' he says. 'I blew most of my savings. Only my family, the Dukes' fans and self-belief got me through. On reflection, the year made me stronger. I sorted out my values. Up until then, my life had been a walk in the park – everything had come my way.'

'It was very much a possibility that the authorities could have banned Gary for life,' points out Allan Ham, manager of the Dukes. 'He was perhaps unlucky in that speedway wanted to make an example of someone. But the Board of Control gave him a second chance and now he's highly respected. He's a classic example of a bad boy come good.'

In March 1990, Havelock returned to speedway – his face harder, his hair inches longer – and instantly recaptured the form that had made him the best prospect since Kenny Carter in the late Seventies. Only an electrical failure came between him and the British Championship two months later. And after ditching his underpowered Weslake engines, he saw the season out almost undefeated as captain at Bradford. 'The club's turned round since he became captain,' says Allan Ham. 'We've had success ever since.'

But as the 1990 season drew to a close, Havelock was back in the *Speedway Star*'s headlines, again 'facing action'. Hauled before the Speedway Board of Control following a complaint from a spectator, Havelock, it was alleged, had exposed himself in public. 'I wasn't even riding,' Havelock protests. 'We'd had a few pints. The meeting was over and we went for a piss against a fence. Next thing I know I'm being accused of running around with my dick out.'

Havelock was promptly banned for five years. While appealing against the Speedway Board of Control's decision, he received yet another summons. This time Havelock was asked to explain his alleged involvement in the wrecking of a hotel room in Czechoslovakia. Havelock protested his innocence and won his case. His ban, meanwhile, was reduced to six months, although he was forced to pay £2,500 in costs.

He returned to race again on May 1, 1991, a week before the British Championship semi-final. Two weeks later, he won the British final after picking up a maximum fifteen points from five rides. 'Winning was a fantastic feeling – a real two fingers to the Establishment,' grins Havelock. 'Afterwards I decided to become Mr Clean. It was obvious someone somewhere wanted me out of speedway. I knew I'd have to be a really good boy to stay riding.'

We leave for Bradford's Odsal stadium, home to the Coalite Dukes, in Havelock's touring van: a Ford Transit converted to accommodate a bed mounted behind the back seats. Scott Trigg, Havelock's blond, 21-year-old New Zealand-born mechanic, sits next to me in the back. Havelock, wearing red jeans, a black long-sleeved T-shirt and an earring, casually swigs from a Lucozade bottle. In less than a year, says Trigg, the Transit has done 50,000 miles. 'It's been 200 kilometres from Chernobyl,' adds Havelock, 'and did a total of 4,000 miles in five days, to Russia, Poland, Czechoslovakia and back.'

Above the van's bed, huge 300-watt Pioneer speakers thump bass. Further back, behind a partition, stand Havelock's three bikes. Methanol-fuelled, like Mansell's IndyCar Lola-Cosworth, they may look like souped-up scooters but are actually precision instruments, costing as much as top-range Harley Davidsons. Their 500cc engines are tuned to perfection by Neil Evitts, an 'expert tinkerer' who now rides for Wolverhampton.

'A good tuner can make all the difference,' says Trigg. 'Gary's bikes are modified, the tread on the wheels changed, depending on the surface conditions of each track. You need a lot of power but also traction to build up speed. Slick tracks without dirt can be dangerous – there's not much grip. Bradford's a good track because there's a lot of different lines and it's wide. The guy out of the gate first doesn't always win.'

As George Michael blares out, Havelock chats about Ying Yang Records, the label he set up last year. The Chinese symbol, he says in his adenoidal Teeside drawl, adorns the sleeve of his first twelve-inch rap single, 'The Champ'. 'I like the image. It's the contrast between good and evil – sort of sums me up,' says Havelock as he lights another Silk Cut and we veer into the A19's fast lane.

The pits at Odsal stadium are not much more than a 100-metre-long corrugated iron shed. Minutes before the first race, Trigg crouches over one of Havelock's bikes, a spanner in his hand, his face a study in concentration. Suddenly, the guttural whine of revving fills the pits. A few seconds later, several mechanics insert earplugs as the din of sixteen 500cc engines at full throttle becomes overwhelming. Methanol fumes begin to poison the chill evening air.

The Reading Racers were the most successful team last season, winning the League and BSPA Cup. In August 1992, their star rider, 27-year-old Per Jonsson, established Odsal's track record of 58.3 seconds for four laps. Tonight, Jonsson swaggers with confidence, his leathers a frenzy of Day-Glo colours and sponsors' logos. Runner-up to Havelock in last year's World Championship, Jonsson is, if anything, a more consistent league rider. The Swede's points average per meeting in 1992 was 10.30 compared with Havelock's 9.32.

Gary Havelock looks tense. As he pulls his face-mask and goggles on and lifts off his pink and black chequered saddle cover, I spot the acid-house Smiley symbol on his knee-pad. He then mounts his bike, threading his scarred right thumb through a loop of string attached to the throttle. Should he crash, the 70hp Giuseppe Marzotti engine will automatically cut out.

At the centre of Odsal stadium, a cavernous bowl of steep grey terracing, a troupe of goosepimpled schoolgirl cheerleaders shiver in the biting wind. A few minutes later, the 3,000-odd crowd stand for the national anthem and then, before the race, Havelock is sworn into the Bradford Dukes' Speedway Hall of Fame.

Pebbles of shale spray spectators as Havelock, riding number three for the Dukes, skids home inches behind Reading's Armando Castagna in the first of his five races. Cowering as near to the trackside as safety permits, I'm splattered by mud and struck by speedway's sheer velocity as Havelock blurs past me sideways at a corner, his agility and balance superb as he 'locks up' at 70mph, his left knee hovering only centimetres above the track.

Several races later, tempers are fraying in the pits. Havelock has just been edged into second place in the eleventh heat by the ice-cool Jonsson. Twenty-two-year-old Sean Wilson, riding number five for the Dukes, is beating a back wheel with a hammer, more in frustration, I suspect, than in an attempt to realign its bent rim.

His blond bob flopping into his eyes, 'Hard Core' splashed across his backside, Wilson is, after Havelock, Bradford's most colourful rider. After beating veteran Phil Crump at his home track during a Test match in Australia in 1987, Wilson was accosted by Crump and knocked off his bike. The incident sparked a mass brawl in the pits, which has since entered speedway legend.

'Gary's a great guy,' says Wilson between drags from a cigarette. 'I've known him since I were six, I reckon. One of me best mates. He doesn't flash off. Got 110 per cent will to win. Good guy to have on your team.'

It's 9.30pm. The Dukes' first home meeting of the season has ended in defeat to Reading by eight points. Havelock has amassed a respectable ten points from his five rides, but Per Jonsson has racked up a maximum fifteen. While Havelock showers, his girlfriend, 22-year-old Jayne Cloney, raps her fingers on his Transit's dashboard, impatient to catch the last hours of Lisa Havelock's wedding reception. Cloney is wearing black leggings and a down jacket, and her eyes are soft, thoughtful and warm, her blonde hair pulled back.

'Living with a speedway rider is a lonely life,' says Cloney. Since she met 'Gaz' in 1985 at a race in Middlesbrough, she has dreamt vicariously, shared Havelock's highs and lows, sobbed her heart out, squeezed his hand on journeys to hospital, longed for his 1000-odd races a season to end.

'Of course, I worry all the time,' sighs Cloney when I mention the death of 23-year-old Wayne Garratt, whom Havelock had known well, after a crash in Newcastle in September 1992. 'But Gary says, "What else can I do? It's my life." After a meeting, I always wonder whether he's going to come into the bar or be in an ambulance.'

'If you take any group, say of three speedway riders,' Havelock had told me, 'you'd find they've broken twenty bones between them. We've all seen crashes and deaths. But hey, when your cork pops, it's time to go. Could happen any time ... All my life, my Dad's always instilled in me that I should win at all costs – that second place isn't good enough ... Fear is something that holds you back ... I once saw a documentary about Muhammad Ali. In his own mind he had the burning belief that he just could not be beaten. Ali didn't know the meaning of fear.

'I now have a few rules in life,' Havelock adds. 'Number one is that you should never underestimate the other guy. Speedway is about such short, sharp bursts, like sprinting, that, if you're not 100 per cent on the job, anybody can beat you. The second comes from the film *Roadhouse*. Someone said they needed to go to bed, and this guy said that you can get all the sleep you need when you die. The other rules I can't repeat.'

At its aptly located AGM in Tenerife last year, speedway's ruling body voted Havelock Rider of the Year. 'The accolade capped a breathtaking year in which Gary may well have been the most successful World Championship entrant of all time,' gushes 22-year-old Philip Lanning, editor of *Speedway Mail* and the son of celebrated Seventies speedway commentator Dave Lanning. Indeed, last year Havelock won the British semi-final, the British final, the overseas title and, of course, the world title. 'I was on the podium for every major speedway event,' he says. But had it not been for an astute physiotherapist and tight bandage-tape, Havelock would still be an unconventional rider with a shady past, earning less than a Bradford rugby league player. Nine days before the Commonwealth final in June 1992, for a split second, Gary Havelock thought he was dead.

Making a guest appearance in the Polish league, Havelock was hit from behind by a 'crazy Pole' at 70mph. 'My whole life flashed before me,' he recalls. 'I did about four somersaults, broke a bone in my hand and ripped my fingers up. My helmet looked like Freddy Kruger had taken a swipe at it. The Pole snapped his arm in two. Between screams he said sorry and that I'd be out for eight weeks. I said, "Not a fucking chance, mate. I'll be riding in nine days."'

His physiotherapist Brian Simpson recommended laser treatment for the swelling on his hand, and Havelock managed to pull through the Commonwealth final, a vital qualifying round for the World Championship, with two taped-up fingers and a thumb gripping his throttle.

Before the overcast morning of August 29, 1992, Gary Havelock was the 'Gazza of Speedway', his nickname 'Havvy', a synonym for wayward potential. By late afternoon in Wroclaw's Olympic

Stadium, he was what he had always said he would be: the best speedway rider in the world.

'It was a fairy tale, the most dramatic win I've seen,' says Philip Lanning of Havelock's World Championship victory. 'If you turned it into a film, it'd be a blockbuster.'

'The morning of the final,' recalls Havelock, 'I just knew something was going to go off. I changed before the first race in a small room on my own where I put my dreads on. I knew if I went to the starting-line for the first race against Per Jonsson and he thought, "Shit, what's he look like?" then straight away his head wouldn't be right.'

Havelock's start was his best. Within seconds he had left Jonsson, the pre-race favourite, trailing metres behind. In the eighth heat, however, 'disaster struck'. Havelock's left leg was clipped by the debris of a spectacular back-straight crash between Zdenek Tesar and Slawomir Drabik. His calf muscle torn, Havelock hobbled back to the pits supported by his father and Brian Larner, a mechanic. Then, as he lay in agony refusing to go to hospital, the 'heavens opened'. For over an hour, a storm washed out Wroclaw stadium.

Inch-deep puddles had been pumped dry by the local fire brigade when Havelock finished second to Drabik in a re-run of the eighth heat. And then, suddenly, victory in his next race over Gert Handberg, a gifted Dane, put the World Championship within Havelock's grasp.

'I just sat very still in the pits, meditating,' says Havelock. 'It suddenly hit me – I only needed third place in my last race to clinch it. Scott [Trigg] told me to get my shit together. I walked to the bike in a daze. As they pushed me onto the track, I thought, "Get a fucking grip, kid." I was out of it. I nearly puked in my helmet.

'I was off gate two, the worst all night. The green light came on,' continues Havelock, tears welling in his eyes as he takes a deep drag from a Silk Cut. 'I dropped the clutch. It flew like a dragster – whoosh. I just thought, "Please keep going, bike, please keep going." And then I'd crossed the finishing line. Union Jacks were everywhere. It was too much. Joy, relief, ecstasy – too many different emotions.'

As Havelock completed a victory circuit, his family and pit crew wept in a huddle. Twenty-four-year-old Brian Larner was, says Havelock, especially 'choked'. Larner had been Yorkshireman Kenny Carter's mechanic in the early Eighties. Carter had been England captain and the great white hope of British speedway, and only the World Championship eluded him before he blew himself and his young wife away with a shotgun in 1985.

Havelock's victory in Wroclaw by three points not only pushed his arch-rival Per Jonsson into second place but also earned him a £3,500 winner's cheque and provided a much-needed fillip for the national side, eclipsed for much of the Eighties by the Scandinavians. 'At 24, Gary's now the oldest rider for England,' points out Philip Lanning, seated in the *Speedway Mail*'s drab offices on a grey industrial estate in East London. 'His victory gave every young rider hope. The Scandinavians had monopolised speedway, passing the World Championship around them for far too long.'

Ironically, Havelock's breezy surfer's image, his garish John Richmond designer 'gear' and dreadlocks, once the emblems of Speedway's Bad Boy Who Threw It All Away, are now being used to draw back the crowds. His cheesy grin has already featured in two million posters pasted up around Britain this season. 'Ivan Major, who was six times World Champion [in the Seventies], said that after I won the World Championship I should not change my character,' says Havelock. 'The last thing I needed, he said, was a suit and a haircut.'

'As long as Gary doesn't make another record and he stays on the bike, there's no limit to what he can achieve,' jokes Radio One DJ Adrian Juste, a lifelong speedway fanatic. 'He's nowhere near his best yet. One day, he could be the same sort of figurehead in speedway as Ian Botham was in his sport.'

But the efforts of GJR-TUSK, the promotion company behind the posters, and Havelock's undeniable appeal may be too little, far too late. The only underground organisation he belongs to, Havelock once joked, is the Save British Speedway Association. Recession has gnawed deep, with four tracks closing in the past year and a pay freeze imposed on riders by promoters.

Gary Havelock may earn £40 a point and could rack up £70,000 this season as World Champion, but most first division riders, says *Speedway Mail*'s Philip Lanning, 'will be lucky to take home £20,000 this year'.

Nor has Havelock's victory in Poland impressed television producers and sponsors as much as was hoped. 'In some ways, Gary's victory hasn't really happened yet,' concedes Tim Swales, chairman of the Speedway Promoters' Association. 'Even when he became champion, I was told speedway was still a minority sport and didn't matter.'

Havelock himself suggests that speedway's current problems stem mainly from promoters who 'got greedy in the Seventies', demanding money from television companies who then turned their cameras on snooker and bowls instead. For his part, Philip Lanning castigates 'second-hand car dealers who ripped the sport off', a 'crisis of credibility' following a 1985 *Sunday People* exposé of rigged races, and the 'changing nature' of leisure.

'People used to watch football on a Saturday and speedway midweek,' says Lanning. 'Now they stay in and watch the wrestling on the box.' Even in Poland, where 40,000 braved grimy Wroclaw to witness Havelock's heroics, speedway's woolly-hatted rattle-shakers are fast ebbing away.

It's 1am at MacMillan's nightclub in Yarm, a village outside Middlesbrough. A tipsy Gary Havelock sits at a Yamaha organ, his arm around Danny Nangolain, a Jakarta-born martial arts expert. Nangolain is crooning Phil Collins' 'In The Air Tonight' and his bride, Havelock's sister Lisa, a poisons expert at Guy's Hospital in London, beams with embarrassment.

'Danny's amazing,' Havelock confides later. 'He spent a year training in North Korea with a Master, running in snow with just his shorts on. He'll stub a cig out on his wrist and not flinch.'

Unlike his new brother-in-law, Gary Havelock does show pain. It's not a physical hurt that I see flicker across his hungover features the following afternoon over roast beef and Yorkshire pudding in a local pub. Nor a malignant resentment of 'just a couple of people high up in speedway' who, he insists, tried to scupper his career. 'Nigel Mansell became a World Champion last year. So did I,' says Havelock with some bitterness as he forks a roast potato. 'I've achieved as much in my sport as he has. But you'd never know it.'

Should Havelock become the first Englishman to retain his world title this August in Pecking, Germany, he will be the last to do so under the present system. From 1994, the World Speedway Championship will adopt a grand prix formula. 'People are talking about six events around Europe and possibly $100,000 as prize money for each meeting,' says Havelock. 'There's also the prospect of real television coverage.'

When I ask about the future, Havelock shrugs his shoulders and sips a Coke. He'd like to try a car out for size, maybe trade speedway, one day, for a different challenge. He just wants to get faster, grow, keep finding himself. In a week's time, he smiles, he'll finally make Bill Beaumont's team on the BBC's *A Question of Sport*. 'I believe in progression, in taking risks, in never getting stale,' he says. 'I'd love to see speedway back where it was when I fell in love with it as a kid. Apart from that, I'd like to get up to Ivan Major's record of six world titles.'

It's high noon on the first day of British summertime. Havelock is driving me to Darlington train station and talking about Bruce Penhall, the English rider who quit speedway after the last World Championship to be held at Wembley in 1981. As a public relations manager for Oakley leisure wear, one of Havelock's sponsors, Penhall now lunches with film stars in Los Angeles. 'Bruce once appeared in the American police show *Chips*,' smiles Havelock. 'His character was called away from a speedway meeting to catch some crook. Bruce made it back to the track just in time to win the day.'

As Gary Havelock leaves me waiting for a train, I notice his gait for the first time. It's that of a cowboy who, mounted on the back of a bucking 500cc engine, has performed more victory 'wheelies' than any rider of his generation. It's the saunter of a man who has finally lassoed his critics, of a reformed outlaw putting a Hollywood fizz of glamour back into a dying sport.

Blood Sports: At America's fifth ultimate fighting championship, above and below, the bare-knuckle savagery knows no bounds. *Barry Lewis/Network*

Escape to Victory: left to right,HMP Kingston's Mick, Bob, Nigel Wheeler (PE officer), Craig Dobson, Andy, Trevor, Kevin Pratt (officer), Phil Sussex (captain), Nigel (surnames withheld at prison's request). *Tim Richmond*

Macho the day: left to right, Neil and Graham celebrate a Santos goal. *John Running*

Mexican Rave: Neil and Graham with a Santos star. *John Running*

Lone shark: Carwyn Williams in the deserted seas off County Kerry, surfing's last frontier. *Conor Horgan*

Speed thrills: horrific injuries, a dope charge and a bad attitude almost wrecked Gary Havelock's career on the track. *Julian Broad*

Death of a boxer: Murray takes a blow to the head from Drew Docherty.
Wattie Cheung

The end: Murray collapses and the referee stops the fight. *Wattie Cheung*

Return to Senna: looking out at his last Grand Prix start, San Marino, 1994.
Dario Mitidieri

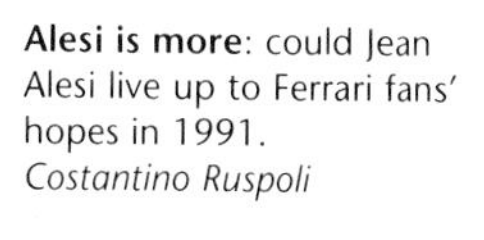

Alesi is more: could Jean Alesi live up to Ferrari fans' hopes in 1991.
Costantino Ruspoli

Cape crusaders: cricket has provided South Africa with a potent symbol of both hate and hope. *Denis Farrel/Associated Press*

Village people: Bob 'Zimmer' Cooper taking a last drag before striding out to the crease – winning isn't everything. *Henry Bourne*

Hit or missile: Australian batsman Dean Jon under fire from Sussex bowler Tony Piggott Hove, 1989. *Adrian Murrell/Allsport*

Ring True: Max Schmeling's victory over Joe Louis in 1936 was hailed by Hitler as a triumph for the master race.
Associated Press/ Topham Picturepoint

Heavy duty: he's British and he's bad. Can Lennox Lewis break America's hold on heavyweight boxing?
Kim Knott

She's got balls: from the *Sport* to Birmingham City Karren Brady is in a league of her own. *David Eustace*

The sky's the limit for Premier League clubs perhaps. But for Third Division Rochdale FC, survival is the goal. *Simon Buckley*

BELLES OF THE BALL

Pete Davies

August, 1994

In the week before the Women's FA Cup Final, the Doncaster Belles joked that since they'd be live on Sky they'd better all get their hair done and put in time on the sunbeds, but there was nothing frivolous about the state of them in the dressing room at half-time. Their knees and thighs were mud-streaked and raw, their lungs hungered for air, and they stared at the floor with red, sweat-smeared faces looking angry and bewildered. They were 1–0 up but they were playing like zombies and they were disgusted with themselves, and their manager Paul Edmunds was disgusted with them too.

Three years a pro, so he knows what he's talking about, Edmunds stood tight-lipped and seething, voice cracked, half gone from shouting in the dugout. 'We've got out of jail there, I tell you, we've got out of jail, 'cause we've played *absolutely useless* out there,' he says. 'You've disappointed everybody – yourselves, me, all the people coming to support us – because we look as though we're *second best to everything*. It's *embarrassing*. We're standing, the ball's bouncing, and they're in and away, *gone*. We went fifteen minutes and we haven't won *one tackle*. All over the field. And *stupid free kicks . . .*'

Edmunds singled out only two players for praise, the two who'd kept them in the game: keeper Tracy Davidson and Louise Ryde at centre half. 'Louise,' he said, 'wants to win so badly, gets there, wins it, gets up and does it again, *and other people aren't doing the same*.' An attractive blonde police officer from Kirkby, Ryde had said the evening before that sometimes, being about the only senior Belle who'd never had a call-up for England, she had a confidence problem. But then her mother told her once, 'You never played for England, so what? You were British Tae Kwon-do Champion for seven years, weren't you?' She was playing like a champion today.

It was April 24, a bright, gusty afternoon at Scunthorpe's tidy new Glanford Park ground, and 1,674 people had come expecting the Doncaster Belles, the best women's football team in the country, to stomp all over Knowsley United from Liverpool. They were undefeated in seventeen games; they'd scored eleven once, scored ten four times (before the cup competition was seeded they once won a game 46–0); and when they met Knowsley in the league they'd beaten them 7–1. But Knowsley were fired up, after half an hour the Belles lost their captain and midfield engine Gillian Coultard with a calf-pull, they were out of shape and nervous – and anyone who says women can't dig in and battle should have watched that second half.

Both sides had a goal disallowed, both hit the woodwork, and when the final whistle blew the Belles remained 1–0 up. Afterwards they said it could only be good for the women's game. If they'd won by a hatful people would have dismissed it, said it wasn't competitive – and they were angry with themselves, sure, but they said they never did seem to perform well in finals 'because people expect so much of us'.

The Belles have been in eleven of the last twelve Women's Cup Finals, and won six of them. They succeed on an abundance of skill allied to unstinting hard work, but more importantly on a family kinship, a collective *joie de vivre* that's jubilant and infectious. In the other teams, they say, players move around, one club to another, always looking for something. But whatever it is, at the Belles they've found it. Once a Belle, always a Belle.

There are now some 12,000 women playing football in England, in approximately 450 clubs. The ten clubs in the Premier Division in the '93/'94 season were the Belles, Red Star Southampton, Ipswich Town, Stanton Rangers, Knowsley and Leasowe Pacific on

Merseyside, along with Wembley, Wimbledon, Arsenal and the Millwall Lionesses in London. The Belles' strongest competition comes from Arsenal, a side widely held to be (surprise, surprise) a joyless bunch of robots – but standards of competition have risen all round in recent years. Compared to other countries – current world champions the US, or the semi-pro set-ups in Italy and Scandinavia – the women's game here is still played on a pitiful shoestring. But if commitment and ability were reckoned in pennies and pounds, these players could never be thought of as amateurs.

They are amateurs, of course – the nearest any Belle gets to the professional game is left back Chantelle Woodhead, who works for Leeds United and has her kit sponsored by Howard Wilkinson. Among the others, there's an accountant and an upholsterer from Birkenhead, two policewomen from Liverpool and Birmingham, two working in the potteries for Royal Doulton and Wedgwood, and another two who work in banks.

Gillian Coultard, who's played for her country 75 times (more than any other woman), and stands exactly five-foot-nothing tall, is a Bryan Robson figure with a shot on her from 30 yards that, if I was the keeper, would send me ducking for cover. She makes gas valves in a factory in Leeds for a living. Like other Belles she's had offers of money to go abroad, but she's turned them down. She says she has a good job and wants to keep it because there aren't that many going. And anyway she is, she says, 'a homely person'.

Work and weather permitting, the players travel to Doncaster twice a week for training on Wednesday night and for matches on Sunday. Striker Gail Borman comes from Hull. 'If I counted up how much I've spent over the years travelling I'd be rich,' she says. 'But if you love something you do it, don't you?' Right back Mandy Lowe, who spends her days putting lids and handles on dishes and bowls at the Eagle Pottery, says: 'I'd prefer to travel and play for the Belles than stay in Stoke and play for some other lot.'

Leading scorer Karen (Kaz) Walker (before whom the others regularly chant, with bowed heads and outstretched arms, 'We're not worthy, we're not worthy') works in Income Support for the

DSS. 'It can be very stressful,' she says. 'It's a relief playing football. It's a relief coming home from work full stop. But I love playing football.' Including the winner in the Final against Knowsley, she'd scored 32 goals in eighteen games, and Andy Gray on Sky compared her to Mark Hughes. 'Nah. I'm better than him,' Walker cried out, mock-outraged. She said she sat next to an England international at a dinner once, and she couldn't believe it. 'He makes all that money and he's that *thick*.'

They had a crew from the BBC living in their pockets through the end of the season. In the Doncaster Moat House on the Saturday evening before the Final, the director, Paul Pierrot, gave them a camcorder so they could make some of their own documentary. They looned about using hotel room keys for microphones, running mock interviews.

'So, are you fit for the game?'

'Yeah, the back's fine.'

'Never mind the back, I meant your head.'

They went off to their rooms early to watch TV. 'Great, innit?' said Dave the cameraman, looking around. 'The women go off to watch *Match of the Day* and the men are left sitting about gossiping.'

In the morning, team jester Joanne Broadhurst took over the camera and said it was 'Anneka's challenge: you've got 24 hours to bring the Cup back to Doncaster.' On the coach coming back after the game, challenge accomplished, she interviewed 'the great Kaz Walker', and asked her to run us through the goal. Walker went into Neanderthal mode. 'I hit it. It went in. We won,' she grunted. And they sang until my ears were splitting:

When we went to the FA Cup Final
We really put on a show
We showed them a brand of football
They really want to know
We're representing Donny
And we're proud to do or die
Arsenal couldn't do it
'Cause they didn't qualify

They had a party at Doncaster's Le Bistro. Women at a disco usually dance around their handbags; this lot had the FA Cup to dance around – when they weren't drinking lager from it, anyway. 'Right. That's one pot out of three,' said Paul Edmunds. Arsenal won the treble last season, and the Belles weren't having that again.

I asked Paul Pierrot why he was making his film, and he said that when he was doing a series about Sheffield United three years ago, he happened to watch a women's international match at Bramall Lane.

'It was really skilful, people taking people on – it brought a lump to my throat,' he said. 'So I went and saw the Belles, and I was captivated. It was at Armthorpe [a colliery pitch where the Belles play when they can't get Doncaster Rovers' ground] and it was lovely. You had the coal mine looking down and the mine was on strike, and there were these women playing super football and all the families coming to watch because it was the one good thing that was going, the Belles giving them a lift each week.

'And when they came off they were changing in the welfare club, and they still weren't allowed to play on the snooker tables, and I just thought that summed it up. Here were these women who for the most part are derided – like, it's not a *real* game – and yet they were bloody good.'

They're long accustomed to leering numbskulls asking if they swap shirts after the game. Before the Cup Final, Louise Ryde said that maybe they should, and give the idiots something to look at. 'But I better not suggest it with this lot,' she said, gesturing at her team-mates, 'because they probably would, too.' When she was at police training college she played in a men's game, cadets versus staff, and at one point, when she got the ball wide, she heard the opposition keeper say, 'Don't worry, it's only a woman.' So she cut in and belted it past him. 'I bent his fingers back all right,' she said, with considerable satisfaction.

Mandy Lowe plays football with men too, lads from her works, in a five-a-side on Friday afternoons at Staffordshire University. Slim, fast, feisty and strikingly good-looking, she juggled the ball round big men with a grin on her face. I asked one of them about her after the game. 'Before she started playing with us, we'd heard she was good, but we didn't expect her to be that good,' he said, with a sheepish smile. 'She's better than the lot of us by far. Fitness, strength, skill – she's got it all.'

Women have, in fact, always played football – a pioneering organiser with the deliciously apt name of Nettie Honeyball played in a North versus South fixture at Crouch End as early as 1895 – and during World War One, women who worked like men (and who wanted to play like men too) began forming teams from Plymouth to Sunderland. They played matches for war relief charities and the premier side of the day, Dick Kerr's Ladies from the eponymous munitions plant in Preston, raised over £50,000 in five years. When they played St Helen's at Goodison Park on Boxing Day, 1920, they drew a crowd of 53,000 – 10,000 more were turned away.

But with the war over, this success began to stick in male craws. In 1921, behind the cover of unsubstantiated and apparently malicious allegations that some of the charity money was going astray, the FA banned the use of league grounds for women's football. Without decent grounds to play on, the women's game was stifled, and they played on in unattended silence.

It took exactly 50 years for the FA to change their mind – they rescinded their ban in 1971. Meanwhile, two years earlier, a teenager named Sheila Stocks was selling Golden Goals tickets at Doncaster Rovers games and decided she fancied scoring a golden goal or two herself. With a group of friends she founded the Belles, her father became club secretary, they started winning five-a-side competitions, and in the club's 25th year, Sheila's still sitting on the subs' bench today. She's also married the manager; they have a beautiful four-year-old daughter, and Paul Edmunds says the only difference between coaching men and women is that in the men's game your players don't too often go and get pregnant on you.

The Belles won their first Cup Final in 1983; in the absence of an organised national side, they also represented England that year. Three years ago, the Women's National Premier League was formed; last year the FA agreed to take over the administration of the women's game. But on the evidence of the first women's Final held under their auspices, the FA still have a bit to learn. Despite the presence of Sky's cameras, neither club got a penny for their efforts; they were given a mere 30 tickets each. More risible yet, it was announced towards the end of play that Kaz Walker was 'Man of the Match'.

They have, in fact, no desire to be compared to men; they play a different game, they play it in their own right, and anyone who sees it with open eyes will become, I'm sure, an immediate convert.

The first women's game I watched was England beating Slovenia 10–0 on a bright Sunday morning at Brentford's Griffin Park. The result put them into the quarter-finals of the UEFA Championship this autumn (if they make the semis, they qualify for the 1995 World Cup), but it was the effervescent style of it that won me over. One thoroughly impressed Brentford man was moved to lean over to where the subs were warming up and say: 'Here, you wouldn't mind turning out for our lot next Saturday, would you?'

The attraction of it lies in the fact that, lacking the driven speed and fanatic physicality of the men's game, women players who are every bit as skilled have more time to apply that skill – so you get more passing, more deftness, more grace and more goals. And second, they don't go out to cripple each other. It's not soft and they're committed, but you don't get the elbow, you don't get players leaving their legs in late; what you get, instead, is people enjoying themselves.

A week after winning the Cup Final, the Belles were back at Belle Vue in Doncaster playing Millwall in the league, and they enjoyed themselves no end. Paul Pierrot miked up the referee and out in the middle Joanne Broadhurst was giving it some lip, so the ref told her she better mind her language because he was carrying the microphone. She smiled sweetly and told him: 'So fucking what?' She's got a touch of Kathleen Turner about the face, this girl, and her through balls are a dream.

Besides, the ref was irking them. The Belles' sweeper Michelle (Micky) Jackson played Millwall neatly offside and the referee said to her: 'That was good. Where d'you learn that? Arsenal?' Word of this reached the dugout, and the man was dismissed as a patronising donkey. 'Does he think we can't work out offside for ourselves?' And being, shall we say, a tad portly, the next time the ref was near a voice rang out: 'Eat salad, fat boy.'

After 30 minutes they were 3–0 up, at half-time it was 4–1, and in the dressing room it was mightily more cheerful than it had been at Scunthorpe. Sheila Edmunds worked over a knock on Tracy Davidson's knee; her husband looked about him and said: 'Right. Everyone else OK? Any knocks?'

Beside him Joanne Broadhurst grinned and said: 'I've jarred me snatch.'

'I can't do nothing about that,' Edmunds snorted.

'Now then, I'm very pleased to be 4–1 up, and as a contest the game should be over with. But don't go out and sit back. After 3–0 we just stood about. I'm sat up in the stand thinking, is the game over now? I couldn't believe it. So lift it, get hold of the ball, shout, encourage. We've done well, played some lovely football, so just lift it and enjoy yourselves.'

'Right,' said Kaz, 'let's lift it. Let's all shout like you want it. Even if you don't.'

Sweat dripped, studs clacked on tiles, hurried fingers checked laces and shinpads. Joanne Broadhurst chanted the mantra ('Enjoy yourselves. Stay on your feet. Watch the line') amid rising cries of 'C'mon yellows'. They bundled out and won it 6–1.

In the other dugout, Millwall's manager was a friendly bloke named Jim Hicks from the Football in the Community Programme. His team will be handy when they grow up – at the moment their average age is about nineteen, and the two subs he sent on were only fourteen. 'Whenever you play the Belles you're intimidated,' he said. 'It was pretty quiet in our dressing room beforehand, because they've got so much respect; at the moment there's no one to touch them.'

He stood on the sideline after the game in the May Day sun, and put the whole business in a nutshell. 'When you come to play the Belles, you could play eight across the back – I suppose you could try and stop them that way. But that's not what women's football's about, is it? They don't get paid for it, so what's the point? And it's very hard as a manager to get negative in this game. They're not playing for greed or ego, the skill element's high, and you don't have that brutal physical element.

'It is,' he said, 'just so enjoyable.'

ONE TRACK MIND

Richard Williams

September, 1991

You're 27 years old, and good-looking: that striking Sicilian mixture of intense blue eyes, thick dark hair and a nice build on a compact frame. You're rich: even after you've insured the £150,000 sports car you have on order, you'll still be a millionaire. There's a pretty blonde girlfriend called Lulu; you'll get married in September, if there's time. You have a loving family that gives you a place where you can always feel safe. And outside this motorhome where you're sitting now, just behind the ranks of giant transporters and the piles of tyres, there's a small red single-seater car with your name painted on the side, next to the yellow shield with a rearing black horse that proclaims to the world that this is a Ferrari. It's waiting for you to get in and win a race. This race. The San Marino Grand Prix, round three of the 1991 Formula One World Championship.

You are Jean Alesi, and it's hardly any wonder that everybody hates you.

Well, not quite everybody. Those 10,000 Italians camped out on the muddy bank above the long, sweeping right-hand bend called Rivazza, for instance. For the moment, you're all they care about. You're their boy.

In these parts, less than an hour's drive from the holy city of Maranello, anybody who drives a Ferrari is their boy. Some more than others, though. Take your team-mate, Alain Prost. He's been world champion three times – but driving for McLaren, your biggest rivals. Last year, in his first season with Ferrari, Prost won five

Grands Prix but couldn't keep the championship out of Ayrton Senna's hands.

So the fans, known as the *tifosi*, aren't too sure about his ultimate commitment. They hear him complaining about the way the team is run, about the handling of the car, about the weakness of the engine compared to Senna's Honda, and they long for simpler days, when Gilles Villeneuve just got into the car and drove the hell out of it, whether it had all four wheels attached or not.

The *tifosi* like you, though. They like how you look, the fact that your name ends in a vowel, the way your driving reminds them of Villeneuve. Most important of all, though, they like you because you haven't had the chance to disappoint them yet.

You like that. You don't mind them tugging at your sleeve and begging for autographs. You can see why your older rivals find it a bore. Your best friend, Nelson Piquet – another three-time champion who right at this moment is making eyes at a nubile girl from behind the smoked glass upper window of his team's motorhome – can act as jaded as they come, while Nigel Mansell, whose seat at Ferrari you took, tends to make his progress even through an empty paddock with the bullocking head-down rush of a man taking on the All Blacks' front row. But you're young, and you're enjoying the warmth of stardom. 'It's not so 'eavy,' you say.

Actually, being a Ferrari driver has never been easy. One by one, Enzo Ferrari fell out with most of them. The great Juan Fangio won a world championship for him in 1956, but they never had a good word to say for each other. Phil Hill followed Fangio to the championship in 1961, but was shown the door a year later. John Surtees took the title for the team in 1964; less than two years later, in mid-season, he was making a hurried exit – another victim of the politics and jealousies that old Enzo encouraged as a particularly diabolical form of creative tension.

Look at the ex-Ferrari drivers hanging around the paddock here at Imola, on the morning of the race. How many of them left with laurels unsullied, with the team's thanks and valedictions ringing in their ears? Over there, talking to a TV interviewer in the McLaren pit, is Niki Lauda, who dragged Ferrari out of the doldrums in the mid-Seventies, permanently disfigured himself in the process and still left the team without honour. Trundling his wheelchair into the Williams team's motorhome is Clay Regazzoni, who brought Lauda to Ferrari but found himself unceremoniously ousted. Here are a couple of Frenchmen, René Arnoux, the quick Grenoblois who flattered to deceive, and courtly Patrick Tambay, who sorrowfully took the seat of the dead idol Villeneuve and immediately won a race in memory of his great friend before losing the job in another political reshuffle.

And talking to everyone, looking to pick up a drive even though we are now three events into the season, there's perky Stefan Johansson, a born racer, whose career has never recovered from a couple of barren years at Maranello during the Eighties.

Of the currently active pilots, three are ex-*Ferraristi*: Michele Alboreto won three races for them in five years, and now galumphs at the back of the field in something called a Footwork; Gerhard Berger, his confidence blown after a mere four Ferrari victories in three seasons, traipses around in the wake of his current team-mate, the near-divine Senna; and Nigel Mansell, who won his very first race for Ferrari to an explosion of joy across Italy, is permanently on the brink of calling the whole thing off if the press won't be nice to him. No, a seat in the Ferrari Formula One team may still be what you'd give yourself, with your eyes open and in full possession of the historical facts, but it isn't something that you'd put your only son down for.

Enzo Ferrari, after all, didn't really like drivers; and when he did take a shine to one he was apt to praise him not only for his 'progressive spirit' and 'the calm assurance with which he drove', but also for 'the equanimity with which he was prepared to face death'. Enzo Ferrari himself may be gone, but the morbid mood lives on.

Jean Alesi knows all this. He knows that the 10,000 fans up on the bank at Rivazza are thinking that no Ferrari driver has won the world championship since Jody Scheckter in 1979. He knows they suspect that Prost is a busted flush, his motivation gone. He knows they've camped out in the mud and spent billions of lire on flags, banners, caps, scarves, badges and stickers at concession stands since Thursday night in the expectation, not merely the hope, that you, Jean Alesi, will win the race and go on to take the title.

So, in the shadow at the back of the pit, you smooth the fireproof balaclava over your head, pull the helmet on, step carefully into the cockpit, wait as your mechanics pull your safety harness tight, and give the hand signal to fire up the engine. You nose car number 28 out into the pit lane, wait for the light and blast out on to the warm-up lap under a lowering sky. And then, two minutes later, just as you come round to take your place on the starting grid, it begins to rain.

At school in Avignon the little French boys and girls called him 'Spaghetti'. He hated that. He couldn't understand it. His father was as good as theirs, with a thriving coachbuilding business employing 40 people.

There was something he could do about it, though. He'd been christened Giovanni, the second son of Franco and Marcella Alesi, immigrants from the little Sicilian town of Alcamo, halfway between Palermo and Corleone. He was proud of that, but he was prepared to make a sacrifice. So, a few weeks short of his sixteenth birthday, Giovanni became Jean Robert. And the insults stopped.

They may have done the work, though, in helping to give the family an unusual closeness. After school each day, Jean and his brother José spent a couple of hours at the body-shop, learning their father's craft. Sometimes they'd help straighten out a car that he'd bent in a weekend rally. Occasionally he'd enter one of the big events – even the Monte Carlo. They couldn't help but be infected by his enthusiasm.

Alesi started racing go-karts at fourteen. Two years later, when he left school, he was taken on by his father as an apprentice. By the age of eighteen he had a certificate and his first car, a white Fiat 500. 'It was quite fantastic,' he says now. 'It was so small you could pass people everywhere. I modified the car, of course. I put in much stronger springs, and I changed the engine a little bit to get more horsepower. In Avignon, I had quite a lot of fun with that car.'

Bearing the dents and dust from Alesi's teenage autocross practice in the field behind the Carosserie Alesi, the Fiat 500 still resides in a corner of the shop.

Eventually the go-kart races were followed by the series for modified Renault 5s, by Formula Renault single-seaters, and by Formula Three. It was then that Alesi came to the attention of Eddie Jordan, the remarkable Irishman who manages individual drivers and now runs his own team of Formula One cars. 'I've always been interested in talent-spotting,' Jordan says. 'We have a computerised system of analysing drivers – what they're doing, what equipment they've got, who they're racing against. A form sheet, if you like. Nobody else does that. All I noticed about Jean in 1986 was that he was very erratic. Then in 1987 he was run by his brother José, who was a calming influence. He won the French Formula Three championship. Then he spent a year in Formula 3000. That was a disaster. There was a considerable difference of opinion with his engineer. It was a major problem.'

At the end of 1988, Jordan and the Alesi brothers bumped into each other at the annual Formula Three jamboree in Macau. Jordan had a budget from Camel for Formula 3000 the following season, and had booked Martin Donnelly for one of the two seats. José talked him into giving Jean the second seat. 'You have to understand that Jean is a special kind of person,' Jordan says. 'His speed is obvious now, but at the time he was very difficult. He'd always been surrounded by his family, and he was used to having things done for him, to getting his own way. Now I have a very strong sense of the way I want things done. I wanted the commitment. I wanted not just his control of his body but I wanted his mind too – because I believed that psychology is such a major part, probably 80 per cent, of current sportsmanship. And there, I felt, was an area in which Jean wasn't doing himself justice.

'He saw what we were doing. We were winning a lot of races. I was under a little bit of pressure from the sponsor to take another driver, but I stuck my neck out in the belief that Jean had the raw talent.

'He was very aggressive, quite arrogant, self-centred, but with a massively kind nature. It was like two different personalities pulling at each other. Jean is the kindest person you could meet, but in the car he's completely ruthless. And that's what you need.'

Two races into the 1989 season, with only a fourth place and a spin-off to show, Jordan lost his temper. 'I went fucking berserk with him. I said right, that's it. You're coming to England. You may be a star in your own environment, but the more you hear people saying, "Oh, you're fantastic," the more likely you are to get carried away.' So Jordan put Alesi up in his own family's house in Oxford, got him a trainer and subjected him to a regime of physical and mental toughening.

'I wanted him, among other things, to see the mechanics grafting themselves to death every day to make sure that he and his team-mate had the best cars. And when we got to the third race, which was at Pau, near his home town, he was refreshed and mentally aware, and he won it. There was no turning back then – he was dynamite after that. It was like turning a switch,' says Jordan.

Only a week or two later, Alesi's career was raised yet another gear. Ken Tyrrell, the veteran Surrey timber merchant who guided Jackie Stewart's career, had fallen out with one of his drivers, and a seat was going begging for the French Grand Prix at Le Castellet. Camel was also Tyrrell's main sponsor, and approached Jordan to borrow Donnelly. No, said Jordan. Donnelly was already down to substitute for another injured driver at the Arrows team. How about Alesi?

'Ken Tyrrell,' Jordan says, 'is the first to admit that he'd never heard of Jean. But I convinced him. And he was very straight with Jean. He said, "You must realise that it's very unlikely that you'll qualify for this race." So it was a great moment when he ran second and finished fourth.'

Naturally, Tyrrell wanted to hang on to such an impressive young man, but Jordan insisted that he complete the Formula 3000 series –

which he won – and take the Tyrrell drive only when he had no clashing commitment. At the end of the season, though, Jordan sat down with Tyrrell and negotiated a three-year contract for Alesi.

Alesi began the 1990 season with one of the most audacious moves seen in Formula One racing. At the first Grand Prix of the season, in Phoenix, he qualified fourth and held the lead for almost an hour. On the 34th lap, though, Ayrton Senna caught up with him and went by on the entrance to a 90-degree right-hand bend.

Such is Senna's psychological dominance over the Grand Prix field that when he overtakes you, you are supposed to stay overtaken. Not Alesi, though; not this day. Within 50 yards the upstart had snapped back at the Brazilian, repassing him into the next corner. Senna, stung by such temerity, used his experience and the greater power of his engine to put an end to the duel, but the point had been made. Then, in May, Alesi took everyone's breath away when he slammed his Tyrrell inside Prost's Ferrari down the hill from Casino Square at Monaco, and again finished second to Senna.

Now, after only a handful of Grands Prix, serious people were talking about Alesi as a future world champion. Talking too much, as it happened. Soon, various team managers were queuing up to meet the young driver behind the Tyrrell motorhome.

Alesi himself was soon persuaded that, with its out-of-date engines and its limited resources, a Tyrrell was not the proper vehicle for a potential champion. And his lawyer told him that in his contract there was a clause allowing himself to buy himself out. So, unusually early in the season, he quietly signed an option to partner Riccardo Patrese in the Williams-Renault team for 1991. But then Ferrari came knocking at his door, and Alesi heard that Frank Williams had been talking to Ayrton Senna and Nigel Mansell. He panicked.

'It was very difficult,' he remembers now. 'Tyrrell said, "You can't leave me" – but it wasn't true, because I had just to pay the buy-out. But he tried everything to keep me. And Frank Williams at this time was not a gentleman. He signed with me, and afterwards tried to have Senna.' Pulled this way and that, Alesi made a bad mistake: on the eve of the German Grand Prix, he called a press conference to ask the media to stop speculating about his future. They thought that was a bit rich, coming from someone evidently capable of having his signature on three contracts simultaneously. 'Fortunately,' Alesi says, 'Ferrari found a solution.' By which he means that Marlboro and Fiat, who bankroll Ferrari's unlimited budget, came up with the several million pounds it cost to pay off both Tyrrell and Williams, and to provide Alesi with his retainer for 1991.

'Those three months were very, very hard,' he says of the period of uncertainty. 'Too hard, because there were no results for the rest of the season. Too much pressure.' Maybe so, but he came out of it a millionaire. And what did he learn? 'A lot. I don't want to be rude but if I explained everything, some people would be a little bit angry.'

Ken Tyrrell's view is somewhat different. 'Jean became dissatisfied with us probably because large amounts of gold were being hung in front of him,' he says, 'and everybody kept telling him that he was going to be a star. To some extent it went to his head. The temptation was too great. He was a very impressionable young man. There was plenty of time for him to go to Ferrari or some other team that he might consider to be better than us.'

Tyrrell remains, though, generous in his opinion of Alesi's talent, unhesitatingly drawing on four decades of experience to compare him favourably with the very greatest post-war drivers. 'I don't know what it is that makes some people able to perform at the top of their profession. It's just a gift. Fangio, Stirling Moss, Jackie Stewart, Jimmy Clark, Alain Prost, almost certainly Senna – they didn't have to try. Life seems so unfair, doesn't it? Jean has exceptional skill and car-control. The physical and mental effort isn't a problem for him. He knew exactly how he wanted his car set up, and he could communicate that to the engineer. The only thing he really lacks is sufficient experience in Formula One racing. When he's got another season or two behind him, he's going to become a very difficult driver to beat.'

Alesi likes his car set up for oversteer, what the old-timers used to call 'opposite lock' or the 'four-wheel drift'. He brakes late, throws the car into the corner under power. It's an extremely exuberant style; a young man's style. Alain Prost, on the other hand, brakes early, feathers the throttle, opts for a softer setting in handling.

Alesi has sometimes said that he prefers the qualifying sessions to the races themselves, which sounds odd coming from such a sharp-toothed competitor. 'No,' he says, 'what I meant was that for me the pleasure is to play with the car. So I don't like to do a race, 70 laps alone, bbrrrrrr . . .' He makes a droning noise. 'But to race with another driver, to try to overtake each other, is another thing. It's fantastic, even if it's 80 laps. You can play, you know?' As he says this he puts his hands out, palms down and parallel, sliding back and forth like a couple of racing cars going neck and neck. 'So qualifying is the same thing. With the qualifying tyres the grip is good, and the special engines are so strong. It means that you can play with the car.'

Is he ever frightened? Some of his top rivals, after all, have said that without constant fear it is impossible to reach the highest level. 'No. Not at all. Well, only when I know that I'm going to go off the track and hit something. *Ça me fait peur, pour un instant – le dernier instant.*' (That frightens me, for an instant – the last instant.) So not when you're sitting it out wheel to wheel with someone, say at 150mph into the fearful Peralta curve at Mexico City, or Silverstone's Copse Corner? 'No! Then I'm happy! That's the difference!'

When he does leave the track, though, the consequences are bleak. 'For one minute afterwards I'm incapable of doing anything at all.' But later he'll go back to the family home in Avignon to hide and take comfort in long cross-country runs.

Alesi has a lot of charm, and it seems unforced. In his suede jerkin, polo shirt, jeans and loafers, he's more like one of the dozens of kids parading in the soft early evening through Imola's Piazza Caduti per la Libertà than a millionaire sporting idol. But you can tell that he really hasn't had an easy time of it lately from the ready way he speaks of getting friendly with Nelson Piquet through mutual need.

'He's a little bit like me. Last year, he was all the time alone in his hotel. He eats alone, he has no friends.' (Hardly surprising, given the widely publicised allegations the Brazilian had made about Senna's sexual preferences, and his remarks about Mansell's wife and other topics.) 'And me, I'm just with my brother. It's difficult for me to have friends because drivers like Ivan Capelli, for example, with four years in Formula One, expect to go to Williams or Ferrari now, and I came after just one year and I take this seat. All the drivers of my age are a little bit jealous. So I can't have a friend. And Piquet was alone, and he spoke a little bit with me, and I had a lot of respect for what he did, and now we're close. We spend a lot of time together.'

The rain lashes down on the starting grid. Mechanics are everywhere, hurriedly fitting heavily grooved wet-weather tyres in place of slicks. But when the 26 cars move off on the parade lap, the Ferrari team-leader, winner of seventeen more Grands Prix than anyone else in history, simply falls off the track, sliding across the grass and stalling his engine. To the dismay of all Italy, Prost unbuckles himself, gets out and begins a weary trudge back to the pits.

The race starts without him. Patrese takes the lead, followed closely by Senna. But on the third lap there is further disaster. Alesi, challenging hard, takes fifth place from Stefano Modena. But just a few seconds later, braking for a left-hander, he gets a wheel on the greasy kerb and slides gently off into a sand-trap.

Less than five minutes into the race, both Ferraris are gone. In the pits, Ferrari president Piero Fusaro puts his arm round the shoulders of his nervy, histrionic team manager, Cesare Fiorio, and leads him away. Fusaro looks like there's something on his mind; in a week's time he will announce the removal of Fiorio, replaced by a three-man committee with Piero Lardi Ferrari, Enzo's son, at its head.

On the bank at Rivazza, the *tifosi* begin to pack up. By the time Ayrton Senna has stroked his McLaren halfway towards his third consecutive victory of the season, all you can see is grass and litter.

UP HILL AND DOWN DALE

Chris Hulme

January, 1996

The chairman of Rochdale Supporters Club is standing inside the giant refrigerator where he prepares the deceased for their final journey. A stainless-steel trolley, a surgical hose pipe and two bottles of bleach sparkle under the bright lights. The walls and ceiling are lined with white plastic, and a drain borders the brown, tiled floor. 'You get some awful cases in here,' says Frank Duffy, 53, grimacing. 'Some that's fallen and cracked their heads. Some whose backsides have fallen out with all the haemorrhaging. Awful. You have to wash it all off.' Duffy, a short, friendly man, is the first to admit that funeral directing is the kind of work that can get you down. If nothing else, the dead are a constant reminder of the Grim Reaper's wanton impartiality – striking us out regardless of the sense of loss we might inspire or, indeed, our own wishes to remain in business.

Duffy copes with the stress of the job by involving himself in the affairs of Rochdale Football Club, four miles down the road. 'The football has always been great for me. When my sons were growing up I could take them to Rochdale. They were able to play football on the terraces while I watched the match – there weren't that many spectators.' He took over running the supporters club five years ago. Over 400 members raise money for the team and travel to away fixtures together. By any reasonable measure, they are a dedicated bunch. Stories of fans who have their ashes scattered at the celebrated theatres of soccer, such as Anfield, are quite commonplace. It happens at small clubs too. 'There was a chappie who died last year,' says Duffy. 'He'd hung on for us to get promotion. He would not die. When he eventually passed away, the club agreed to have his ashes. They wouldn't let us scatter them on the pitch, so we dug a hole and put them under the penalty spot at the home end.' Duffy breaks into a smile. 'The vicar was brilliant. He was one of those who would stand in the pulpit and say: "You should be supporting Rochdale!"'

The Pennines provide commanding views of Rochdale. The hills that landscape much of northern England surround the town on three sides. Rochdale was once an important centre of textile manufacturing and, in 1844, gave birth to the co-operative movement. The history seems long gone, with the centre of town now slowly metamorphosing into a Stepfordesque shopping precinct.

There has been a professional football club here since 1907. The team attracts around 2,000 of the 100,000 people living in the immediate area, though its existence is otherwise scarcely acknowledged. No road signs point the way to the club's stadium, Spotland, and none of the shops sells replica Rochdale kits. Remaining in business in the basement of the Football League has never been easy – but it is especially difficult in this part of Lancashire. Within a radius of 30 minutes' driving, local people can currently reach five Premier League clubs – Manchester United, Manchester City, Blackburn Rovers, Leeds United and Bolton Wanderers. The gates of Liverpool and Everton are just one hour down the M62. To say nothing of Oldham Athletic in the First Division, Burnley in the Second Division, and Bury in the Third Division. Rochdale stands at ground zero in Britain's soccer metropolis.

The club's financial health has been under siege for some time. Changes in the economic structure of English football over the last few years have removed all but a small percentage of a once healthy subsidy. Rochdale fought back by broadening their financial base – launching a lottery and scratchcard business. This revenue, however, has been hit hard by the National Lottery. The fiscal goal posts have been rattled in other ways. In September, the European Court passed the Bosman judgement (due to be confirmed in

January 1996) that makes it illegal for clubs to demand a transfer fee when players reach the end of their contracts. In effect, this presents a club like Rochdale with an unpalatable choice. They can put the entire first-team squad, plus all the youth players, on long-term contracts and so guarantee that they will always be in a position to receive a transfer fee – an impossibly expensive option. Or they can keep footballers on one-year contracts, the norm at smaller clubs, but risk losing them for zero compensation. That, too, is a costly option as the club will often have spent several years developing a player. At a stroke, the judgement has destabilised a traditionally valuable source of income, throwing into yet harsher relief the continuing viability of many small clubs.

There are other problems – but perhaps nothing to forewarn visiting reporters about Rochdale's chairman, David Kilpatrick. Approached for an interview in the directors' lounge at Spotland, the chairman looks at the tape recorder and promptly walks away. He is not upset about the opening match of the 1995/96 season, Rochdale's 3–3 draw with Cardiff City, which has just finished. No, Kilpatrick simply loathes the media, apparently because someone has been making patronising remarks about his club.

After a few moments, Kilpatrick paces back. He is 52 and tall enough to have to lower his head during most conversations, habitually running a hand through his grey hair to keep it off his spectacles. He has contempt for outsiders who criticise the administration of the club. If they are so clever, he says in so many words, they should put their money on the table and see if they can do better. He is open to offers. There is no money in the town. No one should expect them to be like Manchester United. Rochdale is a success on its own terms. The old main stand was horrible, decrepit (we are standing inside its £1.5 million replacement). Kilpatrick shakes his head as if to say, 'You don't know the half of it.'

A group of Asian gentlemen, known in football circles as the Kumar brothers, interrupt to say their goodbyes. (They acquired Cardiff City in July, having previously owned Birmingham City, a club they sold to David Sullivan after losing millions in the collapse of BCCI.) After they leave, Kilpatrick peers from a window at the car park below. 'They've all got Rollers,' he laughs. 'The directors here have only got XJ6s.'

Later, the chairman buys me a drink. Kilpatrick accumulated whatever fortune he possesses in the granite business. He refuses to say how much his involvement in Rochdale costs, but is clearly exposed to a few quid. In today's programme, team manager Mick Docherty writes: 'When you are a close-knit family like we are at Rochdale, everyone knows everyone else's business. The club has suffered financially over the last six months and during the summer it is no secret that David Kilpatrick and his fellow directors paid the wages of all Rochdale Football Club players and staff out of their own pockets. We need to double our gates. I ask that you not only attend next Tuesday's [match], but please bring a friend.'

Thursday, July 27. Rochdale are leading Manchester United 2–0 and are about twenty minutes away from a memorable victory – even if this is a pre-season 'friendly', played behind closed doors at United's training ground. After all, Rochdale have not beaten one of England's leading sides in living memory and only ever fleetingly stepped off the bottom rung of Football League. The team's manager, Mick Docherty, has seven players on the bench, all longing for a taste of the action. Late in the game they take to the field, but McClair, Irwin and Pallister give Alex Ferguson's team a 3–2 victory. Afterwards, Ferguson buys the Rochdale squad lunch, and everyone goes home happy, unaware of the tremendous fuss the work-out will cause. Cantona's appearance seems to have contravened the Football Association ban he is serving. The Frenchman reacts by asking for a transfer. Ferguson has to fly to Paris to persuade his touchy superstar to return.

At least the goodwill generated by the fixture has not worn off in Rochdale. Two weeks later, and with the new season kicking off the next day, Mick Docherty smiles at the recollection. 'Fergie is terrific, a very nice fella. We talked about the season, what players I've got, what I'm looking for. He couldn't have been more helpful. The lads absolutely loved it, too. They were watching the United players running by and going, "Him, fifteen grand a week. Him, twelve grand." Just having a laugh.'

The Rochdale manager has a windowless office in the main stand at Spotland. He shares it with his assistant coach – and with the home and away kits, which are stored on pine shelving along one of the white-painted block walls. Docherty is 5' 7" and in great shape for a 45-year-old. He has spent his entire working life in football, playing for Sunderland, Manchester City and Burnley. So much soccer, but he was still impressed by the visit to Manchester United. 'You look at their training facilities – this wonderful complex, with an indoor and outdoor pitch, a big gym, showers, meeting rooms and upstairs there's food in the canteen. It's another planet. After training, our lads go for a butty at the corner shop.'

Rochdale do not have any training facilities. 'We go where we can . . . schools, parks and council fields. The weather plays a big part. You come in some mornings and it's pissing down; you've got to look for a gym somewhere because all the pitches are waterlogged. Sometimes we can't get anywhere and just end up going for a little road run, or do circuit training under one of the stands.'

The club employs nineteen professional footballers. 'That's not many. If you get a couple of injuries, or a suspension, you're down to the bare bones,' says Docherty. 'We can take a player on loan. But you're only allowed five a season. You've got to use them sparingly because it's a long season and towards the end you might need someone.' Rochdale's top players earn around £20,000. Win-bonuses can add about £2,000 to this figure. Five of the first team were in a strong enough negotiating position when they joined to receive a cut of the transfer fee – adding another few thousand over the length of the contract. The players are not sufficiently famous to be supplied with complimentary boots, let alone paid for endorsing brands. Their perks do not even extend to larking around in hotels. The expense involved (between £800 and £1,000 each night) means that for all but a handful of fixtures, Rochdale trundle to away matches in a hired coach that has to be returned the same day.

Docherty is open and good-natured, apparently none the worse for growing up in the shadow of a famous father. Tommy Docherty managed Chelsea and Manchester United in the Sixties and Seventies. Within four weeks of leading the Old Trafford side to victory in the 1977 FA Cup Final, 'The Doc' was sacked over an affair with Mary Brown, the wife of the club's physiotherapist. Tommy Docherty achieved little with the numerous clubs that furnished the rest of his career and today works the after-dinner circuit. 'My dad was always the first to cross the line,' says the Rochdale manager, smiling. 'I'm a bit steadier. We do have the same values. I like a laugh and a joke, at the right time. My life has mirrored his to a certain extent – playing and then management. I have also been divorced in my forties. I drive over to see him and Mary when I can.'

Mick Docherty has not inherited his father's Glaswegian accent – he was born in Preston. He does, however, share a penchant for short, quick sentences. Docherty only slows down when discussing the recent collapse of his marriage. 'Twenty-four years,' he says. 'There was no one else involved ... simply pressure brought to bear on all fronts. My good lady couldn't handle it any more. I tended to put a lot of my energy into the game. It's sad for me. A sore point.'

Living alone in Burnley, Docherty spends most of his time working. 'I go to as many Premier League matches as possible. Maybe ten a season. I know a lot of the managers because I played with and against them. You can be in and out of a job in such a short space of time in this game. You need to put yourself about. I'm not under contract here. They could sack me tomorrow.' It has happened before. 'I've been hard done by, in my opinion, when I'd felt I'd been very loyal and very hard working.' Docherty pauses briefly, his eyes flaring. 'I left a good job and Burnley to coach at Hull City. I thought I was bettering myself. Going to a Second Division club, with better money, better security. I felt it was the right move for me and my family [Docherty has two grown-up daughters and a teenage son]. It proved not to be. The manager was sacked within six months. His replacement, Terry Dolan, brought in his own people. So I was out of a job.'

Having spent four years as assistant coach, Docherty took over managing Rochdale last January. The most expensive footballers at his disposal both cost £25,000. A much-discussed deal on the day we meet is Andrei Kanchelskis' transfer from Manchester United to Everton for £5 million. Kanchelskis' wages are reported to be £13,000 a week. The entire wage bill for the 42 people employed by Rochdale amounts to only £11,000 a week. Not that any of the Rochdale players are complaining. Docherty has a pile of documents two-inches thick on his desk, detailing the footballers that clubs want to off-load.

The pile may become thicker in the wake of the Bosman judgement. 'It is still early days but if it comes into effect, a lot of clubs will go to the wall,' says Docherty. 'I don't think we'll feel the consequences of the decision until next summer. A lot of players will be out of contract and I think myself and all the managers in the Third Division will be vying for the same fifteen or twenty footballers. Some will already be on our books, some won't. It's going to be very hectic.'

Alan Reeves was the last Rochdale player to depart for the big time. Rochdale acquired him on a free-transfer from Chester City in 1991. Reeves was sold to Wimbledon three years later for £200,000, plus £1,000 for every appearance he makes up to 100 games. The money would be petty cash at most Premier League clubs, but it was a bonanza at Rochdale, representing around two seasons' worth of gate receipts.

The idea that money cannot buy success makes Docherty laugh. 'If you gave me two million quid, I could guarantee you two promotions. I would get you in the First Division with that much brass.' Most of the 72 professional clubs outside the Premier League are, he believes, capable of reaching the top flight. 'If you can get from the bottom division right to the top, you've pulled off a miracle,' reflects Docherty. 'It requires massive investment over about ten years. You need the right backing, the right players and a stadium you can fill. The clubs that have done it, like Carlisle and Swansea, have generally come straight back down again because of money. The players they had were good enough to get them to the top division, but not good enough to keep them there. If you want to stay in the Premier League, you have to pay the best possible wages for the best possible players.' Why bother reaching so high, when Rochdale have never won anything? 'Have you no ambition? I want to do well in this job. If we can create a successful side, it will generate more public interest, which will give the directors more money. They'll give some back to me for new players and off we go.'

Saturday, August 12. Cardiff City have arrived for the opening game of the season. Their fans have a reputation for wrecking stadiums (even their own) and one Welsh radio journalist confides that there might be trouble. 'They were relegated last season and probably think, "We're a big club, we shouldn't have to play in a dump like Rochdale."' An hour before kick-off, a coach packed with Welshmen appears, but empties peacefully into a pub.

To step through the Rochdale turnstiles is to find a clean and well-maintained sporting arena. The four stands face an immaculate green pitch and perimeter advertising along the lines of Jordan's Poultry and Frank Blakes & Son Ltd Engineering helps create the impression that this is all something taken from a model railway of the steam era. If the football is too much for you, the smart main stand, thirteen rows deep, offers views of the Pennines. A season ticket costs £155. The remaining spectator areas are single-storey terraces. The stand behind the 'away' goal is closed, awaiting funds for redevelopment.

People have been watching football here for nearly 90 years. As if to prove that there really is nothing new under the sun, Rochdale's official history, *The Survivors*, tells the 1938 story of how the club tried unsuccessfully to persuade Gracie Fields, the town's most famous daughter, to perform a concert to raise funds for a new stand. At the time, Fields was one of Hollywood's highest-paid actresses, having made her name in British music hall. Steve Warmsley, commercial manager of the current Rochdale administration, wants another local, Lisa Stansfield, to do a benefit at the town's Gracie Fields Theatre. Warmsley grumbles about one recent missed opportunity. 'Lisa Stansfield was sat outside a pub around the corner just the other day. I said to the landlady: "Why didn't you come and *tell* me?" '

Warmsley and Docherty are two of the three people who run the club on a daily basis. Keith Clegg, Rochdale's secretary, completes the simple anatomy. They operate independently and report to the board of directors, headed by David Kilpatrick. Match day is the busiest time of the week. Clegg, 55, a retired Barclays Bank manager, is responsible for financial administration, as well as liaising with the police, the Football League and other clubs. He also checks the toilets are clean. 'It's the kind of job that encompasses a tremendous amount of detail,' says Clegg, modestly.

Gate receipts do not even cover the wage bill at most clubs. In a mediocre Rochdale season, they amount to around £100,000. Handouts from the Football League bring another £150,000 into the business. The biggest source of revenue, however, is Warmsley's commercial department. In the last financial year its lotteries and scratchcards provided nearly 40 per cent (£370,000) of the club's £1-million turnover. The department has been so badly affected by Camelot that the future of Rochdale – and its commercial manager – has been put in some jeopardy.

'The last eight months have been the hardest of my life,' says Warmsley, 41, loudly, and jabbing a finger as often as he blinks. 'In January and February I was really cracking up. The National Lottery has had me in tears. It's made me ill. We lost so much so quickly I thought the whole lot was going to collapse and myself, and my staff of six, were going to be out of a job. We've been out canvassing every night, we've worked and worked. We can't fight against the Lottery.'

Asking Rochdale employees about the future generally elicits silence. There is an understandable reluctance to contemplate the end of the road as a professional club. Everyone knows the club's finances are being stalked from all sides. All hopes are vested in the team finally coming good. Gordon Taylor, chief executive of the Professional Footballers Association, is, however, able to contemplate the worst. He identifies the way money from television is shared throughout the game and the changes to the transfer system as the key issues facing the oldest football league in the world.

'It is sad but somewhat inevitable that the majority of teams in the Third Division will be fortunate if they are still functioning on a professional basis at the end of the decade,' says Taylor. 'That may change if there is some shift in the distribution of income from television rights. But I'm not holding my breath.'

The FA Premier League currently generates £78 million each year from television rights and sponsorship. Only £3 million is passed down to Football League clubs. The Football Association and the Football League are due to re-negotiate this agreement in 1997, but no one is expecting an outbreak of philanthropy. In the meantime, the Football League has been attempting to improve on the £10 million a year it receives from ITV (with two offers on the table that promise to at least double the money). However, the question of how this revenue is shared out remains key. During negotiations, the First Division clubs are reported to have demanded as much as 90 per cent of the income, leaving Second and Third Division teams little better off in relative terms.

Exeter, Hartlepool and Northampton have tottered on the brink of extinction in recent months, while only the eleventh-hour appearance of sugar daddies saved Gillingham and Leyton Orient from joining Aldershot, Maidstone and Newport County in the great football league in the sky. Should this trickle become a flow, history will probably shake its head at the greed of England's leading clubs. The Football League was founded in 1888 on the principle that clubs operate on a mutually supportive basis, sharing a percentage of gate receipts and, later, sponsorship and television revenue. In 1992, the top clubs abandoned this idea with the formation of the Premier League. Their poor cousins in the lower divisions have been left to the law of the jungle.

Taylor believes it is in the interest of everyone in British football to try to lessen the impact of the Bosman judgement. He wants to negotiate with the European Commission next year. 'I hope change will be based on evolution and refinement. I'm quite convinced that complete freedom of contract will lead to a contraction in the numbers of clubs in existence, and therefore to a loss of my members' jobs. The smaller, weaker clubs must be protected.'

So who else cares? The disappointing reality is that our national game has few champions beyond the players' union, some loyal fans, and the people in the lower divisions who stand to lose their jobs. Amid the orgiastic public relations that characterise Sky's coverage of the Premier League, and the rampant consumerism of most of the leading clubs, it is at least worth remembering that more money to the top clubs does not necessarily equal better footballers. 'The Premier League has been great for the clubs that are in it,' says Taylor. 'But without the full-time status of the clubs in the lower divisions, the players coming through into the English game will not be of the same standard. How could they be? It's like asking Nick Faldo to be a great golfer when he's training two nights a week, instead of every day. Over 60 per cent of the players at the top clubs come from the lower divisions and often return there to finish their careers or to get their first jobs in management. It is an absolutely vital breeding ground. We can't take that for granted. We also can't say that the Premier League has raised the standard of football. English clubs are still failing in the benchmark competition, the European Champions League. The English game used to be admired for the standard of competition, the spice and variety. It's our heritage. That's not the case in Italy, Spain, Germany and Holland, where only one or two clubs dominate. I fear we may be going down the same road.'

The Rochdale players are pacing around the dressing room, waiting for the big kick-off. Take That's 'I Want You Back' blares from a ghettoblaster. The music feels good. Everybody wants the positive vibe. Jason Hardy, 25, is one of the few players not dressed for action. He is slim and tanned – a picture of good health. Hardy exists on the fringes of the football world. 'I'm on trial, me. I was at Halifax last year, and know Mick from years ago at Burnley. I rang and asked if there was any chance of a trial. Mick said: "We'll see how things develop."' Halifax fell through the trap door at the bottom of the Third Division two seasons ago, relegated to the semi-professional GM Vauxhall Conference. 'It was a nightmare,' says Hardy. 'You didn't know when your pay cheque was going to arrive. They got a part-time manager. It was like a youth club.' Hardy lives in Manchester and has been a footballer since leaving school. 'I've got no qualifications. If it doesn't work out here, I'll be goosed. I don't know what I'll do.'

John Deary, one of Rochdale's leading players, is also still in his clothes. 'I'm suspended. It's held over from last season. Use of the elbow, they said.' Deary is 32 and looks disappointed to be missing the game. 'This is a very enjoyable way of making a living. I love being out there, playing. I just try to make the most of it. I commute in from Southport every day. There's five of us in one car. It's a great laugh.'

Deary has never played top-level football, but knows Paul Stewart and David Bardsley. 'We were at Blackpool together. They've done very well, both playing for England. Obviously I'd like to have done that, but it's not something that keeps me awake at night. You just get on with it. I've probably got a couple more years playing, then I'll pack up. I've had a double-glazing business for the past four years, which is going well. Most of the older players have got something else. Graham Shaw, one of the forwards, wants to be a lawyer. Steve Whitehall, who also plays up front, is training to be a physio. Dave Thompson is doing a history degree.'

Someone turns off the music. Mick Docherty braces himself for the first team talk of the season. 'It's important to get three points,' he says, standing hands on hips in the centre of the room. 'They're a side that's come down, spent a few quid, people expect them to do well. It means fuck all. How you approach this game individually and collectively counts for everything. You work hard for one another. You fill in for one another. You have a go at one another. You take criticism in the right spirit. Now get out and do yourselves credit.' The players make their way from the dressing room, buzzing with adrenalin. Someone shouts: 'Come on then, we're a good side!' Another voice says, 'Come on lads, we are Rochdale.'

THE BEST OF BARNES

Simon Barnes – GQ Sports Columnist

Simply the worst

November 1994

There came a moment when I had a revelation about Chris Eubank. He is, in fact, Madonna. Perhaps I had better elaborate. Eubank is a boxer and a world champion, though how any boxer manages to avoid becoming a world champion these days is a mystery. Eubank is, in fact, WOCB (or is it the BWW? or maybe the OWB?) light-cruiserweight world champion, or maybe super-upper-middle-bantamweight – well, whatever it is, it is one of the most meaningless baubles in boxing, and the details need not detain us. He refuses fights with anyone who might beat him, and outrages every boxing purist who will listen to him by saying that there is no point in fighting people who might beat you, that boxing stinks, and that he is only in it for the money.

Boxers are traditional losers: manipulated, exploited, and milked of every penny they earn by fighting until their brains turn to mush and they are cast aside to become shambling drunks and appallingly bad gamblers. Boxers are victims. So, for that matter, are rock chicks: exploited by a brutal male world and chucked out when their looks go. But Madonna and Eubank both claim the same achievement: they are victims-turned-victors. They have seized control over their own sleazy, remunerative world. They control their male consumers. Eubank has exploited boxing. What is the next challenge, Chris? 'For me the challenge ith alwayth finanthial,' he answers, in his phony-posh, Inspector Morse voice, garnished with an incongruous lisp. Who do you want to fight next, Chris? 'Anyone I can beat.'

Madonna claims to be the sex goddess who exploited the masters, who seized control of her own destiny, who used the power of her sexuality as an offensive weapon to win her own battles and to make a fortune for herself, not for handlers and middlemen.

Another similarity between Eubank and Madonna: the spectacular modesty of their talents. Madonna became a colossal singing star and a global sex symbol, despite the handicap of being a poor singer lacking any unusual degree of physical attractiveness. Eubank has held on to his bauble and made a fortune – his latest agreement with Sky TV is for eight fights within a year, earning £10 million – without being much of a boxer. 'No one understandsth my limitth like I do,' he has said. Boxing writers find acute pain in all this, but he says they're talking at cross-purposes. 'I'm not looking for glory. I'm not looking for titleth. I'm not looking for the hall of fame. I'm looking for money.'

Further similarity with Madonna: the extreme tackiness of their acts. This demonstrates hatred of their audiences mixed with profound self-love. Both fell in love with themselves at an early age. Eubank turns up to important events in riding boots and a monocle; Madonna also thinks highly of elaborately costumed public appearances. Both rely on appearance rather than substance.

And the odd thing about both is that the more clothes they take off, the tackier their acts become. Madonna's poses have achieved the remarkable feat of making sex unattractive. The lady's private parts are the most public things about her. Eubank's poses in the ring have the same quality of self-parody. His exhibition of body builder's muscles doesn't inspire you with his confidence and strength any more than Madonna's crotch shots make you dream of her beauty and desirability. But they aren't trying to sell these things. They are selling the victory of the poseur, the victory of someone who has conned the world.

Thus Eubank inflates his chest at the end of each round and then takes a few silly, mincing steps back to his corner – his version of the Madonna crotch grab. But he moves beyond her range in the matter of intellect: he's a genius; a cracker-barrel philosopher making speeches about ethics and the meaning of life, full of malapropisms and self-serving nonsense. 'I'm trying to get into Cambridge Univerthity to thtudy pthychology,' he once announced.

Fleet Street Glendas despise him and the boxing establishment loathes him. So he can't be all bad. He is an intelligent man. Somebody once described the cricketer Phil Edmonds as 'a senator who thinks he's an Emperor'; Eubank to a tee.

His finest aphorism was to announce that he would willingly fight a corpse if he was paid enough money. This is a chilling remark when we remember that Michael Watson came close to death after fighting Eubank. But then boxing is human cock-fighting, nothing less. Eubank, as cocksure a man as you could wish to meet, believes it is time that the cocks had their say.

To surf them all my days

September, 1996

I was sitting on a beach in Cornwall, and beside me was a chap wearing glasses. His name was Chris Hines. He was gazing out at the sea. 'The wave has come to you across 1,000 miles of ocean,' he said softly. 'No one will ever ride it except you. Surf it, and it's gone. You have a relationship with a wave, a complete involvement with it, and then it's broken. You know those insects that mate once and die? It's like that.'

'Oh-ah,' I said, giving the sea a bit of a look myself. Was this man beside me very, very sane? Or was he in fact completely barking? 'Only a surfer knows how it feels,' another surfer told me, adding helpfully, 'I read that on a T-shirt.'

Surfing is a mystical matter, an out-of-body experience. It is also a lifestyle, whatever that is, much adopted by male bimbos in those plastic glasses that wrap all the way round your head. But it is also a sport, played out for marks and mere victory, and the August Bank Holiday brings us the British national surfing championships at – where else? – Fistral beach, Newquay, Cornwall. It is part of an event called the Ocean Festival, a gathering of the clans, a chance to buy a new wetsuit, an opportunity for looking cool and eyeing the surf-babes and, perhaps best of all, there will be Dick Dale 'twanging his surf guitar'. But perhaps that's a euphemism.

The entire event is masterminded by a group called, with admirable directness of purpose, Surfers Against Sewage. Its members are surfers, you see, and they are all against sewage. 'And if you've ever been hit in the face by a panty-liner, you'll understand how we feel,' said Nick Green, their events organiser. Quite.

He explained that surfers have a particular reason to dislike raw sewage and infected waters. 'It's not just that you swallow water,' he said. 'It gets fired into your system at some velocity.' There is a raw sewage outlet at St Agnes, near the surfing Mecca of Fistral, and SAS – it likes to be known by these pungent initials – has records of water-users who have contracted hepatitis, gastro-enteritis, all kinds of ear, nose and throat problems and viral meningitis from swimming about among the turds.

The environmental concern is an aspect of the surfing 'lifestyle', and SAS has 24,000 members. British surfers range from professional competitors, through permanent beach bums, down to weekenders from places like Crawley. Surfing is the fastest growing sport in Britain, I was told – but then, ain't they all? Britain has higher-ranked surfers than it does tennis players. Spencer Hargreaves, for example, is the Jeremy Bates of the world of radical manoeuvres. Or Martin Potter, nominally an Australian, but more British than Greg Rusedski, anyway. And the Brits may not be the best, but they are the bravest. British surfers never complain about the cold. They can't afford to. They only complain when the ice that forms about the cuffs of their wetsuits starts to cut into their wrists. And when you get the best seas off Cornwall in January and February, what can you do but freeze and surf?

Surfing is not really about competition. Surfing is about surfing: the idea of competition has been spatchcocked onto the pure pursuit of riding the wave. You get marks for style, and for the radical nature of your manoeuvring on the wave-tip. It is just a little bit like – for God's sake don't tell them I said so – synchronised swimming.

'There is a lot of anti-competition feeling,' Hines told me. Hines would sooner get up in drag than surf in a competition. 'People feel the idea of competition detracts from the whole reason you are out in the surf anyway.' To such as Hines, a surfing competition is something like a praying-contest, or a love-making race. But then all minority movements have all kinds of sects, scions and dogmas – you should hear bird-watchers talking about the twitching tendency. And anyway, they will all be there for the Ocean Festival, some to win, some to pose, some to gather in patronising groups, and all of them to look cool. If you want to make the scene, be seen with a Billabong label on your clothes, or perhaps a Quicksilver. Gorgeous, dumb blondes are highly acceptable, and they come in both sexes. Never take your shades off, best thing is to sleep in them. And if you can actually look good while surfing – a *very* difficult thing to do – then you will have the time of your life.

Oscar Wilde said that a cigarette was the perfect form of pleasure: it is exquisite and it leaves you unsatisfied. Oscar was not much of a surfer, but he caught the nature of surfing. Each wave is exquisite; but it never satisfies. It always leaves you wanting just one more. It is an endless pursuit of impossible perfection. Like all sports.

Wimbledon commoners

August, 1994

At the start of the Grand National, 40 horses line up across the track. Every one of the jockeys, no matter how little fancied his horse, is thinking about victory; every jockey, no matter how lavishly backed his beast, is also thinking about disaster. The race is a handicap, which means that the better the horse, the more weight it has to carry. The aim is parity of competition: in perfect theory, all 40 horses will reach the finish in a single line.

As the football season starts once again, 22 football clubs line up along the start. How many of them believe they have a chance of winning the championship? Two or three. Perhaps half a dozen. A further half-dozen are in contention for the rather wet booby prize of 'a place in Europe', reward for a finish near the top of the league. You hope one of the big clubs at the top wins the Coca-Cola Cup, opening a further place 'in Europe'. It is a feeble business: even leading clubs must be resigned to failure right from the start.

But as for the rest, they are playing in a totally different competition. They play against Manchester United, but they share nothing of United's hopes and dreams. They are playing for different prizes, with different ambitions and different fears. These clubs compete not to win, but to avoid relegation. The only ambition available to them is wholly negative.

Sport is élitist by its nature, but in the Premiership élitism has run riot. And the élitism has been to the detriment of sport and spectacle. For like the Grand National, the Premiership is a handicap, but the handicapper has done the job upside down. The stronger your chances, the more help the handicapper gives you; the weaker, the more difficulties he heaps on your back. Football's legislators have set out to destroy parity of competition; they have succeeded. And football is, for that reason, a lesser game than it should be.

Naturally, I am talking about money. In the mid-Eighties, football changed for ever. Before that, when two football clubs played a league match, they shared the money. That made a trip to United or Liverpool a significant point of the financial season. Now it means nothing. Legislation was introduced to allow the home clubs to keep all the gate receipts.

It sounds innocuous enough, perhaps even fair. But its results have been disaster. The rich get richer, the poor get poorer. The top clubs now all have second teams that are infinitely stronger and more valuable than the first teams of the weaker clubs. In such circumstances, what can the weaker clubs aim for, save survival? One recognised survival ploy is the finding of footballing talent. You encourage, you nurture – and you choose precisely the right moment to sell. The player then goes off to play in United's second team, or maybe as Liverpool's sub.

But one of the truths of football is that any team can beat any other team over 90 minutes. The problem is that turning the odds upside down is seldom possible over a sustained period – unless, of course, you are Wimbledon. Ah! Wimbledon, defiant of the system, heedless of football's law of averages, and of many other of football's laws besides. Football purists curl their lips at Wimbledon. But Wimbledon are in fact the last bastion of the old order: a throwback to the days when teams with consistently poor attendances, or from obscure corners of cities dominated by bigger clubs, could cut it with the mighty week in week out. Wimbledon are without doubt the greatest team in the Premiership. Season after season, they defy the handicapper.

And they get vilified for doing so. 'Wimbledon attract a crowd of 6,000?' asked Howard Kendall, the former manager of Everton. 'I can't for the life of me see how they get that many each week. The fans would be better off shopping.'

'Personally, I take special pride in our low gates,' said Sam Hammam, the eccentric Wimbledon chairman. 'And the fact that we continue to fight against the odds. This we will continue to do as long as we are supported by one person.'

In football, underdogs occasionally win Cup ties. Wimbledon play 42 Cup ties a season, and that's just in the league – overturning the odds is a routine. They do it through defiance, team spirit and cherishing their oddity.

Wimbledon call themselves the 'Crazy Gang' and love to live up to their nickname. Their manager, Joe Kinnear, was asked to comment on another manager's rules on players' dress. 'They can wear jeans and earrings for all I care,' he said. 'But I draw the line at stockings and suspenders. Until after the match.'

That is the spirit of Wimbledon. Their chief delight is cocking a snook. Every time they win three points, it is two fingers to the football establishment, and they love it. They defy logic: they are, despite their flamboyant poverty, fearsomely competitive.

Odd to think that in the US, sports administrators bend over backwards to ensure parity of competition. Every obstacle is placed in the way of successful teams. Whereas the Liverpool of the Eighties acquired a magnificent hegemony over all of English football, in American sport a team that manages sustained success must demonstrate qualities beyond mere excellence. In American football, the worst team of the season gets first pick at the college draft; the Super Bowl winners get the last choice. But in English football, the first shall be first and the last last. Wimbledon may be a glorious exception, but alas that is the rule. It is a system based entirely on self-interest, and the ironical thing is that it actually works against the interests of football. The league season provides fewer and fewer significant encounters, fewer and fewer surprises. It is a system that saps the strength of the top clubs: fewer and fewer matches test them to the limit. Fewer and fewer England-based players are capable of dominating international football. Remember when they called this the world's greatest league.

Cape crusaders

June, 1994

The more the years pass, the odder it all seems. One of the most serious, intractable and deadly conundrums in global politics, one of the nastiest messes of greed and intolerance that the world has come up with in recent years, has somehow got all tied up with sport.

And not just any sport. The hatred and vengeance and forlorn hopes of South African politics are, it seems, inextricably entangled with tea and walnut cake and 'oh well played sir'. While the runstealers flicker to and fro and God's in his heaven, all's right with the world.

Perhaps it is. On June 22, a team of South African cricketers will take to the field with, of all things, the Earl of Caernarvon's XI, and go on to play three Test matches against England. They do so with the blessing of a cricket enthusiast named Nelson Mandela, who in 1950 cheered every stroke of Neil Harvey's great innings of 151 in Durban – an innings played by an Australian *against* South Africa. It was an immemorial South African tradition, after all: the non-white section of the ground always cheered for the opposition, as well they might.

Of all the extraordinary things about South Africa, the most extraordinary thing of all is that the situation there is not worse. The endless predictions of anarchy and civil war have still, somehow, failed to come to pass. Dare one ever, even for an instant, talk about forgiveness?

One dare not. That is far too enormous a thought. But in the infinitely trivial field of sport, you can look for forgiveness, and you do not look in vain. What is more, if ever a sport needed forgiving, it was cricket. The succession of rebel tours was used by the white government as an unabashed propaganda weapon. The idea of boycott-defying cricket tours showed the world that South Africa was happy, contented, or at least stable: that apartheid worked. Lavish sponsors of tours gained lavish tax relief from a grateful government.

The last rebel tour was led by Mike Gatting, and it brought riots everywhere it went. 'As far as I was concerned, there was a few people singing and dancing and that was it,' Gatting famously remarked. Ali Bacher, the tour organiser, shocked by his country's response to the tour, said wearily: 'He has said nothing more stupid than a lot of white South Africans do every day.'

The extent of the opposition stunned cricket people in South Africa. The tour was abandoned. It seemed that South African cricket, like South Africa itself, had painted itself into a corner. The only way out was going to be messy. It looked a lot like the end. In a way it was, but only in a way. As Gatting's boys returned home, so did Nelson Mandela. As Gatting's tour was cast into the stinking cesspit of history, so were 317 racial laws.

And cricket emerged smelling of roses. Despite the dangerous and provocative debacle of the Gatting Tour, cricket has prospered. The cornerstone has been the trust established between Bacher, former promoter for rebel tours and now managing director of the United Cricket Board of South Africa, and Steve Tshwete, chief spokesman on sport for the African National Congress.

During the long years of isolation, England's right-wing cricket fans – which is not quite a tautology, even if it sometimes seems that way – clamoured for the return of South Africa to international cricket in the name of a colonial and imperial past: in the name of apartheid. And now a South African team is preparing to tour England in the name of a multi-racial future. A sport of oppression has become a sport for liberation in what must be the most extraordinary U-turn in sporting history. Nothing less.

Cricket has never even been South Africa's national game. It was the game of English-speaking whites and, therefore, naturally, despised by the Afrikaners. As for the Africans, they had little to do with it. They played, and play, football. It is football, not cricket and not rugby, that was and is the true national game of South Africa.

But changes in cricket have gone beyond pious speeches and window-dressing. The cricket-in-the-townships project began as a photo opportunity; it continues, not just as a development strategy, but as the bedrock of policy in the United Cricket Board. Grassroots cricket, not rebel tours, has become the priority: 'Suddenly, almost without realising the transition, Bacher and his colleagues were thinking as real South Africans for the first time in their lives,' says Donald Woods, the renowned South African émigré.

A cricket team that truly reflects South Africa's racial diversity would need to be three-quarters black. That time lies a long way ahead. But there are now genuine prospects leaping up in junior cricket, even if they are unlikely to be clobbering the English about the park this summer. But when South African cricket people are conjuring with names like Masemola, Mahuwa and Mabena, you know that more has changed in South Africa than cricket.

Bad kids on the block

December, 1995

Drugs. Just when you thought it was safe to get back into the water. Yes, drugs are back, as the world short course swimming championships stretch before us in Brazil. It is a row that will not go away. What's more, it seems that no one wants it to.

Louder and louder the cry goes up: some of China's swimmers are being aided by a state programme of performance-enhancing drugs. From childhood onwards they are stoned out of their little gourds on state-sponsored steroids. Can this be written off as xenophobia?

'You ask me questions about doping because of misunderstanding and jealousy,' says the Chinese assistant-head swimming coach Zhou Ming. 'The sports world has always been the domain of Western people. They just can't tolerate Asian people being good at sport.'

All good stuff. But then seven Chinese swimmers tested positive at the Asian Games last year, which rather knocked the Zhou theory out of the window. The row has grown ever since.

This year yet another anti-Chinese barrage was let loose. It came from the coaches, and was voiced at the Swim Symposium in San Francisco. Phil Whitten, anti-drug campaigner and editor of the leading American magazine *Swimming World*, summed up the feeling: 'After two years of denying there had been cases of doping in China, the Chinese now admit to the fact, but insist these are the actions of individuals. What we're asked to believe is that some naive, mostly rural teenagers from all over a vast nation decided to go into the local village to obtain illegal substances, pay for them and learn how to administer them, all at the same time. It's just not possible.'

Curiouser and curiouser: this year a delegation from the international swimming body FINA went to China, by invitation, to inspect a Chinese dope-testing station. One report reads: 'Practically every testing station was occupied, but they were working with no samples in view. Computers were all on, but no data appeared to be tested. The printers were not printing, the entire staff filed out of the building as soon as we left.' Perhaps they were taking the piss.

The Chinese swimming authority has issued an open invitation to Western journos to come and see for themselves. Whitten took this up. An almost unending correspondence was set in motion. Itineraries and dates changed and changed again. Last word from China to Whitten: 'I'm very sorry to notify you that your planned visit, which has been repeatedly postponed, will have to be cancelled altogether.' Two reasons were given: the busyness of the Chinese domestic season, and the impossibility of meeting all of Whitten's requests.

'I guess it's OK if you agree to be shepherded around, like the IOC [International Olympic Committee] and FINA,' says Whitten. 'That way you relay the message that people want to hear. China never intended to let Western journalists take an honest look at her so-called training methods.' Familiar territory, so far: Western xenophobia meets Eastern xenophobia. But the row gains dramatic intensity with the extraordinary suggestion that there are those who actually *want* a dodgy non-Western superpower at the Olympics.

The 1996 Olympic Games are almost upon us, and vast sums have been paid for the American television rights. The ball continues to roll: NBC have now agreed to pay $1.25 billion for the Olympics of 2000 and the winter Olympics of 2002. And TV is dying to have the Chinese at the Games. Not in the interests of global brotherhood but to play the xenophobia card. 'This is not speculation,' Whitten insists. 'With the demise of the Cold War, in the United States at least, we need a bad guy. We need somebody whom our good girls can go up against – the fight of good against evil and so forth. The Chinese female swimmers fit the bill just wonderfully. It would be great for ratings.' So we not only need Chinese swimmers – we also need dodgy Chinese swimmers. We need the cloud of suspicions, the suggestions of the state-sponsored doping programme.

And as always, of course, there is also the question of Juan Antonio Samaranch, IOC president. Samaranch is strongly pro-Chinese. One of the more remarkable achievements in the power-broking world of international sport was to bring China back into the Olympics without losing Taiwan. That showed nifty footwork.

He also very nearly got Beijing voted in as hosts for the 2000 Olympics. The people of the IOC have pretty strong stomachs, but only 43 of them were able to go along with that one. For the other 46, the memory of Tiananmen Square rather stuck in the craw. Sydney got it instead.

Some believe that for his Chinese exertions alone, Samaranch should get the Nobel Peace Prize. All of which goes to make the Chinese issue still more intractable: the most problematic subject in the permanently problem-plagued Olympic Games. Dope and politics. Politics and dope.

Heigh-ho. Remember when sport was only bothered with things like who could swim the fastest? No, neither can I.

Gentlemen and *Players*

HILL START

Jessamy Calkin

October, 1993

Silverstone, July 1993. There is a question mark over Damon Hill's sideburns. They seem to have been severely modified after looking mean and promising the previous week in France. There is a theory being advanced by drier members of the motor racing chattering classes that Hill won't win a race until he sports a full set of sideburns. Russell Bulgin, a keen observer of Grand Prix racing haircuts and a brave advocate of the theory that Alain Prost has a perm, is troubled at the no-show of the 'burns. 'If a man doesn't have confidence in his own sideburns, has he enough confidence to win a Grand Prix?' asks Bulgin. 'When he's properly bristling, I guarantee he'll win.'

As it transpired, it was not lack of confidence that finished Damon Hill's Grand Prix at Silverstone, a race which he was widely tipped to win after the excellent form he had shown in France. After leading all the way, his race finished on lap 42 with a puff of smoke from a blown engine, and the heart of the whole country went out to him as he got out of the car and walked sadly away.

It is no secret that attendances were down considerably at Silverstone this year, but feelings still ran high. There was not the patriotic hysteria of last year, when 180,000 fans came to witness the annihilation of the opposition by Nigel Mansell; people who, it seemed, had come to celebrate a British victory rather than watch a good race. The recent controversy that has surrounded Formula One has detracted from the sport and left doubts in the minds of the viewing public, already depressed by talk of team orders and confused by technical debate. Nevertheless, excitement was palpable because there was a new British hero in the making.

So there was a healthy sprinkling of baseball caps, T-shirts and Union Jacks bearing the rather formal moniker of 'D Hill', which read more like a new boy's school nametag than the affectionately aggressive home-made 'Our Nige!' and 'Senna, Fuck Off' banners of last year.

Hill, sitting in his Williams car on the front row of the grid, was oblivious to the expectations pressing down on him from all sides. They were nothing compared to his own expectations; this was the most important race of his life. Silverstone is his Wembley, his FA Cup, his Grand Slam. His father competed in the British Grand Prix seventeen times and never won. Nonetheless, to the British public, Damon was under pressure to take up Mansell's mantle, to fulfil the promise of his glamorous heritage and to justify his position in the most competitive team in Formula One.

He made a lightning start, pulling away from Alain Prost – who was being held back by Ayrton Senna – to build up a lead of some eight seconds. When the safety car came out on lap 38 and levelled out the field, Hill was throwing himself into the race of his life against his team-mate, and this was the only real contest. On lap 41 Hill set a new lap record, and then, unbelievably, smoke started to pour out of his engine, and that was that. Not two weeks before he had done three days' testing at Silverstone, covering three Grand Prix distances, and before that twenty days of testing, and in all that time there was no sign of an engine failure.

But in everyone's minds Hill had silenced the critics, justified his selection by Frank Williams, and acquitted himself superbly. 'He drove wonderfully well at Silverstone,' says Jackie Stewart. 'The race was his and he handled the pressure of leading the field in his home Grand Prix beautifully. I think he would have won.'

There had been a big build-up to the British Grand Prix, both in the media and on the track, not least in the previous day's qualifying. Prost had pole, then Hill, then Prost, then Hill. 'Congratulations, Damon,' said an extremely over-excited Murray Walker in a live TV link-up with the cockpit of Hill's car. 'You're on pole position for the British Grand Prix.' Hill's delighted response was interrupted by a crackle of static. In his usual fashion, Walker had spoken too soon, and had the unenviable task of breaking the bad news to Hill and millions of viewers: Prost had just turned in a faster lap. 'I was live on the BBC,' Hill said later. 'It was the opportunity of a lifetime. I should have said, "Murray – you're a cunt".'

Georgie Hill, Damon's sexy, pragmatic, 30-year-old wife, was watching the race from the pits, listening with a headset linked to Hill's car. 'I heard Damon swear, and I thought, "I don't believe it." I saw this tiny puff of white smoke then it just . . . I couldn't believe it. We'd got through all the hoo-ha that led up to it and everything was hunky-dory. Then a puff of smoke and it's all over.'

While Hill walked laconically into the British Racing Drivers' Club for a pint of beer, Georgie burst into tears in the subdued Williams pit. Suddenly, the garage was filled with camera crews and photographers. When Hill got back it was pandemonium, everyone shoving and fighting each other to get pictures. 'Darlin', darlin' – look over here.' 'My name is not darling,' snarled Georgie, but by then they had pushed her out of the way to get to Hill, and the regular motor-racing press were getting pissed off with the tabloid press, and all hell broke loose.

Hill was bemused by this menagerie. 'All that side of it is just as fascinating to me as getting a drive in the top team. I've never seen people behave like that. It shocks me every time. I can't see what all the fuss is about.'

At the moment when Damon Hill was born in Hampstead, in 1960, his father was racing at Snetterton. Two years later, Graham Hill won the world championship for the first time. Damon's early exposure to motor racing did not excite his interest. 'From the moment I was born I was going to motor races and I was chaperoned around the place and told to sit there, don't move, don't touch that, and everyone came up and patted me on the head. Very tedious.'

At the time, Hill didn't appreciate his father's achievements because he wasn't aware of them. 'I just believed he was a better person than most people because a lot of people seemed to be saying that. Growing up as the son of Graham Hill, I could go round and just be normal; but when my father was around, people would behave differently towards each other, and towards me, and after a while I tended to be sceptical of people.'

His father wasn't home much, and motor racing, Hill found, interfered with time that could have been spent with his parents. 'Everyone was telling me how wonderful my dad was, and I was thinking, "Is he? I don't know. I don't see much of him." I don't think we as a society fully appreciate to what degree our lives are shaped by our relationship with our parents in our early years. Before my father died I wanted to have much more of him than I actually got. Whatever it is you're missing in the early days, you end up striving for the rest of your life.'

As a father himself, Hill is extremely sensitive to this. He has noticed that one of his own sons, Joshua, who is only two-and-a-half, starts over-reacting in certain ways if Hill is away a lot. 'I have to be available to him as much as possible in order for him to get the confidence to go out in the world and feel that I'm there for him. If I had spent more time with my father I would have been much more confident in myself, socially.'

It does not seem to have affected his confidence in his ability, or his motivation. 'Well, I wonder how much of my drive comes from some sort of insecurity. Everyone competes for different reasons. Prost is very short. Maybe that's his cross to bear ...'

And Senna?

'God knows. Senna is South American.'

Graham Hill was part of our national heritage. Apart from his remarkable achievements in motor racing (he was the only man to have won the Formula One world championship, Indianapolis and Le Mans), he was articulate and charming in the extreme, the perfect ambassador for the sport, widely loved by the British public. When he retired, he started his own Embassy Hill team. But in November 1975, Graham Hill was killed, along with other members of the team, in a plane that he was flying. It affected Damon very deeply, for a very long time. It transpired, too, that the plane was not properly insured, and after a series of lawsuits on behalf of the families of the bereaved, the Hill family found themselves with no money.

Inevitably, his father's death substantially altered Hill's view of the world. 'Things just happen – I don't think there's any rhyme or reason to it. There was no reason for what happened to my dad – after years of being perilously close to death, he'd given all that up and was looking forward to the rest of his life. And then he has a plane crash. What's the logic in it all? There is no logic, it's just fate, and at any minute something could happen that will completely change your life.'

When Hill was young he wanted everything his own way, and he wanted to do everything himself. Not wishing to emulate his father's career, he chose motorcycle racing as his particular avenue of excitement. On his 350cc Yamaha he was, as any Brands Hatch marshal who was around at the time will tell you, magic, scoring more than 40 wins and becoming Champion of Brands.

Bored of bikes, Hill was sent by his mother to racing car school in France and he made an inauspicious debut at Brands Hatch in FF2000, qualifying at the back and coming off at the first corner. 'My first race,' says Hill, 'was the prime example of how not to start motor racing. The best way is quietly to pick the easiest race you can possibly find and just enjoy it. Instead, I started in a very competitive championship, in a car that wasn't very competitive, with a lot of attention.'

He did fairly well in Formula Ford 1600, where his main rivals are still his contemporaries today – Mark Blundell and Johnny Herbert. In 1986, he graduated to Formula Three, competing in the Lucas Formula Three championship for three seasons, firstly with Murray Taylor Racing and then with the Cellnet Ricoh team, with former Lotus driver Martin Donnelly as his team-mate. Jim Wright, who was consultant to Cellnet for their motor sport programmes, remembers Hill as a very intense, if erratic, driver. 'In those days Damon was quite sporadic and inconsistent in his performances. Some days he was unbeatable, other days he clearly had other things on his mind. You could tell as soon as he arrived if it was going to be a good day or bad – you'd get a cheery hello or a grunt. To be honest, back then he had more poor days than good ones.'

1988 ended badly. Although he'd come third in the Lucas Formula Three Championship, and second in the Macau Formula Three Grand Prix, Hill found himself without a drive for the following year. He had been led to expect the Jordan drive in F3000, but Martin Donnelly had got it. Meanwhile, he had just got married and bought a house, and Georgie was pregnant and had given up her job. 'I didn't know what the hell I was going to do. I began 1989 with a mortgage, no money, no job, and interest rates were going through the roof. Then Oliver was born with Down's Syndrome.' Georgie has spoken of the 'unchallengable love' with which he greeted Oliver's arrival. 'My reaction,' says Hill, 'was that Oliver was the most important thing and everything else was irrelevant; so that helped as much as it might have made things difficult.'

It changed his perspective, but it didn't stop him racing, even with no regular drive. He ended up having one of the best years he'd ever had. 'I drove whatever I could get my hands on, whenever I could, as hard as I could, because I knew that any opportunity was precious. I think I learned at that time that you've got to drive to enjoy it, and that's the way you get the best out of yourself. If you're not enjoying it, you shouldn't be doing it – it's too dangerous.'

In one season he competed in Formula Three, UK Formula 3000, in the British Touring car championship in a Cosworth Sierra and at Le Mans in a Porsche, and finished up in a hopelessly uncompetitive F3000 Footwork. Since it had not previously qualified, Hill did well to get the car onto the grid in each of the remaining six rounds, which made a big enough impression for him to secure a drive in 1990, with the Middlebridge F3000 team.

He competed in the FIA International F3000 Championship, but never actually won anything. It was a very frustrating season because of electrical problems with the car, which kept stopping for no discernible reason. But it was, as they say, character-building. 'Damon really inspired Middlebridge and moulded it into a very good little team,' says Jim Wright. Then it became known that Frank Williams was seeking a test driver. Mark Blundell, Williams' previous test driver, had left for Brabham. 'We were looking for someone to test our active ride programme,' says Patrick Head, Williams' technical director, 'and we gave Damon a test and he did a very good job, so we carried on.'

'Damon is very intelligent and articulate,' says Wright. 'Patrick Head needed someone like that to cope with the electronic drive aids he was utilising.' Hill's job was to test and develop the car to be used in 1992. 'And it was vital for me,' he recalls, 'because the F3000 car I drove that year was completely uncompetitive and I had a dreadful year. But every time I went testing in the Williams, I could prove that I could compete in F1 and come up with good lap times.'

In 1992, Hill took over from Giovanna Amati in the Brabham F1 team halfway through the season. The Brabham was not an easy car to drive. 'It was too small, under-developed, two years old and had no horsepower. Apart from that it was great.' Hill qualified for his first Grand Prix at Silverstone in 1992, finishing sixteenth. Brabham's last race of the season was at Hungary, where he finished eleventh.

Meanwhile he was turning in excellent lap times as he tested for Williams. But he had no expectations of being awarded the Williams drive. He knew that if Riccardo Patrese or Nigel Mansell got flu, there was a chance that Williams might stick him in the car, but there was no clue that they might not be driving the following year. 'In the middle of 1992,' says Patrick Head, 'Damon started deliberately pushing himself a lot harder, getting better and better lap times which were similar to – or better than – those of Mansell and Patrese.'

Then, as the season progressed, there was chaos in the Williams camp. It became clear that Prost had signed for Williams, that negotiations with Mansell had broken down, and that Patrese was going to Benetton. Suddenly there was a drive available, in the car that every Formula One driver wanted.

Martin Brundle was up for it, Mika Hakkinen was up for it, and, orbiting around like an astral presence, offering to drive for nothing, was the threatening genius of Ayrton Senna. Hill remembers it as a very tense time. 'Not least because I came close a few times to everything being settled, and then it didn't happen.' Hill had had an offer from Ligier, and had to juggle carefully. He wanted the Williams drive above all else, but he didn't want to be left with nothing. Ligier were pressing him for an answer. It required delicate negotiating.

Meanwhile, life was hell at home in Wandsworth. 'It was excruciating,' says Georgie. 'Damon was so completely preoccupied with the Williams thing. Neither of us could sleep; it consumed us 24 hours a day. And on top of that I was trying to run a house and look after two children and give them attention.

'I just wanted to run away, it all got too much. I wanted to tear my hair out and scratch my skin off, we were so completely stressed out. I remember saying to him, "If you get this drive, you've got to really enjoy it, for however long it lasts, and you're going to be happy and make up for all we've put up with over the past few months . . ."'

As it transpired, Senna was effectively vetoed by Prost; Brundle was turned down, and Hakkinen already had a contract with Lotus, which Williams wasn't prepared to contest. (The contract was later shown not to be binding.) It was getting very late, and a decision had to be made.

In the end, it was Hill who held the trump card: he was very familiar with the car, he could put down formidable lap times, and he was testing all the time. 'It came to the point where they were going to make a decision over the week of an Estoril test. Frank came down and saw me drive and thought I was doing a good job, and had coped well with the pressure of it all.'

But Hill hadn't won a race since 1988. He may have had uncompetitive equipment, but the fact remained that he had little experience of leading a field. 'Yes, that bothered us,' said Patrick Head.

'Testing is quite a different thing from sitting in the hot seat at Monaco next to Ayrton Senna. So it was a bit of a risk. But after you've assessed a guy's skill and commitment and all those rubbish words, then you take a look at his character – and we decided he was one of those odd bastards who can do it . . .'

On the evening of Friday, December 11, 1992, Hill got a call from Frank Williams, asking him to come up to the factory. 'I said, "Look, it's Friday night and there's tons of traffic and I'm not going to come all the way up to Didcot if you're going to tell me I haven't got the drive . . ."' Williams replied he wasn't going to tell him over the phone, so Hill got in the car and two hours later Williams offered him a contract. 'I said, "I'm not signing that!" No, I'm joking. After a bit of wrangling we had it all sorted out. I would have been happy to sign anything that was put in front of me, to be honest.'

That was that. Hill called Georgie and went home and they drank champagne and had a party and video'd the contract coming through the fax and tried to keep their mouths shut until Monday, when the official press announcement took place. At eight o'clock on Sunday night the faxes went out, and at five past eight the phone started ringing and it didn't stop for four days. And when Hill went to the press conference held for the announcement of his drive, he had a shock. The excitement generated was enormous – here was Damon Hill, son of Graham Hill, who'd only raced in two Grands Prix and never won a championship, stepping into the drive that both Senna and Mansell had wanted. It was incredible!

'Frank had naturally taken a gamble on me,' says Hill. 'It was a case of him sticking his neck out, and I was also sticking my own neck out, but I wasn't going back on it.' There were the inevitable sceptics, but the selection made sense. Hill didn't have an outstanding track record, but nor had Mansell when he signed for Williams in 1985. Hill was getting on a bit, too – compared to Schumacher (24) or Barrichello (21), 32 is quite old for a driver – but, on the other hand, he had paid his dues and his maturity was reflected in the cool and untemperamental way he handled the pressure.

There were also many factors in his favour: not least, that he had been testing the car for two years and was familiar with the suspension system; he was British, which would soothe angry Mansell fans looking for a replacement hero; and he was good, but not yet so good that he would present a major threat to Prost, whose ego had already asserted itself when he had been teamed with Senna at McLaren and Mansell at Ferrari. Hill also came cheap ($400,000 in his estimated salary, as opposed to the $10 million Mansell had demanded) and, lastly, he was intelligent, handsome, with an admirable temperament and an impeccable heritage.

There was another bonus, it later transpired. Hill had a link with Sega, the multi-million-pound computer game company, which had been substantially courted by Formula One. From Sega's point of view, too, Damon was a young, fresh, attractive prospect with no existing 'image'. At the first Grand Prix of the season, Williams announced a sponsorship deal with Sega. 'I think,' says Damon carefully, 'that Sega was encouraged to sponsor Williams because I'd got the drive.'

It's not easy being a racing driver. It can entail having to pose for photographs with a giant replica of Sonic the Hedgehog. This is usually a role adopted by an unfortunate member of the Williams team. ('Come on, who's going to be Sonic today ...?') Sonic is supposed to be 'the hedgehog with attitude', and there is a marked difference between the Canon hospitality suite and the Sega one. At Sega you might come across Betty Boo, Harry Enfield or Paul Simonon. For Hill, one of the high points of being famous (apart from Gene Hackman buying his crash helmet at a charity auction at Gleneagles) was meeting Joe Strummer. 'He wished me luck and I suddenly recognised the voice. That was a big kick for me because I can remember slogging around to Clash gigs in the early days.'

Hill began 1993 surrounded by a fair amount of envy and scepticism. Is he any good? Does he have the lightning genius of Herbert or Schumacher, or the grit of Blundell? He'd got the drive and now he had to prove himself.

And the Canon Williams FW15C is no picnic. It weighs 200lb less than a Citroën AX, and has twenty times the power. It has computer-controlled active suspension, electronic traction control, revolutionary anti-lock brakes, and generates so much downforce that at 120mph it could drive across your ceiling. It travels at well over 200mph, requires 150lb of pressure to work its brake pedal, and when cornering, the G-force is so great that the driver can feel his internal organs move. To drive this car requires more than skill. It requires The Right Stuff.

South Africa's Kyalami Grand Prix was not an ideal debut. Damon spun on the first corner, recovered, and then got taken off by Zanardi. 'That was a low point, definitely,' sighs Hill. 'As a Grand Prix driver you have the Sword of Damocles hanging over your head at every moment.' 'It was on the cards, really,' adds Georgie. 'It was a relief when it happened, because it got it out of the way.'

The incident's only real effect was to compromise Hill's performance in the next race. Like a second serve, his only objective in Brazil was to finish. But he did more than that, he finished second, and – a high point in his career – overtook Ayrton Senna in his home Grand Prix on the Ayrton Senna curve. 'I did think, "Yahoo!" He was a sitting duck really, but I did a quite brilliant manoeuvre on him.' 'I watched it,' says Ken Tyrrell. 'I was very impressed. I was also impressed when he started to ease off when it got wet and let Senna pass. He was criticised for that, but I thought it was a very mature thing to do.' Senna was at home in Brazil, and adrenalin was running high. It would have been a major disaster for Williams, and Hill, if they had tangled.

After Brazil, the jury was still out on Hill. Was he enough of a charger to win? He came second in the wet at Donington (beating Prost); in San Marino he was leading for eleven laps before retiring with a brake problem; in Spain he again started from the front row of the grid, behind Prost, and led for eleven laps before retiring with engine failure. There were no team orders, Prost told *Autosport*, although they agreed that they wouldn't fight during the last ten laps.

Hill came second in Monaco and third in Montreal. In France, he had his first pole position of the season, led for a third of the race and finished three-tenths of a second behind Prost. There were the inevitable murmurs. Were there any team orders in France? 'France was . . .' Damon hesitates. 'France was a good result for the team. It was the first time we had first and second, and there is the possibility that if I had raced harder against Alain only one of us, or neither of us, would have finished. That would have been a disaster, bearing in mind that we have French engines and Elf sponsorship, and Alain's a French driver in the French Grand Prix. I haven't yet got a contract to drive for next year, and it's my first season in Formula One.'

Work it out for yourself, he implies. But after France, the real excitement began; a Hill victory seemed imminent. 'Obviously, I don't want to be second to anyone after a period of cutting my teeth in Formula One,' says Hill. 'And I think that time is getting close. If it's not already here.'

It's here. 'He's obviously ready to win a Grand Prix,' says Ken Tyrrell. 'He'd better let Williams know that he is capable of beating Prost. In the last quarter of the season, he needs to let it rip.' 'I think he's done well,' says Ligier driver Mark Blundell. 'Obviously, he's got a lot of pressure on his shoulders but now he needs to win. I've got no doubts that if I had that machinery I would have won a race by now.'

'Damon's appointment was a calculated risk,' says Frank Williams. 'With every race he impresses us further with his performance both in and out of the car.' Alain Prost, too, has frequently paid tribute to Hill, acknowledging his superiority at getting off the grid first. In his first full season of F1, Hill's goal, says Prost, is not, like his own, to win the world championship. This makes for a healthy balance in the team. 'We get on perfectly well and I am happy to have a team-mate as quick as Damon. He can back me into a corner, which is good for my motivation.'

'Any team atmosphere is good if one driver is ahead of another,' comments Patrick Head. 'But now that Damon is catching up I suspect it might become a little more frosty at race-time. There's not much, "After you, Claude . . ." in this business.'

The general view is that Damon Hill had responded to the challenge,' says Jim Wright, 'and he will work and work at it – he's very much like his father in that way.' 'I've known Damon since he was a wee boy,' says Jackie Stewart, 'and he's a chip off the old block. He has the same dry sense of humour, and the same dedication and total commitment.' Commitment is essential. There are probably more obstacles to success in Formula One than in any other sport. You cannot just get in a car and drive. 'My father,' says Hill, 'felt that he wasn't going to get anywhere unless he tried very hard and never gave up. I think that he probably overworked that side of it; I think he would have enjoyed just as much success if he didn't have the view that it all had to be a slog.

'He used to keep little books, with a record of all the gear ratios from all the races he ever did, and which springs and roll bars he used. He worked and worked and I think that maybe the effort he put in was over and above what was really needed, but he felt that he had to be pushing himself in order to achieve any success because it wasn't going to come to him in other ways.

'The important thing is to realise how much effort to put in and to be efficient with your effort.'

Wandsworth, July 1993. A week after Silverstone, Damon Hill is at home doing the housework. 'Do you think Ayrton Senna empties the dishwasher?' he muses. Georgie mentions her forthcoming appearance at a charity event, at which she will drive a heavy goods truck to raise money for the Tommy's campaign (for foetal research). A poster on the wall announces Damon as patron of the Down's Syndrome Association, and there is a huge colour photo of Damon and Oliver in a swimming pool, next to one of Damon in a pool with his father and sisters. On the table are fan letters addressed to 'Damon Hill, Racing Driver, South London'. We are discussing the price of fame. Yes, they have been asked to appear in *Hello!* magazine. 'But we turned it down because I don't think we're ready to get a divorce yet,' says Georgie. 'We're having a fab time,' she adds. 'The trouble with Damon is that no matter what he's doing, he'd still be like this. He's quite a serious person, but he likes to think about things too much. He's quite funny, sometimes, but more inclined to deep-thinking paranoia. I'd never describe him as happy-go-lucky.'

Georgie has dimples and dark hair. She is articulate and practical, and cuts through all the bullshit. She is quite bossy with Damon, but he is used to it, having been surrounded by strong women – his famous mother Bette and his two sisters Brigitte and Samantha – all his life. 'Damon when he's driving is completely different from Damon when he's at home,' says Georgie. 'I'm not allowed to order him around. For three days over the Grand Prix, I have to do exactly as I'm told. I spend most of the time biting my lip.'

In some ways, she says, their life is much the same. They have perks – Canon Cameras, Renault cars, Sega games. But Hill still spends most of his time at the track and Georgie still spends her time cooking fish fingers and changing nappies. They still live in the same modest house and there are no private jets. 'So most of it hasn't changed, but a little bit of it has changed beyond all recognition.'

Georgie remembers a Renault event, where the three British Renault drivers – Mark Blundell, Martin Brundle and Hill – were signing autographs on a card printed with their photographs. Each driver signed in a different colour pen – Brundle signed in blue, Blundell in red, and Hill in green. 'There were these two girls there, and one of them said, "Come on, we've got to go now," and her friend said, "Hang on a minute, I haven't got the green one yet".' It brought Georgie down to earth. 'You have to remember, when things get too much, that to most people he's just the green one.'

Hockenheim, July 1993. The sideburns are coming along nicely, the track is a fast one and, once again, Prost and Hill are on the front row of the grid. Another fantastic start, and Hill is in the lead, which he loses briefly twice, but by lap 25 he has built up 21 seconds between himself and his team-mate. Prost carves away at this but can do little about it, and two laps before the end, photographers are assembling in the pits and the Williams mechanics are finally allowing themselves to get excited. And then the news comes through. On his penultimate lap, Damon Hill has had a puncture.

Five hours later, on the plane, Damon Hill is friendly and pragmatic as ever. Bitterly disappointed, he recognises that nearly winning is not enough, it doesn't count. 'What do I have to do to win a race?' he asks, but there is no whining, no paranoia, no shifting of the blame. He came very close, and the important thing is that Frank Williams and Patrick Head are still impressed, and basically it's all onwards and upwards from here.

Damon Hill has no doubt that he will be a winner. His determination is more steely than ever. The famous father's son is now famous in his own right. The name, at times a millstone, now underlines both natural talent and inherited traits. In 1969 Graham Hill broke both legs in an accident but recovered enough to drive the following year. He simply refused to accept defeat. 'And I'm very much the same,' says Damon. 'If someone tells me I can't do something, for whatever reason, I just can't accept it. I also think I have a natural talent for driving, because sometimes I amaze myself.

FAST AND LOOSE

Russell Bulgin

April, 1992

The way Eddie Jordan tells it, the dream ended at the Villa d'Este, a wedding-cake hotel of linen sheets and sepulchral charge-card decorum, perched snugly on the shore of Italy's Lake Como. Jordan, founder, guiding light and irrepressibly garrulous force behind the fledgling Jordan Grand Prix team, knew it was over when he saw German racing driver Michael Schumacher walking across the lobby. It was Thursday September 5, 1991, the day before practice began for the Italian Grand Prix at Monza. At the previous round of the FIA Formula One World Championship, at Belgium's daunting Spa-Francorchamps circuit, the 22-year-old Schumacher impressed even the cynics in the Grand Prix paddock by qualifying a Jordan-Ford seventh on the grid in his first Formula One race.

Schumacher had proven himself both composed and quick. Quick enough for Jordan to want to sign him up long-term. Quick enough to invite comparisons with Ayrton Senna and the late Gilles Villeneuve, two other racing drivers who adapted instantly to the mercurial power and epoxy-resin grip of a Formula One car. And quick enough for Jordan, at the Villa d'Este thirteen days after Schumacher rolled out for his first qualifying lap at Spa-Francorchamps in Belgium, to lose his new driver to another team.

'He'd just been flown in by helicopter and I went to say hello,' Jordan recalls, dropping the pace of his Dublin blarney. 'He talked and, you know, just whispered to say how sorry he was.' At that moment, Jordan knew Schumacher was no longer his. 'And then he was whisked away.'

The following afternoon, Schumacher would practice at Monza for the Italian Grand Prix as a driver for the rival Benetton Formula team. He would qualify seventh and finish fifth in the race on Sunday, scoring his first World Championship points in what was only his second Grand Prix.

Schumacher had been a dream-ticket for Jordan. He was fast, very fast. He was young. He spoke good English. He gave precise feedback to his engineers. He displayed high levels of mechanical sympathy. He was even the right size to fit comfortably in the cramped cockpit of a Formula One car. He was everything a Formula One team owner craves. That he was German seemed a bonus, too: German public interest in a new star could generate a serious amount of Deutschmark sponsorship for the team which employed him. In short, Schumacher would have proved a valuable asset to Jordan both on and off the track. But it was not to be.

If nothing else, Schumacher's arrival in Formula One at the end of August 1991 is a microcosm of how Grand Prix racing, its powerbrokers and its sponsors go about their hundred million-dollar global business.

The public perception of what happened at Monza is that Michael Schumacher was spirited away from the Jordan Grand Prix team by its rivals at Benetton Formula.

The truth is, in the inevitable way of motor racing, more complex, involving Schumacher, Jordan, Benetton's new team leader Tom Walkinshaw, Mark McCormack's International Management Group, the Swiss Sauber-Mercedes sportscar racing team, a company manufacturing peppermints and, for Mercedes-Benz, former racing driver Jochen Neerpasch. It also involves a tortuous web of offer and counter-offer, obfuscation and old-fashioned bullshit.

Schumacher is at the tiny go-kart racing track in Kerpen-Manheim, west of Cologne. Above the trackside café is a sign which reads 'prop: E Schumacher': his mother pulls the pils. A tubby, bearded man in a blue boiler suit does odd jobs around the corkscrew circuit: his father looks after the place where his son learnt his craft.

The toytown track, and his parents' enduring links with kart racing, represent what Schumacher's life used to be. The silver, AMG-customised Mercedes-Benz 300CE – chubby-tyred, spoilered, car-phoned and with a fax from the Mercedes-Benz press office lying on the passenger seat detailing today's duties – highlights perfectly what his life is like now. Schumacher is tanned, mid-size, wears a green polo shirt, jeans and a pair of Timberlands. He chats easily, but there's a suggestion of toughness: the more he talks, the more he sounds like Ayrton Senna, without the Brazilian's narcissistic edge. He and Senna both began racing in go-karts: did he, like Senna, drive every day after school? 'Not every day, but when I started to do go-karts I was four, and I remember when I was about seven or eight my father started to work for the [go-kart] club and every afternoon when he came from work, we went to the go-kart circuit and rented karts.' Ayrton Senna, too, first sat behind the wheel at the age of four.

Every racer recalls when he first realised that he was quick, a cut or a corner above the rest. Schumacher allows himself a brief smile: 'I can remember when I was five I got my first real go-kart and when I was six I was, for the first time, club champion.' And how old were the kids he was racing against? 'Nobody was my age – they were between ten and fourteen.' Schumacher was German junior kart champion at fourteen. And at fifteen. At sixteen he finished third in the German and European kart championships at senior level: in 1987, he had won both titles.

Karting was Schumacher's life. He didn't think of moving up to motor racing. His career would centre on squiggling around Europe's kart tracks contesting the purest form of racing. To listen to Schumacher, the hardest part of his career came in the transition from karting to Formula Ford: skinny-tyred single-seaters powered by Ford Cortina engines. Schumacher moved up for the most pragmatic of reasons. He had found a sponsor who was prepared to pay the bills.

Formula Ford might sound prosaic, but the racing is close and this is where young drivers with an eye on a professional career pay their dues. Schumacher graduated from Formula Ford and took second place in the German Formula Three series in 1989, before securing the title in 1990. Along the way, Willy Weber, boss of Schumacher's WTS Formula Three team, became his manager. Weber was a friend of Eddie Jordan. A contact had been made. Weber, in fact, discussed buying Jordan's Formula 3000 team and relocating it in Germany around Schumacher for 1991.

Then an unlikely suitor came on the scene. Mercedes-Benz, concerned about losing image to home-grown rivals Audi and BMW, both of which had successful motorsport programmes, had returned to international racing for the first time since 1955. Guided by former BMW and Talbot competition boss Jochen Neerpasch, who had also worked for the IMG sports management operation, Mercedes-Benz joined forces with the Swiss Sauber sportscar team to build a Mercedes-Benz-powered Le Mans winner.

Sportscar racing was, in the late Eighties, where old Grand Prix drivers often found themselves: when Britain's Derek Warwick or Italy's Mauro Baldi were no longer on the Formula One shopping list, they went Group C sportscar racing. Neerpasch wanted to use sportscar racing for another purpose: to groom young drivers for topline international racing. Implied, but never openly admitted, was the suggestion that Mercedes-Benz, at some unspecified time, would go Grand Prix racing with its own car and drivers plucked fresh from the factory kindergarten.

Neerpasch had noticed Schumacher. 'First of all he has got the talent.' Neerpasch raced in the Sixties for the factory Ford team. His speech is clipped, concise. 'Secondly, he is so strong in the intention to become a professional driver: that's where his priority is. That is his strong side.'

'The first meeting we had with Mercedes was in 1989,' explains Schumacher. 'Neerpasch asked to have a dinner together. Then he told us the situation and what he wanted to do. And I signed the contract in September or October in 1989 for Mercedes-Benz. I was surprised. I mean for a 20-year-old guy to do something like this, it was quite surprising: I couldn't believe it when it was fixed.'

Schumacher was going against racing lore: young hotshots must stick to single-seaters, go Formula Ford, Formula Three, Formula 3000 and then Formula One. 'Everybody told me it was wrong to do it. Everybody said if I do this then Formula One is far away.'

But Schumacher tested for 7,500 kilometres during the off-season, and got used to driving a high-downforce sportscar for a professional team. It was irreplaceable experience; Schumacher also began to understand Mercedes-Benz, to build up a relationship with Neerpasch and IMG. At the same time Jordan and Willy Weber were talking – talking Formula 3000, talking racing, talking Schumacher, talking about the future.

Then on the day in December 1990 when Eddie Jordan was due to make a sponsorship presentation in front of a group of Pepsi-Cola product managers – a compelling spiel-and-slides display which would lead to the company's 7-Up brand becoming the title sponsor of the Jordan Grand Prix team – Belgian racing driver Bertrand Gachot sprayed CS gas into a taxi driver's face after an altercation in traffic at Hyde Park Corner in London. Gachot, already signed to Jordan Grand Prix with a bagful of personal sponsorship, was due to go to the presentation with Eddie Jordan, but police intervention meant that he failed to show. The feeling within Jordan was that Gachot, as a foreign subject and first offender, would receive a suspended sentence and a hefty fine. But when the case finally came to court in the week before the Belgian Grand Prix, Gachot – who had by now driven ten Grands Prix for Jordan – was sent down for eighteen months. Jordan needed a replacement driver, and quickly.

Eddie Jordan notes the progress of young drivers on a computer at home: this is, he says with a grin, his hobby. Schumacher was already occupying hard disk space when the number two Jordan seat fell vacant. 'Gerd Kramer of Mercedes – who's on the PR side – is a big fan of Schumacher's and any time I met him he would always remind me about Schumacher,' says Jordan. 'And he approached me with Willy Weber in Brazil, the second race of the 1991 championship. I told him over the winter that it wasn't possible for Schumacher to join the team, that we needed some people with Formula One experience, particularly in our first year.'

So Mercedes-Benz, through Neerpasch and Kramer, was steadily pushing Schumacher towards Jordan – and to gain more single-seater experience, Schumacher had a one-off Formula 3000 drive in the extremely competitive Japanese F3000 series. He finished in second place at Sugo.

'I didn't believe Gachot would go to prison,' says Jordan now. 'I didn't really do anything.' Nonetheless, there was a sportscar race at the Nurburgring the weekend before the Belgian Grand Prix, which meant Schumacher would be back in Europe, racing for Mercedes-Benz. Jordan approached Weber about the possibility of Schumacher driving for Jordan and was referred on to Neerpasch. Weber himself was enthusiastic and asked Jordan to send a draft contract, which he did, even though at this stage he still thought Gachot would be released on appeal. But Gachot's appeal was turned down, and Jordan got Schumacher. The young German tested the Jordan car three days before practice started at Spa-Francorchamps.

'The first three laps were incredible,' Schumacher says, smiling at the memory. 'I sat in the car and I thought, this is crazy. Because everything happened so quickly and I was so nervous and I thought it's going to be really, really hard to be used to this thing and, at Spa, it would be not so easy. But after three laps, then it started to be OK.'

Jordan is a quintessential Formula One businessman. His teams have won the British Formula 3 series and the International Formula 3000 Championship. Schumacher might have been the next Ayrton Senna, but he would still have to find £150,000 to race for Jordan at Spa-Francorchamps: such is the way of Formula One, where raw economic necessity is frequently all that matters.

In return, Schumacher would receive a specified space on the Jordan car and on his race overalls to display his sponsors' logos. The money was not a problem. Mercedes-Benz would fund his first Formula One drive: Mercedes-Benz would even pay for him to drive a Ford-Cosworth-powered Grand Prix car. The money would be dispatched via the Swiss base of Sauber-Mercedes.

'Under normal circumstances,' Neerpasch says, 'a young driver doesn't have the potential to slip into these possibilities. So that was what we could do. We took the financial risk away and within two days we could refinance ourselves.' In the parlance of the pit-lane, Mercedes-Benz 'sold on' the sponsorship space on the car and Schumacher's overalls to Tic Tac mints and Dekra, a German organisation responsible for the technical checking and control of road vehicles. Ultimately, Schumacher's Formula One debut would cost Mercedes-Benz nothing: it might even have turned a profit.

Schumacher qualified seventh at Spa. He was fast, and classy. He even talked of triple World Champion Alain Prost blocking him on a quick qualifying run. On the grid he felt calm, composed: 'I was surprised that I was so relaxed. I sat there in the car and I controlled my pulse: I would say it was about 100 or 120. I was so surprised because I saw the red lights, then the count – one-two-three – and I said, "Oh, it's gone green . . ."' But Schumacher barely made it around the first corner. 'The clutch was OK after the start, but then I changed down to the first gear, went around the corner, changed into third gear, and when I changed into third gear I had no more drive.'

Schumacher's Grand Prix debut may have proved one of the shortest in history, but Jordan, Schumacher, Weber and Neerpasch had continued talking deals. Jordan would be paid £150,000 a race to run Schumacher in the five remaining 1991 Grands Prix, and $3.5m to provide him with a car for the entire 1992 racing season.

Schumacher remembers: 'I didn't sign a contract before the [Spa] race. He [Jordan] just wanted to have that paper signed: "After the race you have to sign the contract we give you, like this." He wanted that I should sign. This I don't sign. Neerpasch called him and said, change this and this and this. He did and then I signed. And I signed just this: [an agreement] that after Spa we sit together and talk about the contract, and if both sides agree, then we sign the [long-term] contract.'

In the space of one weekend Schumacher had gone from being a respected young driver to an almost-superstar.

Then Jordan made what he admits was a tactical error: he told the world that he was taking a week's holiday: the first time off he had had since October the previous year. In fact, Jordan headed for Japan to discuss the possibility of his team using Yamaha rather than Ford-Cosworth engines for 1992: at this time Yamaha was still the contracted engine supplier to the Brabham team.

While Jordan was away, Schumacher tested for Jordan at Silverstone on the Thursday after the Belgian Grand Prix. He was characteristically quick. He was also uncharacteristically outspoken. 'He expressed some doubts to [team manager] Trevor Foster as to why we were changing from Ford to Yamaha engines,' says Jordan. 'We thought someone had been putting thoughts in his head.'

Jordan's contract had been viewed by both Mercedes-Benz, which would continue to fund Schumacher's programme through Sauber-Mercedes, and IMG: Neerpasch had brought his former employers in to check the fine print of all contractual matters. 'On the day of the Silverstone test,' Jordan says, 'Neerpasch confirmed to [Jordan commercial manager] Ian Phillips, without question, that the lawyers at Mercedes had OK'd the contract for 1991, 1992 and 1993. It would be with us in a few days, we would get his signature and everything would be sorted out. Neerpasch made an appointment for ten o'clock on the Monday before Monza. He would have with him the signed contract, the agreement.' And Eddie Jordan would have Schumacher.

The following day, Friday August 30, the deal turned complicated. Jordan learnt that there was, as he puts it, 'some movement at Benetton with lawyers and Neerpasch in particular'. Weber phoned Phillips with a simple message: 'Something's going on. Watch Neerpasch.' Over the weekend, Jordan goes on to suggest, Neerpasch approached Benetton and offered the team Schumacher's services for 1991 and 1992 with an option on 1993, 1994 and 1995. Both Neerpasch and Schumacher claim that Benetton had approached them after Spa-Francorchamps. Benetton will neither confirm nor deny this.

Benetton's Tom Walkinshaw, who had only acquired a 35 per cent share of the team some six weeks before, is a no-nonsense

Scot, a successful saloon racer turned £100 million businessman: he operates the Jaguar sportscar team, builds Jaguar road cars, creates special vehicles for Holden in Australia and owns a chain of car dealerships. His move into Formula One, mooted for some time, was typically forthright and was widely expected to presage changes at Benetton, which was in some disarray after the departure of designer John Barnard earlier in the year.

Walkinshaw, who has a reputation of playing hard but fair, declined to be interviewed on the subject of Schumacher. He did, however, comment to *Motoring News* that: 'I was only interested if the Mercedes lawyers could give me clear legal evidence that Schumacher was not committed elsewhere. I would want my head examined if I didn't go after a driver of his calibre.' According to Jordan – and confirmed by *Motoring News* – on Sunday September 1, Walkinshaw had asked Benetton team manager Joan Villadelprat to source some Pirelli race tyres and prepare for a seat fitting for Schumacher.

Whatever did or did not happen over the weekend, at 10am on Monday September 2, Jordan Grand Prix, which is based at the Silverstone race circuit, was expecting Schumacher, Weber, Julian Jakobi from IMG and Neerpasch; Schumacher would be officially signed to the team. But on the same morning, at Witney, Oxfordshire, a 30-minute drive from Silverstone, a Benetton-Ford was being readied for Schumacher to test prior to the Italian Grand Prix. Benetton's intention was that Schumacher would replace the team's number two driver, Roberto Moreno, who ironically had come an excellent fourth at Spa-Francorchamps and had also set the race's fastest lap.

But no one from the Schumacher camp arrived at 10am that day. By noon, Eddie Jordan had tracked Neerpasch down through IMG: Neerpasch was in London. 'Eventually he called me back,' Jordan says, 'and everything seemed to be OK. And he then said, "I can't come to you, you'll have to come to me," and I said, "Sorry, I've already made other arrangements, where is Michael?"

'When we found where Michael was,' Jordan continues, 'I said, "Michael, please level with me. What is happening, have you signed the agreement, where is Willy, why are you not here? For heaven's sake we had a test on Thursday. You spoke to us, you're very happy." He cried, virtually, telling Trevor Foster that he wanted to be here, that he didn't need to be in a big team.'

Then Jordan telephoned Walkinshaw at Benetton. 'I said,' Jordan recalls, '"Tom, I need to know what's happening. I've got these contracts and I've got these letters."' Walkinshaw agreed to helicopter to Silverstone the following morning. At 5.40pm Neerpasch and Julian Jacobi from IMG finally arrived at Jordan HQ. There was a discussion. Neerpasch and Jacobi said they would return the following morning. They didn't: Jordan believes they went from his premises directly to Benetton Formula. Schumacher says now that he was told Jordan wanted to change the terms of the contract for 1992 and beyond, apparently insisting that Schumacher's sponsors use different, smaller advertising space on the car for the same $3.5 million annual fee. Jordan dismisses this as 'absolutely preposterous', saying he had no reason to change either the sponsorship space or the fee.

Then there was the contract produced by IMG. Schumacher contends that Jordan refused to sign this: Eddie Jordan concurs, yet suggests that the IMG contract was not so much a refined version of the original, but a completely new document which he wanted some time to scrutinise.

There were, it seems, various sticking points on the IMG contract, which had been quickly drawn up by IMG's Andrew Hampel while he was on holiday in Italy. One was that the contract was made out in Schumacher's name, not Mercedes-Benz's, thus making Schumacher directly responsible for paying Jordan: as Eddie Jordan points out, that meant Schumacher would have to provide bank guarantees to Jordan Grand Prix. And this he could not do. Another concerned the year in which option clauses came into effect. Jordan wanted to sign Schumacher for the remainder of 1991, 1992 and 1993 and on an option for 1994. In other words, if Mercedes-Benz decided to enter Grand Prix racing in 1994, it and it alone had first option on Schumacher.

But there was already gossip that sportscar racing was looking unsteady for 1992: attendances were declining, media interest was low, race entries were pitiful. Jordan thinks that Neerpasch wanted to be able to pull the proposed Mercedes-Benz Formula One programme forward by a year if sportscar racing went soft. 'I said,' Jordan explains, 'that I would negotiate on that issue, and that at the end of 1992, because there was no money for 1993, I would allow him to make the decision: Michael Schumacher and Michael Schumacher only. And it would either be a new team at Mercedes-Benz or at Jordan. I would concede on that issue only. I felt quite confident that if the boy didn't want to be with us then he's better off leaving us.'

Jordan's reluctance to sign the IMG contract appears to have proved too much for Neerpasch, who signed Schumacher to Benetton later the same evening. A fax was sent to Jordan from IMG informing the team that the deal was off.

According to Eddie Jordan, Schumacher's destiny was effectively out of the young driver's hands as Neerpasch allegedly forbade him from attending meetings concerning his racing future. 'Why did they keep Michael Schumacher away from the story? Why did they not let the driver make the choice? That was my argument. If Benetton are better and the driver wants to be with Benetton, I can live with that.'

'That's completely untrue,' says Neerpasch, who nonetheless admits that Schumacher was not present at all of the meetings. 'Part of our strategy is to keep the drivers out of these problems. The success for Michael Schumacher when he was the first time in the Eddie Jordan car was because he was prepared to do this without having had the pressure from the outset. When a driver gets the opportunity to drive, if they have an opportunity like Michael had in Spa, for him then it's everything or nothing. Because of this strategy we tried to keep him out of the very difficult financial and business situation.'

On Thursday September 2, Jordan Grand Prix failed in taking out an injunction in London to prevent Schumacher driving for Benetton in the Italian Grand Prix at Monza: on the same day Roberto Moreno took action against Benetton in a Milanese court, which ruled he did have a valid contract with the team. That allowed Moreno to settle out of court – for, effectively, being dumped in favour of Michael Schumacher – with Benetton for an estimated $500,000.

On the evening of the same day, Italian Formula 3000 driver Alessandro Zanardi visited the Benetton pit at Monza for a seat fitting: if Schumacher was unable to drive, he would deputise. (Ironically, while Roberto Moreno raced the second Jordan in Italy and in Portugal, Zanardi – 'a terrific young prospect,' according to Eddie Jordan – got the drive in Spain, Japan and Australia. This was, quite simply, a game of musical chairs played with million-dollar stakes.)

Then, later in the evening of September 5, came the meeting at the Villa d'Este, arranged to arbitrate the dispute between Jordan and Benetton. IMG representatives, including Andrew Hampel, Benetton lawyers, Jordan, his lawyers, Moreno's lawyer and Formula One supremo Bernie Ecclestone were all gathered in one room. There was one surprising absentee: Jochen Neerpasch.

'I think he was hiding from the flak at that stage,' says Jordan. 'I'd say he was advised to stay away: he had placed Schumacher with IMG before anyone realised what was going on.' Jordan had two letters of intent, one in English, the other in German, and the contract rewritten by IMG, awaiting signature. That, to Benetton, meant Schumacher had been a free agent, seeking to be signed up. Neerpasch subsequently claimed the letters of intent were merely 'an agreement to talk'. Discussions became heated. Ecclestone had to intervene before it was confirmed that Schumacher would drive for Benetton with immediate effect until 1995, with a roll-over option at the end of each year. If Mercedes-Benz wanted Schumacher for Formula One, it must give Benetton six months' notice and also pay the token sum of one dollar.

Whatever the truth, Schumacher's first two Grands Prix, so inch-perfect on the track, were sullied by the off-track politicking. The British motor-racing press ran critical editorials: this was hardly the way to attract sponsors in a time of financial belt-tightening.

Now, Jordan can sit back and take a pragmatic view of the affair.

'This is business at a high level, and I suppose in certain ways it makes the intrigue of Formula One. I have to perform in this situation. Tom Walkinshaw is a hard-nosed businessman: I respect him because he's been successful in his business. I think that he is fair.' As for Neerpasch, Jordan simply says: 'He's not a saint by any means.' Schumacher, by contrast, stresses how indebted he is to Neerpasch and Germany's most conservative car company: 'They showed they believe in me ... I have to say a big, big thank you to Mercedes-Benz.'

There was a triple irony to the story of Schumacher and Mercedes-Benz, too. In late November, the German company announced it would not be entering Grand Prix racing for 'environmental reasons'; Neerpasch had a driver with the necessary abilities – Schumacher took one fifth and two sixth places for Benetton before the end of the season – but no team. Then, in early February 1992, a brusque statement from Switzerland announced that Sauber would go Grand Prix racing in 1993. And Sauber's nominated driver? Schumacher. 'Michael Schumacher is contracted to Sauber,' reiterated Neerpasch. 'Schumacher is released under certain conditions to go Formula One racing [with Benetton]. If Sauber needs Schumacher, Sauber gets Schumacher back.' On February 7, Benetton issued a statement: Schumacher would stay put; the team would only release him to race with Mercedes-Benz. Neerpasch duly disputed this, claiming that what he described as 'the co-operation between Sauber and Mercedes' entitled Sauber to run Schumacher. Enter, once again, serried ranks of lawyers on all sides ...

Jordan walked out of the meeting at the Villa d'Este knowing that he had lost Schumacher. 'The guy was everything that I thought he would be. It doesn't really matter now but there's not another person in that paddock who would have chosen him. As it happens, if he hadn't driven for me he would not be in Formula One and, with the uncertainty surrounding Group C, he could be sitting on the scrapheap now.'

Jordan stood, frustrated, tired and angry, in the palatial understatement of the Villa d'Este. He saw a face he knew, that of Ron

Dennis, boss of McLaren, Formula One's most successful team. 'I think he was dancing with his wife,' Jordan says. 'It was a bizarre situation. There was lovely music playing outside, and there was all this shouting and roaring going on inside. But this was quite late at night and Ron came over and talked.' Eddie Jordan looks up. 'Oh yes, and the other thing he said was: "Welcome to the Piranha Club."'

CAPTAIN SENSIBLE

Matthew Engel

March, 1994

In English cricket, the quest is not so much for the Holy Grail as for King Arthur himself. The men who run our native game engage in a perpetual hunt for our mythical leader of men, parfit and gentil in every way, but capable of smiting the Australians and West Indians to smithereens at a blow.

They never do quite find the king. And most of the time, the England selectors have to entrust their team to someone they know is really only a knight, a senior pro like Mike Gatting or Graham Gooch who is not at all parfit and gentil, and may indeed be regarded as rather oikish. They just hope to blazes he will have some idea about the game's strategy and niceties and, most especially, how to comport himself in the company of barmaids without getting his name dragged through the gutter press.

Once every couple of generations or so, there comes along a figure who seems to be something more than that; someone who rises to the top as if quite untroubled by force of gravity. Early in the century, there was CB Fry, who could otherwise have been King of Albania. In the Fifties there was Peter May, who could on-drive perfectly at the age of twelve and, when he was 25, assumed the captaincy of the England team as if it were his inheritance. May was handsome, May was dashing, May was everything a Fifties schoolboy could ever want to be; and he led the last England team that could justifiably claim to be the best in the world. It was only 30 years later when he himself became chairman of the selectors that it became obvious he was also a bit of a twit.

Now there is Mike Atherton, who is just 25 and is about to captain England in a Test series in the West Indies, perhaps the most thankless job in world sport. It has been obvious for years this was going to happen. It has actually happened sooner rather than later.

I first met Atherton in a heavy metal club in Manhattan, not the sort of place one would ever have found CB Fry or Peter May. It is not quite Atherton's sort of place either. The occasion was a bizarre, not-quite-official, not-quite-rebellious cricket tour of North America and we'd been dragged to the club by Derek Pringle, a cricketer who had himself been earmarked by May as a potential captain until it became obvious that he had far too subversive a cast of mind to be any such thing.

Atherton has got there without being subversive, without being establishment, without really seeming to try, without facing much of a setback, without life ever kicking him in the teeth. If there is a time when you are likely to be kicked in the teeth, it is as captain of England in the West Indies, probably by a short-pitched ball from Curtly Ambrose rearing up and smacking you in the mouth. But Atherton has coped with life so far. He looks at ease with himself, in a heavy metal club or in the Lord's pavilion. He is, above all, young, which is pretty unforgivable. And, in his case, youth is not so much a stage of life as a fixed belief.

It was not a coincidence that when the touring party for the West Indies was announced the players were just about all Atherton's approximate contemporaries. 'Wouldn't you say,' he asked me, though I was the one supposed to be asking the questions, 'that in business it is an advantage to have youth at the top?'

I ruffled my grey hair and floundered. 'Um, um, well . . .' I replied. 'You tend to believe in yourself most when you're young,' he went on. 'When you're older, the doubts creep in. Your drive to success must be greater in your first Test than in your hundred and first.'

To those of us who have grown up with the last generation of cricketers, there is something frightening about Atherton's youth. For about fifteen years, English cricket has been based around a handful of players – Botham, Gower, Gooch, Gatting, Lamb. The first two have retired; none of the others will be playing this winter. And everything has always gone back to one benchmark match: the Leeds Test against Australia in 1981 when Botham turned round an impossible situation and England won, having been 500 to 1 in the betting tent. Atherton remembers that match, too.

He was actually there, the one and only time he had been to a Test match before he was selected to be there. Unfortunately, he was there on the Friday, when Australia were winning and it was dead boring. Everyone with the slightest interest in cricket has a Kennedy's assassination or Thatcher's resignation recollection of where they were when they heard the news of what happened on the Tuesday. Atherton knows exactly where he was too. He was playing for Lancashire Schools. He was thirteen years old.

Fry went to Repton, May to Charterhouse. Mike Atherton was not born with a silver spoon, though it was not quite plastic either. He comes from the northern edge of Manchester and grew up in a nice-ish kind of four-bed detached with a path up the middle of the back garden that was just big enough to provide a decent pitch, if you started your run-up down by the willow tree.

His father, Alan, is now the headmaster of a comprehensive in Bolton. But before that he tried and failed to become a professional footballer. In fact, he was Manchester United's very first apprentice, though only because his name came first in the alphabet. He played a lot for the youth team, when the captain was a lad called Nobby Stiles, a few times for the reserves and once made it to be the actual first team reserve, though that was in the days before substitutes were allowed on and he thinks it was more of a pat on the back than anything else.

Alan Atherton knew Mike was never going to make a footballer, because he never had the pace. Cricket, though, was different. 'I never really coached him,' he says. 'He played a pretty straight bat from the start, at six or seven. And he was a natural leg-break bowler.' Briscoe Lane Junior School in Newton Heath, with Mike Atherton playing just about every role except pavilion cat, won the Manchester Schools Cup four years running.

Then he got into Manchester Grammar School. Nobody from

Briscoe Lane goes to Manchester Grammar any more than boys from Moston Brook, the comprehensive where he would normally have gone, get in to Cambridge. It is an extraordinary hothouse school, an intense, competitive place ('They work your bollocks off,' says Atherton) which only moved out of the state system shortly before his time, when both educational theory and Labour government policy had taken against sink-or-swim schooling.

The boys wear blue blazers with an owl on the crest. Most of them come from posh prep schools like Altrincham Prep (Alty Prep) where they are specially prepared for the experience. It could have been traumatic for an 11-year-old from the wrong side of town, two long and lonely bus rides away.

'Traumatic?' says Mike. 'I'm not the kind that ever thinks of things as traumatic. I just accepted what was happening and got on with it.' But there were problems. One is that the school is near several others that have children with different priorities. 'The local kids round there made their feelings pretty clear,' he recalls. 'I remember several occasions when we were coming out of school and there'd be kids with axes and chains and we'd have escorts on to the buses. I remember a lot of times when there were police around. It used to be hair-raising if you played football and had to walk across the field to the bus stop.'

Atherton rapidly put the other Briscoe Lane kids behind him, not consciously, I think, or snobbishly, but because that was the way it was. They went to Moston Brook, he went to MGS and he has never seen them since. One of the Sunday papers did find all his old team-mates from the Cup-winning side, and Atherton himself was chuffed that they were so generous about his success. Indeed, nearly all of them were: they said how he was nice and polite and a good captain then; and how they knew he would succeed. Mike, being straightforward himself, may have missed the subtext of one of his classmates' comments. 'All I ever seemed to do was field,' said Simon Cropper. 'There wasn't much else left to do after Mike had finished batting and bowling.'

At Manchester Grammar, the rest of his life began. By coincidence, or perhaps not by coincidence, 3 out of 24 in his class are now playing county cricket – Atherton, his Lancashire team-mate Gary Yates, and Mark Crawley, now with Nottinghamshire. Mark's younger brother, John, who is regarded by a lot of judges (Atherton not excluded) as a future Test player, was a couple of years behind.

Atherton was able to play cricket on a flat, well-tended wicket. As a second-former, he was given a couple of games in the first team, in the third form he was a regular. His statistics, preserved in *Wisden*, are almost ridiculous. In 1985, he averaged 187. But old *Wisdens* are full of the statistics of promising schoolboys who are now holding down steady jobs at the bank, if they are lucky.

Atherton, however, knew his destiny as soon as he got to Cambridge (two As and a B at A level, Downing College – which is a midway sort of place, not too academic, not too thicko). His first cricket match for the university was against Essex, then the county champions and playing Cambridge at full strength. The students were 27 for seven. Atherton pulled them round by scoring 73 not out.

At the time, he had never even played county second XI cricket, never been near county players. When he walked out to bat in the second innings, Keith Fletcher, the Essex captain, told his team-mates: 'Let's get this little smart arse out.' That was a very high compliment. Cambridge were 71 all out in the second innings; Atherton made 33 of them.

He knew then he was going to play cricket for a living and was going to be very good at it. 'If I thought I wasn't going to play for England,' he says, 'I don't think I'd have bothered.' Who would have guessed then that Fletcher and Atherton would one day be flying off to the Caribbean together, as manager and captain of the England team? Well, just about everyone actually. It was pretty obvious about Fletcher, too.

Atherton discusses all this with a serenity that is almost frightening. While he was still at Cambridge he had not merely a car – normally undergraduates are only allowed bicycles – but a sponsored one. The only controversy surrounding him was that Lancashire did not rush him at once into the first team every season when he came down from Cambridge. Some of the Lancashire members, who are famously impatient and intemperate, were furious on his behalf.

'I recognised the ability and the class of the bloke,' says David Hughes, then the captain, 'but I wanted to make sure that he felt and everyone else felt that he'd earned the right to play in the first team.' Only one person was unruffled. 'There was no doubt I was going to play eventually,' says Atherton. He finally made his debut against Warwickshire at Southport and scored 53. Everything was just a matter of time.

Atherton still managed to be quite an ordinary undergraduate. He read history, generally when no one else was about because he had to make up for the time he lost leading the Young England team overseas. His special subjects were the Black Death and the gentry in the fifteenth century. Was he interested in them? 'Oh yes. But not slavishly interested,' he says.

He played college football ('left side of mid-field. I was laborious and sluggish but I got stuck in') and water polo. Did he act? 'Only after about ten pints.' But being good at cricket gave him a confidence that affected everything he did, even playing pool in the bar.

There were some who felt that at Lancashire either Hughes was giving him a hard time or that the two hard-school senior players, Graeme Fowler and Paul Allott, were. He never saw it that way. 'Lancashire, more than most, is a hierarchical club. "You're playing for Lancashire, and you should know you're playing for Lancashire," was underlying everything they said.'

By 1989, he was playing for England. His first appearance in an England dressing room was as twelfth man in the Old Trafford Test. England were losing the Ashes that summer as well, even more abysmally than in 1993. And halfway through that game, they announced the names of the players who were leaving for the last of the prop-up-apartheid rebel tours of which cricketers were so fond in the Eighties.

Atherton was watching the names come up on Teletext in the back of the dressing room while everyone at the front was denying the whole thing. David Gower, then the captain, and Ian Botham were left to keep England going. Gower, Atherton recalls, 'was under constant pressure and on a fairly short fuse'. But he had no problems with him or Botham. 'If Both respects you, if he thinks you can play, you're fine,' he says. Atherton was fine.

By 1991, he was vice-captain. But that was when things started to go wrong for the first and only time in his life. He lost form against the West Indies; he needed a back operation. 'I lost my invincibility,' as he puts it. 'My confidence in a whole range of things, on the golf course, everywhere, went as well.'

Alec Stewart jumped ahead of him as heir-presumptive to the England captaincy: Stewart of Surrey, who was seen – in the tired old way that people in cricket look at these things – as the hard-faced professional while Atherton was regarded as the jolly old amateur. This is primarily because Atherton went to Cambridge and Stewart did not.

By the Indian tour of early 1993, Stewart seemed the natural successor to Gooch as captain, while Atherton was struggling to get his place back. When they were batting together in the Bombay Test, they got involved in a horrific run-out mix-up. It was not entirely clear which one was out. This debacle ended with Stewart leaving and Atherton, who had been mysteriously excluded from the previous Test when Stewart had led the team, standing his ground.

The mix-up was seen, in the same tired old way, as Atherton striking back and finally deciding to play hard himself. He denies it all. 'It was a cock-up. I've just written an article for Stewie's benefit brochure, touching on it in a fairly satirical way,' he says. They are friends, both insist; and, indeed, when Stewart lost out to Atherton he was as graceful about it as CB Fry could have been. But the incident did change people's perspective on them.

At the time, Atherton was no more than third favourite to succeed Gooch, behind Stewart and Gatting; a seven-to-one shot according to the *Guardian*. Slowly, subtly, by degrees, the odds changed. By his cricket, by his demeanour, by the fact that people in the end could not find a reason against picking him, Atherton eventually came close to picking himself.

Less than four weeks after he was appointed captain, he had led England to victory in the last Test at The Oval, which meant they only lost the series to Australia four–one. By now, even men like the old Pom-basher Ian Chappell, one of the toughest Australian captains of all, were talking glowingly about his leadership. It was clear, most of all, that he knew what he wanted, who he wanted and how he wanted things done. David Gower was as near as Mike Atherton ever got to having a hero. He was watching TV with his father when Gower played the pull for four against Pakistan in 1978 that constitutes the most famous first-ball shot in the history of Test cricket.

Quietly, he thinks it was a mistake to leave Gower out of the tour of India last year. Equally, he thought it would be a mistake to bring him back to go to the West Indies. Some 75 per cent of the letters he received in the three months after his appointment screamed at him on this subject. He never wavered. Gower retired.

Atherton has firm ideas too about those who can play and those who can't. This suggests a possible end to all the dreadful mucking about by selectors, as long as he can maintain his beliefs and sustain his authority. But there has never been a surer cure for invincibility than captaining the England cricket team in the West Indies, except perhaps for managing the England football team. Atherton knows that good, clever men have been brought down by this job before. This summer, he rejected the opportunity to captain Lancashire, knowing that you ought to take on one challenge at a time and that the Lancashire job may well be there again if, or more likely when, the England job goes sour.

'Sooner or later, you're going to lose the England captaincy, probably in circumstances where things are going wrong,' he says. 'The probability is this will happen to me. I'm not going to be looking over my shoulder. If things go wrong, so be it. You have to stand up and have the courage of your convictions.'

It may go horribly wrong, sooner rather than later, if the West Indies tour lives up to form. But I have never known a time when there was a greater sense that an England captain might have a chance of getting it right, or greater goodwill for him to do so.

On the face of it, Mike Atherton is a very ordinary, very likeable young man. He lives in a tucked-away Manchester flat, stays discreet about his long-standing girlfriend (a medic he met in Cambridge), maintains equanimity and good humour in the face of bores and ruffians, and still drinks a few pints.

I dare say he might still slip into a heavy metal club if he was passing that way, and Pringle insisted. We just have to hope that underneath it all he really is King Arthur.

CAPTAIN BEEFHEART

Mick Imlah

September, 1990

Britain hosts the second Rugby Union World Cup in the autumn of 1991, and everyone will be watching. Everyone will be talking to Will Carling, the man who, two years ago, was given the job of captaining the England side through the most exciting period in the game's history. He was 22 at the time, the 'baby' of the team and the same age as Paul Gascoigne is now – which goes to show that men mature at different rates. His speed, his strength and the skill of his distribution guaranteed his place at centre for the foreseeable future; in addition, there was a quiet intelligence, a self-discipline and a decency about Carling that marked him out as an ideal man to lift the World Cup above his head.

Until March this year, all went well under Carling and Geoff Cooke (the manager who appointed him). England had won their first three games of the Five Nations Championship by emphatic margins, and they travelled to Edinburgh ready to be hailed as a great side by beating Scotland to win the Grand Slam. Such was England's perceived superiority that only two Scots would have got into a composite team (chosen by Englishmen). And one of these, crucially, was their captain, David Sole.

Rugby teams traditionally sprint and scatter onto the pitch like men fleeing the gunfire of their own nerves. But on Grand Slam day, Sole had his players walk slowly out, which was somehow terrifying. You could almost hear the pipes: you *could* hear the pipes. And sustained by what Carling describes as 'the most emotional atmosphere I've ever experienced at a rugby match', Scotland's aggressive defence knocked England out of their imperious rhythm. With twelve minutes to go, and England six points down despite continual pressure, there occurred one of those moments which turn a game as decisively as any score. England won yet another scrummage five yards out. Scrum half Hill picked up and ran laterally, then flung out a long pass to his inside centre, Carling, who took it turning inside, or – in effect – standing still. Scotland's tacklers converged again: Lineen cuffed Carling's legs, Chalmers clung to his body, then Jeffrey, Turnbull and Calder hit the spot in fierce succession. Carling was engulfed and thrown back; the ball popped up like a sweetie and Armstrong thumped it 30 yards up the touchline to safety. The crowd seized on this symbolic tableau of the reversal of Carling's fortunes: England were destined to fail.

It was Carling's bad luck to be the target of the most spectacular of the many tackles which denied his side in that frantic last quarter. But there had been incidents in the first half that prompted much wise muttering about the efficacy of his leadership. There was the indiscipline of the forwards who conceded six points from offences committed when the ball was dead: Skinner for talking, Probyn for stamping after a collapsed scrum. Then there was the running of three easily kickable penalties, a decision which seemed to emanate from the headless chicken of the English pack rather than from the mind of the young captain. For the second of these, pack leader Brian Moore was clearly seen to indicate to the referee *his* choice of a scrum – looking for the boost of a push-over try – before belatedly looking across field to Carling to have the option approved. However it happened, poor Carling got the blame: either he let his team-mate override him with the wrong decision, or he made the wrong decision. England lost their most important match for ten years, and holes were revealed in the myth of the 'great side' being assembled for the 1991 World Cup – an ancient loosehead, an imbalanced back row and an apparent lack of leadership. The first two problems are for the selectors to solve: the last is for Carling, as he enters his third season as captain.

There's no doubt about Carling's qualifications for captaincy: he has, after all, already made a career of it. Like Mike Brearley, the best England cricket captain of the modern era, he studied psychology at university (Durham), where he was sponsored by the army. His military career was doomed the day his regiment denied him leave to play representative rugby (the army's short-sightedness can be measured against the hours of glamorous free publicity the RAF has had from its flying winger Rory Underwood). Now, after a short spell with Mobil, Carling operates what he calls a 'motivational consultancy' of his own, called Inspirational Horizons. The consultancy sends top sportsmen to lecture to captains of commerce and industry on topics such as leadership and teamwork (and occasionally, one suspects, on How We Beat the Welsh). It affords him a spacious office off Bond Street, where he sits with the purposeful ease of a man precociously at home with responsibility.

He is probably sick of How We Lost to the Scots, but he tackles the question head-on and counters criticism of his own role with an alternative notion of captaincy adapted from his own strengths and possible weaknesses. He could never be an inspirational leader on the lines of Ireland's Ciaran Fitzgerald, whose loud exhortation, 'Where's your fucking *pride*!' is said to have won one match at Twickenham. He doesn't believe a captain can have much influence after the kick-off and points out that players generally take the field for internationals with their bloodstreams brimming full of adrenalin, and are more likely to need calming down than psyching up. Preparation is all, and in Edinburgh, he admits that both he and England got it slightly wrong. Carling sees the captain's most important role in today's set up as a link between the management and the players, establishing trust and laying down long-term objectives.

And then there are the media duties which he considers with a frown. Carling calls himself introspective – he likes to have a quiet hour to himself in his room after an international – and press conferences and speech-making don't come easily to him. His anticipation of the World Cup is blighted by dread of the phone and the microphone, and he expects to have to prepare as carefully for the barrage of interviews ('Will Carling, do you think England can bounce back from this triple sending-off?') as for the physical demands of the tournament. It won't help him that rugby is currently shaping up for all sorts of controversy.

Among the issues in line to give the administrators grief, in 1991 and beyond, are the rules of the game. Rugby is imperfect, and its defects are concentrated in the elaborate set pieces – the scrum and the line-out – which contribute so much to the game as a spectacle. (Rugby League has seen fit to get rid of one and devalue the other.) These two phases of play preserve – for the moment – the beloved stereotypes of the fat prop and the towering lock, but from a legal point of view they are close to chaos: the scrum can only be refereed by guesswork, the line-out by degree (*i.e.* penalising an elbow in the face but not a push in the ribs). So matches are won and lost by goalkickers converting penalties for that small proportion of offences a referee is able or willing to detect. Carling partly attributes Scotland's victory over England to the fact that 'they played the referee better than we did', which is not to accuse them of cheating, but to commend them for a superior selection of which laws to break and when. All the talk on the trains back from Edinburgh to London that weekend was of Scotland dropping the scrum to nullify the advantage England had through the work of Probyn. Others say Probyn's angles are such that he should be penalised at every scrum – whatever that means. Don't ask Will Carling – he confesses to having 'not a clue' about front-row play. When crucial areas of the game are conducted in this legal shadowland, frustrations creep in which contribute to rugby's other recurring headache – violent play.

Every three or four years, rugby stamps firmly on its own head, then has to beat its breast for a while. Over the past couple of decades, the most notorious big games have been Canterbury v The British Lions in 1971 (when two halves of punching broke both Sandy Carmichael's cheekbones); Australia v England in 1975 (when each of the Australian forwards celebrated the first maul by laying into the nearest Englishmen); Bridgend v New Zealand in

1978 (when John Ashworth ground his studs through JPR Williams' cheek); England v Wales in 1980 (a general rough-house; Paul Ringer sent off); France v New Zealand in 1986 (when a concussed Wayne Shelford was carefully carried off to have his scrotum stitched); and England v Wales in 1988 (when England came out fighting and Wade Dooley broke Phil Davies' jaw with a punch). This pattern shows that the rotten games are fairly rare and no more frequent than they used to be; it also suggests that we are due for one about World Cup time, which would darken everything.

Meanwhile, players in this country have a running battle with the conservatism of the rugby establishment, and the England captain is at the forefront of the fray. He knows that to appeal to the best young sportsmen the game has to free itself from the grip of the Old Boys. In the face of superstition, he has invited video cameras into an international changing room before a game; and in the face of a new wave of defections to the professional ranks of rugby league, and the increasing demands made on the time of top players, he expresses impatience with union's anachronistic amateur code. 'I never want to be paid for taking the pitch – I still play for fun, and I don't want a sort of rugby employer telling me when and where I have to play, but I think the RFU must relax the rules in other areas. I don't see any harm in a few players being able to make money out of endorsements or advertising. It will only involve a handful of players – Rob (Andrew), Jerry (Guscott), Rory (Underwood) – and me, I suppose – and it won't change the game for the guys at Esher Thirds or whatever. The trouble is that different rules are operating in different countries. Look at the New Zealanders. Companies make them PR executives – they turn up at the odd lunch here and there, and the rest of the time they train. That's professionalism. It's their attitude which makes them world champions – they have a mental and physical toughness we have to learn. But we've had to compete against them with guys who have to decide whether they can afford to play rugby – not how much they're going to make out of it.'

As things are, in the cycle of sacrifices and rewards, it is the players' social lives that come out bottom. Ask Carling about his interests outside rugby and the atmosphere goes slightly glum. In this respect (only), injuries like the shin trouble he had in Australia can be a blessing. Usually, he trains two nights a week with his club, Harlequins, and other evenings he's in the gym with his personal programme. In a couple of years his upper body has zapped itself up two or three sizes and looks impatient for more. 'The whole week is geared,' he says, 'to getting it physically right on Saturday afternoon.' And Saturday night? He shakes his head. 'We just have a couple of drinks and drift away. You can't hope to compete at the top if you're getting hammered every weekend.'

There are those in rugby – even at the top level – who are less watchful of their fitness than Carling. Ireland's forwards, offered a version of the white meat diet their high-tech English counterparts followed throughout the championship, rejected it. Serge Blanco, the greatest of all running full-backs, smokes as many Gauloises a day as he has international caps – 60. And on a Friday night in a pub in West Wickham in Kent, Brian Parsons, the diminutive skipper of Old Beccehamians Fourth team, is limbering up for the next day's grudge match against Westcombe Park. Like Scotland's former captain Colin Deans, 37-year-old Parsons is a double-glazing salesman during the week. At weekends, he enters the comfortable plunge-bath of his club and pub, and sketches out various fantasies about this year's Fourths: one week, they're a class of raw but pacey colts, willing to run all day for their static skipper; next, as players go up and down, a bunch of blokes who've been around, who know all the tricks, who can take the piss out of the opposition's pacey but raw colts. Such formulae give him endless delight, and his winter life revolves no less than Will Carling's around the game.

Next night, in the same pub, and Parsons is the worse for wear. There's an egg-sized bulge on his forehead where a Westcombe Park flanker has 'boshed' him. Old Becs have gone down 17–9, thanks to three second-half penalties; the referee has done them no favours. But the muted percussion of his match analysis is suddenly drowned out by a sudden roar from the bar, as a group of younger Old Becs – good-looking lads with gel in their hair –

sing *You've Lost That Loving Feeling* with brutal togetherness. The local football team look on in dismay; a pair of hockey boys leave. This is tame stuff as yet, but enough to raise, once more, that most difficult of rugby questions: why do so many of the nice, intelligent individuals who play the game feel driven to huddle in a circle chanting about tampons and so on until landlords show them the door?

Meanwhile, a million miles away, Carling studies the personalised wall-chart donated by the England management, which maps out his training schedule for the next thirteen months. Getting to the top in his game – for all its hard-held ethos of playing for fun – is now a gruelling and strangely solitary business. He may be the last amateur of his kind. As Carling is fond of saying: 'There's much more to life than playing rugby.' But not yet.

VILLAGE PEOPLE

Andrea Waind

September, 1993

Church bells are ringing as 'PD' runs in to bowl. A ringed dove coos above the lush Ashby Folville pitch. Two balls to go, the last two men in, and five runs needed.

PD (Phil Lane, after his first two initials) is hit for a soaring six over the horse chestnut trees. The bails fly, the captain swears and Ashby Carington Cricket Club and its three supporters clap off the opposition's batsman, who has his hands down his flannels rearranging his box. What the England team play and are and do isn't cricket. *This* is cricket.

When members of this team are given out by the blind, deaf, 90-year-old umpire who persistently cheats, they don't stand and argue. They wait until they have crossed the boundary marker before they lose their tempers, and rage and stamp around the locker room amid the ancient bats and ripped umpires' coats and dried-up cans of linseed oil. And when they are out and the blind, deaf umpire doesn't notice they are out, they walk.

'I'd walk,' says the wicketkeeper.

'I'd walk,' says the captain. 'I think we'd all walk.'

The Ashby captain is 'Slates' – Richard Slater, 26, whose hobbies are smoking and drinking, and whose other nickname is 'Rigsby' because he takes in lodgers. 'And because he's a scruffy bastard,' says wicketkeeper John Whiting, whose own nickname (they all have them) is 'The Lightning'.

'God knows why,' says Rigsby, wearily.

Ashby Carington CC, whose pitch is a Leicestershire sheep field and whose headquarters is the Carington Arms, where its trophies are on display around the bar, all say the England team is a disgrace to the name of cricket. Mike Gatting putting his fist through a glass door because he didn't like what the umpire said. Players shambling through India unshaved, without blazers, swigging from cans. Players who never walk.

'Would I like to be on tour with this England team? No I bloody wouldn't,' says Rigsby.

Their president, Wing Commander John Smith-Carington – 'Winky' to his friends – is dismissive of the whole international scene. 'Womanising, drug-taking, glaring at umpires – that sort of thing doesn't go on here,' he says. 'We play a civilised game.'

The Wing Commander's ancestors came from Carentan in Normandy: '1066, the usual thing,' he says. They arrived in Ashby Folville in 1352 and now occupy the tombs in St Mary's church overlooking the cricket pitch.

The ground is Arcadian. Ancient chestnuts circle the boundary, and if you hit the oak near the gate, it's a four. (At some local grounds, you can catch off cows.) The river is just visible beyond third man. The team keeps a large net and a pair of waders for when the ball lands in the water (a six). If the vice-president's collie isn't about, they send in 'Pecker' because he's the smallest. Afterwards, the ball is spongy and hard to grip, and the Ashby batsmen grin at each other across the crease, Ashby being a batting side.

The only other building is the black-and-white village hall where the team serves ham teas. But the more meaningful assembly point is the Carington Arms, where the Quorn, Prince Charles' favourite hunt, meets. In the cricket season, and out of it, they hold meetings, play skittles, run books and get blind drunk. 'With two weekend league matches, two evening league matches, cup matches, and knocking up and mowing the wicket on Fridays, we can be playing and drinking seven nights a week,' says Nigel Hubbard ('Hubcap'), who captains friendlies.

The Wing Commander's red-and-black coat of arms, the Smith

peacock and Carington unicorn, is up outside. 'I own the pub,' he says, standing by his study window in the Manor Gate House. 'I'm lucky enough to own the village. And the land about. It means the village remains unspoilt.' John Smith-Carington is sturdy, resolute and dressed in an immaculate blazer and navy tie. His study is alive with paintings of flying Blenheims and Mitchells and Mosquitos. In the Second World War he was a Pathfinder in Bomber Command. 'We led night ops by planting flares on targets.'

Before sorting out the Hun, he played for the team. Now he uses it as a test of character. 'When I was looking for joint tenants for one of my farms, the Smith brothers attracted my attention because they play cricket.' David and Alan Smith are reliable opening batsmen who live twenty yards apart and are both known as 'Smiggy'.

The Ashby Carington wicket is safe and true, and favours batsmen. 'We haven't got any bowlers,' says Rigsby, who is a bowler.

'Well, he runs up and turns his arms about,' says Hubcap.

Early friendlies are called off to protect the pitch. Twice last winter the river flooded the field and road. The sheep were swimming and calves waded across the ground.

'I did point out the risk of flooding when the club chose that field,' says the Wing Commander, whose grandfather diverted the river in front of the Manor last century. Another of the Wing Commander's ancestors won a duel with spears at the top of the hill: 'The usual argument about land. Of course, he had to go into exile for a time because, even then, killing your opponent wasn't considered quite cricket.'

Groundsman David Favell ('Plum' because he is five-foot-four and seventeen stone) adjusts the wheels on the sightscreen, tries out the roller the team got from the council in exchange for a bottle of whisky, and checks the outfield for signs of moles and the opening batsmen's sheep.

Later, in the Carington Arms, he raises his pint of bitter. The team is celebrating its first league victory of the season: seventeen points without playing a ball because its opponents couldn't raise a side. Robert Woods (woodpecker, thus 'Pecker', he insists) reckons the team is top of the table.

Pecker wears a gold chain under his leather jacket, has spiky black hair and is a welder. When he heard the match was off he went to Garthorpe point-to-point with six of the lads and lost his money. 'My record is 22 bets without a win,' he says.

'Beer and gambling is all these lads think about,' mumbles one of Ashby Carington's fourteen vice-presidents (you only have to buy a round to be elected a vice-president). Five of the team once bought a greyhound, but it didn't win much. Hubcap has still got it.

Pecker and the 43-year-old chairman and emollient solicitor PD (or 'Petal' – 'because he's so nice and refined') are discussing practice.

Pecker: 'We don't do any. We did nets once and we didn't get any better, so we stopped.'

PD: 'The beginning of the season's a lottery with soft wickets and the ball not coming through. When we did nets we were all out for nought first game.'

Pecker: 'Nets gets you looser, but the ground's hard in nets. So I don't think practice is good for you.'

'*This* is practice,' says Rigsby, raising yet another glass of Guinness.

He is at a corner table playing three-card brag, a Benson & Hedges fug above him. Rigsby is discussing the team's switch to the Rutland League with umpire Mike Home, who, although in his fifties, still turns out as a player for the side.

'I only make up the numbers these days,' says Mike, 'but I'm younger than "Zimmer".' Zimmer, 54, is Bob Cooper, who also umpires. (Bob is father of another player, Ian Cooper – 'Cutie', because somebody thinks he looks cute.) Mike is also younger than 'Denzil' (Derek Cooper, no relation) who bowls and umpires and is the current holder of the silver Duck Trophy for most ducks in a season.

Ashby Carington umpires are never accused of cheating ('except by us,' says The Lightning, 'because they try to be so fair'). But the village cricket can be brazenly incestuous. 'There's a Rutland bowler,' says PD, 'who has been known to shout "Howzat, Father?" To which the invariable reply is "Out, Son".'

This is their first season in the Rutland League. They resigned from the North Leicestershire League (where they were the Wimbledon Football Club of their day, rushing up through the divisions) because they want to play village cricket and compete against village cricket teams.

'A lot of good village sides moved out [of the North Leicestershire League], leaving just park and recreation-ground sides,' says Rigsby, who is pulling his own pint. 'Townie grounds are diabolical, not to mention dangerous. One of them's by an aerodrome with remote-control aircraft flying about, and there's usually another game going on behind you so you can get brained by somebody hitting a six.'

Rigsby doesn't like townies. 'Most of 'em wouldn't even have a drink with you. And they never field the same side twice.' (Most of the Ashby team have been playing together for six years, some for fifteen, PD for twenty.) 'They only play for league points, say "Thank you very much", and sod off.'

'They don't start hitting you or anything, but you can feel the aggression,' says The Lightning. 'Some of us can be aggressive, but they are different people. They think we're country bumpkins. Do we think of ourselves as country bumpkins? Yes. Yeah.'

One of the Ashby vice-presidents thinks village teams are more tolerant. 'At least two local country teams have players who are what you might call a bit slow, and the lads accept them.' Another vice-president says: 'If you mean village idiots, we've got eleven playing for us.'

An evening league match at Wymondham on the edge of the Vale of Belvoir is under way. Last season Wymondham won promotion to the first division of the Borrough League for teams around Melton Mowbray. 'Six years ago all our matches were friendlies,' says Rigsby. 'Then all the teams we want to play signed up for leagues, so we had to as well.'

Around the ground, the hawthorn is thickening and making bursts of flower. The Wolds villages are ochre brick with greens tended like Ashby's wicket. 'Beeks' (Stuart Beeken), the evening league captain, is polishing the inside of his box with his elbow. Beeks takes his cricket seriously: he hates losing more than anybody. 'Perhaps he's sulking because he's lost the toss,' says a voice from the locker room.

It's eighteen overs a side – more or less a thrash. Pecker, off to open the batting, breathes deeply of the chilly air, and slips on a fourth jumper. The only sounds are the breeze in the oaks and four boys knocking a ball about. 'Just beautiful. Leather on willer,' says Pecker in broad Leicestershire. On Sunday he was out for six in a friendly against Houghton-on-the-Hill.

A few minutes later, he is walking back to the pavilion, out for two. 'I chased a wide 'un again,' he says.

Rigsby, at the door, takes a long pull of his cigarette. 'Two, Robert,' he says.

'Yeah.'

'Total eight, Robert.'

'Yeah.'

'Average four for the season, Robert.'

'It'll pick up.'

'It better.'

Fifty goes up on the scoreboard. 'Deals' (Steve Dealey) says his girlfriend moans about the time cricket takes up. 'I just tell her, if I'm playing, I'm playing.' Someone says the Smiths' wives do not allow them to play twice in a weekend. 'When I was courting it was difficult to get to all the matches,' says Rigsby. 'Now I've no problem.'

'YEAH!' Miff, the Wymondham umpire, holds up his index fingers and both teams cheer Beeks' six. Miff has been playing and umpiring at Wymondham for 39 years. Someone points out 'WG', from a rival village team, by the pavilion. WG has been flattered by his nickname for years, not knowing it means 'Whingeing Git'.

Later, Beeks, bowled for 41, scowls like a melodrama villain during his long walk to the lockers. Not hearing the applause, his only consolation is the traditional post-innings scratch down the front of his flannels. Pecker scratches violently in sympathy in an unusual two-handed style.

Tall and bearded Nigel Hough, nicknamed 'Rough Hough' because his language gets crude when he's on Hofmeister, is the team's slogger. 'I'm noted for going out and getting a lot, or getting nothing at all,' he says. Tonight he gets out first ball. So, in the next three balls, do three more batsmen, falling victim to Wymondham bowler Andrew Ruddle.

'If three out in three balls is a hat-trick,' calls a gleeful fielder, 'what do you call four out in four?'

'Crap batting,' mutters Rigsby, pulling out his crumpled Benson & Hedges.

'Just prod it about a bit. Get a few singles,' Beeks tells Deals, off to bat. 'People who play because it's a game have no idea,' he says with sudden disgust. 'If you don't play to win, it's a waste of time. I never play friendlies unless they're desperate. YEAH, AND BACK!' he yells to Deals as a fielder misses the ball.

Ashby makes 97. Despite the team's bowling – Rigsby, in a T-shirt which shows off his windmill action, bowls a lot of wides because he has not had enough practice – it is enough: Wymondham only makes 90. Undefeated in both leagues, Ashby celebrates with its opponents in the Berkeley Arms.

It is still an easy social mix, on and off the field. Zimmer says that when he was a boy, the squire played, the blacksmith, the baker and, on occasion, the vicar. The mix is as egalitarian today. Zimmer is a factory manager, Plum a farm worker. Beeks is clerk to the works with the council. Rigsby a lighting sales director. Rough Hough drives a school bus, Nigel is an accountant.

Even the Wing Commander's grandson plays occasionally. 'He took five wickets once, and had to buy a jug,' says Rigsby. (You also buy a jug – $5\frac{1}{2}$ pints – if you score 50.) 'And we've got a boy wonder who's at public school. He's going to be a fantastic player if he keeps away from booze and women.'

Bert Slater, 87, a Smith-Carington tenant farmer and former team member, remembers when Teddy Gutteridge, the odd-job man at the Manor, and the chauffeur, Hake Baker, started the team in the Thirties. 'We played at the bottom of the hill then,' he says. 'Twenty-three of us worked on the estate – bricklayers, farmers, gardeners. It was strictly a village team.'

Bert Slater thinks village cricket is dying. 'Twyford, South Croxton, Barsby – none of them have teams now,' he says. In his tweed jacket and knitted waistcoat, he sips on his Manns bitter and remembers such great England cricketers as Jack Hobbs, Maurice Leyland and Billy Gunn. 'Even county cricket isn't what it was. Goggles and mouth shields! Least we're still in pads and gloves.'

Zimmer says village cricket is becoming more professional. 'The surviving sides are better, and the grounds are better quality,' he explains. Poaching is rife. Rough Hough left his home village team because a lot of money came into the club.

'I was brought up in Barkby, but now they don't want local lads,' says Rough Hough. 'Ashby is on the up, but there's a good atmosphere, we have a laugh. At Barkby you've just got to win. I don't call that cricket.'

Two days later, Ashby comes up against semi-professionals in a cup game against the hamlet of Pickwell. Pecker is wearing five jumpers because this is the highest, coldest ground in the country. It has an astonishing view of the Wolds.

Pickwell bats. It is soon obvious Rigsby, Cutie, and PD (who wears a floppy hat and bowls deceptively fast off five paces) will have a hard time shifting the opening batsmen.

'The lad batting at the far end plays in the Bradford League alongside Vinod Kambli,' says the third Pickwell bat. Vinod Kambli scored a double century for India against England. At the other end of the crease is the best batsman in local cricket, borrowed from Billesdon. The third bat settles comfortably for a long wait. When the Billesdon man is out for 60, there's no griping from Ashby. Both teams cheer him off.

'We don't get many spectators,' says Hubcap. 'More dogs really. On sunny days we get "Handtrap Sam" [a former player who called corsets "handtraps" when he was a lad], and a chap who lies on a sunbed, puts a hat over his face and goes to sleep.'

Pickwell sets an unobtainable target and puts Ashby in. Steve Barnes ('Salty the Sea Lion' because of his clapping action when catching) is run out. 'Run out on his first game of the season without facing a ball,' says Cutie, gleefully. Salty is a run-out merchant.

Rigsby is sitting on a log, smoking. 'Everybody has a go at everybody,' he says, 'but there's no ill-feeling. The odd time somebody goes mardy, but it don't last long. We don't let it.'

The rest of the team are keeping warm in the pavilion, trying not to get too despondent at the prospect of a heavy defeat. 'Looks like we've qualified for the Wankers' Cup again,' says Pecker. Last time they won it, Hough drank the pub out of Hofmeister and Plum opened his bedroom window to throw up, forgetting he had double glazing.

At an acrimonious club meeting behind velvet curtains in the Carington Arms, the team is discussing the Ashby pavilion. Beeks came across a Portakabin going cheap; Plum has installed a kitchen.

'Now the team have extended their field of operations by joining the senior league, we have to provide facilities,' says the Wing Commander, who is chairman of the parish council and has a particular interest in planning. The club has bought a second Portakabin to house some showers and toilets.

Beeks complains that pillocks like him are doing all the pavilion fund-raising, while others, the ones at the front when the team photographs are taken, are doing sod all. The Lightning says people have to decide whether they want to play for a poxy village side or if they want to improve standards and have a shower after playing. But he isn't knackering himself raising 'a poxy ten quid' on a sponsored bike ride. Someone says if Mike Home joins the bike ride, he'll have a sponsored heart attack.

'Where is the second Portakabin anyway?' asks the chairman through a giant sausage cob. On Sunday, Handtrap saw it going the wrong way up Ashby Street, but now it is in David Smith's farmyard, which Pecker says is a long way to go for a wash.

The new pavilion faces the ramshackle old pavilion by the river, where rats recently ate a pair of wicketkeeper's gloves. After that the team got changed in a henhouse. The Wing Commander remembers the old pavilion appearing on Easter Sunday twenty years ago: 'I stepped out of church and there it was, so Christ wasn't the only one who rose early that day.' There will be no problem with planning permission. 'I'll class it as a temporary building, like the last one,' he says. 'I'd say twenty years is pretty temporary.'

The other item on the agenda is the tour. Nigel wants to go to the Harrogate Cricket Festival, but Pecker says the object of the tour 'let's face it, isn't cricket'. On the last tour, Rigsby lost two front teeth – playing golf. Most of them want to go to the seaside: 'Ain't there some dossy oily beach somewhere?' says Pecker. Nigel says he will investigate dossy oily beaches.

Ashby is in the Carington Arms 'preparing' for a match at home to a Northamptonshire side. The team is in high spirits – last week it lost by only six runs to one of the strongest sides in the new league – but, as yet, its members haven't had many drinks. 'They're never drunk at lunchtime,' says one of the vice-presidents. 'It takes them all day.'

Rigsby, though, sitting at the bar, is looking forward cheerily to another day's village cricket. 'Two pints before, two pints after,' he says, summing up the Ashby philosophy. 'We're going to have a good time.'

SWINGS AND ROUNDABOUTS

Ben Webb

August, 1993

The first day of the BMW International Open in Munich was blindingly hot. Liam White, already sweating, took careful aim down the narrow fairway. His focus switched to the little white ball that was perched on a tee in front of him. Slowly, he brought the club head back, then accelerated it down towards the Maxfli. He heard the crack as the ball flew, ruler straight, down the centre of the first fairway.

The thin line of spectators applauded. The desultory clapping, so typical of the early tee-off times during the first two rounds of a tournament, had little impact on him. His face was set.

He picked up his bag of clubs (a caddie costs money: playing without one saves £300 a week, but means there's no one to consult before each shot or to provide a boost after a bad one – you are on your own). Eric, White's usual caddie, would be hanging around at home in Nottingham waiting for good news. White yearned for a win, but he was pressured now, rushing his bag around and tending the flag himself.

A naturally confident player, his mind was fixed on one thing – making the cut: qualifying for the final two days of the four-day competition when the prize money is shared out. Only players placed in the top 65 make it, but all are guaranteed a part of the pot – if only between £600 and £1,500 for coming in 65th. The rest count their losses. Top players assume they will make the cut and aim for the higher positions and the big money. The lesser players often just judge the score required to make the final two days, and aim for that. White knew that if he did make the cut, then he could push himself to climb the leader board, assured that he was, at least, guaranteed a cheque – and enough cash to play another event.

And he desperately needed a win. The season had started out well – brilliantly even for a rookie on the European circuit. He had beaten Sevvy Ballesteros twice in early tournaments and pocketed earnings of more than £7,000. But a sequence of missed cuts had eaten into his cash reserves. He was under pressure to win some money – not the sort of money that buys Ferraris, but enough to cover his expenses and a bit more so he could afford to get to the next event. And he owed his father £800 already, cash he had borrowed just to get to Munich. He didn't like to borrow his parents' money, or gamble with their savings. They weren't well-off, and while he knew they didn't begrudge it, he wanted to return their trust and generosity by winning some prize money to repay them.

White knew the Munich course was not difficult and that he would need a sub-par score to make the cut. In practice, he had been playing well; he was hopeful. As the holes passed, he got into a rhythm and scored two birdies. But the pressure was turning the round into a leaden ordeal instead of an enjoyable morning's golf. He finished the final holes and returned to his hotel with a 69 – three under par. Tired but relieved, he flopped onto his bed and gazed at the ceiling. 'So far, so good,' he thought.

Later, he went to the bar. Two other young players congratulated him on his score. But, as the other golfers rolled in, White realised that the scoring had been low. It had been a day of birdies, and more than 65 players had scored 69 or better. He would have to do it all again the next day. His nerves fluttered, replacing the ebullience that had filled him all evening.

Despondent, he phoned his parents. He didn't want to give the impression he was down. 'Mum, I played really well,' he said. 'I shot 69, and it could have been a lot better.' His mother, Margaret, was excited. 'Fantastic,' she said. 'Do you think you'll make the cut?'

'I think so.' He tried to sound confident. 'If I play as well tomorrow as I did today, I can make it.'

'Good luck,' she said. 'Fingers crossed.'

White returned to the bar and ordered a beer. It didn't taste as good as he had hoped. The second round was going to be make or break. One bad hole, one bad shot even, and, instead of a fat pay cheque, he would face the lonely flight home. He estimated he needed three birdies to make the cut.

That night he slept poorly. He woke early and went to the course. The pressure mounted: a gut-twisting, mind-wrenching tension. So far, his swing was standing up to the strain. He knew that just one tense muscle in the hundreds that must co-ordinate to create an effective swing could send the ball hurtling into a bunker or the rough. Every shot was potential disaster. He had to relax.

He started the round well and, at level par, was in contention as he approached the ninth, a par five – and a birdie chance. His drive had left him on the fairway, 265 yards from the flag. It was at the limit of his range, even with a wood, and it was into the wind. He had a choice: one risky shot and two putts for a birdie, or two easy shots to the green for a par. Should he? Shouldn't he? He pulled the driver from his bag.

The sparse line of spectators noticed nothing unusual. A player was selecting his club and confronting a dilemma typical for a par five. But for White, it was a decision that might determine whether he played another competitive round that season. He was all alone, without a caddie to offer reassurance. Characteristically, he gambled.

To drive the ball accurately from the fairway is tough. He tried to wipe his problems from his mind. He thought back to recent rounds on his local course, when he had tracered similar shots to the pin. He swung and made good contact – but the club head was a couple of degrees off dead straight. He had hooked it. The ball flew towards the green, began to curve away, cracked into an advertising board and ricocheted six inches out of bounds. A two-shot penalty. White, knowing his chance was gone, salvaged a double bogey seven.

He went back to his hotel and packed quickly. A series of 'if onlys' flitted through his mind: the putts that had grazed the hole, the unkind bounces, the dire ninth hole. All he knew was that it was too late. He returned to his parents' home in Nottingham.

That night, instead of analysing his third round with the pros, he had a few drinks at the club with his mates. He said to a close friend: 'It's a nightmare. My dad went and earned the money and I've gone and spent the bugger.'

Liam White is a natural. He first picked up a golf club at sixteen, when he was caddying for his father. He sprinted after his father's ball, put down a spare, and cracked it 180 yards onto the green. His bemused dad – a veteran of years spent endeavouring to perfect his own swing – asked him to try the same shot again. His son swung the club a second time and sent the ball fizzing towards the flag.

Since then, White has joined the golfing fast track. Three months later he had reduced his handicap to twelve and a year later was scratch. In 1991, at 22, he fulfilled every amateur player's ambition when he played in the biannual Walker Cup, the amateur equivalent of the Ryder Cup – a match between the British and Irish team and the traditionally cocky Americans.

The precocious White grabbed the headlines. The *Daily Mail* splashed 'THE CHARGE OF THE WHITE BRIGADE' after he won a gruelling battle with the top American, Phil Mickleson. The two players were all square at the par five sixteenth. Both reached the green in two. It was the young rookie who broke the stalemate. Stooping over his ball, he knew that if he could sink the 25-yard 'monster' putt it would be a killer blow. He stroked the ball, and the spectators erupted as it curved across the subtle contours and dropped into the four-and-a-quarter-inch cup. White leapt into the air, fists clenched – a pose that dominated the *Daily Mail*'s back page. And White had still never had a golfing lesson in his life.

His manager, Anthony Hoffman, was so impressed when he first met White that he immediately gave him £3,000 of his own money to play in Monte Carlo. Hoffman, who works with sports personalities every day, raves: 'He is electric on the course. He has an aura which few sportsmen have – charisma and a remarkable talent.' White has that hair-prickling ability to hit the difficult shot with apparent ease that attracts the spectator. Like his snooker-playing namesake, Jimmy White, he attacks. A birdie and bogey man, he likes to entertain.

But Hoffman feared White might waste his talent because he had never struggled to play the game. He lacked the steel and self-awareness to maximise his potential. Hoffman didn't want him to join the litany of wasted sporting talents, the mavericks who didn't train hard enough or lost themselves in drink. He explains: 'I had to get involved because he needed someone to keep his feet on the ground, not a bunch of backslappers around him.'

After White's Walker Cup success, it was a natural step for him to turn professional and join the circus of players who circle the globe, playing on the Volvo European Tour – the series of events run by the Professional Golfers' Association (PGA). It is a big-money, high-glamour life for the successful. But the pressure to win week in and week out, away from home and family, with only fellow professionals as company, is draining. While thousands dream of success on the circuit, only tens make a fortune.

Playing professional golf is not simply about turning up at a tournament and having a go. It is a huge financial and physical commitment. Just to play the year will burn a £35,000 hole in a competitor's pocket. One week the army of professional golfers and their caddies invade Dubai, the next Spain, the next Rome. The events are sponsored by huge companies like Mercedes, Lancôme, or Johnnie Walker. It is an arduous trek through hotel lobbies, airport lounges and stuffy golf clubs. Simply to survive on the tour a player must win £1,000 a week to fund the nomadic quest for a share of the total £22,300,000 prize money. As PGA tournament director Mark Stewart says: 'It is a different world. The pressures are vast.'

In a typical week, the players will often arrive in droves, ferried by tour operators who offer package deals to the players. Everything is laid on, from hotels to the daily transport to the golf course.

Players can save money staying in cheap hotels, but, after sweating around the course all day, a good dinner, a cool beer, and satellite TV help stave off the ennui. If players are not in prime physical and mental condition, the £20 saved each night could cost hundreds in dropped shots. Competitors practise at the beginning of the week and walk the course. On Thursday, the tournament starts. On Saturday and Sunday, the players who survive the cut play for the prize money.

The stars, the ones who swan around in private jets, can pick and choose their events, confident of winning enough to take time off should they need it. They are often paid just to turn up; they flourish on huge sponsorship contracts. Last year, Nick Faldo, the world's best player, and a golfing automaton, took home roughly £1 million in prize money and probably five times that amount off the course.

At the other end of the scale, first-year professionals need to win money just to survive on the circuit, as well as find the cash to pay for a roof over their heads at home. It is survival of the fittest.

White's first step, in 1991, was to go to the tour school with about 600 other hopefuls to compete for a tour card, essential in order to be part of the European tour. He had to undergo two qualifying stages, after which the numbers had been whittled down to just 40.

White qualified in fifteenth place; he was one of the highest ranked first-year professionals, or rookies. It was a good sign. Previous highly placed rookies have made an immediate impact on the professional circuit. Steven Richardson, for example, made more than £100,000 in his first year, 1990. A year later, he made £393,000. White hoped for a similar record.

Because it is expensive, many players are wary of trying out for a card. White had no doubts. 'I was on such a high after the Walker Cup that it was an easy decision to go professional. Getting my card in my first year – no bad achievement – proved it was a good one.'

White's next goal was to start the 1992 season well, to ensure that he could get into the more popular, big-prize-money events later in the year. The problem for White, as with other young and lower-ranked professionals, is that there are more players than spaces in each event. The 40 qualifiers, added to the number of pros who already have cards, swells the pack of cardholders to more than 200. And there are only 144 places available in each tournament.

A complicated system of ranking and categorisation determines which players have priority. Everyone is ranked according to how much money they have earned, or how well they did in qualification. The more you win, the higher your position in the pecking order. The list is updated twice during the year and, to guarantee entry, White needed to climb the table until he was higher than the 140s.

White had another overriding reason to climb the rankings. At the end of the season, the top 120 players retain their cards and can come back the following year; otherwise, it's back to the tour school.

With his newly acquired card, White flew to Thailand for his first chance to rub golf bags and discuss the run of the green with tournament-winning personalities. It was the Johnnie Walker Asian Classic in sweltering Bangkok – a chance to compete against Faldo, Ballesteros and Ian Woosnam, everyday people hurled into the public domain by golfing talent. He was nervous but optimistic. His six-year-old goal had been achieved.

He first encountered Ballesteros on the practice ground. White was cocooned in a private world of concentration, grooving his swing, when he heard clicking cameras and the jabbering of a gallery of fans. Ballesteros, a man with an almost tangible aura, began playing a bare six feet away. White felt weird; he couldn't concentrate. For the next twenty shots, he felt as though he were trying to hit a marble with a stick. But the feel came back to his swing. He could hardly wait.

In the tournament itself, White kept to the fast track. He played solidly, concentrating on his own game. He didn't want to be intimidated by the roar of the crowds as the stars scored birdies and eagles. After two rounds, he was four under par, and just made the cut. It was an eye-opener; in amateur golf the cut is often at four over par. In the third round, he shot a 71, which put him among the big names. On the tense final day, he scored a 68, after starting with an eagle, and beat Ballesteros (69) and Woosnam (72). White recalls the confusion and exhilaration: 'I thought: "What's happening? It isn't right. I've done something wrong here."' He hadn't. White had won his first serious prize, a cheque for £3,400, in his first week on tour – not at all a bad pay day.

A fortnight later, he played in the Turespana Masters in Malaga, Spain. On home soil, Ballesteros is always determined not to let down his adoring fans. But again White beat his hero. In appalling conditions, he started with a disastrous 81. He wrote off his chances and went for a drink in Torremolinos. Relaxed, on the second day he shot a 68, making the cut easily. He went on to score 73 and 67, one of the best final rounds. He came seventeenth, and scooped £3,600.

A few weeks later, while practising bunker shots, he hit the pin and heard a shout of 'Olé! I like it.' Ballesteros strode over and gave White a few tips on how to play from the sand. 'I'll never forget that,' White says. He began to feel at home.

The gregarious White swiftly gained a taste for the touring, the hotels, the evenings that turned into early mornings spent leaning on bars with the seasoned pros. White, who enjoys a good time, remembers Richard Boxall – who 'likes his pop' – sinking a few beers the night before the final round of a tournament he went on to win.

The high-profile life suited White. If he ever had doubts about being a professional, they were swiftly quashed. 'What I really like is the glamour side, to be up there in the public eye, signing autographs,' he says. 'It makes me feel good. To be the best on a given day; that makes you feel fantastic.'

The chance of making a few bucks also motivated a young man who likes Boss jeans and apologises for his ageing Vauxhall Astra. 'You can't avoid the big numbers,' he says. 'The money's dangling there like a huge carrot, and you want to grab it.'

But life on the tour is not always jolly anecdotes of success. A few poor performances, and the high life becomes a struggle to cover the costs of a caddie. Every year, only about a third of the 40 qualifiers make the top 120 and keep their cards. In doing so, they can shunt as many as fifteen other pros off the list – players who may be lumbered with mortgages and families. For White it had started well. 'Twice in my first three weeks I had beaten Sevvy. I was on top of the world.' He had proved he had the ability to win money. He was on the verge of establishing himself in the professional ranks.

But he soon experienced the tug of gravity. Missed cuts began to erode his bank balance. And the harder he tried, the worse he played. Short of cash, he began to miss tournaments. In practice, he was playing as well as ever; on the course, his game went into decline. He was experiencing the downside of what he calls 'golf's rollercoaster'. Searching for funds, and withdrawing from events for which he was eligible, sapped his resolution. His self-belief evaporated. 'I knew I had to play well to get to the next event. I couldn't just play twenty tournaments and have a good bash. I was playing one week, and then not for six weeks. I started getting nervous.'

Robert Green, editor of *Golf World,* had seen it happen before. 'The pressures depend massively on the level of financial backing,' he says. 'If you play knowing that missing the cut means you have wasted £1,000, and that the bank manager has only given you a £5,000 overdraft, then that is real pressure.'

After Munich, White's life returned to normal. He spent a lot of time practising at his home club, and played well. But frustration began to replace the swagger. His practising became sporadic. He was stuck at home, unable to compete on the tour. His card was redundant. Bullishly, he had gone headlong into the cauldron of professional sport, had proved he had the ability, and it had all gone wrong. Heel-kicking at home for the first time in his life, he almost gave up.

Etched on the oak panelling of the plush Wollaton Golf Club in Nottingham are lists of the winners of the club trophies. The name of Liam White is prominent. The lists represent exploits he has consigned to the sunny days of his past.

White himself is gazing at the deer which roam over the course, and plotting his campaign for this year. He has just finished one round and is relaxing before embarking on a second eighteen holes in the afternoon. Recently, he has been practising harder than ever. He has just gone round the course in 63. His manager is delighted. White is annoyed it wasn't a 59.

He talks with a maturity acquired from the shock of failure. He has, he feels, recovered from the rise and fall of 1992. His preparation for this year has been professional, the cavalier spirit of the newcomer banished. 'It's got to be a reassurance year,' he says. 'I've got to get my confidence back to where it was.'

He sips tea in the club lounge. He is surrounded by mostly middle-aged men. He doesn't conform to the traditionally staid image of the sport. His stockiness, which belies a smooth coordination, suggests rugby is his game. And his bleached hair would blend easily into football's Premier League. He is brusque, sanguine almost to the point of cockiness, a function of finding a difficult game easy. But he is amiable, too. One of the lads.

It is easy to envisage White strutting around the green with a broad grin, chatting and chortling with fans. He is more a Lee Trevino character, chirpy and full of natural vigour, than a Nick Faldo, ordered and contrived. His attitude is straightforward. 'Coaches work for some people, but I like to keep the game simple,' he says. He has, however, turned to psychology.

In an attempt to unravel the reasons that lie behind last year's troubles, White has been reading Timothy Gallwey's *The Inner Game of Golf*. 'It's very interesting and helpful,' he says animatedly. He leans forward. 'The book helped me understand things that had happened to me – about how I had lost confidence and become anxious through self-doubt.'

White is convinced the book has already made an impact. 'I am aware of how you must programme yourself to be concentrated on what you can do, and not to allow fear of the unknown to creep in. I don't feel I did myself justice last year, but I learned what pressure is about. I have not come across it before, and I can tell you it's not a nice thing.'

Golf is not like most other sports, where surging levels of adrenalin and nervous tension help athletes run faster, rugby players tackle harder, and cricketers bowl quicker. There is less palm-bashing self motivation in golf. It is about control. It's good to be keyed up, focused, and determined. But if tension creeps into the swing, shots will be dropped. Many immensely skilful players who fail to win major trophies are dubbed 'chokers', because their games fall apart when the pressure is on.

White, not content to train his mind, has also subjected himself to a strict diet. His weakness for a few beers – 'I love to party' – has been controlled by the rigours of his new fitness regime. Already, his stout frame has shed a stone. The new Liam White may neither be entirely teetotal nor a ten-hour-a-day practiser, but he is certainly a lot more committed. 'It was obvious I had to make some changes,' he admits.

Anthony Hoffman has noticed the transformation. 'Liam's dedication to his game and personality changed after last year, but the change is still not as big as I would like.' Hoffman has pulled together a couple of deals which should make life a little easier. He has signed a contract with Nike, which started on January 1 this year. He is negotiating with Imperial Tobacco and with a business consortium who, he hopes, will sign a few cheques. White is guaranteed a good run this year.

He will play in at least seven invitation tournaments on the Volvo European Tour, and he will be competing in the Challenge Tour, a satellite series for those bubbling under that sought-after top 140. A top-ten position in this year's Challenge Tour, brought about by coming 180th in the Volvo order of merit, was a stroke of luck for White. One position lower, and he would have missed out, and then 1993 would have been a total waste of time. 'It was a bit of an omen for me,' he says.

Back in the Wollaton club's old changing room, with wooden benches and lockers varnished to a dark patina, White pulls on his studded golf shoes. Over the years, the boarded floor has been worn down by the trudge of golfers marching in and out. Casual players, untying their laces, nod at White and comment on their rounds, their babies and the weather. White is a gregarious man and has an answer for everyone. His chirpiness is back, a sign that the pain of 1992 is overcome, if not forgotten.

'I ended up at a stage I never thought would happen to me,' he says. 'I got very disheartened. I almost gave up. It was a total all-time low. I pitied myself. "Why me?" I asked. At times like that, you get a bit selfish.'

The well-documented saga of Ian Woosnam's struggle to succeed helps White to keep faith in himself. Woosnam spent his early professional years living on cold baked beans in a camper van. Ten years later, Woosnam was probably still eating beans, but in the comfort of the private jet he now flies around the world. And fellow rookies Jim Payne and Gary Evans, who both played in the Walker Cup with White, did well last year. Payne, who qualified behind White at the tour school, was Rookie of the Year, winning £148,352 on the Volvo European Tour, and has just bought himself a BMW. Gary Evans made nearly £150,000.

'I couldn't be more pleased for them,' White says. 'It gives you a boost.' The rehabilitation is almost complete. Hoffman has no doubts: 'I'm over the moon about Liam. Once he realises how good he is, then someone better look out.'

White looks around the changing room he knows so well. He is pleased to be back on track again, albeit a slightly slower one than before. 'My heart lies in golf; it is what I love, what I want to do, and what I will do,' he says. 'One day, I can't say when, I will be back on the tour and doing well. There's no way I am going to let myself fall by the wayside; it means too much to me.'

He hoists his bag onto his shoulder and leaves for the first tee. Last year, he would have been sinking snooker balls on the club table, a pint of bitter sitting under the scoreboard.

THE MARK OF A MAN

Dave Hill

November, 1990

In the end, it was all a false alarm – we should get that straight from the start. But for a while it seemed that this encounter with the team manager of Glasgow Rangers Football Club was going to be more perfunctory than I had hoped. Something had come up, a personal matter: and given that Graeme Souness is, by his own description, basically a private person, due consideration lies behind the decision to relate the story at the beginning of this piece. However, what follows is an attempt to capture the spirit of a man. And, given that our subject is all too frequently portrayed in a stereotypical way, the personal matter in question seems a reasonable place to start.

It concerned Souness' eldest son, nine-year-old Fraser, and a spot of trouble he was having with his hip. A conscientious doctor had rung with the news and expressed the opinion that there might be complications. Young Fraser and his stepsister Chantelle, fifteen, attend a boarding school in rural England. On receiving the message, Souness beckoned me into a chamber of Ibrox Stadium's inner sanctum. He was sweating, doing sit-ups, squat-thrusts and other things that involve pain. Without stopping, he explained, politely, that he was already booked on the first available plane south. He could give me only an hour – maybe we should make another date? This was a disappointment. But it bolstered the assessment of his own priorities that Souness would subsequently make: Rangers is his *near*-obsession (his qualification, my italics), but in the end 'the most important thing in my life is my family'.

A cynic could be forgiven a scoff. The received wisdom about Graeme Souness is that he is totally ruthless. As a player, his ferocity in the tackle was famous. As a manager, he marshals his teams with an apparently remorseless lack of sentiment. As a human being, he is often described as inspiring – but among opponents, what he frequently inspires is fear.

It is a reputation that has seeped into the tabloid story of his private life, a tale that has all the ingredients of a modern soap opera: husband with high-octane temperament and awesome will to win puts work before all else; beautiful wife reaches end of tether and slings hook with children in tow; husband fights (not 'pleads') for reconciliation and access to his beloved babies (there is a third, Jordan, aged five); wife's horror story of a man possessed by the demon football appears in the *Sun*; there is talk of an expensive, though amicable, divorce. Would the next episode be the story of Fraser's dodgy hip and his daddy's dash to his bedside? Well, no, not in the end. Moments before leaving for the airport, he received an update from the doctor, Fraser's ailment was minor and perfectly routine. Normal service could be resumed. The paradox of his character thus established, the manager of Rangers Football Club breathed a sigh of relief and invited me into his office for tea and a plate of baked beans.

Baked beans, indeed. What has this least-elevated dish done to merit being served in surroundings that ooze a sumptuous gravitas, befitting the biggest, richest and, arguably, most venerable institution in British football? The carpets are a gorgeous azure. Just the thought of walking round the manager's handsome desk gives me visions of oxygen tents. The beans seem slightly out of place. But there is a lesson in this. Researchers at Strathclyde University have commended the baked bean for its value in lowering cholesterol levels. As such, they have a value to the playing-side staff of Rangers Football Club. And Graeme Souness is not the sort of man to care if they clash with the furnishings.

Souness joined Rangers four years ago, when the board invited him to leave Sampdoria of Genoa and take up the post of player-manager. His mother, Elizabeth, the parent who influenced him most during his Edinburgh childhood, had once told the youngest of her three boys, 'there'll never be a dull moment when you're around, son,' and so it has proved. When Souness returned to Scotland, Rangers was a moribund organisation, a truth that could no longer be concealed by clinging to the emperor's old clothes. Souness' declared aim was to compete with the best in Europe. He took the place apart.

Rangers have always had money, but Souness made it talk. Dissatisfied with the players he inherited, he committed his first acts of sacrilege by signing a series of Sassenachs. Chris Woods, England's first-reserve goalkeeper, came in July 1986 for £600,000; Terry Butcher, England's centre back, arrived the following month for £750,000 million. The robust former Tottenham Hotspur Graham Roberts arrived in December for £450,000. Souness planted himself in the middle of midfield, and, at the end of his first season, Rangers won the Scottish League. All told, the manager has purchased more than 30 players, about half of them Englishmen, plus a couple of Israelis and a Dane. As I write, he is trying to complete the defection – not literal – of a Russian, Oleg Kuznetsov, from Kiev.

But cosmopolitan though these acquisitions have been, two of the new Rangers stars represented a breach of barriers even more profound than those of nationhood. In December 1987, Aston Villa received just over £500,000 in exchange for a deliciously skilful winger called Mark Walters; he became the first black player ever to wear a Rangers shirt. Walters quickly acquired a nickname which shows why the second of Souness' most controversial recruits had even more iconoclastic import. 'Jaffa Cake' was what they dubbed the little Brummie: chocolate on the outside, orange in the middle.

Unmoved by the long-standing ecumenicism of Celtic, their traditional Catholic rivals, no man open to the derogatory epithet, taig, had ever carried his kit through Ibrox's wood-panelled corridors of unofficial Scottish Protestant power, or warmed up beneath the portrait of the Queen that adorns the wall of the home team's dressing room. So, when Souness raided the readies yet again last summer to buy striker Maurice Johnston from Nântes in France, it was like passing holy water in a roundhead's swimming pool.

And what a Roman conquest Johnston was! Not only a Catholic, but a former *Celtic* hero who had been negotiating a possible return to his erstwhile employer just a few weeks before. Souness admits the club took 'an enormous risk': sectarian Rangers diehards burned their season tickets, the only time Johnston was seen parted from his security guards was when he ran out on the pitch; the 'Gers chorus would never summon a refrain of 'we are the Billy boys' with quite the same conviction ever again. Catholics, baked beans, Jaffa Cakes – where will it all end?

'I'm an optimistic person,' Souness says. 'Whatever I've gone into, I've approached it in a positive manner. I was prepared to fall on my backside, which you always must be. I was prepared to fail.' These observations are made with the comfort of hindsight. Following that first League title, Rangers have taken the championship twice more and won the Skol Cup three times (the prestigious Scottish Cup still eludes Souness). But this procession of domestic domination has not always been glorious, and it says much about the make-up of this frustrated family man that not all his public deeds have been fit for family viewing. Sent off twice in the first season – most memorably during the match against Aberdeen in which Rangers finally clinched their title – Souness was accused of ostentation, arrogance and a pathological recklessness in his desire to win. Dovish introversion has not exactly been a characteristic in the career of this handsome man of 37 who pines for the times when he gets to bounce his two wee laddies on his knee. At Liverpool, with whom he enjoyed six great years before heading for the lucrative Italian league, he built a kind of composite reputation – half Flash Harry, half Hard Man, a beautiful, measured passer of the ball who could scrap with the best of them, an assassin with velvet feet.

You get a sense of this duality when you meet him. The first look is not very friendly: a stare of curt appraisal. Yet the brogue is accommodating, almost mellifluous. Though he denies he suffers from self-doubt, he concedes the pressure to prove himself at Rangers may have contributed to his failures of discipline. 'I would say that is possibly correct. But that never concerned me. It wasn't a case of my coming back to show these naive Scotsmen how it's all done. But the thing I have found here, and I have found hard to handle, is that there is a fair bit of bitterness and jealousy, bordering on hatred, from people within the game towards this club. I think I increased that hatred and I admit I should have handled myself better. But there were a few people trying to make their mark. I would respond with no worse a tackle, then get booked or sent off. I felt I was set up slightly,' he remarks, but adds hastily, 'not that I would ever ask for special treatment.'

There is a great deal of pride about Souness, the sort manifested in a desire to make light of life's reverses and see triumph as the just reward for commitment and hard labour. Souness' rise from rags to riches – his fortune is estimated at £5 million, his salary about £150,000 a year – has been dramatised by the fact that he was brought up in a prefab, but Souness does not describe a life of denial: 'It was a very happy childhood. I seemed to get everything I ever wanted.' He says there was none of that traditional working-class parental pressure to get out and improve himself – his decisions were his own. 'There were several clubs I could have gone to as a boy, including Rangers. They left it up to me, so any mistake I made was my mistake.'

Souness chose Tottenham and had his nose put out of joint. Simultaneously obstreperous and homesick, at nineteen he thought he should have been in the first team. Manager Bill Nicholson, a short-back-and-sides type and a legendary 'boss', was not impressed. Souness transferred to Middlesbrough, a second division team about as far removed from the London glitz as you could get. It did him good. Jack Charlton became his manager there, and, true to legend, laid it on the line: 'Basically, you can go far in this game, or you can piss it down the drain.' Souness admires Big Jack. 'He's very much like that, very harsh. There's a lot to admire about him.' There is a pause. 'He's a *man* – you either do this or you don't. Truthfulness, that's what it was.'

To be called 'a *man*' by Graeme Souness is a substantial compliment. I asked him about his reputation as a hard man and his celebrated duels at Liverpool with Leeds United's Terry Yorath. There is a story about how Souness once honoured Yorath with one of his most cultivated fouls, bent down to the Welshman prostrate in the mud and said proudly: 'That was me!' Souness corroborates the episode without shame: 'He was one I admired. We had great games together. I honestly believe that's part and parcel of the game. He and I were as friendly as anything [off the pitch]. I could phone him right now and chat with him for an hour. He never hid behind anyone. You know, he's a man.'

He bestows the same honour on David Murray, Rangers' young chairman. Murray's buy-out of the club last year was completed with Souness' help, including £600,000 of Souness' money (he owns 7 per cent of the shares). Since then, improvements to the stadium have proceeded apace, as has the manager's spending on the fabric of his team. On the face of it, they make unlikely partners. Murray, whose business interests are wide and varied, lost both legs in a car accident when he was still in his early twenties. 'I very much doubt if I could approach life in the manner he does,' Souness says, his admiration plain. 'He's on sticks, he's never in a chair. It's an inconvenience to him, and that's all it is . . . He's larger than life.'

Souness is rightly seen as a new breed of football 'gaffer' (as his subordinates call him). Modern values and a changing code of soccer economics have dissipated some of the uglier post-war criteria for assessing a player's worth. Crude superstitions about race and religion are a hindrance to the meritocratic ideology of someone like Souness (this extends beyond football: his wife is a Roman Catholic divorcee). He defines his responsibilities simply – 'to produce quality football' and, most of all, 'being a winner. That's all I'm interested in.' Unlike managers of earlier generations, Souness has no financial need to work again. His footballing desire, therefore, is remarkably uncluttered. He does it for no other reason than the very thrill of competing.

But isn't there more to it than that? In his office stand photos of his children – one of the three altogether, another of a smiling dad with a lad cradled in each arm. That's one image. Yet the word 'arrogant' has pursued him through his career, and he was never the most popular of players either on Merseyside or in a Scotland shirt. He dedicated his autobiography – *No Half Measures* – to his mum.

Top football is a demanding business. To glimpse the reflective, even sentimental streaks in Graeme Souness – and the expression partly denied them by his marital problems – is to wonder at his apparent equilibrium. Is it real?

'I've mellowed a lot in the past four years,' he declares, pounding on the pedals of an exercise machine. But it was only in May the Scottish Football Association fined him £5,000 for his second breach of a touchline ban originating in a verbal set-to with a hapless referee. Souness denies he is 'a Billy Big' or unduly confrontational. He doubts, though, he will ever learn the art of strategic retreat. As a player, he always shook hands with his opponents when the final whistle went, but 'I've always found it hard to socialise with people I was competing against. In the bar afterwards, I felt I couldn't go over to the other players ... Don't exaggerate that point. I wasn't unfriendly, but I wasn't *over*-friendly. It's only half an hour after the game, your adrenalin's still pumping. It was a bit too soon.'

Still, today's Rangers wait for no man, and the Ibrox revolution rolls on. Ground renovations to the tune of £14 million are underway and should render the stadium close to the best continental standards. Forthcoming European Cup games will tell us whether Souness' team can do it justice on the field.

As for the manager himself – and, for the record, I liked the man – he is impressive in his capacity to rationalise his own fallibility; and to do so armed with an eloquent understanding of football's enduring power to engage the passions of men, for better or worse. 'I would not approach the job any differently if I had the chance again,' he says, ''cause I had to show a certain amount of aggression. I never went out of my way to upset people – I'm like that anyway. I'm twenty years past caring what people think of me.'

'Football ... it's basic. It's like opening yourself up to a psycho-analyst. I can tell people's characters by watching them play foot-ball – the way they react to a foul against them, or to the referee or when they score a goal. You can't tell everything, but you can tell a lot. I can ... I think I can.'

HEAVY DUTY

Ian Hamilton

May, 1993

When I first met Lennox Lewis he was dressed up as Father Christmas and he had a gold crucifix hanging from one ear. A six-foot-six man-mountain, he was encircled by a small congregation of admirers: a dozen or so disabled infants from the Freddie Mills Boys' Clubs, each of them kitted out in a T-shirt made by SPX, the clothing firm that sponsors Lewis and exclusively supplies his gear – though not, one guessed, the ill-fitting scarlet cloak that he was sporting on this day, nor the cotton-wool whiskers that he was having such trouble securing to his chin. As Lewis moved among the damaged kids, sparring up to one or two of them, tousling hair, dropping the odd word, his expression was properly Santa-like. But it was also detached and self-aware. Lewis looked as if he had been doing it for years.

The occasion was the 1992 Sky Sports Christmas Party, being pre-recorded on November 29, less than a month after this same Santa had savagely clubbed Razor Ruddock to the canvas at Earl's Court – clubbed him not once, but three times; Razor Ruddock, who once went the distance with Mike Tyson!

It was on that day, November 1, that Lennox Lewis had become a bona fide British star. A one-time Canadian Olympic champion, the London-born heavyweight could now be safely hailed as a phenomenon not granted to this country since the last years of the nineteenth century: a genuine world championship contender, a puncher who could hang in there with the New Yorkers and the Philadelphians. To us, it no longer mattered that Lewis had learned to box in Canadian gymnasiums and been groomed in the hills of Pennsylvania. He was still the holder of a British passport and 'with one hammer blow, lethal Lennox – the kid from London's East End – had punched his way into the hearts of the nation'.

So said the *Sun* on the morning of November 2. And there was Lennox over two pages, wielding a champ-sized Union Jack and managing to look both gratified and faintly scornful, as if to say: you lot may be surprised, but I'm not. Lewis knew well enough that if he had lost to Ruddock, it would have been a different story; words like 'carpetbagger' and 'flag of convenience' had already been whispered, and there was never much chance that Lewis would fit into the loveable-loser bracket that we reserve for the likes of 'Enery Cooper and Dame Bruno.

Close up, he has little about him of the pug: no broken nose, no vulnerable scar tissue. His skin looks more pampered than pummelled. At first, the stare he greets you with seems meant to disconcert, but it's actually quite neutral. It's a celebrity stare, the stare of one who expects to be stared at. At the same time, though, the eyes are rather kindly and amused. The message seems to be: Relax, shorty, I only *use* all this muscle-power when I'm at work. Off-duty, I'm just another extraordinary guy.

Lennox Claudius Lewis was born 27 years ago in Forest Gate, east London. His parents split up when he was six, and at the age of twelve Lennox's mother Violet took him and his older brother Dennis to settle in a small town just outside Toronto. His mother has recalled: 'Things got difficult and I couldn't manage to have the boys with me, so I sent them back home to their aunt in London. It was a very difficult decision ... All my friends called me the weeping mother – I used to cry all the time when I was apart from the boys. I phoned them every day ... [but] when Lennie returned to Canada, he was angry with me. Somehow that anger always seemed to be in him.'

Lewis' anger found an outlet in the playground. He was a big boy and was growing fast. At his school in Kitchener, Ontario, he came in for a lot of teasing: he was the school's only black and he had a Cockney accent. 'I was at an awkward age,' says Lewis, 'I was an outsider. They didn't treat me badly but I did run into, you know, certain different cases there, and I used to get into a lot of fights. My school principal, after the third time giving me the strap, we got on pretty well because of the fact that he understood, you know, my language thing and that I looked at things differently. So we became good friends and he encouraged me to go into a contact sport, which is boxing. He told me where to go. It could have been basketball – that's a sport at which I always thought I would go far – but I excelled so much at boxing.'

Lewis was coached at the local Police Recreational Center and was soon winning local and then national tournaments. At sixteen, he won the World Junior Championship in Santo Domingo and 'after that, I thought, I'll see how far I can actually go'. Under the guidance of Romanian coach Adrian Teoderescu, he progressed to become the world's best Intermediate (under-twenties) and represented Canada at the Los Angeles Olympics. He lost there in the quarter-finals, but four years later, after lifting the 1986 Commonwealth Games title, he won the gold at Seoul. His opponent in the final there was Riddick Bowe.

The offers to turn professional poured in, but Lewis already had a money problem. In the run-up to the Olympics he had no income apart from a niggardly $450 a month stipend from the government agency Sport Canada, and in order to finance his training, he entered into a punishing loan agreement that left him with a debt of more than $150,000 by the time he won his medal.

On his return from Seoul, Lewis hired a lawyer and put his services to auction: 'I wanted to not take any chances. I wanted to get involved with the right people, 'cos a lot of people don't know how to bring up a champion with the pedigree, or how to bring up a boxer.'

Even before his triumph at Seoul, Lewis had toyed with the idea of returning to England. There was the British title to go for, and also the Commonwealth, the European. In Canada, he felt neglected. In the States, he feared that he would be exploited, then neglected. England 'just seemed like the best place' from which to make a start. Happily, it turned out that the English offer, when it came, topped anything that had been tabled from the States. Bankrolled by the Levitt financial services group, which was then, according to the business press, 'moving aggressively into sports management', the deal guaranteed a $200,000 signing-on fee (enough for Lewis to dispose of his Canadian debt), a company house, a company car and the hire of a tutor to help Lewis with his reading, never his strong subject at school. The split would be 75–25, but Levitt would cover all expenses, including the salary of a full-time trainer. And, most important of all, says Lewis, 'they also gave me control of my own career. I realised that I would be used in professional boxing, but I didn't want to be used a lot. I wanted to be the founder of my own destiny.'

By the time the Levitt group collapsed, in December 1990, Lewis had already moved to England and had won some fights. He is now backed by a London accountant whose speciality is liquidation and, says the *Independent*, 'by another backer who doesn't even like his name mentioned'. His brother Dennis serves as his financial adviser, and his mother also seems to have a formidable say. And Frank Maloney, his original Levitt contact, has been retained as manager. A former amateur flyweight, this amiable hustler runs a pub in Crayford and had contacts in the murky world of 'small-hall' boxing. He has worked for Frank Warren and Micky Duff, both of whom presumably now view him with some envy. Duff is said to have sneeringly predicted that Maloney would do a Cecil B DeMille on Lewis, in reverse: he would take a star and turn him into an unknown.

Maloney may be inexperienced but he has sense enough to recognise that: 'I'm only in the position I'm in because of Lennox Lewis ... I work for Lennox, Lennox doesn't work for me.' He has been mocked for giving Lewis too much control, but looking at the pair of them, the eagle and the sparrow, Maloney all fuss and bother and Lewis so lordly and composed, it is pretty obvious who is, and has to be, the boss. Maloney's account, to *Boxing Monthly*, of the build-up to the Ruddock fight, well captures how the power seems to be balanced:

'I walked over to Lennox's hotel and went up to his room and he was just sitting there, laughing. I said: "In a minute you're going to have the hardest fight of your life." But he just shrugged his shoulders and said: "I'm going to win, don't worry. Relax. Meditate."

'I stayed with him for about twenty minutes then I went to the arena. When I got there you could sense the build-up and everything, people coming up and asking how Lennox was. It was tense. But the atmosphere in Lennox's dressing room was so calm. I've been in a lot of big fighters' dressing rooms in America, but I'd seen nothing like this. It was just like sitting in someone's front room. Lennox was just sitting there with his dark glasses on and the camp were just talking among themselves. That's what Lennox injects into people. Calm. You can't have all this excitement around a fighter's dressing room. I tend to stay away from him because I'm a bit excitable, to be honest.'

Lewis knows about this 'calm' and values it. He calls it 'being focused' and speaks of himself as a 'foreseer'. Before the Ruddock fight he was, he says, tuned into the 'low heartbeat' of Bob Marley's 'Crazy Baldheads'. By the time he got into the ring, even his movement was linked to Marley's bassline. 'That's what you call rhythm,' said Lewis; or did he mean: 'That's what *you* call rhythm'?

Watching Lewis go about his saintly business for Sky Sports, I could more or less see what Maloney meant. His smile was never more than a half-smile, but he did what he was told. He fooled about in a bouncy rubber boxing ring, he exchanged blows with a legless robot, he bantered in near-Cockney with one or two of his 'old mates' – including Arsenal's pugilistic Ian Wright – and he was politely indulgent to John Conteh and Billy Walker, two bruisers from the past, who were brought on at the end as mystery guests and may well have been as mysterious to Lewis as they were to most of the audience. He was required, as a climax to the show, to fun-fight one of these illustrious has-beens in the bouncy ring, and it was rather sad to overhear a now less-than-husky-looking Conteh getting ready to do combat: 'Maybe,' he said. 'I'll catch him with a lucky punch.'

He didn't, but then so far no one has. Lewis has had 22 fights as a professional and has won all of them, eighteen by KO. It is true enough that his opponents, pre-Ruddock, have been more nuisances than threats, but even a Mike Tyson can get knocked out by a nuisance. Lewis, however, is no brawler; he leaves nothing much to chance. At school he was nicknamed The Scientist – 'because I'm the kind of guy who likes to sit back and observe things' – and he still relishes the label. He speaks of his adversaries as 'puzzles to be worked out', and to date he has had no trouble coming up with the right answers.

In the ring, Lewis uses his high-speed, high-precision left to keep his opponent at arm's length, to wear him down with stinging jabs and also, while he's at it, to measure him for the kill. There is a marvellous arrogance in the way Lewis now and then freezes the action, shoves a squashy left into his victim's nose and holds it there for just long enough to take a glance along the length of his own arm. It is as if he is rechecking the arithmetic. And the sums usually look good. Lewis has an 82-inch reach.

The kill is likely to happen when the other man presumes to land a punch, or a near punch. Flicked by an opponent's hopeful glove, Lewis appears to snap out of a studious half-dream: who is this guy that he should so interrupt my calculations? He has been riled by an impertinence, but mostly he seems keen to get this last, messy bit settled quickly. A ferocious three-punch combination tends to do the job. If it doesn't, and Lewis has to batter his opponent on the ropes, there is no discernible blood-hunger. The attitude seems to be sorrowing contempt: can this man see that the puzzle has been solved?

It was probably this failure of blood-lust that led people to assume that Lewis, for all his stylish ringcraft, had no killer punch. The guys he knocked over were dismissed by pundits as journeymen, bill-fillers, Mexican roadsweepers and the like. By contrast, the 40-year-old Mike Weaver, the punchbag Tyrell Biggs (who beat Lewis at the Los Angeles Olympics, when Lewis was nineteen), the immobile Gary Mason: these were name-fighters, names enough, anyway, to generate real money from TV, but none of them was reckoned to be hard to floor. Pre-Ruddock, Lewis' cerebral approach was still thought of as a liability – OK for the Olympic Games, but unlikely to upset a mongrel pro.

For a time, under his former trainer, the American Marine John Davenport, Lewis was encouraged to exhibit more animal aggression, to rush out from his corner at the bell and act very, very angry. In this role, he looked – and no doubt felt – a bit ridiculous, and against the short, squat, flailing Levi Billups he came close to getting caught. It taught Lewis a few lessons: 'I did more fighting than boxing. I should have boxed more, moved backwards, analysed it. That's why I changed my trainer, because he was making me get into a fight when I didn't need to. I've got enough mobility in my feet to stay on the outside and just work it out that way.' Under his new coach Pepe Correa, who used to handle Sugar Ray Leonard, he is always urged to 'work it out', to have a 'gameplan' and to be ready to make 'sacrifices' in the interests of a chosen strategy – in other words, to take no notice when the critics accuse him of being passive or switched-off.

The other lesson Lewis learned from Billups is that he should never go into a contest without having done his homework on the opposition. Billups was a late replacement for Tony Tucker, and Lewis had but three days' notice and no videos. Today he would refuse to take this kind of risk. Before Ruddock, Lewis says: 'I watched so much tape on Razor that I had it all stored in my head. I could see him box in front of me, exactly the way he boxes. So when I went out there and presented him with something he wasn't used to, he starts doing things that he *doesn't* do, and then I take advantage.'

Like Mike Tyson, Lewis spends a lot of time watching boxing videos, but Lewis believes his interest in the past is more constructive than Tyson's: 'Tyson is not a student of boxing, he is a student of boxing *history*. When I watch an old Ali fight, for instance, I try to incorporate his style into my style.'

Against Ruddock, this kind of scholarship certainly paid off. Lewis and Correa worked it out that Ruddock had one genuinely fearsome weapon, his big left, but that when he wasn't using it, he kept it hanging low. The gameplan seems to have been for Lewis to keep moving clockwise, to avoid the left, and force Ruddock to attack his body. It was this that Razor 'doesn't do'. To body-punch, Ruddock was obliged to bend into his opponent and thus set himself up for Lewis's pulverising right, which – when it came – must have seemed to have dropped down on him from the sky. 'Razor wasn't expecting me to be so quick. He threw a couple of hooks and I wasn't there. Not only my anticipation was good, but my balance was, too. Ruddock was too sure of himself. The press believed he was going to knock me out. They didn't realise that I thrive on the thrill of competition.'

Certainly, Lewis doesn't seem all that competitive. His Christmas video is subtitled 'I'm British and I'm Bad', but he doesn't usually pitch as the snarling type. When it comes to the routine pre-match slag-offs, he prefers on the whole to let the other side spit venom. 'My insults,' he says proudly, 'are reality insults. When I said Gary Mason had a big head, I meant that he had a big head. My insults are meant.' But why bother with that sort of thing; why not say nothing? And why all this preening and parading that goes on before a fight? 'You say those things to pester, to get under a guy's skin. It's part of the psyche game. And the parading is an animal instinct that comes out in us, in the almost ape-ian side of us. All animals do that. The human animal is not known to do that and yet it is, if you want to look at it in true respect. We all kind of parade. We want to impress, what do we do? We've gotta walk right, whether we model or whether we're athletes in front of our audience. You have Chris Eubank that does this (he mimes the Eubank strut), or you have the Lennox Lewis who does a little dance before the fight.'

Many sports heroes speak of themselves in the third person, but Lewis does it more than most, as if to acknowledge a discrepancy between the real man and the packaged star. He talks unblushingly of Lennox Lewis' marketable attributes: the looks, the personality, the mid-Atlantic accent. 'People find me easy to talk to. I don't look like boxers are supposed to look like – rough guys that cause trouble and fight all the time. In one sense, I'm an ambassador of my sport in the best way I know how. Plus with the help of my mother bringing me up the right way.' And what about his life when he retires? 'It should be filled with me touching people's lives in different ways. Whether it's as a sporting champion or whether it's as a businessman. I think I spread a certain kind of positive energy around. I want when people talk about me for them to say: "yeah, he's a good, solid person."'

It is this kind of piety which has led Lewis' enemies to deride him as a softy, a 'hairdresser' – and it must be said that his flat-top is almost pedantically well groomed – or to chuckle about his pet poodle (name of Tyson), his tropical fish, his mother love. When asked about his 'outside interests', Lewis is likely to assume that the question is about money: after all, he once took a course in business studies. And when he does name his hobbies, there is always a sense that the list is meant to sound impressively unboxerlike: he plays chess a lot (because it teaches him to be 'cunning') and when he reads, he reads usefully: 'I don't read fiction. I like things that educate you, that you can learn and put to work. I'm studying black history because a lot of things weren't taught to us in school. You read about Christopher Columbus and all of those things, but you don't read about Africa, where we originated from – those kind of things.

'After a time, you have to start educating yourself – for instance, when I get married and have kids I'm going to be part of the programme of educating my children.'

Get married? Lewis is not known to have a girlfriend, and if he does he's not telling. When the *Evening Standard*'s Daisy Waugh tried to cajole him into a confession on this topic, the exchange went as follows:

Wasn't his girlfriend jealous of his relationship with his mother?

Lewis: 'I guess a girlfriend would get jealous.'

Was he ever teased for being a mummy's boy?

Lewis: 'Would you tease me?'

Violet is often in residence at Lewis' small, mock-Georgian house in Bexleyheath, but on the day I visited she was away. It was easy to tell this because the living room was a shambles of scattered videos, remote-control guns, tracksuit tops, newspaper cuttings, mail. There was no tea or coffee left, and Lewis was touchingly triumphant when he unearthed a bottle of Asti Spumante from the fridge. Violet, we know, is a stickler for tidiness and a terrific cook. There are photographs of her on the walls and Lewis invariably speaks of her with reverence. When I ask about his father, he cuts me short: ask mother. Does Violet mind him being a boxer? 'No. She sees me travelling the world, not getting hurt, and she knows where I am.'

Will Lennox Lewis get hurt? Quizzed about Mike Tyson, he is uncharacteristically tentative. He has seen the bull-man dismantle quite a few well-trained defences and he knows that Tyson's headlong style would be difficult for him to cope with. 'If ever I was to go against Tyson, what old fight would I turn back to? Ali-Frazier. But I believe I can knock anybody out, including Tyson. If they just stand there for one second and let me generate all my body mechanics.'

Before Tyson – if that ever happens – Lewis' body mechanics will presumably have to apply themselves to Riddick Bowe. When I met Lewis, the haggling over Lewis-Bowe had just begun. The insults were flying: Lewis was calling Bowe a 'chicken', Bowe was calling Lewis a 'faggot', and so on. Bowe contemptuously surrendered his WBC belt – in a waste-bin. Lewis picked it up, the press cheered – a world champion at last! – but everybody knew that it was really Bowe who held the crown: he was the man who beat the man who beat the man.

The fear was that by isolating Lewis and the WBC (Bowe held on to his three other titles), the Bowe handlers had outmanoeuvred Frank Maloney. Certainly they seemed to have achieved what they wanted: an indefinite postponement of the Lewis-Bowe match (thus freeing Bowe to milk his title against a procession of no-hopers). How could Lewis as WBC champ go up against Bowe, who had denounced the WBC prize as 'dishonoured, a piece of tainted trash'? Must Lewis relinquish *his* title in order to win Bowe's?

If these doubts have substance, Lewis can look forward to some domestic entertainment but not to a real breakthrough in the

States, at least not yet. There will be Lewis-Bruno, Lewis-Foreman, Lewis-Stewart and, this month, Lewis comes up against Tony Tucker.

For Lewis, though, the big one is still to come, and the big one is Riddick Bowe, the *real* world champion, the man he has already floored. As so often before, Lewis believes he has the psychological advantage: 'Yeah, Bowe's gonna have to second-guess himself. I don't. He has to remember. I don't have anything against Riddick Bowe. He's just someone I'm competing with. Whether he wants to turn it into a grudge match and call me names, that's his prerogative, but it's a waste of energy on his part.'

At this, Lennox Lewis sprawled back, gave a contented yawn and then hoisted his massive size-fifteens onto the coffee table. He has wasted enough energy today. 'I'm only saying something that is reality, you know. I don't think he has enough heart to hang with me. All the things I say I believe.'

BAT OUT OF HELL

Matthew Engel

January, 1991

One of the most recognisable faces in British sport was at that moment about as incognito as it could get. Graham Gooch had had a shave and, for the second time since starting his cricket career, he had, on a whim, shaved off his moustache. The most persistent designer stubble in the known world, ranking alongside George Michael's and Yasser Arafat's, had temporarily vanished. He seemed to look younger, thinner ... different, anyway. Even some of his team-mates started to walk past him before doing a double-take.

There was another reason for Gooch's anonymity. He was perched on a rolled-up mat of Astroturf in the Exhibition Stadium, Toronto, where an unofficial, but almost full-strength England team was playing the West Indies on an artificial wicket in a sort of one-day international for the benefit of Toronto's substantial West Indian immigrant population.

The authorities back home at Lord's had disowned the enterprise, saying they were fearful that the players would get injured immediately before the Ashes tour to Australia. But Gooch was, aside from the wicketkeeper Jack Russell, the one significant absentee from the England team. He was already injured; the best year of his career also brought him three separate hand injuries, the last of them, in Australia, leading to serious infection. But Gooch had come along to Toronto anyway, taking advantage of the chance of a free holiday for himself, his strapped-up thumb, Brenda and the three kids. They were on their way to Disneyworld the following day.

The setting was strange, but what Gooch was doing somehow summed up his career as much as anything he could have done on the field. He was antagonising cricket authority in a small way and he was putting his family first. Our conversation in the dugout was delayed because he was taking little Hannah to the lavatory.

As England captain, Gooch is heir to the greatest names of cricket's golden past. Did Douglas Jardine ever spend his time on a cricket ground taking his daughter to the lavatory? Did the Hon FS Jackson ever sit in a baseball dugout? Did CB Fry ever have designer stubble? Gooch is not quite in the mould of the ancients.

But he is unusual among the moderns as well. In the past ten years, ten men have captained England. Only one was considered a success: the cerebral and enigmatic Mike Brearley, who was in command when Ian Botham played two of the greatest innings in Test history (against Australia in 1981) and managed to be elsewhere whenever England played the West Indies.

Excluding Allan Lamb, who only got the job as Gooch's deputy, every one of the others was sacked, David Gower twice. Yet they virtually all came in amid loud hosannas and high hopes . . . Ian Botham, Keith Fletcher, Bob Willis, David Gower, Mike Gatting, John Emburey, even, for heaven's sake, Chris Cowdrey, who was appointed primarily on the hereditary principle. Except one.

No one expected much of Gooch. When he was first appointed to the job, in the summer of 1988, the cricket correspondent of the *Sunday Mirror* wrote that he felt as though he had been slapped in the face with a wet fish. By the autumn of 1989, the same correspondent, one Ted Dexter, had mutated into the chairman of selectors and was obliged – in the absence of any other viable candidate – to make Gooch his captain for the tour to the West Indies.

By that stage, every cricket follower in the country felt as though he had been slapped by a trawler-full. The England cricket team has always been a bit of a joke. That is its fascination. If we always beat the foreigners at the game we invented, there would be no point in playing them. But by that stage the joke had gone too far.

Players had been caught up in various scandal-ettes (Botham and the cannabis, Gatting and the barmaid) that had been made infinitely worse by the fatuously hysterical reaction of the game's administrators. There had been five captains in one year. The team had been not merely beaten but humiliated by both the West Indies and Australia. Half the established players had opted out and signed up for a rebel tour of South Africa. The remnants were going off on the hardest tour of all, to the Caribbean, with everyone expecting them to be on the receiving end of the biggest shellacking of all time.

And the rest is history. England spectacularly won the opening Test in Jamaica, were diddled out of victory in Trinidad and only lost the series in the last two games when Gooch was absent injured. They came home and won series against both New Zealand and India. The win over India at Lord's was achieved after Gooch had scored 333, the sixth-highest score ever in a Test match.

As he sat in the Toronto dugout, no one knew what might befall Gooch next. He had learned better than most that a cricketer's career has downs as well as ups. But at that moment he was more pre-eminent, as a player and a leader, than any Englishman in three decades. And nothing could ever take away the fact that he had presided over the return of English cricket's self-respect.

This little jingle kept going round my head. It was composed by Clement Attlee, perhaps Britain's most improbably successful Prime Minister, about himself:

> There were many who thought themselves smarter
> Few thought he was even a starter
> But he ended PM
> PC and OM
> An earl and a Knight of the Garter.

I might have mentioned it to Gooch, but he would probably feel insulted to be compared to a Labour politician. The *Sunday Telegraph* called him cricket's Thatcher: 'forceful, plebeian, undeferential, a winner'. That is more his mark.

Gooch is 37 now. He has spent his life in that Thatcherite tract of land where east London and Essex meet. He was born in Leytonstone, hard by the old ground at Leyton where the Essex cricket team used to play, before, like much of the population, it moved farther east to a posher, less metropolitan address. He grew up among those places that only Ian Dury has ever bothered to celebrate.

His father Alf played a lot of club cricket. Graham worked briefly, but he was playing first-team cricket for Essex before his twentieth birthday and inside two years he had won an England cap. In one of their regular desperate moments, the selectors plucked him from obscurity, sensing unusual talent. They were right about his talent, wrong in their timing – Gooch got two noughts in his first match and was sent back to his country for three more years to learn his craft.

Cricket's first great rebellion – when the Australian Kerry Packer set up his rival cricket circuit in 1977 – gave Gooch his opportunity. He was a powerful hitter of a cricket ball but with enough inhibitions to succeed as an opener. He established himself as Geoff Boycott's opening partner and looked set to be a fixture of the England team indefinitely. 'Those of us who enjoy exciting and entertaining cricket,' said *Wisden* in 1980, 'will be grateful for that.'

Gooch himself, however, proved less grateful. Those of us who will never play cricket for England assume that anyone who gets the chance to do so should have no other ambitions in life and play as often as he is invited. But modern Test cricket, with its relentless schedule and long months spent far away from home, is a uniquely stressful way of living, one that is carefully crafted to kill anyone's sense of romance, both about travel and the game itself.

All of England's great modern players have felt the need to climb off the madly spinning whirligig at some point. But for much of the Eighties, Gooch's absence was as frequent as his presence. His form has come and gone, like anyone's. But since 1978, no one has doubted that, all other things being equal, he is one of the best two opening bats in the country and since Boycott retired (well, more self-destructed), his pre-eminence has been beyond dispute.

But he always seemed to be somewhere else. In the spring of 1982, he joined the first rebel tour of South Africa. When the players refused to accept Boycott as captain, the mantle fell on him, and it became known as Gooch's tour. At the time, he was palpably clueless about cricket tactics and ill-equipped to be the leader of any enterprise above a shopping expedition, particularly one as high-risk as that tour. He was banned from Test cricket for three years, along with the rest, and nursed his grievances with a pathetic injured innocence, as he still does: 'I was just taking up a private offer to go and earn some money,' he will intone, if he has to.

Insecurity led Gooch to South Africa. And all along, insecurity seems to have been the prime motivation. No one could really dislike him. No sportsman has ever been quite so publicly and touchingly obsessed with his family. And from that butch and usually hairy visage comes this surprisingly reedy voice; WG Grace apparently was just the same. Most players mimic him affectionately. But among black activists on five continents, who knew nothing of the man, he became an absurd hate-figure.

When he was allowed to tour again, in the West Indies in 1986, he was abused by politicians, chanted at by demonstrators and burned in effigy in Trinidad, while Allan Lamb, a real South African, walked around unnoticed. Gooch tried to go home instead of returning to Antigua, whose deputy prime minister Lester Bird had been more than normally unpleasant; the Test and County Cricket Board, whose chief mission often appears to be to stop anyone saying anything, declined to let him reply. He made it clear he would not be back.

After two seasons, he gave up the captaincy of Essex, saying the pressure had affected his form. He refused to tour Australia the following winter: 'My twins had just been born. I got slated for it. I put my family first. It was very hurtful.' The next year he would do only half the tour to Pakistan and New Zealand. In 1988, he signed to play provincial cricket in South Africa but was talked out of it when, having again taken charge at Essex, he was offered the England captaincy. However, he was now regarded as such a bulwark of apartheid that the Indian government refused to accept him; the tour was cancelled and the following summer Gower displaced him. By now Gooch seemed to wear a permanently hard-done-by look. When another South African tour was rumoured in 1989, it was generally assumed Gooch would be the first on the plane.

But he wasn't. Had he been bribed with the captaincy again? Or did he feel that all his mucking about had tarnished his career, that he still had something left to prove? The truth remains unclear. 'I want to play as long as I can,' he insists, 'as long as I'm good enough. It's an honour to play. I've worked an apprenticeship, I enjoy this.'

Really? Whatever might be said about Gooch's cricket, enjoyment has for some years not obviously been part of it. Throughout the Eighties, the strokes were played less frequently, while the determination became all the greater. An American watched him face down Malcolm Marshall at his fastest in desperate light at Lord's in 1988. 'You could hear his brass balls clanging,' he remarked, awe-struck.

When Gooch did play, he felt like the boy on the burning deck. One began to sense his growing impatience with the likes of Gower and Botham, who were much more ready to turn up physically wherever in the world they might be required, but often seemed only half-there in spirit. The doggedness of Gooch's batting and his obsessive concern with his family rather than cricket began to build into that mysterious quality known as professionalism.

He began to prepare for a day's work with a quite extraordinary meticulousness: box-briefs, chest-protector, thigh-pad, helmet, visor, arm-protector, pads ... everything in its place and put on with an air of one going out to war. A soldier's life is terrible hard, says Graham.

But when he took his raggle-taggle army to the West Indies, the troops responded to this set of attitudes. They quickly realised there was no hypocrisy in the man. He expected nothing from his players he would not give himself. 'Gatting would sometimes bollock players for not wearing a jacket and tie to a function,' said one county captain, 'then a week later you'd see him doing the same thing himself. Gooch would never make that mistake.'

There was also the matter of fitness. Micky Stewart, the frustrated PT instructor who became England manager, found in Gooch the perfect soul-mate. When the Australian party went to the National Sports Centre at Lilleshall last October to have their fitness tested, Gooch, even with his broken thumb, came out as far sharper than men ten and fifteen years younger than him.

This did not happen by accident. In Toronto, he was, in effect, on holiday. But both mornings he was there, he went for a half-hour run down by the waterfront. Then he went back to the hotel and ran ten times up the fire escape between the mezzanine and the sixth floor, taking the lift back down again – sort of skiing in reverse. 'What I say is, if there's no pain, there's no gain.'

Old-time cricketers – and cricket writers – are still pretty scornful of this. We all look back to the more relaxed days of Denis Compton, who would wander into cricket grounds still wearing his dinner jacket, and Colin Ingleby-Mackenzie, who led his county Hampshire to the County Championship in 1961, reputedly on a regime of wine and women, though he insisted he never let them sing.

On being told by the county secretary that all the players should be in bed by eleven o'clock, Ingleby-Mackenzie said that was bloody silly because the game started at half-past. The philosophy, if not quite the timings, lingered on in English cricket until last year. Now, anyone not willing to play it the Stewart way is keeping quiet.

It may have helped both mentally and physically for England to be fitter. Certainly the connection with Gooch's own performance can hardly be ignored. Traditionally, marathon batting has been the preserve of very young men; weight-for-age, Gooch's 333 at Lord's last year was an absolutely astonishing performance. 'You're as old as you feel,' he says. 'I felt very tired at the end of the first day, because we'd had a hard game against Lancashire at Colchester the previous day. It was hot and we'd had a run chase. But I wasn't tired at the end of the 333. Your reactions do get slowed, your arms get tired. But that's why you train.'

His team-mates could not criticise a man who led so spectacularly from the front. And he is now surrounded by players who were not part of either the old England set-up or the clique that usually surrounded the leader. Gooch's only clique is his family. And for him, the lads will run the extra half-mile. They will even tell you what fun he is.

It is a side of his character that hardly ever transmits itself to the wider public. Just as much of the joy of the young Gooch's stroke-play has been lost under the weight of worry, so the lightness of his character has seemed to go too. He used to do wonderfully comic impressions of other bowlers to enliven those wretched dead afternoons when matches are doomed to be draws. He is more prepared to make fun of his new lugubriousness – 'I know I look a thoroughly miserable sod on telly but I can't help it' – than change it.

In 1990, he went from being mildly famous to very famous. If Goochymania never quite took off like Gazzamania, it still made him feel uncomfortable: 'Everyone in the streets walks up to you. You can't disappear into a corner without someone bothering you. That's the price you pay. It used to happen quite a lot. Now it's every time.'

And he has never learned to cope with the press. All captains of England prefer to be at arm's length, even the most affable; Gooch would rather use a bargepole. A journalist who asked in the autumn whether the beard had gone for good was told it was none of his business. At home, he only gets the *Mail on Sunday*, yet somehow he always seems to know when he is being criticised. 'My job is to captain Essex, captain England and concentrate on the cricket. They can write what they like. But if they write what they like, don't expect to come to me. And if they write something libellous, I'll sue 'em.'

If he was paid a baseball salary – three or four million dollars a year – then, he says, he would be more cooperative. Gooch, by employing a cold-eyed agent and putting himself about, can perhaps earn £100,000 a year as England captain. But his poisoned finger in Australia could easily have ended everything. Even a bad run with the bat could put him back on a county pro's pittance. Gooch, without the financial insecurity and his fears for his family, might be a happier and more cheerful man. He would probably be a far less effective cricketer.

The nation will probably never take such a withdrawn man to its heart. But if he can complete England's turnaround from shambles to champagne, the Attlee rhyme will apply. An earl and a Knight of the Garter? Baubles have been handed out for less.

BAIZED AND CONFUSED

Julie Welch

August, 1995

It is half past seven in Northampton and Ronnie O'Sullivan is on his way to play Jimmy White in the Doc Martens European Snooker League. O'Sullivan has two rules of the road: 1) set off late; 2) go very fast. He drives a black convertible BMW M3 and a few days earlier he was all over the tabloids, nicked for giving in to the temptation of a cloudless night, empty motorway and brute horsepower. The only other car on the road was driven by the cops who clocked him at 135mph.

He's still 19 and already has a fairly good record with cars, cutting swathes with them through car parks, wrapping them round lamp-posts: 'Ain't got no mortgage – I don't take no drugs or anything. All I like is a few clothes and bits and pieces and a car.' But though you might not want O'Sullivan to drive your grandmother home from bingo, you should go anywhere to watch him play snooker. As sure as you can be of anything in these times, O'Sullivan has the hands, the eyes, the genius and the lack of fear to become world champion. Clive Everton, the *Sunday Times* snooker correspondent and the editor of *Snooker Scene*, describes him as a 'bloody brilliant player whose very best is better than Stephen Hendry'. Anything else? 'There's not enough of it yet. But I think he's realising now what he needs to do.'

The Doc Martens is an event promoted by O'Sullivan's agent, Barry Hearn, and is being broadcast on Eurosport. It's bread and butter snooker; the tournament doesn't affect world rankings, but there's £50,000 waiting for the winner. The event is run on a league system between seven of the world's top players – O'Sullivan, Hendry, Ken Doherty, Steve Davis, Jimmy White, Alan McManus and John Parrott. There are eight frames in this match, but a draw is no use for O'Sullivan. He needs to be beat White if he's going to make the play-offs.

In the Diamond Club, Nene Park, 200 Northampton necks crane as O'Sullivan prepares to enter the auditorium. He wears the snooker player's uniform of plain black waistcoat, bow tie, white shirt and evening trousers. But despite the formal attire, O'Sullivan looks young and graceful with a fringe that flops over his forehead, giving him the look of a young Paul McCartney. He's tallish, slim, late-bedtime pale, hairy-armed but with the delicate, pianist's hands that all great snooker players have and no one notices. He chalks his cue, gives his slow easy smile and steps forward. The MC turns up the volume. 'One of the most explosive young stars ... full of self-belief and attitude ... From tomorrow's world – the Rocket himself – Ronnie O'Sullivan!'

God knows if the 'Rocket' nickname will stick. Luke Riches, the laconic PR at Barry Hearn's Matchroom outfit, says they'd been racking their brains for a suitable handle for months: 'All the barometric names – Whirlwind White, Hurricane Higgins – have gone.' Then just as someone said, 'Eureka – Rocket!', Ronnie Rosenthal unleashed three goals for Tottenham against Southampton in the FA Cup 5th round and there he was in the headlines the next day, 'Rocket Ronnie the Spur'. 'We were really cheesed off,' says Riches.

But the kind of snooker O'Sullivan plays is definitely turbocharged – expressive, fluent, adventurous, above all instinctive. What he possesses, perhaps more than any other player in the game, is the most extraordinary natural talent, that fabulous hand/eye co-ordination that can't be learnt. There is also a whiff of danger about him. You get the impression that he has only one speed, flat out, which is the way he tends to live his life – Rocket Ronnie, 135 miles an hour.

Back at the Diamond Club, O'Sullivan clears the table briskly to win the first frame. Second frame, White gets a break of 39 but then O'Sullivan's in there again, walking and chalking at the same time. He's really flying, 61, 64, 68, 70, blue, pink, 79, black, two frames up. Third frame, White stops at 47. Here we go again. O'Sullivan's three frames up and it's only ten to eight.

Crowd voices swell: 'Go on Jimmy, go on Jimmy.' The MC intones: 'This is a very important frame, please cease the comments.' White takes it all the way through to win the frame: 3–1. O'Sullivan takes the next: 4–1. But then White starts to play at the top of his game and squares the match at 4–4. O'Sullivan's payday is cancelled.

Owning such prodigious gifts has its drawbacks: O'Sullivan can play so brilliantly and effortlessly so often that he can't understand why he can't do it all the time. He is still finding out that what wins matches is absence of mistakes on shots *within* your normal ability range, more than spurts of brilliance. But the signs are that he is learning. In the UK Masters at Wembley earlier this year, he really concentrated in the crunch match, the semi-final against Peter Ebdon, who played out-of-this-world snooker and still lost. In the final against John Higgins, O'Sullivan really stuck to it, not trying to take the match with spectacular one or two-visit frames, but applying himself to the slow grind.

'Ronnie is a bit inclined to think "I don't deserve it, let it go," when he's not playing well,' says Everton. 'It's not in him yet to try and drag the other guy down. He's like Jimmy White when he was 19, very cavalier. People to whom sports come easily are different. They think differently. No cunning. They almost think they don't need it. But look at Steve Davis. He can still beat Ronnie, even now.' So what's O'Sullivan got to learn to do? 'Crush the ego. Make dents in it.'

Ronnie O'Sullivan junior was born in 1976 under the sign of Sagittarius (likes a bet) to an Italian mother ('my fiery temperament') with some Scottish/Irish on his father's side. He first saw light of day in the Midlands but is essentially an Essex boy. 'Funny old story. My dad didn't have any money so he had to live in Birmingham. Job on the ice-cream vans, couldn't handle it so he went back to London and, when he could afford it, brought me and my mum down to join him.'

At first they were crammed into a little flat in Dalston but three years later his mother Maria, 'a brilliant saver', played her ace. 'She'd saved up £11,000, brought it out from underneath the floorboards, the fireplace ... My dad couldn't believe what he was seeing. It got us our first house, in Ilford,' says O'Sullivan. Now he lives in posh Chigwell with his mother and younger sister Danielle.

He played his first snooker at the Ambassador's club in London's West End. They had five tables, and Ronnie junior was soon making a name for himself. 'My dad used to finish work and take me in for a couple of hours. It was difficult at first because I was only eight or nine at the time but they'd get to know me dad and he'd leave me there all day.'

At thirteen, he spent weekends travelling on his own, coming home with 1,500 quid in his pocket. Alone at an early age, a child prodigy among adults, O'Sullivan developed the open, confiding manner that stays with him now: 'If someone's nice to me, I'll talk to them,' he says. But his early life was not without strangeness. 'I didn't have my first real girlfriend till fifteen or sixteen. Only in the past two years I've realised there's other parts of life than snooker.'

There is one part of O'Sullivan's life away from snooker that threatened to overshadow his success at the table. Ronnie O' Sullivan senior, the father he worships, is serving a jail sentence for stabbing to death a former driver of the Krays. When Barry Hearn first became O'Sullivan's agent, he went public with the information straight away, knowing that was preferable to the boy carrying round a dark secret the tabloids were bound to dig out. Further devastation was to follow – his mother is under investigation for VAT fraud. 'When they took me mum in, they wanted 200 grand bail,' says O'Sullivan. 'I rang Barry and he said, "I'll be twenty minutes," and he got on a train and stood up in court and said he'd stand bail. Lots of people come up and say, "He [Hearn] ain't doing enough for you." But it's only because they want to upset the applecart.'

Does he miss his father? 'Cor, yeah. Sometimes I just wish I could be in there with him. He says to me, "Just crack on and do your bit. This place isn't for winners." I don't know how he copes with it, he must be very strong. I know how hard it is for him.' He phones his father every day and says O'Sullivan senior is managing to keep the family together. 'He's there. He's given so much to me and when I do something wrong I don't feel bad for myself, I feel bad for him.' At tournaments, O'Sullivan senior's always ringing the press room, sometimes twice within the same frame. He buys *The Times* for its snooker coverage, taking pleasure in being the only inmate who reads it. Two days after Northampton, O'Sullivan is off to play the Thailand Open in Bangkok, one of nine events that dictate the world rankings. He should be trying to acclimatise, practising, resting in his hotel room, frowning over chess or Scrabble like Steve Davis, but decides he can't be bothered. His first round opponent is Doug Mountjoy, whom he treats with complete and utter disrespect, taking outrageous risks when there is no need. This lack of awe for older, fading players is nearly to undo him later in the season but for now he gets away with it, and goes on to his crucial second-round bout against Stephen Hendry.

Blank-faced and chilly at the table, Hendry is a different man when he isn't playing. Over the last year, the Scottish world champion has become a good friend of O'Sullivan's, who describes Hendry as 'a bit shy maybe', but 'one of the only ones [snooker professionals] who's halfway decent. I've never met a nicer fella in my life. What a diamond. I went up to Scotland to play and he picked me up at the airport, took me for a cup of tea. Some of them get jealous of him, of what he's got. He's got, what, ten million, and it hasn't gone to his head, he's more dedicated than ever. People like him are the best, because they play the game for love, even if they've got bundles.'

But what do you do when your friend is also your biggest rival? In recent matches, the warmth with which O'Sullivan regards the Scot has got in the way of the need to destroy him at the table. In Thailand, O'Sullivan sits in his room, stares in the mirror, tells himself to be as hard as granite, to hate Hendry as long as the match lasts and give him hell.

It works; he beats Hendry 5–2. This is his first important tournament after the UK Masters and, as he goes through the ensuing rounds, it looks as though he's on the brink of a fabulous win double. But then tiredness and jet lag begin to erode him. He needs to sustain momentum one more match and he can't. He loses in the final to local hero James Wattana. 'By the semis I started to feel really knackered,' he says later. 'I was petering out and by the final I felt really weak.'

By this time, he's also brushed with the *News of the World*, which has sent a team over to Bangkok there to work on a story that the organisers naively believe is about the explosion of snooker in Thailand. At first, they trail Cliff Thorburn, Dennis Taylor and Tony Drago, who, disappointingly for them, all lead blameless existences. Then they nail Jimmy White with two girls, pictures, the lot. O'Sullivan is implicated with a 'raven-haired temptress'. He gets a bit upset with the *News of the World* guy and before leaving pours a jug of water over him.

When he gets back home, he sets off to play the Benson & Hedges Masters in Dublin and the *News of the World* is still on his back. After going out of the tournament early to John Parrott, O'Sullivan returns home and the hacks get their story: 'Cue's A Bad Lad,' reads the headline. 'Snooker Kid Ronnie in cells after boozy row with cabbie.'

O'Sullivan had been to celebrate a mate's birthday in the West End and there was a taxi driver who didn't fancy taking him back to Chigwell. Was it a Dennis Wise job? 'Nah. You're joking!' he says. 'Can't even remember what happened, I was enjoying myself so much.' He got a formal warning for being drunk and disorderly, then the police gave him a ride home. And the *News of the World*? 'I suppose I'm an idiot. I know they're waiting for me. I don't even like the taste of drink but if I'm in a club and on water all night, everyone else is having a good time and I just feel like an ice-cream stand, a doorman.'

A few days after he gets back from Dublin, O'Sullivan and I meet for lunch at La Famiglia (he likes Italian food) in west London. He arrives with three mates in tow, asks if it's all right if they sit at a nearby table; we end up eating together. He introduces them: 'My friend Jamie. My mate Ricky. My mate Nicky.' Nicky Thurbin is a boxer, light-middleweight; he looks slightly older than the others, tough, well-sorted. 'Going to be British champion one day soon,' says O'Sullivan who's in jeans, dark T-shirt and black loafers. He looks rosy and relaxed; they've been doing an hour's circuit training and running. At the moment, fitness is his thing. 'I was finishing the snooker at midnight and going straight down the curry house, doing myself no good. So these boys are helping me get fit. They're natural fit boys. We don't drink. Except on Friday nights.'

The feel-good buzz of fitness can only be good for O'Sullivan. 'He's such a bright kid in the here and now, but has no talent for introspection,' says Everton. 'He's had a background in which introspection and repose don't come into it. But what does he do with the rest of his time? He can't practise sixteen hours a day. He's realising what he wants to do, and on the other hand he wants a good time. He can't shut himself in a house and practise. He's got to practise in a club.'

Everton also wonders if O'Sullivan suffers from what he calls 'a depth of depression'; the symptoms are quite pronounced, he says. Last year he won the UK Open and got to the final of the European Open straight after. Then he came down to earth and couldn't lift himself off it. He lost in the 1994 Masters, couldn't string three balls together, could have lost to anybody. Dennis Taylor was tripe and he won 5–0. In November, he lost in a big quarter final to Ken Doherty and announced he was going to pack it in. But then Ronnie O'Sullivan senior changed his mind.

'There's nothing worse than going to a tournament and not being prepared,' says O'Sullivan. 'There's been times when I've not put in enough work and it's been my turn to win and I haven't been up to it. If you ain't prepared, you're going to miss the boat. I was getting to quarters and semis and not winning. I was prepared to give up and then my dad said, "It's your turn." And it all happened in a month. I won the UK, the Benson, got to the final in Thailand.'

It's half past seven, another month, another city. Plymouth is where the British Open takes place, in The Pavilions, a grey brick roundhouse blending into the greyish dusk. In the press centre – that has, as ever, become an unofficial players' lounge – Jimmy White sits in silence by the window, having a smoke. Stephen Hendry is parked in front of the TV set, watching John Parrot suddenly doing not very well against a 500–1 bottomweight, Suriya Suwarinasingh. Next to him are James Wattana, Tony Drago and a man from Bolton.

O'Sullivan pulls up a chair. On a table in front of them stand three glasses of Budweiser and the menu from a nearby tandoori takeaway.

'Whoo-hooo! Through the gap, through the gap,' says Hendry, eyes on the TV. 'There's only 40 in it.' He's getting quite excited. 'This would be a dish. In the gap between the black and the red, that's it!' Steve Davis joins the game: 'This looks intrestin'.' Ronnie leans forward, grinning, and lays a twenty note on the table next to the bottle of Bud.

You suddenly realise what snooker is really like, behind the iridescent highs. A lot of grind, several terrible curries, endless hanging about. The most poignant thing O'Sullivan says is when I ask him if there's anything he doesn't like about the life. 'Sometimes, being stuck in a room. You watch a football match and see them running out in the fresh air and you think, "I'd like to do that."'

Instead, he has two days to kill until his match against Dennis Taylor, a former world champion. Taylor needs to win in order not to suffer the ultimate indignity, having to qualify for the world championship in Sheffield. And it's here that it happens, what you might call the revenge of the ageing gunslinger.

O'Sullivan's such a candid guy that he sometimes can't hide his real thoughts; sit him at a press conference and he's meant to come out with something deferential about older players he's just trashed, and he tries, but you can tell he thinks they've played rubbish. But Taylor doesn't play rubbish. At one stage Ronnie trails 4–3 and at 0–57 in the eighth is resigned to going out. Taylor only needs one more black and he'll have got his place at Sheffield sewn up. It will be the worst career humiliation that O'Sullivan will have ever been handed.

Taylor rolls the black towards a pocket. It goes in. But the white goes in after it, taking with it Taylor's chance of a shock victory. O'Sullivan goes on to win 5–4. So it isn't the worst thing that's ever happened to him in snooker after all.

That was the time when, as a 16-year-old, he was beaten by Cliff Wilson, an old pro at the end of his career. The match was in front of a big betting crowd, O'Sullivan was 12–1 on, not a profitable bet in itself but they all had him in their accumulators, £10,000, £50,000 riding on O'Sullivan. 'Drove me mad,' he recalls. 'Wilson was going blind. He beat me 9–8, must have pulled every stroke in the book. Clunk, he'd spilled the ice bucket. Clink. Filling his glass with ice. Wouldn't sit in the chair, he stood in the middle. They let him get away with it because he was old. I'd won eleven rounds to get there and I had Stephen Hendry in the next round and I got fuckin' beat. Anger – anger – in me chest. Then I went back to my room and started crying. He went round saying, "Ronnie O'Sullivan, he's no good," for months after.'

And the best moment? 'Winning the UK and the Benson. There was about a hundred people there who I knew. And, when I won, Nicky and Jamie came running down the stairs and the steward had to stop them.'

You start imagining the scenes when O'Sullivan finally wins the world championship ... Whoo-hooo! Now that *would* be a dish.

GOALS TO NEWCASTLE

Alex Kershaw

January, 1993

'I didn't want to come back into football,' insists Kevin Keegan. 'Sure, I'd been offered loads of jobs. But Newcastle was the only club I would ever have considered.' The former Liverpool and England footballer is sitting in his spartan office at St James's Park, Newcastle United's ground, an hour before the club's first game of the 1992 season. Wearing a bespoke suit and what look like Gucci loafers, he has every reason to be nervous, but appears relaxed, bullish even. The last time Keegan was on Newcastle's payroll it was as a player nearing the end of his professional career. Now he is midway through his first full season as manager, and if he succeeds in taking Newcastle back to football's top flight he will have defied all the odds. Already worshipped with the kind of religious fervour normally associated with Latin American saints, he will again be heralded as the Messiah who restored pride to a North-east for so long engulfed in gloom as thick as Tyneside fog.

Since the North-east's industrial base collapsed in the early Eighties, there has been little else save Newcastle United around which Tyneside's hopes of regeneration can crystallise. Yet Newcastle United is no ordinary football club. It has always thought itself a cut above, and its fans have always demonstrated a unique loyalty: the club is, as Keegan has said, 'the heartbeat of a great city'. But its rapid decline has stretched even the tolerance of its long-suffering fans a defeat too far. And the longer the fans have had to wait for a revival, the more savage their despondency has become.

When Keegan returned from football exile on the Costa del Sol to manage the side in February 1992, he found a club languishing at the bottom of the Second Division, technically bankrupt and dazed by years of divisive boardroom battles. There had been so much blood spilt on the boardroom carpet that Keegan's first managerial decision, joked the fans, would be to add red to the club colours of black and white. Many pundits wondered whether Keegan, now 41, had downed one too many sangrias under the Spanish sun. Despite his popularity and astuteness, he has taken on a Herculean task – to save the club in its centenary year from what looked like certain relegation. Others predicted King Kevin's reign would end before it had barely begun.

When Newcastle avoided the 'drop' by just one place last April, the sighs of relief on Tyneside could be heard in the basin of every dry dock. Although Keegan's record in his first season in football management was one of the worst of any Newcastle manager, he had, as far as Tynesiders were concerned, performed a life-saving miracle; relegation to the Third Division would have been the death of the club. Not for nothing, quips Jack Charlton, himself a previous incumbent of the St James's Park hot seat, have Geordies since nicknamed Keegan 'Golden Bollocks'. 'If Keegan fell in the Tyne,' says Charlton, 'he'd come up with a salmon in his mouth.'

Now the talk on the terraces is of promotion to the Premier League. The beautiful game has at last, claim the purists, returned to Gallowgate. Not since Newcastle won the FA Cup in 1955, their last domestic honour, has there been such expectation at St James's Park. With eleven successive victories, Newcastle have never started a season so well.

But is it all another false dawn? Despite three successive defeats in late October, many think not, among them John Gibson, the engaging sports editor of the *Newcastle Evening Chronicle*. We are sitting in the early hours at the dimly lit bar of Edinburgh's Royal Hotel after Newcastle's pre-season friendly at Hearts. Keegan had played for twenty minutes before substituting Lee Clark for himself in a lacklustre 1–0 defeat. His touch, however, had been as good and his crosses as accurate as when, as a Liverpool player, he picked up every winner's medal in football.

In his prime, Keegan was as famous for splashing on the Brut as for scoring sensational last-minute goals. Almost everything he did seemed to 'come off' – the most impudent flick, the most courageous diving header, the most acutely angled shot at goal. At his best, Keegan won balls, particularly in the air, which players a foot taller could not reach. 'I just try and exploit what is there,' he said.

Gibson saw Keegan score twice for Liverpool against Newcastle in the 1974 FA Cup Final. 'And I've only just forgiven him,' jokes the North-east's most respected football commentator. As a lad, Gibson was one of the 50,000 who would regularly turn out in the Fifties to watch Jackie Milburn net 200 goals. He says he could reminisce until dawn about the greatest of all Newcastle managers, Joe Harvey. Since Harvey resigned in 1975, Gibson has seen eight others, some just as talented, pass through the revolving door at St James's Park. He can recall the playing debuts of Malcolm 'SuperMac' Macdonald, Peter Beardsley, Chris Waddle and Paul Gascoigne, he says, a passionate glint returning to his blood-shot eyes, 'as if they were yesterday'.

'Without a doubt,' says Gibson, 'Keegan's job is one of the most difficult in football. He's expected to achieve success almost overnight. As Jack Charlton says, it takes three seasons to build a side. But at Newcastle the fans, after waiting so long, expect success today, not tomorrow. And success at Newcastle United doesn't mean mid-table respectability. A job well done means winning the championship and the European Cup.'

Along with self-delusion, Newcastle United has always had a talent for under-achievement. At board level, it has for years been a case study in how not to run a football club. For too long, it has been afflicted with that classic English disease, short-termism, the kind of financial myopia that closed the shipyards on the Tyne and led to home-grown talents such as Chris Waddle and Paul Gascoigne being sold 'to save the club'. Every Newcastle manager's greatest problem, agrees Gibson, has been bridging the gap between reality and aspiration at a club which still thinks of itself as a Liverpool or Manchester United. In fact, Newcastle has no more glorious a past than Stoke City. But such is the prominence of football in the city's psyche, there is no greater chasm between success and failure than at St James's Park.

'Keegan has many of the qualities of great football managers,' says Gibson. 'He's a great man-manager. Players want to play for him. That hasn't always been the case at Newcastle. And his enthusiasm and personality were, some say, the only reason why Newcastle avoided relegation last season.'

As he downs his last drink, John Gibson tells me that Real Sociedad manager and former Liverpool player John Toshack supports his view of Keegan as a manager who still exploits 'whatever there is'. 'He's not the type to bet against,' Toshack told the *News of the World* last August. 'Kevin has always been able to climb to the top.'

Kevin Keegan, OBE, has, of course, scaled the heights at St James's Park before. In 1982, in the twilight of his career, he moved from Lawrie McMenemy's Southampton to Newcastle and less than two years later inspired the side's promotion to the First Division. For sheer instant and explosive impact, English soccer's first millionaire was United's greatest signing. Keegan joined a club then, as now, rich in promise. In Keegan, manager Arthur Cox had secured for just £100,000 the perfect front man for a side which ranked alongside the best to have donned the black and white shirts: the Newcastle eleven that won promotion in 1984 boasted Terry McDermott, Peter Beardsley, Chris Waddle and David McCreery.

Before retiring from professional football in 1984, Keegan appeared one last time at St James's Park, scoring against his old club Liverpool before 36,722 emotional fans. And then, almost as dramatically as he had arrived, 'Special K' was gone, whisked away, apparently never to return, by a helicopter which swooped onto the hallowed Gallowgate turf and left as fireworks lit up the Geordie sky.

The brilliant but wayward Terry McDermott's departure from St

James's Park a year later, following a dispute over pay, was less ostentatious. But Keegan has brought him back as assistant manager. 'It's great to be back,' says Terry 'Mac' as he leads me through the players' tunnel, past the 'Howay the Lads' sign and onto the pitch. His scouse drawl seems to echo around the eerily silent ground. The ankle-length Gallowgate grass has yet to be mown and lovingly chalked, and the steep grey terraces are oppressive with the air of expectation. 'I'm telling you,' McDermott adds, 'when this place comes alive, there's no place in football you'd rather be. A good home crowd is like a goal's head start.'

McDermott and Keegan signed three-year contracts last May. Known as the 'Twin Perms' to some of the fans, the pair have since forged an inspiring partnership. 'The place was like a morgue,' says McDermott. 'Kev brought me in to put a spark back in it.' In McDermott, Keegan knew he had an ally of unswaying loyalty and commitment. In Keegan, says McDermott, he had a 'great mate', one of the few people in football for whom he would 'bust a gut'.

Keegan, jokes McDermott, has had to turn to the bottle – Grecian 2000, that is, not booze – since coming back to St James's Park, and indeed, he needs to: the trademark perm that spawned a generation of shaggy Seventies lookalikes looks distinctly more grey. But rumours of Keegan returning to football had been rife since he was found brutally beaten in his Range Rover near the M25 in April 1991. He had been attacked by a young man with a baseball bat as he slept. The story in Spain was that he had been on his way to talk to a club about a comeback.

If his wife Jean had not agreed to the move, Keegan swears he would still be wintering in Spain. 'She knew before I even met the board that I'd take the job. Jean knows me better than myself,' said Keegan of the woman he met at the St Leger in 1970 and who remembers being surprised by the young player's modesty. Keegan didn't admit on their first dates to being a professional footballer. That, he thought, was too flash. The Cortina parked in the drive, he blushed, was his Dad's.

Keegan's first game as manager was a dream start. Newcastle beat Bristol City 3–0 before an ecstatic home crowd of 29,000 and

Keegan, choked with emotion and relief, struggled to remember his players' names at the post-match press conference. But Keegan's honeymoon was to last just 39 days. After a 3–1 win over Swindon at St James's Park in late March, fans were stunned to see their tracksuited saviour storm out of the club, jogging through the ground's main entrance as he headed for the 5.30pm London flight. Promised £1 million for new players, Keegan had tried to buy David Kerslake, Swindon's £500,000-rated full-back, only to be told there was actually no money.

'You can't sign a manager and expect him to produce miracles out of nothing,' snapped Keegan. 'There was only one man who did that. And he wasn't in football. It's not like in the brochure.' But before the week was out, Newcastle's chairman handed Keegan, whom he claimed had 'held a gun' to his head, a personal cheque for new players.

'The first months were a baptism of fire, to say the least,' smiles Keegan. 'It was a nightmare start to a management career.' Indeed, the struggle to avoid relegation only ended when a Steve Walsh own goal gave Keegan's emotionally drained side a 2–1 victory in the last minute of the last game of the season against Leicester City.

John Toshack, for one, had predicted all along that if anyone could save Newcastle from 'the drop', it would be Keegan. He had shared many a round of golf in Spain with the homesick former European Footballer of the Year during which they would talk about their glory years at Anfield, about Keegan's race horses and football management. A couple of days after Keegan's return to St James's Park, Toshack rang his old team-mate. 'I suppose you're calling to welcome me to the funny farm,' replied the novice manager.

Newcastle reveres its footballing heroes like no other employment black spot. Even those who desert the club in search of a greater honour than wearing a Magpie shirt are treated as prodigal sons, one day to return to a forgiving Gallowgate. In the many pubs and working men's clubs of Newcastle's depressed Wall's End, unemployed fitters and turners still splutter into their pints at the very mention of Peter Beardsley, Chris Waddle and Paul Gascoigne. They have still not forgiven the 'board' for selling all three. As far as they are concerned, it was as if the 'gaffers' had supped too long on their sponsor's special brew – Newcastle 'Broon' Ale, the 'loony broth' that fuelled many a pitch invasion in the Seventies.

In retrospect, success at the club seemed not to disappear with Beardsley to Liverpool nor even when Terry Venables bought Gascoigne for £2.3 million, but on that balmy night in 1984 when Keegan made his operatic exit. But things looked different, of course, back then, even when Arthur Cox resigned in 1985 as manager, complaining of contractual disagreements with the board.

Tyneside's mourning of Cox had turned to joy when Jack Charlton replaced him. Although he had never played for the club, Charlton was a Newcastle man born and bred. He hailed from the same clan in Ashington that reared the club's most prolific number nine, Jackie Milburn. Jack's mother, Elizabeth Charlton, was in fact 'Wor Jackie's' cousin. Legend has it that when Jack, as Leeds and England centre-half, made Elizabeth a grandmother in the Sixties, a neighbour asked how her grandchild was. She replied: 'Ee, the bairn's lovely. And his feet are fine, too.'

But Charlton's time at St James's Park, like that of so many before him, was destined to end in bitter disappointment. For all his Geordie pedigree, Charlton's approach to the game quickly alienated the fans. His early conversion to the long-ball game infuriated a crowd soon yearning for the flamboyant United of the previous season. Charlton's abrasive style also frustrated the blossoming talents of Waddle and Beardsley. And when Waddle moved to Tottenham at the end of the 1985 season, the fans were inconsolable. The local press dubbed his transfer not the sale but the 'crime of the century'. 'Joe Harvey once told me, "If the fans get on your back it's time to leave." So I did,' recalls Charlton, who quit in 1986 after a dismal pre-season friendly against Sheffield United.

Under Charlton, Newcastle had finished tenth in the league, the club's highest placing since the Thirties. It was a post-war zenith to which Newcastle has yet to return. Just three seasons later, despite the emerging genius of Paul Gascoigne, the club was relegated for the second time in less than a decade.

In 1988, the fog of despair that seemed to have settled on the city was about to become a pea-souper. Local tycoon Sir John Hall began ruthlessly to purchase shares in Newcastle United, initially offering £500 for each of the 2,000 50p shares, then upping the ante to £1,000. The son of a Northumberland miner, Hall had been the developer behind Europe's largest shopping complex, the Metro Centre in Gateshead, one of a series of property deals that had amassed him a personal fortune estimated at £50 million. Last year, Hall was knighted for his contribution to the region's faltering regeneration, and for him, a successful Newcastle United had always represented the last piece in the jigsaw of his plan to revive the North-east.

Hall was backed in his takeover bid by a coterie of local business associates calling themselves the Magpie Group. Newcastle's then chairman, 63-year-old Gordon McKeag, led the boardroom counter-offensive. Well respected in football's inner circle, McKeag was the son of an ex-mayor of Newcastle and came from a family of solicitors. An enthralled city watched as Hall the meritocrat took on 'gaffer' McKeag in what the *Sunday Times* called 'the richest poker game in football'.

'Hall meant business, all right,' says a former aide-de-camp. 'He hired private detectives to track down shareholders as far-flung as Alice Springs. Motorcycle couriers were dispatched with blank cheques to OAPs in Gateshead who suddenly discovered a Newcastle share certificate was worth as much as a winning Pools coupon.'

Inevitably, as the stakes got higher, some participants were tempted to throw in their hand. When the share price peaked at an incredible £7,000, two directors in the McKeag camp folded to Hall. One of them, vice-chairman Ron McKenzie, then retired to the Costa del Sol with £640,000 as a lump sum – a healthy return on shares worth £200 at most two years earlier. But McKeag somehow held out. By 1990, after spending more than £2 million, Hall still hadn't acquired control of the club. Stalemate followed, broken only in August 1992 when McKeag, now president of what remains of the Football League, finally capitulated.

The takeover battle left McKeag, according to one source, 'beggared by the ordeal and physically broken', and it brought Newcastle United to its knees. Playing veterans of the 1987–8 season testify that the most immediate effect of the Magpie Group's bid was to make relegation the next season almost a foregone conclusion. And the Group's unsuccessful attempt to float Newcastle United on the Stock Exchange in 1991 only capped a disastrous half-decade. On the field, the club's drive for promotion had been just as ill-fated. In April 1990, Jim Smith's side had finished third in the Second Division, only to lose to local rivals Sunderland in the promotion play-offs. Eight months later, hamstrung by lack of money for new players, Smith resigned in abject frustration. 'I just felt I'd had enough,' he said. 'If you make a mistake here, it's not just a mistake – it's a disaster.'

Smith's legacy was a flourishing 'grow-your-own' youth policy which has nurtured Lee Clark, the slightly built 19-year-old local lad now hotly tipped to fill Paul Gascoigne's boots. And great things were expected of Smith's replacement, Ossie Ardiles. Within months, though, Ardiles' young side crashed to the bottom of the Second Division.

In January 1992, with Ladbrokes making the club odds-on favourites for the Third Division, Sir John Hall was still standing publicly by Ardiles despite Newcastle's worst run of results since 1938. The club's new chief executive, bluff Glaswegian Freddie Fletcher, was less loyal. 'I felt the club was going down,' recalls Fletcher, who had earned a reputation as a financial hard man under Graham Souness at Glasgow Rangers. 'Much as I admire Ossie, no one person is ever bigger than a club. It was a case of doing whatever had to be done to survive.' Fletcher phoned former Newcastle Breweries executive Alasdair Wilson, who had brought Keegan to St James's Park in 1982, and asked him to contact Keegan on his stud farm in Hampshire. The next day, Keegan met the Newcastle board in London. By Wednesday, Ardiles, the Argentine 1978 World Cup star, had cleared his desk.

Six months on, the sun is shining again on the funny farm. The training ground has been fumigated, the club given a lick of paint. 'You're now sitting in potentially the biggest club in Britain,' says Keegan, the Yorkshireman who began his football career kicking widgets around a Scunthorpe brassworks and who has now moved into a cottage with stables on the estate of Hall's nineteenth-century home, Wynyard Hall. 'I honestly believe that when we hit our targets this club will be bigger than Liverpool. If we clinch a Premier League place next spring, it will make St James's Park a more exciting place to be than Anfield. This club's greatest asset is the fans. Through all the disappointments, they never stopped believing that one day the golden era would dawn again. I never stopped believing it either. This club will go back to where it belongs.'

During the closed season Keegan spent £1.5 million of Sir John Hall's money on new players, snapping up John Beresford for £650,000 from Portsmouth, Barry Venison for £250,000 from Liverpool and Paul Bracewell for £250,000 from Sunderland. This inspired defensive troika has proved an inspired buy and has shown Keegan can play the transfer market with the best.

On a hot Wednesday lunchtime, a fortnight before the first game of the season, Keegan and McDermott are putting their summer signings through their paces at the club's Durham training ground, whose car park is crowded with BMW coupés. Bracewell's fabled dodgy knee seems to be holding up. 'Goldilocks' Venison looks as sharp, his hair as peroxide-blond as when he used to make the Liverpool first team on a regular basis; he still wears Versace suits and Mexican heels. A sweating Beresford, the star of Portsmouth's FA cup run last season, glistens with promise.

'You really want to know why I joined Newcastle from Liverpool?' asks Venison, fresh from a shower. 'Because of Keegan and only because of him.' Born-again Christian Gavin Peacock, the side's top scorer with 22 goals last season, is equally enthusiastic about the 'boss', having turned down 'serious' offers from Middlesbrough, Chelsea and West Ham to stay. 'Keegan's a man you want to stay around,' says Peacock. 'His ambition and vision are infectious. He made me feel like I'd be mad to leave.' With Lee Clark, who has also decided his future lies at St James's Park despite being approached by 'several agents' over the summer, Peacock has formed the most effective goal-scoring partnership since Beardsley and Waddle.

Saturday August 15, 1992. It is 5pm and Keegan is surrounded by a huddle of local reporters looking for good quotes for Monday's papers. Newcastle have beaten Southend United 3–2 in the first game of the season. Bracewell, the ex-Sunderland captain, has scored on his debut with a spectacular fifteen-yard strike.

'Yeah, we gave away two silly goals,' smiles Keegan chirpily. 'But then again, as you know, I've never had an easy game here. We've proved one thing – we can play as good a game of football as anyone in the country with the players we've got. Sorry it couldn't be 8–1, lads. But, hey, all dreams have to be shattered at some stage.'

For the time being, the Geordie faithful's reverie has yet to be disturbed. At times vindictive and brutal, as Jack Charlton well knows, the fans have seldom been deceived. In Keegan, they see resurrection personified. It used to be said that they would turn up just to watch the Gallowgate grass grow. That may still be the case. But with receipts of more than £250,000 every home game and the highest average attendance in the country this season, the club's financial survival depends on them more than ever.

'Clubs with our debts but without our support would be almost impossible to turn around,' admits Freddie Fletcher. The club's shortfall this season is budgeted at £1 million, to which have to be added a £5 million debt and mortgages on a £10 million ground redevelopment. 'On the credit side,' says Fletcher, 'the boardroom conflicts are over. We're busy restructuring debts. Newcastle Breweries are as supportive as ever and gate receipts have exceeded our wildest expectations. Keegan alone has considerably eased the financial crisis.'

Sir John Hall, who now owns three-quarters of the club's shares, also has the money to revive Keegan's promotion drive should it need resuscitation. He may have spent as much as £6 million – or half what the club was worth in 1988 – acquiring control, but Cameron Hall Developments, despite the recession, is still cash-rich. 'Hall's no Jack Walker,' says the *Evening Chronicle*'s John Gibson, referring to the Blackburn chairman who spent millions building Kenny Dalglish's new side. 'But he's not a miser either. There's no other man with as much money, with as good a name at the bank, in the North-east. Without Hall, there would be no Newcastle United for Keegan to revive.'

Hall is in many ways the quintessential football director derided by Arthur Hopcraft in his study of Sixties soccer, *The Football Man*. He's a superfan anxious for success because it gives him enviable social cachet, because it nourishes his own ego and, crucially, that of the local community. Nonetheless he is also too shrewd, believes Gibson, 'to allow his heart to dictate to his head. He sees Newcastle as a business with huge potential. With the best support in the country, he knows it could be a gold mine. He's here to finish the job, all right.' The question the impatient Gallowgate end now asks is whether Hall, as far as ever from his dream of democratising the club, will put enough of his money where Keegan's mouth is. It will need Jack Walker-style wedges to realise Keegan's recent claim that Newcastle can 'do a Leeds' and win the Premier League title within three years.

As for Keegan, there seems little doubt that he can succeed in his first management job where Arthur Cox, Jim Smith and Ossie Ardiles failed. He has claimed he has 'a better chance of success than any post-war manager at Newcastle'. But he is also the first manager, certainly since Joe Harvey, who cannot cast the board as scapegoats for failures on the pitch. Hall, likewise, is the first Newcastle chairman with no self-made Geordie to blame for the club's precarious financial position but himself. It is said that when Sir John seeks divine inspiration, he wanders into Wynyard Hall's baroque chapel and stands beside the tomb of the third Marquis of Londonderry, who fought alongside Wellington. Both Hall and Keegan may yet find themselves kneeling together before the marble grave on Saturday mornings before the season is out.

CENTRE OF ATTENTION

David Jenkins

November, 1992

At what he does, Jeremy Guscott is the best in the world. And what he does, time after time, is contrive the irregular, inventive, breathtaking back-play that electrifies the rugby aficionado. He scores three tries on his debut for England. He celebrates his promotion to the British Lions with a try-scoring gem of impudent spontaneity that changes the course of the match. He drops, from nowhere, a crucial goal against Scotland. He floats through indiscernible gaps. He is an automatic selection for any putative World XV. He has what George Bush calls 'that vision thing'. 'He is,' enthuses Will Carling, his England captain, 'the best centre I have ever played with. When he gets the ball, you see the panic on the opposition's faces.' He is also black, good-looking (he does a little modelling on the side), presents a television show and has rugby league clubs waggling gargantuan cheques in front of him. He was, he says, 'born to play rugby'.

Which should be fine and dandy. But the British mistrust flair. Politicians are damned for being too clever by half; cricket and football selectors opt for biddable diligence over God-given genius. 'People in this country are so *down*,' Jeremy Guscott complains, a fleeting petulance marring his fine-boned features. 'If you're American, it's everybody's dream to be a sporting hero, a Joe Montana or a Michael Jordan. No one goes around saying you've got a big ego – *of course* you've got a big ego.'

And that, in rugby's blokeish milieu, has been Jeremy Guscott's problem. *Sprezzatura* – effortless superiority – may be the Italian ideal; over here, we call it cocky. 'He was impetuous,' says Gareth Chilcott, his Bath club-mate and a former England pack member. 'Jeremy's not everybody's cup of tea,' observes Simon Halliday, Guscott's friend and England team-mate. 'He came across as conceited in his early days,' remarks Richard Hill, the erstwhile England scrum-half. 'You've got to have some arrogance,' says David Trick, the Bath and England winger, 'but he had too much. "You're a great player," I told him, "but you're a prat to yourself." '

But Guscott, they agree, has matured. 'He's like a fine wine,' says Chilcott. 'He's got better with age.' He may keep a lot to himself; he may be difficult to know; but he's a team player now and they all really, really like him. Guscott has bitten the bullet. Or has he? 'I'm not,' he says, 'as outspoken as I was. You've got to be more devious.' And being devious involves being one of the lads.

Bounding through the bar at the Lansdown Golf Club, Bath, no one could be more of a lad than 'Jer'. Seal on the stereo, Ray-Bans on the dashboard, a wodge of Wrigley's Spearmint perpetually on the go, he has roared down from a marketing conference at the Excelsior Hotel, Heathrow, in his white, sponsored, Rover 220 GTi. Pastel yellow shirt, discreet tie, dark slacks, brown suede brogues – he's the model of a young British Gas executive. Six-foot-one, with a 42- to 44-inch chest, a 33-inch waist and a 32-inch inside leg, he moves with the low-slung stride of the dangerous athlete. The handshake is confident, the eye contact full, and he's off like a startled pheasant to find partners for his medal round.

Golf is his new big thing. Celebrity brings with it trunkloads of invitations to pro-am frolics. Jeremy enjoyed 'just trying to melt the ball down, to send a vapour trail as far as I could hit it. There's not a lot changed.' Now his handicap is down to fifteen and he was off at the weekend for a return visit to the Terry Wogan golfing jamboree in Dublin. 'Lots of fun, lots of Guinness – which is not what the coach ordered. It's great to see the stars close up. We got friendly with Hale and Pace last year, had a real laugh.'

He likes to have a laugh, a great raucous, roaring, libidinous, bar-room laugh. His humour, say his friends, is coming through. Well ... 'I wish,' says one of his golfing partners, 'my lawn were like this green.' 'If my lawn were like this green,' quips Jeremy, 'there'd be no work for the wife.' Which, I suppose, is marginally better than Richard Hill's memory of the Leicester v Barbarians match: 'We were in this hotel and they were trying to warm the disco up. And this woman comes up, she's not the best looker in the world, and asks Jeremy to dance. And he turns round and says to her, "I didn't know it was Halloween tonight."'

Well, that's rugby and that's laddishness. Out on the golf course, there's plenty of breezy banter and a façade of seeming casualness. But when he has tried to kill the ball and sent it scuttling out of bounds, you see it: the tightening of the features, the controlled wrath of the very gifted at perceived inadequacy. For gifted he is, caressing chip shots and soothing balls from the bunkers in a display as delicate, as silken and as satisfying as his running on the rugby field.

He more than satisfies his colleagues. Critics assert that Guscott was last season muted by tight marking, but for Will Carling: 'It's his balance in attack, not only physical, but mental. And his tackling! People think he's just a pretty boy centre, but he's a terrific tackler, tremendous.' To Simon Halliday: 'He's a special, massive natural talent. In terms of complementing each other, Will and Jerry are marvellous – Will has the power, Jerry the grace. No one holds a candle to him.' According to Gareth Chilcott: 'He's proven he can do the nitty gritty, play in all weathers, get under high balls, defend. But it's the way he expresses himself. So many players in his position are stereotyped. They play to a team pattern and that's all they can play. He can play to a team pattern *and* turn on that bit of magic.' And as for Richard Hill: 'Jeremy can take two or three players out of the game with his *presence*. And he's still got talent to fulfil. We'll see an even better Jeremy Guscott these next two years.'

That's devoutly to be wished for. Right now, Jeremy Guscott is fiddling with his food and sharing the knowledge.

'Scoring a try. That's my greatest satisfaction. It's a split second ... it's just ... it ... it fills all your body and every time I score, it comes in, *zap*, and it goes away. It's a rush. It's totally unlike anything else, anything else I've experienced.' Jeremy Guscott is struggling to articulate his gift. In general, he is self-possessed, authoritative, practised in his patter. Suddenly he's tentative, even metaphysical. 'It's not an aesthetic pleasure. You can't enclose it like that. There's this gap and you can actually feel yourself ... *glide* through it. It's there, I've *got* to go through it.' He pauses. 'Why *shouldn't* I go through it?'

Go through it he does. Score tries he does, in abundance. And, since that British Lions try against Australia, 'things have been very different for me'. So different, in fact, that he now has little time to call his own. Last year's World Cup brought 'media, media, media'. And rugby, although nationally an amateur sport, is voracious of its stars. Guscott helped his club, Bath, win the Pilkington Cup (rugby's FA Cup) in May. Five weeks later he was back lifting weights and enduring the agonies of running up and down countless Jacob's Ladder steps with Richard Hill, the archetypal bullet-headed glutton for training punishment. 'I wouldn't say he enjoys it, but it has the desired effect,' says Hill. 'His gifts are speed and power – which for his position is fine. But for the England squad, we're also tested on stamina – not that he needs it. But England demands it now.'

England demands. Exactly. For years, England demanded a forward-orientated game, and all we got were guttering glimpses of Guscott's brilliance. The game plan, he says, revolved around 'steamroller ... grind the opposition into the ground'. He endorses it: results count. Last season England opened up and dazzled in their defeat of Ireland. 'Yeah, that was incredible. But we set ourselves such high standards that what stands out now are the faults. At our meetings, it's not going to be, "Gaw, look at that, rewind the tape, look at the way the forwards are interpassing and then it's out to Dewi Morris, on to Rob Andrew, and Rory Underwood ends up scoring in the corner" – we don't watch *that*. The coach says *these* are the mistakes you made and everybody's head drops. In modern-day rugby you tend to forget about the good things you have done.'

Which prompts the question – why not get paid for this? Guscott admits he would adore the money Steffi Graf and Nick Faldo get for doing 'what they love'. But he's realistic enough to know that rugby is, relatively, a minor sport. The bucks will never be big enough. They are, though, in rugby league.

'How much did they offer you?'

'It was a lot of money.'

'Quarter of a million?'

'More than that.'

'Half a million?'

'A bit less than that, but with what could have been made from sponsorship ... let's say it was very *substantial.*'

His wife, Jayne, fancied it, Jerry didn't. 'Had I gone, I would have missed out on things like World Cup Finals, Grand Slams, the British Lions Tour in 1993. Rugby for me is entirely enjoyment. I'm so happy with what's going on at the moment.'

The garden cannot always have been so rosy. He lives just two minutes from where he was born in Bath in 1965, the son of a Jamaican immigrant and a local girl. They met, he claims, when his mother knocked his father over with her bike, 'but I've never checked'. School was a frost: 'I did not take to education, and education did not take to me.' He was constantly in trouble, and was expelled for walking off in protest at a football referee's decision. He was a South-west Judo champion but had a 'personality clash' with his coach. Cricket? Replay that personality clash. It was at this period, says his drinking buddy Peter Blackett, that, even on the rugby field, 'he sometimes seemed like he couldn't be bothered'. He drifted from job to job, 'working on building sites, stacking shelves, log chopping, selling logs, then building sites a little longer'. But rugby was going well and 'a lot of influential people are involved. Anyone with half a brain could take advantage of the contacts.' Now he is a rising executive with British Gas. 'There's nothing better. You come back to earth with a bang. On Saturday, you're in the World Cup final. On Monday, you're in the office. Back to reality.' Should his TV work lead to Jim Rosenthalean grandeur, splendid. But 'ordinary is everything'.

Ordinary means a terraced house with two bedrooms, a car for him and a car for Jayne. Ordinary means jaunts to Bali, Australia, America, Jamaica. Ordinary means underwear from M&S and 'stuff' from Blazer and The Gap. Ordinary means a fondness for telly and having Jayne plop dinner on his lap. (They met when he accused her of kicking him. It was, in fact, her friend who wanted Jeremy's handsome attention. Still, it was Jayne's number that he took. They've been together seven years.) Ordinary means still having to save. Ordinary means a predilection for pissing around with the forwards when the lads are playing away. ('Jerry likes hanging around with the donkeys, as we call ourselves,' confirms Gareth Chilcott, a prime and portly specimen of donkeyhood. 'Forwards tend to be streetwise, they know where things are happening. Jerry enjoys that.' It makes a change, at least, from rooming with Rory Underwood, the illustrious winger: 'Rory,' Guscott exclusively reveals, 'was so homely, always making tea.') Ordinary does not ring true of the man Simon Halliday dubbed 'the future of British rugby'.

Over dinner – smoked mackerel, fettucine, lager – Guscott is as composed and as elusive as he is on the field. Politics? 'I voted for the first time in the last election.' For whom? 'Not saying.' Well, was he pleased that Chris Patten (then MP for Bath) was defeated? He roars with laughter. Being black? He's been lucky in being around people who do not have a problem with colour. Yes, it is true that Scott Hastings, the Scotland centre, did say 'something relating to me and something I wasn't too keen on . . . But it was during the 1990 Grand Slam decider and the Scots, and the English, were pumped up to a level I've not seen since. There's nothing I'll ever hold against anybody unless they really mean it.' Criticism? Guscott has no dark nights of the soul. He can fall asleep anywhere, any time. He is charming, fluent, full of fun – and canny. 'There's an ongoing joke between me and rugby journalists. They don't know how to take me. And that's the way I like it.'

Guscott runs his life the way he likes it. 'This,' he says, 'is the happiest time of my life.' His first child, Imogen, was born back in the summer. He has played for England 22 times. He has scored fourteen international tries. He relishes the communality of his club and sport. He relishes his skills and the showcases he adorns. 'We have redemption through his blood,' shrieks a rooftop sign in Bath. Jeremy Guscott's redemption has come through rugby. Conceit has become confidence, big-headedness, balance. He is the cynosure of the decent chap.

And the cost? '*Of course*, you've got a big ego.' Rugby, and the British, allow him to temper his basic instincts, not to flaunt them.

More's the pity.

THE PAWN KING

Dominic Lawson

February, 1989

The King's Head pub in Bayswater is a good example of the sort of low-life hangout in which that part of London has always specialised. At the bar, an attractive black girl is being chatted up by a not so attractive and much older white man. A stag's head on the wall stares down on this episode with a 'seen it all before' look. Through the fug of smoke and alcohol it is possible to observe a few men playing chess. It is that sort of a pub.

In the corner of the room sits the pub champion. He looks like the classic chess bum. Untidy hair. Big beard. His possessions in a white polythene bag by his feet. The chess board is also made of polythene, and the pieces of plastic. The 'table' is an up-ended keg of beer. The pub champion is playing some kid genius from out of town who has just won a London grandmaster tournament. He is called David R Norwood (I know. The boy wonder, all of 19, gave me his business card. It said 'David R Norwood. International Chess Master'). Now David R Norwood is, as he will be the first to admit, one of the hottest properties on the international chess circuit. But something funny is happening in his games – played at the rate of about one every ten minutes – against the champion of the King's Head pub. David R Norwood is not winning any. And he is not merely losing. He is being taken a-p-a-r-t. In the argot of the chess player, he is being 'busted'. But David R does not seem too worried about this denouement. Occasionally he will say, with a smile, 'Hey, you're not such a bad player.' His opponent, Jonathan Speelman, the King's Head champion, only laughs and sets up the pieces for the next act of slaughter. It is a joke, of course. He is not merely 'not a bad player'. He is possibly the best player in the Western world. He is officially world-ranked number five. A month before, he had won through to the semi-finals of the world chess championship, the first Briton ever to reach the last four in an event which makes the Olympic marathon appear an afternoon stroll by comparison.

It is, needless to say, odd to find a chess player of such eminence playing what can only be described as ping-pong chess in a pub, and ... for no money. The other chess players of this rank, who are called 'super grandmasters', play only for money, and then only in well-appointed hotel rooms where the public, if they are allowed to breathe at all, are certainly not allowed to smoke while doing it. But Jon Speelman shows up night after night at the King's Head, and takes part in all its chess events, including the 'drinking chess championship', a knock-out event in which it is necessary to consume two pints of ale while winning each game.

After Jon had finally exhausted David R Norwood's enthusiasm, I asked whether he would mind playing me. Not at all, he said, and played game after game against me until I became more bored by losing than he did by winning. Why, I asked, do you put up with playing chess jerks like me? 'Because I like to play with the pieces,' was the instant and unanswerable reply. My impression while playing Jon was slightly different, namely that the pieces enjoyed playing with him. He gives them the time of their life. These plastic pieces, property of the King's Head, had probably never before experienced more than the intellectual equivalent of being cooped up in a shed. With Jon, they were roaming free across vast expanses.

Last August, Jon was in the uncomfortable position of having to play another Englishman, Nigel Short, in the quarter-final round of the world championship. Uncomfortable because they are friends, and fellow residents of West Hampstead. Nigel Short, a prodigiously gifted 23-year-old, nine years younger than Speelman, was the favourite. He was ranked third in the world, behind only the world champion Gary Kasparov and his predecessor as champion, fellow Soviet Anatoly Karpov.

In recent games, Nigel Short had handed Jonathan Speelman some severe beatings, and some grandmaster pundits had given the older man about as much chance as Pee Wee Herman arm-wrestling Arnold Schwarzenegger. But Speelman's chess drinking partners from the King's Head made the unfamiliar journey to the hygienic wasteland of the Barbican to cheer their man on. After crushing Short by two wins to nil, Speelman declared, 'I need a drink,' and was dragged off back to the fastnesses of Bayswater by his friends, who, unlike the grandmaster chess journalists, had never doubted that Jon would win.

His friends, incidentally, do not call him Jon. They do not call him Speelman either. They call him 'Spess'. This stems from a report in *The Times* about ten years ago of a chess tournament in which Speelman was taking part. But, *Times* sub-editors being *Times* sub-editors, his name came out as 'Specimen'. In view of his rather weird appearance, fellow chess players decided that this was, if not his real name, at least descriptively accurate, and so Specimen, and then later Spess, he became.

In those days, he had much longer hair. But it is still hardly short, and now, as then, he has an unruly beard and a manic grin. He still dresses in what might be described as chaotic student mode: T-shirt bearing legends in a foreign language, age-old corduroy trousers, boots that are made for walking. (In the first game of his match against Short, Jon wore a suit, stretched most uncomfortably over his six-foot-two-and-a-half-inch frame. 'That's the first time I've seen Jonathan in a suit since his barmitzvah,' said his mother with evident astonishment. By game two, the jacket had disappeared, and by game three, the old scallywag had returned.)

But most striking of all are Jon Speelman's eyes. When he takes his spectacles off they are revealed as a penetrating bluey grey. But Jon Speelman rarely takes his spectacles off. It is easy to see why. They are thick, like glass bricks. I once sat next to Jon – near enough to touch him – and asked him to take off his spectacles. I held up a hand with three fingers extended. 'How many fingers?'

I asked. 'Two,' he guessed. Now Jon Speelman is not so short-sighted that he cannot play chess without the aid of spectacles. But problems with his eyes almost finished his career, and the end of those problems has much to do with his sudden breakthrough into the elite of world chess.

Until two years ago, Speelman suffered from haemorrhaging in his eyes. The blood vessels would burst regularly, and during games, so that the blood would flow in front of his eyes. The result was that he played many quick draws against players he really should have beaten. Only a few friends knew of his problem, and his foreign opponents simply put it down to laziness on his part or good fortune on theirs.

As recently as the Hastings Grandmaster Tournament of January 1987, a distressed Speelman, eyes bleeding, told the organisers he would have to withdraw. They gave him the good practical (if not medical) advice to agree a series of quick draws, and try harder when the problem eased. This he did to such effect that he almost won the tournament.

Knowing of their great expertise in eye surgery, Speelman sought advice from the Russians – he is a fluent Russian speaker. He was told that the bursting blood vessels were not part of some degenerative condition, but simply the result of the extreme nervous stress which he suffered in the early stages of a chess game. Speelman, greatly relieved, responded by attempting to relax more before games, and, true to the Russian doctor's prediction, the haemorrhaging has stopped. 'Ever since then,' says Ray Keene, a chess grandmaster and friend of Speelman, 'Jon has been unbeatable.' Speelman himself does not like to talk about the matter. 'Let's just say that I have an idea what it's like not to see. I was scared.'

On this, as on many other personal matters, Jon Speelman is difficult to interview. He is very self-conscious, a keen practitioner of self-psychoanalysis. The result is that he is only too aware of the implications which might be drawn from anything he might say. Worse, he was so concerned about what I was writing down that he would stare at my pad when I noted anything, attempting to read my scribble upside-down. In an effort to counter this awkward turning of the tables, I began deliberately to write in messier and messier scrawl. Afterwards I was quite unable to read many of my own notes. Later I surmised that the chess player in Speelman had calculated that his scrutiny of my notepad would have this effect, and that it was a deliberate attempt to reduce the number of personal details I would be able to decipher.

If that sounds convoluted, it is quite in character with Speelman's way of playing chess. Some great chess players reveal their greatness through the simplicity of their methods. This is true of Nigel Short, and it is true of Karpov. Others, more unusually, have a genius to confuse, an ability to generate chaos, out of which only they can perceive a clear path to victory. This is Speelman's method.

In the eighteenth century, the equivalent of the King's Head pub was the coffee house. And chess players there tended to thrive in complex positions, being gamblers by nature rather than scientists. This way of playing thus became known as 'coffee house chess'. But when I told Speelman that he played 'coffee house chess', he replied with one of his manic grins, 'my style is closer to another South American export.' Now it should be explained that Speelman is a fanatical devotee of *The Times* crossword, and frequently speaks in crossword clues. What he meant is that his chess games are so bafflingly surreal that they sometimes appear to have been played under the influence of narcotics. Yet operating on adrenalin only, his chess is like Coleridge writing 'Kubla Khan' without recourse to an opium pipe.

But such a style is, as the Russian doctor must have noted, one which makes enormous demands on the exponent's nervous system. When he plays, Speelman is all nervous twitchy movement. His hands play with his beard, his glasses, anything they can reach. He makes strange clicking noises. He will get up from the board and stand over it and his opponent, nodding his head as if checking through the variations. ('He goes there, I go there, he goes there . . .')

I asked Speelman how many moves he can see ahead. 'It's a silly question,' he replied, 'but it's not too difficult to imagine a position in which one could calculate 25 moves ahead.' 25 moves on each side, he means. That is 50 moves in total. Try saying 'he goes there, I go there' 25 times. Now you get the picture.

William Hartston, the former British chess champion, told me that playing Speelman was like playing 'an old fridge, one of those where the door shuts with a big clunk. You can't see inside, but the thing is whirring and shaking and something is certainly going on in an undirected sort of way.' The fridge is, of course, an innocent and harmless object of domestic pleasure, and Hartston chose that metaphor quite deliberately. The point is, as Jon Speelman explains, 'I do want to win at chess, but I don't want my opponent to lose.' (How very different from the home life of Bobby Fischer who declared on coast-to-coast US television 'I like to crush the other guy's ego.')

Speelman does not view chess primarily as a competition. 'It is like meditation,' he says, 'a way of attaining a higher state of consciousness. It is a bit like making love.' The last time Speelman said something like that he ended up in *Private Eye*'s Pseud's Corner. But he is unrepentant. 'I'm not saying that chess is mental masturbation, but a lot of libido is involved. Chess involves the emotions, and anything which involves the emotions involves sexuality.'

Sex is clearly something Speelman thinks a lot about. According to friends, his biggest passion outside of chess is writing poetry, and by all accounts his poems contain the most lurid sexual imagery. There is, at the moment, no one person with whom Speelman shares his sexual drive. He has had many girlfriends but few long relationships. 'Chess players can be hard to live with,' he admits, 'but so, I imagine, can bankers.'

If Jon Speelman ever does manage to persuade a woman to marry him, then one of her tasks could be to prepare vegetarian meals for Jon when he finally gets home after closing time at the King's Head. For years, Speelman has been a vegetarian, with a particular emphasis on the aubergine as the basis of his diet. This faddish regimen is also very much in tune with his character. For not only does he feel sorry for his opponents when they lose, he hates to do or say *anything* which might hurt or offend. And this seems to extend to all life forms. 'There is enough blood spilt on the chess table,' he told me. 'I don't see why I should extend it to the food table.' In fact, Speelman does not appear to take great pleasure in the food he does eat, and when I told Bill Hartston that I thought Speelman was a reluctant vegetarian, he replied, 'Jon eats his food like that because he feels sorry for the vegetables he is biting into.'

I invited Speelman to my home in order to interview him at leisure, and to provide a meal which I knew he would not feel betrayed his dietary principles. He arrived about a quarter of an hour late and explained, 'It took longer to walk from West Hampstead to Highgate Village than I thought.' It is, as it happens, the best part of an hour's walk, and I was incredulous that Jon had not paid the £3.50 it would have cost for a short taxi ride. (Needless to say, Speelman is not the type that could ever pass a driving test.)

But Jon Speelman likes to walk everywhere, in rapid massive strides. When I asked a friend of Jon's about this habit, he replied that 'Jon is incredibly tight with money. He's a sweet man. He'll always remember your birthday. And he'll always give you some book which no one would ever want to read, something you just knew had been remaindered.'

I prefer to think that Speelman is simply the perpetual student, and that he has not yet realised that he is making enough money (probably over £25,000 a year) to abandon some of the privations of the student's life-style. I remember when we were at university together, both playing for the Oxford chess team. We both had long hair, both wore corduroys and T-shirts and both walked everywhere. Now I – and probably every other member of that chess team – wear a suit, short hair, and jump into taxis. But Jon Speelman, who now has the possibility of earning more than any of us – if he beats Karpov in the final he will pick up a prize of at least £500,000 – will continue to behave as he did when an undergraduate at Worcester College, Oxford. This rather endearing trait caused some consternation during the quarter-finals of the world chess championship. It was held at the Barbican, and the manager at the Barbican Hotel asked Speelman if he would like a room in the hotel rather than have to trek back to West Hampstead to bed. 'Don't bother,' said Speelman. 'My assistant already has a room here. If I feel like sleeping, I'll crash out on the floor in his room.'

Jon Speelman is, in fact, the very sort of chess player who, 20 years ago, would probably have stayed at university and remained, quite literally, a perpetual student, commonly called a lecturer. In Speelman's case, as with many other chess players, the subject would have been mathematics. But Mrs Thatcher, quite accidentally, is probably the main reason why Britain – or rather England – is now the strongest chess-playing nation in the world after the Soviet Union, with three players in the world's top ten. Grandmaster Jonathan Mestel is the type of chess player that Britain always used to produce. Mestel is admissions tutor at Christ's College, Cambridge. He is also the reigning British chess champion – actually the British chess championship was one of the very few tournaments he was able to play. Although he has the talent, he will never – by choice – be a world-beater.

By contrast, the career of Dr John Nunn, Britain's third-strongest chess player, and the tenth-strongest in the world, is more up-to-date. A mathematics prodigy, the youngest undergraduate at Oxford University since Cardinal Wolsey, Nunn completed his PhD just at the wrong time, as Mrs Thatcher's cutbacks began to bite at Oxford. He was unable to get a permanent lectureship, and after some teaching in Kent, left the academic world for good. The result of his full-time devotion to chess was astounding. From being merely yet another competent international master, he turned into a ravening grandmaster who has regularly subjected the world's best to humiliating losses. (John Nunn failed to qualify for the finals of the world championship by only the narrowest of margins.)

But if this budgeting serendipity accounts for the new professionalism of British chess masters, it is less clear why Britain turns out such an array of individuals, like Speelman, Short, Nunn and Mestel, with such freakish ability. With the Soviet Union, it is easier to work out its extraordinary strength at chess. In part, it is the result of organised state sponsorship. In part, it is because

Russia is a slow-moving country, and people therefore have time for slow-moving pursuits. But the real point is that chess is one of the few areas in Soviet life in which intellectual endeavour is not – cannot – be constrained by ideological proscriptions. There is no such thing as a socialist way of playing chess. There is only good chess or bad chess.

Perhaps the alternative British advantage is geography. We are a small country largely lumped into one or two massive conurbations. Few places in Britain are so remote that a chess-playing child's parents cannot take their little prodigy to London, where all the top players live. Speak to any American chess player, and he will talk with envy of London as the new chess centre of the world, an intellectual melting pot that simply does not exist in his own, hopelessly extended country.

Beyond that, it is difficult to explain the British chess phenomenon. Except to speculate that we have always been a great nation of inventors, and in even earlier times, of piratical adventurers. The second trait is now most clearly seen in the success of our merchant banks, who can offer nothing but their wits and their opportunism.

Now if there is a better description of chess than a game requiring invention, opportunism, and just a bit of piracy, I should like to hear it. It may be that this is the real reason for our chess success. And it may be too that, despite all his fads and eccentricity, Jon Speelman is only another in a long and very traditional strain of buccaneering British heroes.

RACE RELATIONS

Richard Williams

March, 1996

He had barely lifted himself out of the cockpit of car number 27 in Victory Lane at the Indianapolis Motor Speedway last May, when a microphone was thrust at him and a voice asked how he'd felt as he crossed the finish line of the great 500-mile race, just 24 years old and the winner at his second attempt.

'Were you thinking about your father?'

'No! I don't see why I should have been thinking about my father! I don't race for him. I race for me, and for my team.'

The words came fast and even. And they didn't stop.

'Sure he'd be proud of me, and it would be neat if he were here, but I don't see why I should be thinking of him. I know a lot of people would like me to think of him now and say to him, "I won it for you." But that would be ridiculous. It's not right to live in the past. If I'd started to race during his lifetime, maybe it would've been different.'

'And to have won with the number 27?'

'The number doesn't matter. What counts is that the team is good enough to win. For some people, the most important thing this season is that I'm racing with the number 27. But that's just coincidence. Last year, I had the number 12, and my father finished second in the world championship and had some of his finest hours with that number. People only concentrate on 27 because that's the one he had when he was killed. They'd like to see him brought back to life through that number. But that's not what I'm racing for.'

It wasn't Jacques Villeneuve's first win of the season, and it wasn't the first time he'd been asked these questions. Four months later, after he wrapped up the IndyCar championship, becoming the youngest man ever to win the series, they'd stopped asking about his father. But by then Villeneuve knew he was on his way to Formula One in 1996, which meant he was in for another year of telling people that, no, he doesn't carry his father's memory around with him like a holy relic every time he steps into a racing car.

He was in the Williams factory at Didcot, small and quick and bright-eyed, having a fitting for the customised seat of his 1996 car, when I asked him more or less the same question, prefacing it with a sheepish disclaimer to the effect that maybe in a year's time we would be able to have a conversation without the subject coming up.

'Yeah, but it's OK,' he said politely, in his strange polyglot accent. 'I'm used to it. It's been more positive in that respect since I started winning races. The first time I was asked, it surprised me. The thought just hadn't occurred to me. I mean, I think about my father when I'm with my mother or my sister or with people who knew him when he was alive. But when I'm working, there's no room for that. I wouldn't be thinking about him at that moment if he were alive, so why should I think about him just because he's dead?'

It makes a great story, of course, and an even better one for this coming season, when the son of the late Gilles Villeneuve takes his place in the Williams team alongside the son of the late Graham Hill: two highly professional young men forced – well, maybe not forced, exactly, but finding themselves with no choice other than to measure themselves against the reputations of their charismatic fathers. For Damon Hill, this inner struggle appears to have been at least as intense as the external one he has been waging for two years with Michael Schumacher, and it may have been largely responsible for the frequent and well-publicised disturbances in the balance between his skill and his self-belief. For Jacques Villeneuve, it would seem that such self-examination has barely begun.

'Look,' he told me later, 'for sure I'm super-proud of my dad. Of course I am. But what exactly do they want me to do? Burst into tears at the thought of his memory every time I see the chequered flag? Ridiculous.'

The trouble is that his dad was the most beloved of all recent Formula One stars. Not by any means the most successful – Gilles Villeneuve won only six of his 67 Grands Prix – but undoubtedly the most spectacular, and held in universal affection throughout those parts of the world in which Formula One has an audience. It was Gilles, a baby-faced little French-Canadian, who drove an unforgettable lap on three wheels after his left-rear tyre had exploded at Zandvoort in 1979 and who, in the same year, banged wheels with René Arnoux for the last three laps at Dijon in a bare-knuckles battle for second place that had the crowd in ecstasy and the two drivers saluting each other's courage and chivalry on the slowing-down lap.

Whatever the race, and whatever his position in it, Gilles drove with his heart and soul. Born to race, brought up competing in snow-mobiles on frozen lakes, he loved the feeling of machinery sliding underneath him; even in Formula One his car would spend most of its time in lurid power-slides that were usually caught at the last minute but that often took him beyond the limit of control. He was fearless, but he was also undoubtedly foolhardy, and he was killed at Zolder in 1982, still in a hot rage two weeks after his team-mate Didier Pironi had tricked him out of an important win at Imola. It was Gilles' doomed flamboyance that did much to create the modern legend of Ferrari as a team condemned to endure a permanent agony of promise betrayed, and the number 27 has since assumed a weirdly iconic significance; you see them still at Imola and Monza, the *tifosi* with 'Forza Gilles' and the sacred number on their banners, daring his successors – Arnoux, Alboreto, Mansell, Prost, Alesi, Berger, now Schumacher and Irvine – to wrestle with his inviolable memory. Such a fuss did Enzo Ferrari make of him that it is almost a surprise to enter the tightly guarded Ferrari family tomb in Modena and discover that there is no place within it for Gilles' mortal remains. Only Senna's death, twelve years later, evoked similar emotions, similar visions – even in cynical hearts – of an unvanquished spirit racing on through the heavens.

When it became clear, in the middle of last year, that the great romantic hero's son was heading for Formula One, Ferrari's interest was immediate. Jacques, however, knew better than to fall into the most obvious of honey-traps. He and his manager, Craig Pollock, went straight for Williams, the class of the field, with the encouragement of Bernie Ecclestone, the Formula One ringmaster, who sees Villeneuve as perhaps the only man capable of mounting a real challenge to Schumacher's pre-eminence (and, perhaps, of reawakening North America's dormant interest in the series). A Silverstone test proved the young man capable of jumping straight into a Formula One car, mastering its complex driver aids, and lapping within a second of an established ace (Hill, in this case). Both sides took little time to make up their minds, which sent Williams' existing number two, David Coulthard, off in the direction of a McLaren drive.

For Villeneuve, it was the next in a series of logical (although not always obvious) career choices that began soon after his father's death, when he decided that he, too, wanted to be a racing driver. After burying Gilles at home in the town of Berthier, 40 miles north-east of Montreal, Jacques and his mother and his little sister Melanie returned to their home in Monaco, where Gilles had made his base after signing with Ferrari. Jacques, then aged twelve, was sent to school at Villars in Switzerland. There in the Bernese Alps he honed a talent for skiing that had been sparked by his father's friendship with the downhill champions Steve Podborski and Ken Read, the 'Crazy Canucks'.

A natural on skis, it could well have been skiing that provided Jacques his destiny. But in his sixteenth year, on a visit to family in Quebec, he took a summer course at the Jim Russell Racing Drivers' School at the Mont Tremblant circuit, where his father had briefly been a pupil. His mother, who had spent several years travelling North America and Europe in a motor home while her husband built his career, was not keen. 'She didn't really want me to race,' Villeneuve said. 'She was hoping I'd do something else. I don't know why, really. I don't think it's because she was scared that I'd get injured or anything. After all, for her it was a normal world. I think it's more that she was afraid I wouldn't succeed, and that the pressure would be too much.'

Two years after the course at Mont Tremblant he was out of his Swiss classroom and racing Formula Three cars in Italy, an apprenticeship which lasted three seasons before he accepted an offer to spend a year contesting the parallel series in Japan. 'That was like my university year. You know, like when you see a movie and kids are just having fun. In a way, outside of the racing, I was living a little bit like that, like you do at university, which I hadn't done because of the demands of racing.' It was in Japan that he bumped into Pollock, a half-Scot, half-Swiss who had been his ski instructor at Villars. Pollock had moved into the commercial side of motor racing, and Villeneuve persuaded him to take over his management. Together they devised the timetable that took the driver to North America for a reconnaissance year in Formula Atlantic followed by two seasons of outstanding success in Indy-Cars with a Reynard-Ford. Named 'Rookie of the Year' for his second place at the 1994 Indy, last year he ran a brilliant race to scoop the million-dollar pot, despite a two-lap penalty for a technical infringement.

That opened the gates to Formula One, and he saw no point in delaying his entrance, although well aware that the last man to attempt a direct graduation from IndyCars to Formula One did not succeed. Michael Andretti was the US series' golden boy when he joined Senna at McLaren in 1993. Despite being the son of a former Formula One world champion, and widely tipped for similar distinction, he never came to terms with the technology or, more particularly, the culture of the Grand Prix paddock, and was humiliatingly dismissed in mid-season. Villeneuve shows no fear of a similar fate. 'The difference is that he'd lived all his life in the

US, and even when he was racing there he was still living in Pennsylvania and taking the plane Sunday nights to go back home, so there's no way he could adapt to Europe. He couldn't get all the testing he needed, so he wasn't ready. He couldn't reach his own standard.'

Villeneuve, on the other hand, is completely acculturated to the Grand Prix world. 'Look, I've lived in Europe since I was six,' he said. 'Deep inside, I feel very Canadian, I'm proud of it. It's something you belong to, not something you can chop and change. But that doesn't mean my culture or my mentality are Canadian, or North American. I'm happier in Europe, I know it better. I feel better here.' His business affairs are being handled by the London-based Julian Jakobi, once Senna's right-hand man, and his own centre of operations will be a newly acquired apartment in Monaco, not far from the home in which his mother is bringing up a second daughter, three years old. (Melanie, her daughter by Gilles, is now 22 and lives in New York studying composition at NYU: another link with their father, who loved music and was a recreational trumpeter. Music, too, is Jacques' chief off-track interest: 'It's my drug,' he said. Lately his listening has encompassed 10,000 Maniacs, the Cranberries, Erasure, and various Japanese and French-Canadian bands.) He met his girlfriend, Sandrine Gros d'Aillon, in the principality. Another French-Canadian, she is currently studying communications and TV production at university in Montreal.

Europe was where his father was best known, and it is where Jacques himself will come under far greater scrutiny. Already people are saying that although the son might be fast, he hasn't inherited the irresistible recklessness that lifted Gilles beyond statistics and into immortality. 'On the driving side,' Jacques said in a coolly appraising tone, 'I think we're very different – from what I've seen on tape and from what I've heard people say. Although, of course, the cars were different then, and maybe if he were driving now he'd be more similar. I don't know, and I don't really care to know. It's not important to me. What is important is that he was one of the best, and now he's a legend. That will always be there. Now

I'm on my own road, and I want to do it in my way. If that's like him, great. If it's not, it doesn't matter.'

Too young to have known much about what his father was doing in the cockpit, later on he admired Senna and Prost, 'for different reasons because they were entirely different drivers, but they were both impressive. It's difficult to judge from the outside, so I could be totally wrong, but Senna seemed to be very aggressive and very in control and sure of himself, and he seemed to get more out of the car than the others. I'm not saying that includes Prost, because he got a lot out of the car as well. But Prost seemed to be a little bit calmer and more strategic than Senna. He could be aggressive and set a quick lap in qualifying, although he wasn't aggressive at all times – whereas Senna was aggressive from the first lap to the last. Even with a 40-second lead he would still be doing qualifying laps.'

So you don't just take the example of one person, your hero, and fall in love with everything about him? 'No. Even heroes will do something that isn't good in your eyes. Everybody has good sides and bad. Even the best drivers make mistakes.'

Somehow, at this point, the impression begins to form that perhaps giving entertainment is not as important to Villeneuve as it was to his father. 'Not being sideways just for the sake of it, no. When you can see that a guy is coming back through the field, or he's riding a good strategy, yes. But when a guy's got a 40-second lead and he's still going sideways just for the sake of it, I don't think that's any use.'

Jody Scheckter and Patrick Tambay, respectively Gilles' team-mate and his successor at Ferrari, had helped Jacques' mother through the early years of her widowhood, advising on schooling for her children and so forth. Had Jacques sought or received advice on his driving from members of the earlier generation? 'I spoke with Tambay a little bit, before I started racing. But I don't think you can really learn from the others, because everybody's situation is different. The only way you can learn is by your own experience and making your own mistakes. Someone can tell you something, but once you're in the car, how can you transfer what you've been told? Everything happens so quickly. You have to be able to understand your own mistakes, to feel what you can do to correct them. That's the only way to progress to the next level. Anyway, I hardly ever do what I'm told just because I'm told.'

His father was often criticised for losing races through rashness, for spending too much time entertaining the crowds and not enough time winning. 'I don't think he was doing it to entertain people. He was doing it to entertain himself. And he didn't care what people thought. He was doing what he wanted to do. So, he would just go out there and go over the edge, and when he crashed a lot of people would blame him but he didn't care. That was the way racing was for him.'

I told him that my own best memory of his father was of his least characteristic race, the 1979 Italian Grand Prix at Monza. Villeneuve and Scheckter both had a chance to win the championship; Scheckter if he won that race, Villeneuve if he won that and two subsequent rounds. Team orders dictated that whichever of them took the lead should hold it to the end. Scheckter got ahead at the start and Villeneuve, while clearly the quicker of the two, never budged out of his slipstream. It was perhaps the most outstanding display of sportsmanship in Formula One since Stirling Moss testified on behalf of Mike Hawthorn at a stewards' inquiry in 1958 and thus handed the title to his chief rival.

Jacques was eight at the time, but he knows the story of Gilles' unselfishness. 'If my father had overtaken him, he could have won the championship. But he was a real racer: very clean, very straight. That's the way it was. He wasn't ever going to cheat. Not to copy my father, you know, but that's something I believe in as well. There's nothing to compare with being straight. What goes around, comes around. I still believe in those virtues.'

I replied that it's a bit hard to imagine a place for that kind of sportsmanship in the Formula One of the mid-Nineties. Only the day before we met, his new team-mate had been holding forth in the newspapers about the need for the team to put its effort behind a designated number one – by which he meant Damon Hill – rather than dissipating it on two drivers with equal status.

'There's no way I would race as a number two,' Villeneuve responded with some briskness. 'Although I don't want to be a number one, because I think the two drivers should always be treated at the same level. If you think you're the best then you don't need the other driver to be a number two in order to beat him. If you believe in yourself, why should you bother with stuff like that?

'I don't want to be a number two driver. First of all, everybody compares you to your team-mate. And everybody expects you to be slower because you don't get the same treatment. But if you're slower, everybody blames you. It happens all the time. The only reason I'm going to race next year and in the future is because I want to win. I want to be able to fight. So I want everything to be on my side. That doesn't mean I want more than the other driver; I don't really care, as long as I don't have less. That's all.'

But Senna, of course, and now Schumacher, began the business of establishing an advantage by insisting on the best equipment, the most attention, the newest modifications. 'Of course, if there's only one piece that's made, you'd rather you had it than your team-mate did. And if one of you is leading the championship and the other is nowhere, it's obvious who should get it. But if there are two pieces, you don't want to keep them both for yourself.'

All this stuff was much less political in Gilles' day. Or so we can tell ourselves until we start examining the circumstances leading up to his death, and the never-to-be-resolved rift with Pironi, himself killed in a powerboat race five years later. All sorts of memories are distorted by the passage of time, or erased altogether.

People tell Villeneuve that his relationship with his father was a troubled one even in its brief span; that the adult put pressure on the small boy and made him so nervous that he could barely function when they were together. Villeneuve doesn't remember that. 'I know it because my mother told me, but personally I don't remember. Maybe it's a blockage, or maybe it's something I just forgot.' What does he remember about the relationship? 'Not much. There wasn't much of a relationship. I looked up to him because he was my father, but the few times I was seeing him it was holidays or in the mountains for Christmas, stuff like that. And at Christmas when you're a kid you have presents, and that's all that matters. A few things that I did with him, when we went out on his boat or in a four-by-four or on skis, it was a lot of fun. Always out over the edge, I remember that side, and that's all I remember.'

Damon Hill, whose father died when he was fifteen, once said that he's spent the years afterwards getting to know him, which might seem to be something the two 1996 Williams drivers will have in common, besides the colour of their driving suits. 'Yeah, probably true. My father died when I was twelve. What do you know at that age? All you see is Father Christmas. The rest of it is very important, but you just don't pay attention to it – unless it's really terrible, of course, and I can't say much on that. I know more now because I've been told so much. It's as if people talk three or four times more about a person after he's dead. But I honestly don't know my father.'

There's a fine posthumous biography of Gilles Villeneuve, written by a Canadian journalist, Gerald Donaldson, and published five years ago to widespread admiration for its honesty and accuracy. People who knew Gilles say that it gets him right. Jacques has never read it.

'No – well, the first couple of chapters. But since then I've been reading other stuff. It's not because I'm against him or anything like that. I just haven't read it. It sounds stupid. I know I should have, I've never brought myself to read it, that's all. I've been wanting to for a while. Perhaps I should, so that when people ask me questions about it, I'll know ... But maybe I don't feel like reading a book about racing. You have so little time to do the things you really want to do.'

also available from

THE ORION PUBLISHING GROUP

The Discovery of the Titanic £6.99
DR ROBERT D BALLARD
1 85797 660 6

Shanks: The Authorised Biography of Bill Shankly £5.99
DAVE BOWLER
0 75280 246 1

Diaries £7.99
ALAN CLARK
1 85799 142 7

As It Seemed To Me £7.99
JOHN COLE
1 85799 425 6

Sean Connery £5.99
MICHAEL FREEDLAND
1 85797 871 4

The Riddle of the Titanic £5.99
ROBIN GARDINER & DAN VAN DER VAT
0 75280 167 8

Football Against the Enemy £6.99
SIMON KUPER
1 85799 469 8

☐ **Ian Fleming** £7.99
ANDREW LYCETT
1 85799 783 2

☐ **Brando** £8.99
PETER MANSO
1 85797 733 5

☐ **The Big Yin: The Life and Times of Billy Connolly** £5.99
JONATHAN MARGOLIS
1 85797 738 6

☐ **Cleese Encounters** £5.99
JONATHAN MARGOLIS
1 85797 963 X

☐ **Lenny Henry** £5.99
JONATHAN MARGOLIS
0 75280 358 1

☐ **Confessions of an Actor** £5.99
LAURENCE OLIVIER
1 85797 493 X

☐ **For God, Country & Coca-Cola** £12.99
MARK PENDERGRAT
1 85799 180 X